IKEBUKURO & ENVIRONS

ASAKUSA & RYŌGOKU

WEST TŌKYŌ

OUTSIDE TŌKYŌ

YOKOHAMA

KYŌTO

ŌSAKA & KŌBE

HIROSHIMA

KAGOSHIMA

SENDAI, MIYAGI

TAKAYAMA, GIFU

SAPPORO, HOKKAIDŌ

NAHA, OKINAWA

DRINKING JAPAN

A Guide to Japan's Best Drinks and Drinking Establishments

CHRIS BUNTING

TUTTLE Publishing

Tokyo | Rutland, Vermont | Singapore

居酒屋

CONTENTS

Published by Tuttle Publishing, an imprint of Periplus Editions (HK) Ltd

www.tuttlepublishing.com

ISBN 978-4-8053-1054-0

Distributed by
North America, Latin America & Europe
Tuttle Publishing
364 Innovation Drive
North Clarendon, VT 05759-9436 U.S.A.
Tel: 1 (802) 773-8930; Fax: 1 (802) 773-6993
info@tuttlepublishing.com
www.tuttlepublishing.com

Japan
Tuttle Publishing
Yaekari Building, 3rd Floor
5-4-12 Osaki, Shinagawa-ku
Tokyo 141 0032
Tel: (81) 3 5437-0171; Fax: (81) 3 5437-0755
sales@tuttle.co.jp
www.tuttle.co.jp

Asia Pacific
Berkeley Books Pte. Ltd.
61 Tai Seng Avenue #02-12
Singapore 534167
Tel: (65) 6280-1330; Fax: (65) 6280-6290
inquiries@periplus.com.sg
www.periplus.com

14 13 12 11 10 9 8 7 6 5 4 3 2 1

Printed in Singapore

Page 2: Izakaya sign, Shinjuku, Tōkyō. Right: Bar in the Golden Gai drinking district, Shinjuku, Tōkyō.

6
お飲物
キリンビール大
ほっとするね

Japan: A Drinker's Paradise

Salarymen enjoy a cheap drink after work in Shinjuku, Tōkyō. Social drinking has been an important part of Japanese business life for centuries.

The idea first struck me while walking through Tōkyō's Shinjuku district. I had just left a whisky bar stacked with more than 500 bottles of single-malt whisky and I was heading to another which specialized in Japanese whiskies, of which it offered more than 250 varieties. En route I had noticed a *makkori* bar, which I was later to discover offered a world-beating selection of the Korean rice wine *makkori*. Within a kilometer of where I stood, there were at least three superb sake pubs, another bar laden down with more Scotch whisky than you could sample in a lifetime, a Bourbon bar with a stock of 400 premium American whiskies, and a hotel which boasted the best range of American wines in Asia. And this wasn't even particularly unusual for Japan. For drinkers in Roppongi, Shibuya, Ginza, Akasaka, Ōsaka and Kyōto, such drinking opportunities were commonplace. Many of Japan's provincial cities were not far behind. Japan, it occurred to me, was the best place to drink alcohol in the world.

Unlike most grand theories cooked up in the rosy glow of a good evening out, this idea did not immediately crumble in the sober light of morning. In fact, it has grown into a conviction. Visitors who know their way around the bars perched in Japan's high-rise drinking districts, each stacked with hundreds of bottles of their chosen drink, can access a range of whiskies, beers, wines and spirits that I believe is unrivaled anywhere else in the world. Of course, there are better places to enjoy particular types of alcohol. If you want a wine holiday, for example, you would do better traveling to France or South Africa than the back streets of Shinjuku. If you like whisky, take a trip to Scotland or Kentucky. For beer, try England, Belgium or Germany. But if you want to try them all or just want to explore a little beyond your usual tipple, I believe there is no better place than Japan.

The claim that Japan has a uniquely rich alcohol culture is not original. Long before my epiphany in Shinjuku, Taylor Smisson, the doyen of Tōkyō whisky drinkers, had already convinced me that Japanese whisky bars were the best in the world. He called Tōkyō "the Scotch single-malt drinker's heaven on earth" and also introduced me to many of the non-whisky bars featured in this guide.

"Tōkyō is probably the best place to drink Scottish single malts, not to mention Japanese single malts, as well as many other alcoholic beverages," Smisson says. "But most visitors from overseas are not aware of this and come and go without taking full advantage."

Nicholas Coldicott, who writes about alcohol for *The Japan Times*, says, "Tōkyō has a more diverse drinking scene than any city I've been to. You can drink Suntory Kakubin whisky highballs in a hole-in-the-wall, or Château Pétrus by the glass in a Ginza salon. I've seen 50 yen glasses of quasi-beer, and a 1919 Springbank for seven million yen. From cocktail bars to *izakaya*, from 'snack' pubs to roof top beer gardens, there seems to be an unusually wide array of drinking venues here."

John Gauntner, a leading authority on sake, says he sometimes has problems getting foreign visitors to understand just how devoted to good alcohol Japanese bars can be: "I was taking a group of 15 people around and I found myself having to chide them. We were waiting for a taxi

生ホッピー

BLUE
DRAGON

Left: The Golden Gai drinking district in Shinjuku, Tōkyō, is home to dozens of tiny bars.
Below: Atsushi Horigami's Shot Bar Zoetrope (page 190) offers an astonishing selection of about 250 types of Japanese whisky and 100 other Japanese alcohols.

at a hotel lobby, and one guy orders a martini. The taxis come soon here; the martinis take 20 minutes. They don't just pour you a martini. The attention to detail is such that it has to be made perfectly."

Of course, the proposition that Japan is "the best place to drink alcohol in the world" goes considerably further than mere admiration for a rich drinking culture. I spent a wonderful year up and down the country meeting hundreds of brewers, distillers and bar owners trying to marshal the evidence for my over-reaching claim. Each trip seemed to open a new field of inquiry and a fresh pile of Japanese language histories and guides to be laboriously deciphered. I have some wonderful memories: the rasp of untouched snow under-foot at the Yoichi distillery; the haunting bird song deep in the forest at Kagoshima's Manzen distillery; a plastic glass of *awamori* poured for myself on an empty white beach near Nago; and the subtly different rich, sweet smells of all the brewing and distilling halls I visited from Okinawa to Hokkaido.

Mine is the sort of far-reaching claim that will always leave room for dissent. Indeed, I expect more people to be vaguely annoyed by it than those who accept the case. New Yorkers no doubt had a thing or two to say about the claims of 1960s London to be the world's capital of music and fashion. The international media was full of debate a couple of years ago about whether Tōkyō had indeed surpassed Paris as a gastronomic capital, just because it had earned more Michelin stars. Similarly, I have had numerous spirited arguments with people reluctant to accept the idea that Japan is also a land of rare alcoholic opportunity. In one sense, this book really just offers my final tuppence worth to all those debates: for the fellow who assured me that Japanese beer was always dull, the chapter on Japanese beer will hopefully open a few doors to all the smoked brews, *yuzu* ales and imperial stouts coming out of the independent makers. The lady who insisted all Japanese wine was sweetened bilge water drove me on while I was writing about wine, and the whisky chapter goes out to the Scotsman who sent me a three-page long poem/invective assuring me that whisky could only properly be made in Scotland!

I have had many enlightening conversations with Japanese bar tenders about specific shortcomings in the Japanese scene and Nicholas Coldicott of *The Japan Times* has pointed out the relative immaturity of the rum (see page 235), tequila (see page 222) and gin markets (see also Coldicott's excellent analyses of Japan's cocktail scene, page 221). But there perhaps lies the key point and the reason why I am serious about the claim that Japan is the best place to drink alcohol in the world at the moment: the fact that a debate can even be entertained over whether the Japanese cocktail scene is superior to that of the United States, whether its rum and tequila bars surpass those in other countries, or whether Tōkyō and Ōsaka offer better ranges of Scottish whisky than anything to be found in London or Edinburgh, must put the issue into

Yorozuya Matsukaze in Ikebukuro, Tōkyō (page 73), has known various incarnations since its opening in 1955—as a sweet shop, a coffee shop, a restaurant and now as a traditional izakaya.

some perspective because, of course, Japan also offers a whole world of superb alcohols that are almost completely inaccessible in any of these places.

Most people have heard of sake, though fewer will have experienced the thousands of sublime *jizake* lining the walls of Japan's sake bars, but there are other interesting drinks to be tried. *Shōchū*, Japan's indigenous distilled spirit, has its own traditions in the southern part of the country, stretching back centuries. There are six major types of premium *shōchū*, all using different ingredients. The products of hundreds of small distilleries can be sampled in the specialist *shōchū* bars. There is also *awamori*, a separate distilling tradition on the islands of Okinawa, where people have been making and long-aging their spirit for centuries. When you have exhausted all that, there is a well-established wine industry, a thriving craft beer sector and the second largest single-malt whisky industry in the world. Japan's whiskies are currently shaking up international competitions in much the same way that New World wine did to the wine industry in the 1970s.

Why is contemporary Japanese drink culture so rich? All sorts of theories were put to me during my year-long research and many struck me as convincing. Certainly, historical factors played a part in ensuring the survival of the country's own alcohol traditions. Japan was never colonized and was largely isolated from the international trading system until the Meiji period (1868–1912). Unlike rums, whiskies, brandies and wines, the major Japanese alcohols never became internationally traded commodities and still remain largely unexplored outside the country. But Japan's unusual resistance to Western colonization had benefits too: its premium markets were never completely dominated by foreign tastes and its alcohol industries were never swamped by foreign capital. Japan retains a domestic industry, which is still, in many sectors, based on small- to medium-sized producers. This is particularly the case in its indigenous alcohol industries—sake, *shōchū* and

くわ茶割り
月の桂
手取川
神亀

awamori—where the most interesting makers are often very small indeed.

There are also economic and cultural forces at work: the country has a mature and prosperous consumer economy and, unlike many developed, non-Western countries, has been importing high-quality alcohol from across the world for more than a century. Interest in these alcohols goes back to the opening of the country in the late 1800s and, while not eclipsing the native traditions, has strongly influenced Japanese alcohol culture. The chapters on whisky, wine and beer in this guide tell various parts of the story. In recent years, tariff barriers have tumbled and a diverse drinking-related media has helped to inform young Japanese consumers, often in extraordinary detail, about the flood of new, relatively cheap imports. These people are demanding higher quality from both importers and domestic alcohol makers and this demand is both supporting and being supported by Japan's innovative and highly professional bar owners and staff. In Chapter 7, I take a closer look at the historical development of bar tending in Japan and the profession's key role in developing the myriad of drinking opportunities now on offer.

Twenty years ago, the drinking districts of Japan did not offer the quality they do now. Twenty years from now, I have a sneaking fear they may not offer the bustle of activity that overwhelms the visitor these days. There might be something evanescent about this "golden age." Post-war Japanese business culture was at least partly built on hard drinking and, while money has been short since the 1990s, we are still riding on the coattails of that booze-fueled epoch. In

"Hanami" cherry blossom viewing parties began as an aristocratic pursuit in the Heian period (794–1185), but now much of Japan can be found under a cherry tree in March or April enjoying the season's ephemeral beauty and free-flowing alcohol.

the 1980s, and to some extent this is still the expectation in some workplaces, the cultural norm was for salarymen to spend endless long evenings out on the town with colleagues and clients. It wasn't an option. In many companies, it was part of the job, and that culture was critical to building and sustaining the tens of thousands of bars in Japan's cities. If you visit any whisky bar, you will see salarymen still doing their bit for the alcohol business, but younger men are increasingly resistant to devoting their entire social as well as working lives to their companies. Such changes may turn out to be more deadly to the Japanese drinking districts than any of the short-term issues caused by temporary economic problems. On the other hand, as I explore below, Japanese culture has always found a prominent place for drinking and the same social shifts that are starting to see men demanding more time with their families are also bringing more women into the workforce and therefore the drinkforce. Nobody really knows what will happen from here but, right now, I believe Japan offers a uniquely rich and diverse drinking culture. I hope this guide will open some doors to new experiences.

Japan's Drinking Culture

Detail from "Seven elves getting drunk" by Kitagawa Utamaro (1753–1806).

At the height of the prohibition era in the United States, a few voices in Japan hesitantly suggested that their country should impose a similar ban. Japan had been assiduously copying its neighbor across the Pacific since the Meiji reforms of the late 19th century. Perhaps the next enlightened thing to do was to follow America in outlawing alcohol?

The opposition was immediate and vociferous. The *Japan Chronicle*, a leading English-language newspaper at the time, reported people driving around cities throwing pro-alcohol leaflets onto the streets. The propagandists claimed that there was no example of an advanced civilization that had not embraced alcohol. Booze was essential for progress! Of course the claim was false, but it is a measure of alcohol's place in Japanese culture that its proponents were considered mainstream while the prohibitionists were widely dismissed as extremists. The idea of a ban never really got off the ground. A law was introduced in 1922 forbidding children from drinking and a grand total of 17 villages nationwide went "dry," but the rest of Japan spent the prohibition era picking the bones of America's alcohol industry, shipping over second-hand equipment from defunct US firms to help build its fledgling beer and wine sectors.

The Japanese people seem to have been enthusiastic about their alcohol from the earliest times. The first written record of Japanese drinking is actually found in China. *The History of the Kingdom of Wei*, written in AD 297, reported that the Japanese were "fond of their alcohol." At funerals, the Chinese observer wrote, "The head mourners wail and lament, while friends sing, dance and drink liquor."

In the oldest Japanese chronicles, the *Kojiki* (c. AD 712) and the *Nihon Shoki* (AD 720), there are drinking songs, stories of intoxicated emperors ("I am drunk with the soothing liquor, with the smiling liquor," he sang) and several bloodthirsty tales of getting the better of opponents with alcohol. In fact, if the chronicles are to be believed, serving sake to unsuspecting foes and then skewering them was a very popular ruse indeed: an eight-headed serpent meets his death after getting plastered on eight buckets of sake, a murderous soldier is stabbed as he lifts his cup, and a group of enemies are made drunk by the emperor's men only to have their heads cracked with mallets. ("Ho! Now is the time/Ho! Now is the time/Ha Ha Psha!/Even now, my boys/Even now, my boys," sings the Imperial commander as his warriors bludgeon the tipsy tribe.)

Ordinary Japanese people seem to have acquired their taste for alcohol early. Some established accounts would have you believe that alcohol was restricted to the elites and to festivals where the rich doled the good stuff out to commoners. It is certainly true that the officially sanctioned sake made by the religious foundations and, later, by commercial firms was far too expensive for most people to drink regularly until quite recently. But there is plenty of evidence of a popular drinking culture. Some working-class consumption in the towns hung on the coattails of the sake industry. Poor housewives would offer to wash the bags used in sake making, from which they squeezed a weak brew for their families, and there is a genre of jokes from the Edo period (1603–1868) about eating solid alcoholic sake lees (the friends of one notoriously penniless drunkard ask: "How much did you drink?" He replies: "Half a kilogram").

大猩々酩酊之図
哥麿酔中筆

Office workers raise a toast at Kaasan, Shinjuku, Tōkyō (page 59).

The importance of being frank

Many Japanese people look upon office parties as a sort of safety valve. The theory goes that lowly workers should be able to talk honestly to their bosses about feelings they would not normally be able to express. Everybody is supposed to relax, act and talk freely and forget about any indiscretions in the morning. But tread carefully! There may be more politics going on than you think.

In 1323, courtiers acting under the auspices of the Emperor Go-Daigo started organizing *bureikō* parties. *Bureikō* meant "putting aside rank" and is still the term used for the frankness encouraged at office gatherings. At Go-Daigo's original *bureikō* parties, humble warriors and priests were allowed to mix with favored members of the court. Sake and food were consumed in great quantities. Everybody let down their hair, dressed simply and were prompted to speak honestly about their frustrations, politics and hopes for the future. These curious events were not taken seriously by the Kamakura shogunate, the warrior government which had a stranglehold over the Imperial state at the time, but were the first steps in building support for Go-Daigo's long and eventually successful campaign to smash the shogunate.

In the countryside, the peasants were more proactive. The *Zōhyō Monogatari*, a sort of management manual for *samurai* officers published in the mid to late 1600s, advises against giving too much food to the lowest rank of soldiers drawn from the peasantry. "You can give rice enough for three or four days but not more than five days. If you give ten days worth of rice they will put eight or nine days of it into making sake. If you let that happen, they will starve and die," the guide advises. "With three or four days of rice, they will still make their unrefined sake but they will not starve."

In the villages themselves, a cat-and-mouse game with the authorities continued well into the 20th century. One old woman interviewed in *Nōka ga Oshieru Doburoku no Tsukurikata* ("Farmers teach unrefined sake making"), a wonderful little book published in 2007 about the Japanese home brewing scene, said she still brewed late at night because of memories of police raids in her childhood. The Japanese sake writer Hisao Nagayama recalled that, in his own village in the 1950s, farmers would ring bells, blow conch shells and clang pots if any official-looking stranger came into the area. (At the time, about 40,000 people a year were being arrested for illicit brewing or distilling.) Nagayama's parents kept their home brew in the ceiling above the toilet because the stench there disguised the smell of the alcohol from prying noses.

If there is a theme running through Japanese alcohol history, it is the people's endless inventiveness when it comes to obtaining drink. The established view is that Japanese alcohol culture begins and ends with the rice wine sake, but the rural brewers interviewed by the authors of *Nōka ga Oshieru Doburoku no Tsukurikata* revealed recipes using just about any ingredient that came to hand. In fact, more obscure ingredients may have been easier to use than the heavily taxed and regulated rice. One 91-year-old, for instance, recalled a recipe for *yamabudō* sake, a wine brewed from mountain grapes. Other villages used other fruits, millet, corn and even sweet potatoes. Home distilling also seems to have been common. The *Koume Nikki* ("Koume's diary"), kept by the wife of a school headmaster in the 19th century, records the use of a family still to give a bit of oomph to unsatisfactorily weak sakes.

There have been numerous attempts to suppress alcohol in Japan. Buddhism, one of Japan's two main religions, takes a far dimmer view of liquor than Christianity and most other religions. The prohibition efforts of the 1920s were, in fact, just the latest in a long line of campaigns by religious and government leaders. There were Imperial decrees against alcohol in AD 722, 732, 737, 758 and 770 and similar proclamations recurred regularly throughout the succeeding centuries. The problem has been that normal Japanese people have consistently ignored or sidestepped these regulations, tending more towards a philosophy of life encapsulated by the 8th-century poet Ōtomo no Tabito: "Rather be a pot of sake than a human being/To be saturated with sake."

Customers at the Daizen sake bar, Chiyoda, Tōkyō.

The folk religion Shinto and indeed much of the fabric of traditional Japan incorporates alcohol consumption at almost every turn: the most sacred part of a Shinto wedding is the *san-san-ku-do*, where the couple ceremonially drink alcohol to bind themselves in matrimony; the Girl's Festival in March is toasted with the sweet, low-alcohol *amazake* (March was a prime time for home brewing when arrests were still common because the booze could always be excused as *amazake* gone bad); the coming of the cherry blossom brings *hanami* picnics celebrating spring with enthusiastic drinking; in autumn, full moon viewing parties are also soused and the New Year celebrations are incomplete in many families without *toso*, a herb-infused sake thought to guarantee health in the coming months.

The details of these traditions vary widely between different localities but a common feature is that the consumption of the alcohol often seems to be as important as the excuse for it. The American scholars Robert Smith and Ella Wiswell, describing 1930s rural society in Suye village, Kumamoto prefecture, quoted a Mrs Toyama, who was organizing a cherry blossom party: "It is called *hanami* (flower viewing) but, since the cherry blossoms are gone, we will look at the violets in the fields instead."

Smith and Wiswell were astonished by the Bacchanalian energy of the Japanese farmers they studied: "The people of Suye were always ready for a party, and one cannot but be impressed by their seemingly limitless capacity to find occasions for them. Most parties, whether attended by both women and men, or by men or women only, involved dancing, singing, eating, and heavy drinking, and almost invariably considerable sexual joking and play. There were parties given to mark the naming of a new baby, returning from a visit to a shrine or temple, celebrating a variety of festivals and holidays, sending off conscripts and welcoming them back, dedicating new buildings and marking the end of rice planting and the harvest, the completion of the silk-producing cycle, and every other enterprise involving more than two or three people."

An Encouragement of Learning

The statesman and scholar Yukichi Fukuzawa is chiefly remembered today as the founder of Keio University and for his presence on the 10,000 yen note, but his tremendous energy produced an English–Japanese dictionary, best-selling books on Western culture, influential political and philosophical works, children's textbooks, a national newspaper and the 17-volume *An Encouragement of Learning*. His own method of keeping himself at the scholarly grindstone was more carrot than stick: he would put a bottle of sake on top of his oil lamp as he studied. By the time the sake had warmed up, it would be midnight and he would relax with a drink of the hot sake before retiring to bed.

On one occasion, Wiswell attended a "vaccination day" at a school: "Mothers came from all directions, and the school room looked like a nursery with babies crawling all over the place.... When I left all the older children had got their vaccinations and the doctor was well through the babies. On my way down the stairs I met the custodian with a barrel of *shōchū* and bottles of beer. 'The drinking is starting,' he said. It had not occurred to me, after all these months, that even a vaccination clinic calls for drinking afterwards."

Alcohol was a part of life for almost all adults. If anybody tells you that Japanese drinking was traditionally only for the men, ask them to explain this account by Wiswell of a "baby naming party" in Kumamoto: "Everyone got very drunk. The old grandmother became very playful with Masakichi, and Ichiro's father was pawing one of his sisters-in-law. Mrs Wauchi was very far gone, and the two of us must have made a funny sight coming home huddled under her shawl, as I was without a coat. We stumbled along, talking loudly, and she kept telling me how good it felt to be so drunk. [Later] Mrs Hayashi stopped by completely drunk, saying how sorry she was that she had not left the party when I did. Her husband will be angry at her at being kept waiting, she said, but she does love to drink, and just could not tear herself away any sooner. She was sure her husband will divorce her, she laughed, for coming home late and drunk again. Today the women were discussing the Kawaze women's escapade of the night before (which we don't learn more of) and how drunk they were and where they finally went for their after-party."

This all comes from a description of peasant life in southern Kyūshū in the 1930s. Middle-class city dwellers at the time and farmers in other parts of Japan may have had quite different norms (at one stage, Wiswell quotes a school principal's wife from outside the village finding the antics of the village women "quite surprising"). It was certainly perfectly normal for respectable women in post-war Japan to largely abstain from drinking, and we are currently in the grip of a moral panic about younger women who like to drink. There were, and still are, all sorts of drinking cultures in the country. Today, if you look at a map of Japan's alcohol consumption, you will find the people of Kyūshū (including Suye village) drink nearly twice as much *shōchū* per person per year

Sakamukae

Traditionally, when a traveler was expected back from a long pilgrimage, friends and family would wait at an incline at the border of their village to welcome him home. It was customary at these *sakamukae* to drink sake while waiting. An early Edo-period account has it that one fellow got a little too drunk waiting for an unpunctual friend. He began groaning loudly and his worried friends told him to stop drinking. "What are you talking about?" he said. "I am groaning because the intoxication will go away so soon."

as the rest of the Japan and four times more than parts of Kansai. The heartland of sake is the center and north of the main island. In Niigata prefecture, they drink about 16 liters of sake a year, while in Okinawa and Kagoshima in Kyūshū, they drink about a liter. The same goes for other alcohols: Northerners like whisky, Kyōto and Ōsaka are big on liqueurs, Yamanashi likes its wine. Two prefectures, Tōkyō and Hokkaido, drink just about everything to excess. Perhaps the only generalization that it is possible to make is that, wherever you travel in Japan, you are in the midst of a complex and deeply rooted drinking culture. There are new things to be discovered at every turn.

Detail showing revelers from "A willow tree by the gateway of Shimabara" by Ando Hiroshige (1797–1858).

The Main Types of Drinking Establishments

The first and perhaps the biggest obstacle to exploring Japan's drinking districts is just getting through the right doors. The best bars are not always the ones that you can see into from the street, and it takes a bit of courage to dive into an unfamiliar establishment with no clear idea of what it sells and how much it charges. Here is a bestiary of the most common types of pubs and bars and some tips on how to identify them.

Izakaya 居酒屋

The three most useful Japanese characters for anybody going drinking in Japan are 居酒屋 for *izakaya*. The word is probably best translated as "Japanese pub."

Historically, *izakaya* seem to have evolved in the 18th century out of alcohol shops that began to sell food and provide seating to customers who wanted to drink on the premises, but nowadays there is as much diversity among *izakaya* as there is among Western pubs. Some *izakaya* are very friendly, some are not; many are cheap, but others are trendily expensive. A few are just grim. In general, though, a sign for an *izakaya* fairly reliably indicates a shop where the main business is food and drink, rather than, say, female friendship (see below). There is usually an entrance charge, but it is often relatively low compared to the more exclusive bars (see page 26).

You will be expected to order a little food to go with your drink. Many of the dishes on the menu will be small *otsumami* intended to be eaten while drinking. Here are some fairly standard options:

Edamame (boiled soy beans in the pod). A tasty, cheap and commonly available snack.
Yakitori (grilled skewered chicken).
Hiyayakko (cold, fresh tofu). This often comes with fish flakes, so the *edamame* are a more reliable vegetarian option.
Shiokara (fermented seafoods). A lot more challenging than the previous three options, but a classic Japanese drinking food nonetheless

Izakaya will often have a red lantern outside called an *akachōchin*. Unfortu-nately, not all shops that have red lanterns are *izakaya*, so it is good to be able to recognize the Japanese characters.

Other pub-like establishments

There are a number of other Japanese words that are either used interchangeably with *izakaya* or are very close in meaning to it. The situation is similar to the overlapping meanings of "pub," "bar," "inn" and "tavern" in English. Sometimes

The Kanayama Johnny shōchū bar in Hiroshima (page 95) allows customers to serve themselves from the hundreds of bottles lining the walls. Waitress Asaka Kōno, shown here, says dishonesty is rare.

izakaya-like establishments will sign themselves as 酒場 (*sakaba* or "alcohol place") or 飲み屋 (*nomiya* or "drinking shop"), which is sometimes written as 呑み屋). The words *sakaba* and *nomiya* seem to have slightly wider ranges of meaning than *izakaya*, encompassing bars without the food menu you would expect in an *izakaya*, but there is no reliable distinction.

There is another sub-set of Japanese pubs describing themselves as 立ち飲み屋 (*tachi-nomiya* or "standing drinking shop") or スタンディングバー (*sutandingu* bar or "standing bar"). These places, as their names suggest, serve drinks to standing customers. The English and Japanese versions of the name are applied fairly indiscriminately, although more modern-styled places, serving wines and posh sakes, are more likely to be *sutandingu* bars while traditional drinking stands tracing their roots back to the post-war years are more likely to be *tachinomi*.

Pubs パブ

When I first arrived in Japan, I used to walk around looking for "pubs" on the theory that I knew what they were. It is not as simple as that. In Japan, the word "pub" can refer to various types of drinking establishments, not all of which serve reasonably priced drinks. There are "English pubs" and "Irish pubs" offering exactly what you might expect, but there are also "sexy pubs" that sell something else. All sorts of legitimate *izakaya*, bars and "snacks" also use the word. It is usually obvious when you are dealing with a legitimate drinking establishment but the general advice is not to regard the word "pub" as a guarantee of something familiar.

The English used on Japanese bar signs does not always carry the same meaning it would back home. Clockwise from top left: an "emotional bar" in Takadanobaba, Tōkyō; a "snack" in Toshima, Tōkyō; a "sexy pub" in Shinjuku, Tōkyō; and a jazz bar in Setagaya, Tōkyō.

Bars バー

The word "bar" has as many meanings as "pub." Many of the places featured in this guide call themselves "bars" but there are also hostess bars and snacks that go under the name. There is so much variation that any generalization is going to run into contradictions, but for me an archetypal Japanese "bar" tends to put much less emphasis on food than an *izakaya* does. The barman or woman is much more likely to be serving from behind a bar top, will probably be offering Western drinks of some description (although there are also sake and *shōchū* bars), and is likely to be charging a heftier entrance charge than your average *izakaya*.

"Snack" スナック

The "snack" is a peculiarly Japanese institution. It is typically a small bar run by a woman. Part of the attraction for customers can be the conversation with the *mama-san*, although, in many places, couples will go to a snack and treat it as their local bar. Originally, snacks emerged out of regulations that forbade hostess bars from opening late at night. Women running snacks could argue that they were doing bar work and not hostessing, which allowed later hours. It is a misunderstanding to see all snacks as sleazy operations. Most are not. However, you are usually paying in some way for the personal attention—either through some sort of entrance charge or a relatively expensive food dish that you are expected to accept. These charges are often higher than in a standard *izakaya*. A snack is never, as I mistakenly thought on arriving in Japan, a cheap place to go for a bite to eat.

Soba restaurants, oden stalls, etc.

For the Japanese, drinking and eating go together and there are many types of restaurants that are associated with alcohol. Two of the more classic choices are *soba* restaurants and *oden* stalls (see page 64). *Soba* (そば) shops, serving buckwheat noodle dishes, are traditional places for daytime tippling. A glass of sake, *shōchū* or beer with your noodles is quite the done thing. Drinking too much, though, is seriously uncool. *Oden* (おでん), an assortment of vegetables, fish cakes and eggs cooked in a light soy-flavored stew, is another time-honored drinking food and the best places to try it are the rickety outdoor stalls set up in some parks. They usually serve cheap sake, *shōchū* and beer. The modern preference is for drinking with various types of grilled meat. The drinking quarters are full of *yakiniku* (焼肉 or 焼き肉, grilled meat); *horumonyaki* (ホルモン焼き, beef and pork offal); *gyūtan* (牛タン, grilled beef tongue), Mongolian barbecue (using lamb and mutton and often referred to as *Jingisu Kan* (ジンギスカン)), as well as Korean barbecue restaurants.

The law

Drinking age

The minimum legal drinking age in Japan is 20.

Disorderly behavior

The Law to Prevent Drunk and Disorderly Conduct (1961) empowers the Japanese police to arrest people for disorderly speech or behavior in public places.

Drunk driving

Anybody who tells you that Japan is lax on drunk drivers is seriously ill-informed. It now has some of the strictest drunk driving laws in the world. You can be imprisoned or heavily fined not only for drunk driving yourself but for being in a car with a drunk driver, lending a car to someone who has been drinking or serving alcohol to a driver. Enforcement is highly effective: police routinely block roads and test everyone who comes by. You don't have to be driving irregularly to get caught.

The legal limit is less than .03 blood alcohol content, which is significantly lower than in many countries; one small beer will get some people over that limit. Indeed, one Western executive was taken to court for driving the morning after drinking. The maximum sentence is five years in prison and a fine of 1,000,000 yen. Although the sentences will not be that tough for most drink drivers, it is worth remembering that Japanese law routinely enforces large compensation payments upon people who cause harm to others or damage to property on the road. If you are under the influence, you will almost certainly be judged to be at fault, and that could mean life-ruining debts.

Emergency service telephone numbers
110—Police
119—Ambulance

Kimiko Satō, owner of Juttoku, Shinjuku, Tōkyō *(page 58), pours sake for customers.*

Pouring for others

It is customary when drinking in a group in Japan to pour other people's drinks, and it is polite to wait for others in the group to pour yours. This may sound overly formal to the uninitiated, but can be a great way for foreigners having difficulty with the language to interact and make friends. I have known this custom to be used to strike up conversations with people in adjoining groups too. If you want to be really polite, pour while holding the bottle in two hands and hold your glass in two hands when receiving. If possible, try to accept drinks offered by people in the group who have not poured for you and swiftly pick up the bottle and pour for them (in many cases, people are pouring because they want their glass refilled). None of these drinking customs should be taken as being set in stone. Plenty of people pour their own drinks in group situations. In general, it is not the done thing to drink directly from bottles, although there are young people's hangouts where this is de rigueur. Where a glass is provided, it is best to use it.

Cautionary notes

A yakitori (grilled chicken) restaurant in Shinjuku, Tōkyō. Grilled meats of various sorts, ranging from yakitori to grilled beef tongue, are popular drinking foods in modern Japan.

Drinking too much

Drinking in a new environment has a way of making idiots out of people. Familiar cues that rein in excessive drinking are not present. Bars in Japan, for instance, open very late compared to many pubs in the UK, where I come from. British people often start drinking quite early in the evening, forgo food and drink at a breakneck pace because they are used to pubs closing between 11 and 12 pm. This kind of approach is likely to lead to embarrassment (or worse) in a drinking culture where many bars are still serving drinks at 4 am. The hazards will vary depending where you come from, but it is a good idea to take a conservative approach until you get your bearings.

Another major cause of stomach-heaving *futsukayoi* (hangovers) is unfamiliarity with the alcohol being consumed. Sake is one of the world's strongest brewed beverages. Knocking it back like beer will end in disaster. If the clear liquid you have been poured is *shōchū*, a distilled spirit weighing in at anything from 25 to 40 percent alcohol, you really need to be sipping, not gulping. Even some of the craft beer bars recommended in Chapter 4 can catch you off guard: a 9 percent Special Brown Ale from Hakusekikan, for instance, is a very different beast from a 4.7 percent London Pride.

Japanese drinking customs can sometimes push you into drinking too much. As I mentioned on page 23, it is common to pour drinks for other people in a group and you can find your glass being filled fairly constantly. In some circumstances, fellow drinkers may ask you to drink up before they pour for you. It is difficult to offer general advice on what to do in this sort of situation, because it really depends on who you are drinking with and how intoxicated they are, but three points to remember are: (1) You do not have to empty the glass before someone pours for you. It is very common indeed to take a small sip and offer a half or even three-quarters full glass to be topped up. (2) If you have had enough, it is not rude to say so (*Kekko desu*—"I'm fine"). (3) The custom of pouring drinks is supposed to be about shared conviviality. If you are feeling pressurized to drink more than you want, then the pourers are making the faux pas, not you.

"Kampai!"

Many Japanese drinking sessions will start with a toast and it is polite not to start gulping until the customary loud chorus of *Kampai!* Another drinking exclamation is *Banzai!*, which is far less popular than it once was but is still occasionally heard near the climax of an evening, particularly at company parties. *Banzai* does not mean that everybody present is about to fix bayonets, as some aficionados of John Wayne films may mistakenly believe. It literally means "10,000 years" and toasts the emperor's long life (or, indeed, the longevity and prosperity of other, non-Emperor related pursuits).

The use of *Kampai* and *Banzai* as drinking toasts appears to be a relatively new phenomenon. Wherever there are drinkers there is always going to be someone who thinks a few words goes well with the first glass (see *otōri*, page 120) but it was the arrival of Western diplomats in the Meiji period (1868–1912) that formalized Japanese toasts. The foreigners were forever toasting their kings and presidents and so, not to be outdone, the Japanese representatives started shouting alcohol *Banzais* to the emperor. Later, in the 1910s and 1920s, *Kampai!* (from the Chinese exhortation *Kampei!*, "Drain your glass") began to establish itself as a less Emperor-centric alternative to *Banzai!*

Drinking in public

Legal restrictions on drinking in public are looser in Japan than in many countries, but social codes in this area are actually less forgiving. The general view is that food or drink should be properly appreciated while sitting down and that it is

vulgar to walk around stuffing your face. The omnipresence of convenience stores and vending machines is starting to break down these social expectations among certain groups, but it is still crass to walk down a road swigging beer.

There are times when it is acceptable to drink in public places. Part of what is special about *matsuri* (festivals), *hanabi* (fireworks displays) and *hanami* (flower viewing picnics) is that the normal restrictions on the street can be transgressed.

Practicalities

Tsukidashi, otōshi and other entrance fees

Entrance charges are a source of much misunderstanding between foreign customers and the bars that levy them. Most bars in Japan have an entrance fee and many charge this fee by giving a small dish of food—called a *tsukidashi* or an *otōshi*—that has not been ordered by the customer but is put on the bill. This is not a sneaky way of separating you from your money. It is built into the pricing of most Japanese bars, and all Japanese customers expect it.

The original theory behind these snacks was that any order of food would take some time to be made, so the *tsukidashi* was a pre-prepared dish that would keep customers happy while they waited (this illustrates how important food is to drinking for many Japanese people). Nowadays, *tsukidashi* or *otōshi* are best regarded simply as a charge. In most places, it is going to cause more hassle than it is worth to attempt to refuse the dish.

From the point of view of foreigners who are unfamiliar with the practice, the fact that a dish is provided actually seems to cause more aggravation than if nothing were given at all. The misunderstanding most often occurs when customers find the *otōshi* on their bill, think it is a mistake because they did not order it and ask for the charge to be subtracted, only to be met with incomprehension and apparent defiance from their previously friendly hosts. Atsushi Horigami at Bar Zoetrope (page 190) says: "I had a Dutchman in here who got quite angry about it. He said I was a thief and threatened to call the police!"

One way to get one's head around these charges, particularly relevant to drinkers from the United States, is to see them as substitutes for tips. It is not normal to tip in Japanese bars or restaurants. If you stay in a bar for any length of time, the 500–1,000 yen usually levied through the *tsukidashi* will often be equivalent to or less than what you might have paid the barman or waiter as a tip. You can always inquire on entering a bar how much the charge is: *Tsukidashi wa o-ikura desu ka?* ("How much is the tsukidashi?").

Drinking in an unfamiliar environment can be hazardous. Sake is one of the world's strongest brewed beverages and bars in Japan open later than in many other countries.

Credit cards

An increasing number of Japanese bars and restaurants now accept credit cards, but Japan is still very much a cash society. It is safest to assume that credit cards will not be taken. I have tried to indicate which bars do take cards in the guide, but I have not been able to give a detailed list of precisely which cards are accepted in each establishment. If you are planning to use a credit card, you really need to find out if you are going to be able to use it before ordering: *Kono credit card wa daijōbu desu ka?* ("Is this credit card OK?")

Holidays

I have tried to provide accurate information on the opening hours of bars and on the days or periods when they will be closed. However, there are two times of year when almost all of Japan closes down: New Year (December 29–January 5; most businesses close between January 1–3) and Obon (middle of August, though some regions celebrate it in July). You can assume that most of the bars included in this guide will be shut for at least some days during these periods. I have not specified these holidays on every bar listing to avoid repetition, and also because the bars often change which particular days they take off from year to year.

To clarify the rather vague dates for Obon: the festival is held on the 13th to 15th day of the 7th month of the year. Unfortunately, the conversion from the old lunar calendar to the modern calendar is done differently in different areas and, since Obon is about returning to your family home, that means lots of people in the cities work on different timetables. There is no national holiday, but businesses do tend to give staff leave. Some people return home between August 13 and 15, some between July 13 and 15 and some according to the old lunar calendar, which hits a different date every year. The August dates are the big ones: any visit between August 8 and 16 is likely to be affected by Obon.

Shōchū Bar Gen, Shibuya, Tōkyō (page 107).

Bottle keep

Some bars in Japan provide a service called *botoru kiipu* ("bottle keep"). The customer buys a whole bottle of alcohol but does not have to drink it in one sitting. Instead, it is marked with a name and kept at the bar for the customer's next visit. Nowadays, the bottle is bought from the bar itself, but *botoru kiipu* has its roots in the 1950s, when some drinkers would bring their own bottles to bars, pay a corkage and return to drink the contents over many sittings. In those days it was hard for some bars to get good whisky, but they offered their customers a pleasant atmosphere, proper glassware and ice. Suntory's tremendously successful Torys Bar chain adopted the idea (but insisted that you had to buy their whisky), and helped spread the practice across the country. In most bars, the price of the bottle should work out slightly cheaper than buying by the glass. A good rule of thumb is to expect the bottle to cost about 10 times the price of a single shot.

Costs

Japan has a reputation for being expensive. In truth, it really depends on when you come to the country and how your home country's currency is doing against the yen at the time. When I first arrived in Japan, the yen was weak and the conversion I got used to at that time made Japanese prices seem pretty reasonable. When I began researching this guide, the yen was stronger and therefore costs seemed higher, though still fairly acceptable. The subsequent collapse of the dollar and the pound against the yen made almost all prices seem frightening for a while. The situation will almost certainly have changed again by the time you read this.

There are bars in this guide that are expensive, but I have made an effort to include a good

The Watami chain has more than 600 outlets across Japan.

Chain pubs

There are a growing number of chain *izakaya* in Japan. Independent bar owners complain such chains are squeezing out the little men. Few of them offer the range of alcohols offered by the best independent establishments, and the quality of the service is often noticeably worse. If you are near an independent *izakaya*, I would recommend giving it a try before trooping into the chain. However, it has to be admitted that the ubiquity of the chains can offer reassurance in an unfamiliar location. Some relatively small chains like Kaasan, Himonoya and Komahachi have found their way into this guide on their own merits, but the most successful *izakaya* chain in Japan is Watami, with more than 600 outlets. It is not at all bad and is definitely worth considering as a back-up. The drink list is not particularly extensive, but there is always some high-quality sake and *shōchū* available. I have noticed some good Japanese whisky creeping onto the menu in the last couple of years. Watami styles itself as a "family friendly" *izakaya* and my wife says she often opts for Watami over the more atmospheric independent bars if she is having a drink on her own out of town. The interiors are usually open and well lit, and there is a slightly more anonymous feel to these places, which she says lends itself to having a quiet drink and bite to eat as a solitary woman. The group uses various logos for different parts of its chain, but look out for its name: Watami (わたみ or 和民).

number of cheaper bars in every section. In general, if you are traveling on a budget, a willingness to try indigenous alcohols like *awamori*, *shōchū* and, to a lesser extent, sake will throw up more bargains than foreign imports like whisky, beer and wine.

Read more

The more I have studied Japanese alcohol, the more I have realized that it is not possible to do justice to the topic in a single volume. There are dozens of bars and many topics that I would have liked to have covered here but which had to be chopped out in the final edit. The following English language sources will take you further:

Books

The Sake Handbook by John Gauntner (Tuttle, 2002). An interesting, authoritative and comprehensive guide to sake.

Sake's Hidden Stories by John Gauntner (ebook, 2009). Reaches beyond technical explanations, uncovering the human stories behind sake. Available only as an ebook: www.sake-world.com/html/sakeshiddenstories.html.

The Insider's Guide to Sake by Philip Harper (Kodansha, 1998). Slightly older than Gauntner's handbook but offers an extremely informative survey of the topic. The writing is lyrical in places.

Sake: A Modern Guide by Beau Timken and Sara Deseran (Chronicle Books, 2006). Much less detailed than Gauntner's and Harper's books but has an appealing introduction that communicates the essential information in a clear and entertaining way.

Japanese Whisky: Facts, Figures and Taste by Ulf Buxrud (DataAnalys, 2008). A comprehensive and detailed guide to the Japanese distilleries.

Other media

Anything by Nicholas Coldicott, the drinks writer of *The Japan Times*, is essential reading.

Metropolis Magazine. Good features and bar reviews.

Websites

Sake world (www.sake-world.com). Another mention for John Gauntner. His website is full of information about sake, as well as details of his seminars and professional courses, which have trained many of the leading figures in the international sake scene. Gauntner's email newsletter is also packed with information.

Bento.com (www.bento.com). The leading English-language guide to eating and drinking in Tōkyō, Yokohama, Ōsaka, Kyōto and Kōbe. Its regularly updated restaurant and bar reviews are informative and reliable.

Brews News (www.bento.com/brews.html). Brews News is hosted on the www.bento.com servers but offers such a good coverage of the Japanese craft beer scene that it deserves separate mention. Maintained by Bryan Harrell, the leading expert on Japanese beer.

Boozelist (www.boozelist.blogspot.com). A constantly updated list of craft beers on tap in the Tōkyō and Yokohama area, plus beer and bar reviews on linked websites. Maintained by Chris "Chuwy" Philips, who taught me most of what I know about Japanese beer.

Beer in Japan (www.beerinjapan.com). Very good coverage of the Japanese craft beer scene.

Tokyo Foodcast (tokyofoodcast.com). A consistently interesting blog about Tōkyō food and sake by "Et-chan and Te-chan."

Tokyo Through the Drinking Glass (www.tokyo-drinkingglass.blogspot.com/). "Life, wine, and the pursuit of sake" by Melinda Joe, who writes for Bento.com and *The Japan Times*.

Urban sake (www.urbansake.com). A great resource for US-based sake fans. Includes guides to drinking and buying sake in several major American cities.

Nihonshudō NYC (www.nihonshudo-nyc.blogspot.com/). A blog about New York's flourishing sake scene.

Drinking Japan (www.drinkingjapan.com). My own website. It offers news and updates relating to this guide, and detailed referencing to the sources used in its preparation. The website also carries links to www.nonjatta.blogspot.com, a website I edit about Japanese whisky.

A warning and an appeal

Everything changes and few things are in such a constant state of flux as the Japanese drinking scene. I visited every one of the bars in this guide at some time between the end of 2008 and August 2010. By the end of my research, I discovered that some of the bars in this book that I had visited at the start of my travels had closed or changed radically. I was able to remove these from my recommendations, but I am sure others listed here will close, raise their prices, drop their standards, change their opening hours, move or employ spectacularly obnoxious bar staff by the time you visit. If you do find things significantly changed, I would first like to apologize and would also appeal to you to contact me at www.drinkingjapan.com, where I will try to post details of important changes. If you find an excellent bar not included here, please send details! Any information given will help improve the next edition of this guide.

Sake bottles at Donjaka, Shinjuku, Tōkyō (page 52).

Chapter 1 **Japanese Sake and Sake Bars**

The Art of Japanese Sake

Keisuke Terada, head of the Terada Honke brewery in Kozaki, Chiba, where they have been brewing sake since 1673.

In September 1699, the low-ranked *samurai* Bunzaemon Asahi confided to his personal journal: "I got back at night. I had drunk so much I puked a lot." Bunzaemon's diary, the *Ōmu Rōchūki* ("Diary of a Caged Parrot"), has left us a wonderfully vivid and vomit-stained picture of the Genroku era, a time of relative peace and prosperity when it seems the life of a warrior was largely about downing vast quantities of sake and suffering the inevitable consequences.

Bunzaemon and his friends were allowed to drink on their night shifts and liked to get properly drunk on their days off. Since only one out of every nine days was spent on guard duty at the castle (the euphemism for the other days was

Sake casks.

寺田本家
寺田本家
五人娘
寺田本家醸
香取

"training at home"), they had plenty of time to carouse. "Around 2 o'clock in the afternoon, Shinzō came around," Bunzaemon writes. "We drank together and then went out. Then to 'Jinsa'. Had sake and warm *tōfu*. Got back home at dawn." Another entry: "I got so badly drunk and puked so much, I was almost beside myself. Choked and took a big breath. How stupid!"

I introduce Bunzaemon at the start of this chapter because foreigners like myself, given to overly romantic visions of Japan as a land of light-dappled *shōji* screens and Zen stripped interiors, can sometimes get the wrong idea about sake. I have often caught myself adopting an oddly one-eyed view of Japan's national drink: as a particularly refined alcohol, connected umbilically to Japanese religion and national identity, a liquid of such delicacy that some people devote good parts of their lives to its appreciation. Of course, sake is all of that, but it is something else too and, in a way, something more: Japan's bog-standard brew. It is the drink of the common people, Japan's beer, if you like, and the drinking culture has often had more in common with the 14-pint-a-night lager swillers of my hometown in Yorkshire than the sniff-and-sip connoisseurship you will find in some of the better sake bars today.

Take, by way of illustration, the *sake kassen* or drinking contests of old Japan. In 911, eight hard-drinking courtiers at the retired Emperor's palace played a game in which they passed around 20 cups of sake. Everyone drank in turn and the cups just kept going around the circle. One drinker ended up face down outside the palace, another threw up all over the floor, but Korehira Fujiwara drank eight rounds without getting unseemly. He was awarded a swift horse for his prowess.

The participants were less aristocratic in 1648, when 16 "Eastern Army" drinkers fought 14 "Western Army" drunkards at the famous Daishigawara drinking battle in Kawasaki. They drank until they dropped and there is still dispute about which "army" won. In October 1815, four months after Waterloo, the Senju district of Tōkyō hosted its own battle: between 100 local soaks. The contestants could choose to quaff from a range of cups: from a relatively small 5-gō vessel (900 ml, more than a bottle of wine) to the monstrous "Green Haired Turtle Cup" (4,500 ml) and "Red Crowned Crane Cup" (5,400 ml). The winner was said to have filled and emptied the "Green Haired Turtle Cup" three times, equivalent to seven and a half of the big double-sized "Isshōbin" bottles in which sake is now sold. In 1927, second place in a similar contest went to a woman called Otome who stomached 34.5 liters of sake in a single sitting. These quantities verge on the unbelievable (and anybody trying anything like this with modern strength sake would risk killing themselves) but, even allowing for some exaggeration, they do show that sake drinking, like all alcohol cultures, has never been a wholly civilized affair.

There are endless accounts of these drinking contests, but I will introduce just two more, held at the Imperial court in 1474, to clarify my point. In the first, called *Jūdonomi*, two groups of 10 men competed with each other to see which team could neck their sakes the fastest. The second game was called *Jusshunomi*. Again, two groups of 10 competed: each drinker was served three types of sake and then had to try to identify the samples they had tasted from a range of 10 sakes. These two themes—sake as an object of connoisseurship and sake as an uncomplicated intoxicant—run throughout sake history and have helped shape a modern market in which, as the Kyōto sake bar owner Yoram Ofer said to me, "There is a lot of garbage and a lot of heaven."

Preparing the organic rice used for sake making at the Terada Honke brewery.

A brief history of sake

Beginnings

Sake was probably not Japan's first alcoholic drink. That honor probably belongs to prehistoric fruit wines (see page 196). Rice-based alcohol had to wait until the arrival of rice cultivation from the Asian continent between 1000 BC and 300 BC. The earliest sakes would have been quite different from today's refined drink. They were probably made by villagers chewing rice to promote fermentation and then spitting it out (*kuchikamizake*). There is a report from the 8th century of peasants in southern Kyūshū still using the chewing method, and Hateruma Island in Okinawa prefecture was holding a chewed sake festival until the 1930s. It would have been an opaque whitish color and quite sour. Some of it may not have been a drink at all: one early account appears to describe a semi-solid alcohol served on a tree leaf.

By the 6th century, *kōji* molds (see below) imported from the continent were offering a slightly more sanitary way of breaking down the starches than peasant spit. There are also records of priests making and selling sake as a commodity from the next century. Some of this alcohol was quite sophisticated: in the early 900s we know that aristocrats were warming sake, which would have required highly filtered beverages to taste good. Some of the ruling class became very fond of a tipple. When the nobleman Michitaka Fujiwara was on his deathbed in 995, his priests told him to face west toward heaven and chant a sacred prayer. He flatly refused:

Company employees play drinking games at a party in the Nishiura Hot Spring resort, Aichi Prefecture, in 1961.

The since-closed Shikishima sake brewery in Kamezaki, Aichi Prefecture, in the early 1960s.

"What is the point of going to heaven when there is nobody to drink with?" Less wealthy drinkers who got a taste for the cripplingly expensive temple sake faced bigger worries than a lack of drinking buddies in the afterlife: there is a ghost story from the 9th century about a man who bought 37 liters of alcohol from a temple on credit but was unable to pay his debt. He was reincarnated as an ox and had to return to the temple to work off his bill.

The Kōji riot

From about 1200, sake began to be sold as a commodity to commoners in the cities, and over the next three or four centuries this growing popular market transformed the industry. The grip of the religious foundations on sake making loosened slowly and commercialized, commoner-run businesses began to dominate. The transition was never more dramatically illustrated than in the Kōji riot in Kyōto in 1444.

The famous Kitano shrine had a legal monopoly on Kyōto's production of *kōji*, the mold used to prepare sake rice for fermentation. But for many years the city's 340-odd sake makers had been complaining that the supply provided by the shrine's guild was not meeting booming demand and that the prices were grossly inflated. They started building their own "moonshine" *kōji* rooms which, throughout the 1420s and 1430s, were periodically smashed by soldiers sent to enforce the monopoly. In 1443, the situation came to a head when the sake makers simply stopped buying the shrine's mold.

The shrine petitioned the shogunate and, in a sort of strike to put pressure on the authorities, its *kōji* makers locked themselves in their sacred precincts while they waited for the decision. Initially, the shogunate seemed likely to back the shrine and the status quo, but popular protests in the city and the lobbying power of the sake makers (who were among the richest citizens and the main money lenders) brought a dramatic change of policy. Soldiers were sent, not to break the moonshiners' *kōji* rooms, but to root the *kōji* guild out of the shrine. The scene quickly turned ugly. Forty people were slaughtered. Kitano shrine and other buildings in the area were torched, and the priests' domination of sake brewing was smashed forever.

It took centuries for the transfer of power to be completed, but the trend was toward secular commerce. In the Muromachi period (1392–1573), we see increasing differentiation between sake makers, distributors and shops selling to the public. Brands start to emerge and, of course, we get the fitful, often barmy government regulation that seems to be a feature of any mature drink market. At one stage, the shogunate even tried to legislate what commoners could eat at a party: they could either have three different food dishes and one soup or one soup, two dishes and three glasses of sake. Needless to say, no one seems to have taken much notice.

Edo sake

In the 17th and 18th centuries, the population of the city of Edo (modern-day Tōkyō) grew from about 400,000 people to more than a million. Bunzaemon Asahi, the vomiting *samurai* we met at the start of this chapter, was typical of the population: a man from the provinces living on his own in the big city with money burning holes in his pockets (there were 1.5 times as many men as women). At the peak of Edo's binge, at the start of the 19th century, the revelers were drinking one barrel of sake a year for every man, woman and child in the city (about 200 ml per person per day). Much of this was a cheap, unrefined style of sake called *doburoku*, which would have been consumed cold. There were more than 1,800 *doburoku* makers in the city in 1837. But more prosperous drinkers were drinking warmed sake made out of much more refined brews imported in huge quantities from Kōbe, Ōsaka and Kyōto in western Japan. You will sometimes still hear modern Japanese call poor quality goods *kudaranai*. The phrase literally means "did not come down" and refers to the Edo view that if something had not "come down" from Kansai's prestigious production centers it was not worth buying. The view was particularly strong among drinkers, and Kansai's sake (*kudarizake*) overwhelmingly dominated Edo's market, accounting for about 70–90 percent of refined sake consumed in the city.

It was a formidably sophisticated industry. When patronizing Westerners arrived in Japan during the Meiji period to "teach the natives" about modern science, they were astounded to learn that the Kansai brewers had been heating their sake to destroy microbes for more than 250 years before Louis Pasteur's discovery of "pasteurization" (Pasteur had initially been working for the wine industry). Charcoal filtering was also common practice. The story went that a worker at an Ōsaka sake *kura* in the early 1600s had become angry with his master and dumped ash from a stove into a batch of sake. The *kura* owner made a fortune when he discovered that the alcohol rescued from the barrel was of unusual clarity.

A quick guide to sake

When the sake bug gets you, the seemingly endless variety of types of sake is great fun to explore. But, for the newcomer, these different categories—*ginjōshu*, *honjōzōshu*, *junmai* and *yamahai*—can be a little overwhelming. So, what do you really need to know to make a start in sake?

Basically, sake is a brewed rice beer (though much more alcoholic than beer, so be careful). It is usually called *Nihonshu* in Japan, not sake. To find good sake, you need to look for *junmai* or pure rice sake (with nothing else added). The characters for *junmai* (純米) should appear somewhere on the bottle. The other type of sake that is highly sought after is *ginjō* (吟醸), which is made from highly polished rice. You will sometimes hear people talking about *daiginjō* (大吟醸), which is a more refined version of *ginjō*. You can drink any sake at any temperature you like, from hot to refrigerator cold. For more information on getting by in Japanese shops and bars, see the Appendix (page 253).

Modern sake

The taste, appearance and ways of serving sake have been in constant flux throughout its recent history. In a similar vein to the American economist George Taylor's famous theory that women's hemlines rose and fell with stock prices (miniskirts in the boom times, ankle lengths when the crashes come), the Japanese food historian Osamu Shinoda suggested that sake's sweetness varied with war and peace. Indeed, records do seem to give the theory at least superficial credibility. In the relatively peaceful 1870s, a typical sake seems to have been quite dry by modern standards. In the war years between 1915 and 1920 and from the 1930s to 1940s, sakes became very sweet.

We currently seem to be headed in the opposite direction: away from the obsession with the super-dry sakes of the 1990s. (Maybe it's all those North Korean missile tests?) Other tastes wax and wane as well: cedar wood smells and flavors imparted by sake barrels were valued in the Edo period—the bottom of a sake barrel could have a positively gin-like spiciness—but the rise of bottling has led to these tastes falling out of favor for the very best sakes.

The most significant change over the past 100 years has been a dramatic shift in the geography of sake. In the 19th century, the dominance of Kansai's brewers seemed unassailable. Not only did they sell more than anybody else, but their sake was acknowledged to be of a higher quality. They swept the board at the first national sake tasting competition in 1907. *Rakugo* performers, Japan's traditional sit-down comedians, used to tell jokes about the poor quality of *jizake* (地酒, local sake) from local breweries. But, in 1913, the New Sake Tasting Competition ("Shinshu Kanpyōkai") dealt a stunning blow to these preconceptions: provincial sakes from Akita, Okayama, Ehime and Hiroshima shared the top prizes with Kansai's famous Fushimi and Nada districts. Worse, a detailed look at the results revealed that only 60 percent of Nada and Fushimi's sake had earned top medals, while Hiroshima boasted an 80 percent success rate and Okayama 70 percent. The country hicks kept on winning big prizes and, by 1919, the Nada makers had become so angry that they refused to take part.

These competitive reversals had little immediate impact on Kansai's dominance in the real market, but impending war in the 1930s brought long-term changes that still shape contemporary sake. A government push to reduce rice use hurt the *jizake* makers in the short term. Half of the smaller *kura* were closed, and those that were left were given strictly limited rations of rice, which made it virtually impossible to expand. It was the big Kansai makers who invested in mass production and made most of the cheap, adulterated sake that was all that was available to most people during the war. Disgruntled drinkers talked of "goldfish sake," which had so much water added that fish could live in it. After that was regulated out of existence, a more potent but equally knavish innovation called *zōjōshu* hit the shelves. It had so much distilled alcohol and sugar added that rice use was cut by more than two-thirds.

Just as *zōjōshu* tended to give wicked hangovers to its consumers, so its production affected the industry long after the end of rice shortages. The basis of some of the big *kuras'* businesses was no longer making the highest quality sake in Japan, as was the policy in the Edo and Meiji periods, but the mass production of plonk. For many years, the Japanese tax regime favored these cheap drinks and this legacy still marks the industry. The most inexpensive sakes contain added alcohol and other additives, which are there solely to increase the yield. "Nihonshu was dealt a very, very raw hand by the big makers," says Yoram Ofer. "Today you have everybody from the industry carrying on about falling sales but they have only themselves to blame. They got themselves a terrible image. It is foreigners and the young Japanese in their twenties who are most enthusiastic about sake now because they have not been put off by this foul stuff."

Far left: The Terada Honke brewery in Kozaki, Chiba.
Left: Terraced rice paddies in Saga prefecture.
Below left: Rice planting at the Terada Honke brewery.
Below: Steaming rice at Nakashima Shuzō, Gifu.

Happily, the post-war period also saw the rise of *jizake* of unprecedented quality. It would be wrong to claim that Nada and Fushimi do not make good alcohol. Many makers in these areas have never compromised their principles and the mass-market makers still have very good products at the top of their ranges. However, the stark reality is that Kansai sake is no longer synonymous with quality in the way it was 100 years ago. Regions like Niigata and Akita have gained powerful reputations since *jizake* started to assert itself in the late 1970s, but great drinks are now coming at us from all directions: Aichi, Chiba, Fukushima, Hiroshima, Nagano, Saitama and Yamagata. Indeed, just about every prefecture would claim to be producing some good sake.

Sake making

Fortunately for the sake industry's profits, enjoying sake does not require a detailed understanding of how it is made. After all, most drinkers only have the vaguest notions of how wine and beer are brewed. So, if the technicalities bore you, just read the "Quick guide" box on page 35 and skip ahead. For those who do like to know the technicalities, however, here is a quick, potted explanation of how that ricey goodness gets from the paddy field to your glass:

Sake rice has larger grains and is much more starchy than the rice Japanese people eat. It tends to be quite tall, often exceeding a man's height, and is notorious for its vulnerability to storm damage. "Yamada Nishiki" (山田錦) is the most famous variety. Although particularly difficult to cultivate, it is still a favorite with many *kura* because of its flexibility and the complexity of its tastes. According to the sake writer John Gauntner (whose books are a must for anyone learning about sake), Yamada tends to produce drinks with fruity, lively and layered flavors—"a biggie in terms of enhanced sake flavor and fragrance profiles." There are lots of other varieties, including the very popular "Gohyakumangoku" (五百万石, light and dry), "Miyama Nishiki" (美山錦, strong flavors and acidity) and "Ōmachi" (雄町, full and smooth) rices.

The first stage of sake production involves milling or polishing the rice so that the outer portions are removed. More expensive sakes will have more of the outer layers of the rice taken off. The weight of the polished white rice as a percentage of the raw brown rice is called the *seimaibuai* (精米歩合) and is often displayed on bottles (see *daiginjō* and *ginjō* below). A low percentage generally means a more refined sake.

The white rice is washed, soaked, steamed and then cooled to prepare it for brewing. About 20–30 per cent of this rice is then cultivated with mold spores called *kōjikin* (麹菌) for two or three days in a heat-controlled room. The resulting mold-covered rice (*kome kōji*, 米麹) is vital to sake making because, when it is added to the rest of the rice in the fermentation vat, it breaks down rice starches into sugars, which can be turned into alcohol by the yeast (*kōbo*, 酵母). Before the main business of fermentation begins, however, the yeast is given a chance to propagate and establish itself in a smaller vat. The yeast, small amounts of water, *kōji* rice and steamed rice are mixed in this side vat for 2–4 weeks to produce an extremely yeast-rich liquid called the *moto* or *shubo*. Lactic acid is often also added at this stage to suppress unwanted micro-organisms (*yamahai* and *kimoto* sake *motos* are different, see page 41).

Fermentation proper begins when steamed rice, *kōji* rice and water are added to the yeasty *moto*. The rice, water and *kōji* are usually added in three stages over four days, to give a chance for the yeasts to do their work (distilled alcohol and other additives are put in at this stage in some breweries). This *moromi* is then left to ferment for 2–5 weeks. Philip Harper, the first foreigner ever to earn the title of *tōji* (master brewer), described what happens next in a wonderfully lyrical passage in *The Insider's Guide to Sake*: "The tank appears to contain a great swollen heap of very thick porridge. After a couple of days, the moist surface begins to crack in places, and a thin foam appears there. The mash begins to bubble.... The first fine, watery foam changes into a much thicker, creamier layer of bubbles. At its peak, this foam rises well over a meter above the surface of the mash.... This recedes a few days after reaching its peak ... the mix is much lighter and more obviously liquid by now, and it bubbles and seethes frantically for several days. Gradually, the activity subsides." The sake produced can reach up to 19–20 percent alcohol and is called *genshu* (原酒) if it is bottled at this strength. Most sake is diluted to about 16 percent alcohol for sale.

What are the different types of sake?

The six main categories

Although the term "sake" is in such wide use among foreigners that it is impossible to avoid using it, "sake" is not a precise term. It is actually the general word in Japanese for any alcohol, including beer, whisky, wine, etc. *Nihonshu* (日本酒) is usually the term used if you want to refer specifically to the brewed rice beverage (although some *shōchū* makers don't like it because it implies that sake is the national drink. "Shōchū is Nihonshu too!"). A more technical term is *seishu* (清酒). These two characters are useful, because they are printed on the labels of all refined sakes. To the uninitiated, sake and *shōchū* bottles can look quite similar, but *shōchū* always has 焼酎printed somewhere and sake almost always carries the characters 清酒.

At the Terada Honke brewery, preparing the rice for sake making is still done using equipment and techniques that have changed little over the centuries.

You are going to have to know a bit more than that if you want something interesting, however. As Yoram Ofer bluntly put it, there is a "lot of garbage and a lot of heaven" in the sake world. Let's begin with the "garbage."

Zōjōshu 増醸酒 The cheapest sake and the close bosom friend of technicolor hangovers. Hundreds of liters of distilled alcohol can be added for every tonne of white rice used in making this stuff. Other additives such as glucose are also often used. Since 2006, these products have been forbidden from calling themselves *seishu*, the technical name for sake, and are instead classified as a type of liqueur. They still sit on the sake shelves, though. Don't touch the stuff.

Futsūshu 普通酒 The *vin ordinaire* of the sake world. *Futsūshu* accounts for the majority of sake sales. It contains much less added alcohol than *zōjōshu*. Like *vin ordinaire*, the *futsūshu* category encompasses tedious mass-market bottlings, but also quite interesting brews. It really depends on who is making it and for what reason. There are some bargains to be had, because prices are not being ramped up by prestigious classifications.

Honjōzō or Honjōzōshu 本醸造 or **本醸造酒**
These are premium sakes made with polished rice, but with small amounts of alcohol added in the production process. The polished rice's weight is a maximum of 70 percent of its unpolished weight and fewer than 117 liters of distilled alcohol per tonne of rice are added during fermentation. Unlike the cheap *zōjōshu*, the alcohol is not added for economy reasons. It helps the brewers create light but aromatic sakes. Fragrant components in the *moromi* dissolve in the alcohol and are brought into the final sake rather than staying in the lees.

Junmai or Junmaishu 純米 or **純米酒**
Junmaishu is pure rice sake: only rice, *kōjikin*, water, yeast and perhaps a little lactic acid to help the yeast are used in production. Not all *junmaishu* use *ginjō* or *daiginjō* polished rice, but this does not mean they are necessarily of inferior quality. In fact, there has been a recent trend towards favoring the robust tastes often associated with relatively unpolished *junmaishu*.

Ginjō or Ginjōshu 吟醸 or **吟醸酒** Sake made of very finely milled or polished rice. Polishing reduces the rice to 60 percent of its unpolished weight. A lot of *ginjō* is *junmaiginjō* (純米吟醸) made of pure rice, but some *ginjō* have a small amount of added alcohol, like *honjōzō*. They are not usually labeled as *honjōzōginjō*. You have to look at the ingredient list to see if alcohol has been added.

Daiginjō or Daiginjōshu 大吟醸 or **大吟醸酒**
Ginjō's more polished sibling. The *seimaibuai* (精米歩合), the weight of the polished rice as a percentage of its original weight, is less than 50 percent and in some extreme cases can go as low as 10 percent. Small amounts of alcohol are sometimes added.

Opposite: Priests prepare doburoku unrefined sake at the Shirakawa festival in Gifu prefecture.
Left: The promise of free doburoku sake at the Shirakawa festival draws hundreds of visitors to the remote mountain village.

Other numbers on labels

We have already dealt with one of the important numbers often listed on sake labels, the *seimai-buai* (精米歩合) or degree of rice polishing. There are three more figures that you will often find on labels, which may help you understand better what you are buying. One is the *Nihonshudo* (日本酒度, sometimes called SMV or "sake meter value"). This measurement is usually between -4 and +15 (but can range much more widely). Put very simply, this measure shows whether a sake is dry or sweet: -3 is sweet, 0 is sweetish and anything above 4 is getting dry. Of course, other taste components influence the perception of sweetness/dryness, so the *Nihonshudo* is not always a reliable guide. (For example, a +10 sake with a very full body may not taste very dry at all.)

The acidity of a sake (酸味) also affects its flavor and labels often carry measurements of this tangyness (typically from a lowish acidity of 1.0 to highs in excess of 2.0). They will sometimes also measure amino acids (アミノ酸味), high levels of which can give the sake a feeling of body (again, 1.0 to 2.0 is a normal range). But all these figures can be very confusing. Personally, when I am in a liquor shop, I generally take a glance at the *Nihonshudo*, and do the rest with my tongue when I get home.

Seven variations

If sake could be reduced merely to six levels of purity and refinement, the world would be a dull place. In fact, there is endless variety in the methods of making and storing sake. Here are some interesting variations to explore:

Yamahai and Kimoto sake *Yamahai* (山廃) and *kimoto* (生酛) sakes are known for the wildness and richness of their flavors. *Yamahai* makers do not add lactic acid when they are making the *moto*, the yeasty liquid that powers fermentation. Lactic acids are usually added nowadays because they suppress wild yeasts and other microorganisms that might create unpleasant flavors. *Yamahai moto* making instead relies on naturally occurring enzymes and lactic acids. It takes up to twice as long and involves additional stages of heating and cooling.

Kimoto sake is made using an older method closely related to *yamahai*: brewery staff work in freezing temperatures for hours on end with long, flat-headed poles to grind the *kōji* and water into a paste. Until 1909, this was the way that all sake was made: they thought the back-breaking work was necessary for getting the *kōji* to work on the rice so that the yeasts could be nourished and protected. Historically, *kimoto* came first, then the *yamahai* method dropped the pole work by using a slightly different *moto* mix and warmer temperatures. The benefits of lactic acid were discovered in 1911, allowing today's warmer, quicker and more reliable *moto* making. However, many *kura* are exploring the complex, untamed tastes that the old natural methods tended to promote.

Namazake (生酒) Most sake is heat-treated twice, once immediately after the sake is pressed from the *moromi* and once when it is bottled. *Namazake* is not heat-treated at all and it can smell and taste quite different to your average dry sake: boisterous, nutty, fruity, herb-like, and even spicy tastes can be brought out by the extra life non-pasteurization allows. The usual instruction is to make sure your *namazake* is carefully refrigerated so that all that microscopic partying does not get out of hand, but Yoram Ofer served me a *namazake* that he had kept at room temperature for three years. It had a wonderfully mild and honeyed taste. "The industry will tend not to want to do that because it is too risky. You will get

Above: Isshin, a sake pub in Sendai prefecture (page 57), has a special annex, equipped with "chirori" heating flasks at every table, for customers who want to warm their sake.
Left: Koshu aged sakes, such as these at Shusaron, Shinagawa, Tōkyō (page 68), are enjoying a revival.

the bottles that will go off but it is not true that it always goes bad," he says. There are two halfway houses to *namazake*: *namachozō* (生貯蔵), which is not pasteurized after filtering, and *namazume* (生詰め), which is not pasteurized at bottling.

Muroka (無濾過), **nigorizake** (濁り酒) **and doburoku** (濁酒) Most sake is charcoal-filtered. *Muroka* is not and therefore tends to retain some of the heavier flavors and yellowish/green coloring that the filtering is designed to remove. *Nigorizake* takes the unfiltered thing a step further. Rather than pressing the sake out of the *moromi* through a fine filter, the *nigori* makers use only a wide-holed mesh or, alternatively, filter the sake clear and then reintroduce *kasu* from the *moromi* afterwards. Either way, some of the solids in the *moromi* are present in the final alcohol and *nigorizake* range in appearance from cloudy to positively porridge like. The tastes vary considerably too but there is often a strong acidity. Unpasteurized *nigorizake* is called *kasseishu* (活性酒) and can sometimes have a slight fizz to it. At the extreme end of the spectrum, *doburoku* is not filtered or squeezed at all. It looks like porridge and can be quite hard to like, with a strongly acidic taste. I once spent some time teaching English in a beautiful village in the Japanese Alps called Shirakawa. They have a festival there every October where you can drink free *doburoku* made by the villagers. It is a religious occasion but, when, in the middle of the festivities, an old Japanese man grabbed my friend by the testicles (just, he said, to "size him up"), I realized people can get seriously drunk on anything if need be.

Fizzy sake Fizzy sake brands such as "Suzune" (すず音) from Ichinokura (一ノ蔵) in Miyagi and "Puchipuchi" (ぷちぷち) from Suehiro Shuzō (末廣酒造) in Fukushima have recently been gaining popularity. They usually contain a lower alcohol content than standard sake because making the fizz requires that the tank fermentation be stopped earlier than usual. The bubbles are made by a secondary fermentation in the bottle. These brews are usually filtered (so are not *nigorizake*) but significant amounts of sugar and yeast must be allowed into the bottles for the secondary fermentation to take place. They are, therefore, usually cloudy and quite sweet.

Koshu The rediscovery of long-neglected traditions of maturing sake is, for me, one of the most exciting developments in the contemporary sake scene. There are diaries and letters showing that aged sake, or *koshu* (古酒), was valued highly as early as the 13th century and Edo-period shop records tell us that 3–9 year old sake was two or three times more expensive than *shinshu* (new sake, 新酒). The *Honchō Shokkan*, a food encyclopedia published in 1697, says: "After 3–5 years the taste is rich and the smell is wonderful and that is the best. From 6–10 years the taste becomes thinner and yet richer. The color darkens and there is a strange aroma. Better than the best!"

Yet, when pioneering makers tried to resurrect *koshu* making in the 1970 and 1980s, they were sometimes met with outright hostility. The traditions of aging had died out so completely and had been replaced so thoroughly by the modern interest in young sake that *koshu* was seen, at best, as a gimmick and, at worst, a worrying subversion of "proper" sake values.

Why did *koshu* almost disappear? The growing popularity of wooden barrels for storing sake in the Edo period may have been partly to blame. The barrels allowed much more exposure to the air than the pottery vessels they replaced and therefore increased the risk of spoiling. They also imparted woody tastes that may have become overpowering after long aging. More lethal to the tradition, however, were tax laws introduced in the early Meiji period (1868–1912), which forced sake makers to pay tax on their sake as soon as it was made. Cash-strapped *kura* needed to get a return on their investments as soon as possible and this factor, plus faster distribution networks and wartime shortages, discouraged

The basement at Isekane, Takadanobaba, Tōkyō (page 240) is packed with premium sakes.

Shingen Takeda

Shingen Takeda, known as "the Tiger of Kai," is still remembered as one of the greatest *samurai* generals. He once led an army against the Hojo clan in freezing conditions in the middle of January. His troops were cold and facing a well-defended enemy on the top of a hill. Takeda is said to have ordered a large amount of sake to be heated in cauldrons and given to his men. "Do you feel warm now?" he shouted. "No," they said. He replied: "You see those men on top of that hill? Imagine how they feel!"

A ukiyoe print of Takeda Shingen by Kuniyoshi Utagawa.

long storage of sake to such an extent that it became almost unknown.

The modern *koshu* scene is rediscovering the complex tastes, fragrances and colors that aging adds to sake. Nobuhiro Ueno, a leading figure in the movement and manager of the Shusaron bar in Shinagawa (see page 68), says *koshu* can be classified into two broad types: air temperature-aged sake and refrigerator-aged sake. The air temperature *koshu* is often dark in color, with blood reds quite common (the color usually comes from reactions between sugars and amino acids in the liquid rather than from the barrels or pots used for storage, as is the case in whisky or rum aging). This type has a very wide range of tastes, including drinks reminiscent of sherry or Chinese Xiaoxing wine. Refrigeration, on the other hand, often produces sakes which are lighter in color, ranging from almost transparent to golds and greeny yellows. The taste is usually much closer to the *ginjō* sakes, with roundness, as well as biscuity and nutty flavors, often added by maturation. The sector is such a hive of innovation that Ueno admits any strict classification is doomed: combinations of cold and warm storage temperatures are being played with, as well as all sorts of storage containers (steel, glass and enamel-lined tanks; bottle aging, barrels, earthenware and ceramic pots) and a seemingly endless variety of brewing techniques (*namazake*, fortified sakes and even rice wines made with grape wine yeasts).

Mirin In the 1980s, the Japanese media was swept by a moral panic about alcoholic housewives. Shocked newspapermen reported that some of these women were so desperate they were known to drink *mirin*, a fortified rice wine that is commonly used in Japanese food. It was the ultimate sign of degradation, like lounging around the house in pajamas, swigging the cheapest cooking sherry while watching daytime television. But if the journalists who reported these horror stories had been a little more familiar with their alcohol history there might have been less sneering. *Mirin* does not mean "low-quality cooking wine," although there are plenty of low-quality products describing themselves as *mirin* on the market. In fact, certain types were considered the height of sophisticated drinking in the Edo period (1603–1868); only in the 20th century did *mirin* come to be seen almost exclusively as a cooking ingredient. It is probably best thought of as "Japanese sherry" (although the production method is closer to port): rice and *kōji* are used, just as in normal sake making, but *shōchū* is added during the fermentation, suppressing the conversion of sugars into alcohol and producing a sweeter drink. Most cheap *mirin* in supermarkets are not really *mirin* and are solely intended for cooking, but drinking *mirin* is currently being rediscovered. Look out for glass-bottled (rather than plastic-bottled) *mirin* and for the words "Hon Mirin" (本みりん). Sometimes, the drinkable stuff is bottled under the Edo-period names "Hon Naoshi" (本直し) or "Yanagikage" (柳蔭).

Shirakawa festival, Gifu.

Drinking sake

My wife's grandmother did not allow her husband to drink cold sake. In the 1960s and 1970s, it was considered very uncouth, the sort of thing a laborer might do on a building site. Even in the most oppressive months of the Japanese summer, the poor fellow, and many like him, had to drink his sake warmed.

Then the temperature police started getting into refrigeration. There was a time in the 1990s when it seemed everybody who was anybody was drinking a cold sake from Niigata. Heating up some sakes was deemed the height of bad form. There is a lovely story told by the *manga* writer Akira Oze about a *kura* owner he knew who asked for his own sake served *kan* (燗, "warmed") at a sake pub. The landlord, not knowing who he was dealing with, refused, saying heating that particular sake was a heresy. The *kura* owner ordered the sake cold with a hot *tōfu* stew and then plonked the sake *tokkuri* in the stew, drawing aghast looks from other patrons and a derisive snort from the landlord.

The moral of the story is never to let others dictate how you enjoy your drink. You can have great fun playing with sake's temperature. Unlike beer and wine, many sake will play fairly freely up and down a whole scale of temperatures. Finding out what temperature you think best suits a particular sake is part of the enjoyment of drinking. If my wife's grandfather were still alive, he might have rediscovered the delights of *kanzake* (燗酒) at Isshin in Sendai (see page 57), where customers are encouraged to heat their own sake, monitor its temperature themselves and explore their own preferences freely.

At Isshin, they break their temperatures down to the nearest five degrees centigrade (ranging from 5 to 55 degrees centigrade). The more commonly used categories include *hiyazake* (cold sake, 5–15 degrees centigrade), *hitohada kan* (skin temperature, c. 35–40 degrees), *nurukan* (lukewarm, c. 40–45 degrees), *jōkan* (well-warmed, 45–50 degrees) and *atstukan* (hot, 50–55 degrees). Many premium sakes are very nice chilled just slightly (10–15 degrees, warmer than fridge temperature) but there are sakes that really come alive at much higher temperatures.

It is worth saying that, though this is a matter of personal taste, many sakes are served either too cold or too hot in Japanese restaurants in the West. I remember one particular occasion when the sake was just off boiling. There are two good ways of warming sake: you can warm a pan of water to the right temperature first and then put the sake jug in (harder to overheat the sake) or you can put the jug in a pan of cool water and then very gently heat it (which gives less of a shocking heat). Each has its adherents and they bicker with each other like English tea drinkers over the ancient question: "Milk, first or last?"

Ajihyakusen 味百仙 011-716-1000 ajihyaku.exblog.jp

B1F, Miyazawa Kōgyō Biru, 4 Kita Nana-jō Nishi, Kita-ku, Sapporo, Hokkaido
北海道札幌市北区北七条西 4 宮澤興業ビル B1F
Open: Weekdays 5 pm–12 pm; Saturday 5 pm–11 pm; closed Sunday and national holidays
Booking recommended? Booking recommended on Fridays and weekends Credit cards? Most major cards
English menu? No Table charge: 500 yen

There was a time when Hokkaido sake did not have the best of reputations. Minoru Nagashima, owner of Ajihyakusen, has been working for 25 years to dispel that image in this small basement bar out the back end of Sapporo Station. He serves 30–40 types of *jizake* with some meticulously prepared *izakaya* fare. Both the food and drink menus change with the season, but when I visited Nagashima-san recommended the mouth-watering *kaki to gorgonzola hoiruyaki* (oysters and gorgonzola cooked in foil, 650 yen) with a potato salad (500 yen) and the "Kita Sekai" (北世界), a fruity, slightly dry *daiginjō* from Nippon Seishu. Nippon Seishu has a different sort of history to the old family businesses you will often find on the main island of Honshu. In the 19th and early 20th centuries, Hokkaido was Japan's New World, a land of opportunity (and bankruptcy) where business capital flowed freely across all sorts of bright ideas for developing the frontier. Nippon Seishu was a product of that business environment, emerging from a co-operative venture between seven local sake makers in 1897 and then a formal merger of eight companies in 1928. It is now a large company pumping out extensive ranges of *miso* and wine as well as sake, but a clear-sighted view of the future of sake seems to have brought a greater commitment to high-quality sake production. Its main sake brand is "Chitosetsuru" (千歳鶴), but "Kita Sekai" was a premium sake project close to the heart of Nippon Seishu's old master brewer, Wataru Tsumura. Unfortunately, Tsumura-san died suddenly before he could see it to fruition, so it bears the signature of the current master brewer, Kazuyuki Satō. "Kita Sekai" is almost impossible to find on the open market.

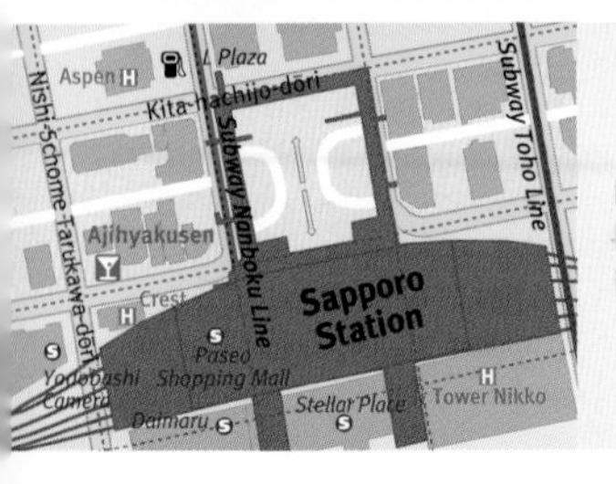

DIRECTIONS: Sapporo Station, North Exit. Immediate left out of the North Exit. It is in the basement under the AU mobile phone shop and is directly opposite the Hotel Crest.

Akaoni 赤鬼 03-3410-9918 www.akaoni39.com

2-15-3 Sangenjaya, Setagaya ku, Tōkyō, 154-0024
〒154-0024 東京都世田谷区三軒茶屋 2-15-3
Open: Weekdays 5.30 pm–12.30 am (last orders 11.30 pm); Saturday 5 pm–11.30 pm; Sunday and national holidays 5 pm–11 pm Booking recommended? Yes Credit cards? No English menu? No Table charge: 500 yen

Akaoni is probably the best-known premium sake pub in Tōkyō and the range of more than 100 types of sake easily justifies its reputation. It first opened in 1982 and has been a major force in the rise of *jizake*. Manager Nakamura-san says the sake market has changed radically: "In those days sake was not a young person's thing at all. We now get very knowledgeable young people in here, and they are driving changes in sake. Overall, sales have gone down in Japan, but if you are offering good sake then you are actually seeing popularity going up." With sakes like the *junmai ginjō* "Kameizumi CEL-24" (亀泉 CEL-24, 650 yen) in stock, Akaoni has clearly got nothing to worry about. It may sound like a Star Wars droid but "CEL-24" is actually the name of a yeast known for producing fragrant and acidic drinks. This unpasteurized "Kameizumi" is fragrant, fruity and sweet (-10 *Nihonshudo*). Many drinkers will prefer it served cold so that the sweetness does not become overwhelming. Another unpasteurized sake, "Kozaemon" *junmai ginjō* (小左衛門純 米吟醸), from the young brewing team at Nakashima brewery in Gifu prefecture, offered a total contrast: clean and clear. Quite a few sake and spirit makers all over Japan play music to their fermenting alcohol in the belief that it influences the fermentation, but at Nakashima, according to "Et-chan" of the excellent www.tokyofoodcast.com website, they play hip-hop. It is not clear whether this is for their own enjoyment or the yeast's. The sake world is getting younger!

DIRECTIONS: Sengenjaya Station (Tōkyū Den'entoshi Line). Go out of the central gates of Sangenjaya Station and take North Exit A. Walk straight ahead across the side road, then cross the main road to Big Echo Karaoke. Bear right toward the Carrot Tower. Go left just after the bicycle park, right at the T-junction and right again at the end of the block beside the car park.

Amanogawa 天乃川 03-3344-0111 (main hotel reception) www.keioplaza.co.jp/rb/bl05.html

Keio Plaza Hotel, 2-2-1 Nishi Shinjuku, Shinjuku-ku, Tōkyō, 160-8330
〒160-8330 京王プラザホテル 東京都新宿区西新宿 2-2-1
Open: 5 pm–10.30 pm Credit cards? All major cards
English menu? No Booking recommended? Yes Table charge: 577 yen

Koji Maruoka, the sake sommelier (*kikizakeshi*) at Keio Plaza Hotel's Amanogawa sake bar, compares trying a new sake to meeting a new person. "Often people who are very forceful or a bit different will put you off when you first run into them. They might not seem like your sort at all, but once you have got to know them, you grow to like all their differences. You love them because of their differences." He says some customers at this stylish 10-seat sake bar arrive determined only to drink very dry sakes served very cold. "A lot of that has come from the *shōchū* boom. People want very clean, cold tastes." Another type of customer wants their sakes boiled until dead. "In truth, the best temperature depends on the particular sake. It is going to be in a moderate temperature range. The style of sake that best suits the moment is also going to depend on what you are eating it with." During my visit, Maruoka served a three-food plate (*chinmi omakase sanshu*, 2100 yen), which changes every day and may vary in price. Our plate featured *tōfu*, the classic drinking snack *shiokara* (salted and fermented seafood) and a dish made of cream cheese and sake *kasu* (the rice waste from sake making). Maruoka-san recommended an "Okuharima Jyōho" (奥播磨 誠保) *junmai kimoto* sake, a pure rice *junmai* sake, from his constantly changing line-up of around 30 sakes, which he tries to source from small *kura* rather than the big players. "Okuharima Jyōho" is a fascinating pick. It is a *kimoto* sake (see page 41). The rich, almost milky tastes represent a step back to a time when all sake was produced by a back-breaking process of mashing rice by hand. It is extremely hard to get hold of. The two expressions released so far by Shimomura Shuzō of Hyōgo prefecture have sold out almost immediately. Maruoka also recommended a "Retsu" (洌) *junmai ginjō* from Kojima Sōhonten in Yamagata prefecture. Kojima have a reputation for very dry, clean tastes. Most sakes at Amanogawa cost in the region of 900 yen and are served in 90 ml measures. Maruoka-san will sometimes serve two 45 ml measures of different sakes.

DIRECTIONS: Shinjuku Keio Plaza Hotel, Main Tower, Second Floor. From JR Shinjuku take the West Exit, straight up Chūō-dōri. The hotel is on your left and is hard to miss.

Buchi ブチ 03-5728-2085

1F Nomoto Biru, Shinsenchō 9-7, Shibuya-ku, Tōkyō
東京都渋谷区神泉町 9-7 野本ビル 1F
Open: 5 pm–3 am Credit cards? Most major cards
English menu? Yes Table charge: No charge

Let's be honest, some premium sake pubs can be intimidating. The staff and customers are almost always incredibly friendly if you actually take the plunge, but everything that makes these places picturesque and appealing—the grizzled old men slicing *sashimi* behind the counter, the *kanji*-covered paper hanging from the ceilings advertising a multitude of unknown drinks and dishes—can also make them feel like too much hard work. Foreigners can be turned off by the suspicion that these places are really aimed at connoisseurs and/or crusty salarymen with drinking issues. Fortunately, many Japanese people, particularly women, have similar feelings and that is probably why places like Buchi are thriving. When Buchi opened in 2004, it was one of the first of a new wave of *tachinomiya* (standing bars) that have since swept Japan. Standing bars have long been part of Japanese drinking culture—cheap, no-nonsense places where drunk men can get more drunk—but the shiny new *tachinomiya* of the Buchi school offer modern interiors and sophisticated menus aimed at young professionals. The wine (60 bottles, 10 glass wines) and *shōchū* (50 types) on offer here might have earned Buchi a mention in either of the chapters devoted to those drinks, but the 30 types of "cup sake" (カップ酒) provide an excellent way to try a range of good sake in a very low-stress environment with an English menu. The cup sake is itself a reinvention. This most unpretentious of serving vessels was developed by the makers of the cheapest plonk. Nowadays, though, an increasing range of premium sakes are available in cup form. When I visited, they had an "Okuharima" (奥播磨) *yamahai junmai* from Hyōgo prefecture (600 yen). The Shimomura brewery is known for its dry, well-balanced sakes, but this bottling (like the *kimoto* "Okuharima" we met at Amanogawa, page 48), is a bit special: the labor-intensive *yamahai* method (see page 41) gives richer, wilder tastes than the normal "Okuharima." The first bottling of this sold out as soon as it was released in 2007. Buchi say it works well warmed or otherwise and recommended their *senba dōfu* (*tōfu*, 500 yen) to slip down with it.

DIRECTIONS: A bit of a walk from Shibuya Station. From the Hachikō statue (a statue of a dog used as a landmark in Shibuya's chaos), head west up the road to the right of the building containing L'Occitane en Provence and then bear to the left of the Shibuya 109 building up Dōgenzaka (Dōgen slope). When you reach a large overpass, do not go under it but bear to your right past the AM/PM convenience store. Buchi is to your right when you come to a wide junction.

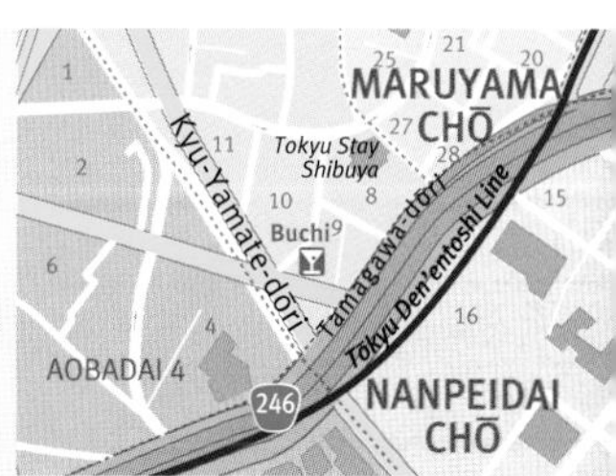

Buri ぶり 03-3496-7744

1-14-1 Ebisu-nishi, Shibuya-ku, Tōkyō
東京都渋谷区恵比寿西 1 丁目 14-1
Open: 5 pm–3 am Booking recommended? No Credit cards? Major cards
English menu? No Table charge: 200 yen

Like Buchi in Shibuya (see page 49), Buri is one of the new breed of standing bars that have been opening up since 2004. In fact, Buri and Buchi have the same meaning in the Hiroshima dialect (approximate translation: "very") and, although not the same chain, there is some unfathomable link between the investors in the two projects. The concept is also similar: a modern, casual environment serving cup sake of high quality and good, no-nonsense food. There are usually 30–40 types of *shōchū* and about 20 types of sake on the menu. A fun diversion is their "Majikōru" refrigerator, which cools 12 types of sake so that it is turned into a jelly-like consistency. I can't say I understand the science behind the trick but Buri claims it produces a very mild-tasting drink that works well on one of Tōkyō's grimy summer days. The food is a mix of Japanese standards (a delicious smell of *yakitori* met me as I entered) and Western dishes ("Rebā Pēsuto", chicken liver pâté, 450 yen), but the beauty of these standing bars for me is that you are not expected to gorge yourself while you are drinking in the time-honored Japanese fashion. Owner Mitsuyuki Shioiri recommended a "Hitakami" (日高見) *junmai* cup sake from Miyagi prefecture. It is named after an ancient, semi-legendary kingdom in the north of Japan, which is mentioned in the old chronicles as being particularly fertile. The makers, Hirakō Shuzō, use long, low-temperature fermentation, meticulous washing and steaming of the rice (which they say determines 80 percent of a sake's flavor) and refrigerated storage to produce polished and refined sakes that are designed to go particularly well with seafood (try the *kimoiri surume*, dried cuttlefish, 500 yen). Buri's restroom is a little hard to find. A hint: look carefully at the cup sake-covered wall.

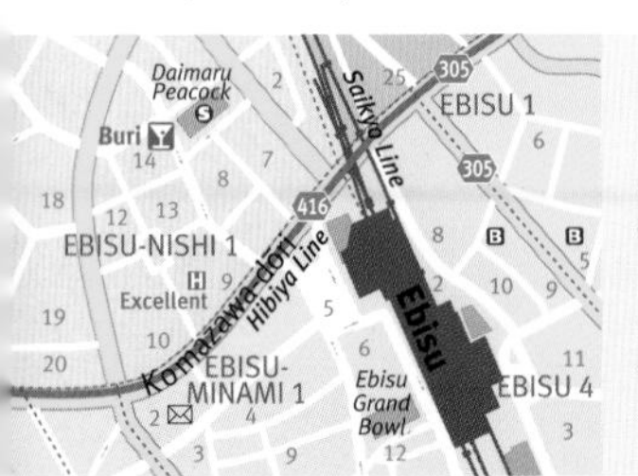

DIRECTIONS: JR Ebisu Station (Yamanote Line), West Exit (west side). Cross to the right of the taxi ranks, with the fountains beside you. Cross the big road and continue down the street beside the KFC. Follow the road for about 150 yards. Buri is on your left. From Ebisu Hibiya Line Station Exit 1, reverse your direction as you come out of the exit and follow the instructions above.

Chokottoya ちょこっと屋 082-245-7770

12-26 Kanayamachō, Naka-ku, Hiroshima-shi, Hiroshima, 730-0022
〒730-0022 広島県広島市中区銀山町 12-26
Open: 7 pm–5 am, occasional irregular one-day holidays Credit cards? Visa, Master and JCB, not Amex or Diners
English menu? No Table charge: 300 yen

Chokottoya is in a seedy part of Hiroshima. It faces an establishment offering "school girl play" and I am pretty sure we are not talking cat's cradle and skipping games. The *izakaya*'s multicolored, corrugated scrap metal façade adds to the slightly bizarre first impression. Inside, though, the aesthetic is more country farmhouse than Mad Max and the selection of more than 120 Hiroshima sakes is unrivaled. The staff are knowledgeable and friendly. If in doubt, I recommend leaving the selection of sake to them. They may surprise you. "The image is perhaps that Hiroshima sake has a sweet taste, but that is a thing of the past," Chokottoya's manager Yasutaka Sakumoto says. "Nowadays, it really varies with the *kura*. There are some very dry Hiroshima sakes." By way of example, he recommended "Ryūsei karakuchi junmai" (龍勢辛口純米) from Fujii brewery in Takehara city. It is quite dry but has a mildness to it that really develops when warmed. Sake drinkers talk about *kan agari*, the quality in some sakes of developing new, alluring tastes with heating, and this one is definitely *kan agari*. It is designed to work with food and there could be no better accompaniment for a Hiroshima sake that the local speciality, *anago tempura* (conger eel tempura, 680 yen). Also try the *gyū no yukke* (raw seasoned beef, 800 yen).

DIRECTIONS: Kanayama-chō Hiroden tram stop (Station No. M5). Head down Yagenbori-dōri (the road with the UCC coffee-sponsored gate). Take the fourth left (at the crossing with the K2 building). The sign is entirely in Japanese characters, but the corrugated iron-covered shopfront marks it out from the sex traders.

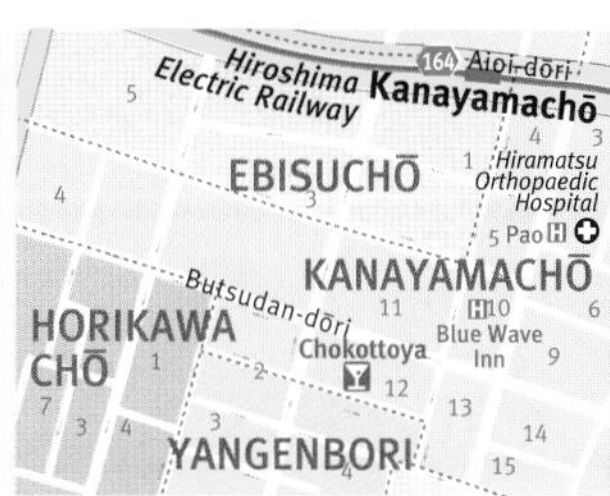

Donjaka 呑者家 03-3341-2497 r.gnavi.co.jp/g873801

3-9-10 Shinjuku, Shinjuku-ku, Tōkyō, 160-0022
〒160-0022 東京都新宿区新宿 3-9-10
Open: **5 pm–7 am** Booking recommended? **Yes** Credit cards? **No**
English menu? **No** Table charge: **400 yen**

This place is part of a group of very reasonably priced *izakaya* in this area of Shinjuku. There is another branch around the corner in Suehiro-dōri with 65 seats and a nautically themed variation, called Dora, a few paces down the road with 100 seats. Together with the 45 seats available at this branch, you would have thought there would be plenty of space for Donjaka's customers. You would be wrong. Booking is definitely a necessity on Fridays. Donjaka's alcohol and food menus are well-judged and fairly cheap. Manager Kazutoyo Uematsu recommended the *yakitori* set (*yakitori moriawase*, 500 yen) and, for those who like small fry, the potato and fish fry (*chirimen jyako to potato no kara-age*, 550 yen). Both the *shōchū* and sake selections are excellent, offering between 20 and 25 bottles of both types. The sake-tasting set, with generous samples of a varying line-up of three *jizake* (*kikizake seto*, きき酒セット, usually around 650–750 yen but varies with the line-up) represents a particularly good opportunity to expand your Japanese alcohol horizons. You might also take the opportunity to try "Denshu" (田酒), a very highly respected pure rice *junmai* sake from Aomori prefecture (特別純米酒 田酒, "Tokubetsu Junmaishu Denshu," 650 yen). Around the turn of the millennium, Nishida Shuzō, the 130-year-old sake company that makes "Denshu," were picking up so many gold medals at the national sake competitions for this fruity but well-mannered sake that they didn't know where to put them.

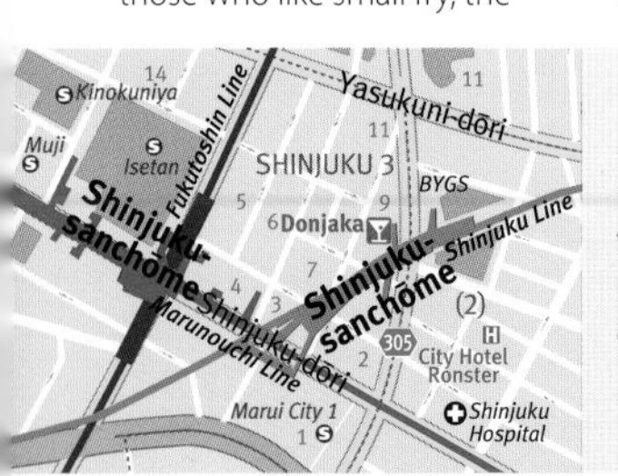

DIRECTIONS: Shinjuku-sanchōme Station, Exit C6. Turn left out of the exit (reversing your direction). It is about nine yards along on the right—the *izakaya* with a bamboo-barred window under a sign for another shop saying Amigo.

Galali

03-3408-2818 www.gala-e.com

3-6-5 Jingumae, Shibuya-ku, Tōkyō
東京都渋谷区神宮前 3-6-5
Open: **Weekdays 6 pm–4 am; Saturday, Sunday and holidays 6 pm–11 pm**
Booking recommended? **Yes** Credit cards? **Most major cards**
English menu? **Yes** Table charge: **800 yen**

You could almost mistake Galali for a residential house, which is apparently what the local residents think. There have been complaints from neighbors about the din through the thin walls. This is, therefore, not the best place to come for a noisy night out, but, if you are up for some serious sake drinking (at some moderately serious prices), Galali has an original approach. It is a sister establishment to the nearby Garari *kokuto shōchū* bar (see page 93), which serves its spirits with an unrivaled range of *miso*. At Galali, the featured combination is salt and sake, a traditional favorite. Twelve different types of salt line the bar, ranging from quite sour *umejio*—salt that has been used to pack *umeboshi* plum pickle barrels—to a delicious sweet sea salt from Ishikawa. Each has a unique taste and, if you ask, they will give you selected salts to taste with your sake free of charge. Salt also features strongly in the menu (for example, *Jidori no shioyaki*, grilled salty chicken, 1,200 yen), and they recommend it as an accompaniment for their *sashimi moriawase* (raw fish selection, 2,700 yen). I was recommended the Honjōzō Tamagaeshi "Jū Yon Dai" (十四代) from the extensive sake menu. In my experience, any bar that has a good supply of "Jū Yon Dai" will want to shout it from the rooftops. It has an almost legendary status but is actually a very young brand. It was first released in 1993 by the 15th-generation head of Takagi Shuzō, Akitsuna Takagi (the sake's name means 14 and is a tribute to his predecessor). Akitsuna was educated at Tōkyō Agricultural University, which has become a major force in modern Japanese alcohol, turning out a generation of highly educated, innovative alcohol makers (for example, the *shōchū* innovator Yoichiro Nishi of Nishi Shuzō (see page 98) was a classmate of Takagi's). The "Jū Yon Dai" *honjōzō* is made by introducing a small amount of *kasutori shōchū* (see page 81) into the fermentation tank, both to lighten the taste as well as to bring out flavors. It has a gentle vanilla sweetness but no cloying aftertaste.

DIRECTIONS: Gaienmae Station (Ginza Line), Exit 2. Walk down the right side of Route 246 to the southwest. Turn right onto route 418 just after the Bell Commons building. Cross the road to Starbucks and continue to the pedestrian footbridge. Turn left immediately after the bridge. Galali is hidden behind a cycle shop in what looks like a residential alley across the road from the Oakwood Residence building (just before the Moritex building).

Ginjōtei 吟醸鼎 011-261-0720 www.ginjyoutei.com

Basement, President Matsui Biru 100, 5 chōme, Minami Ichijō, Chūō-ku, Sapporo
札幌市中央区南 1 条西 5 丁目 プレジデント松井ビル 100 地下（電車通り沿い）
Open: 6 pm–11 pm; sometimes closes at 8 pm if empty; closed Sunday and national holidays
Booking recommended? Yes (booking requested by the owner) Credit cards? Most major cards
English menu? No Table charge: 500 yen (sometimes there are special events with a higher charge)

When you write a book about alcohol and bars you get used to marathon nights on the town, but nothing prepared me for the evening I spent with Phred Kaufman, the legendary owner of Mugishutei (see page 154), and Kjetil Jikiun, the man behind the Norwegian beer brewery Nøgne Ø.

We were still out at 6 am, long past my bedtime! Somewhere in the middle of that hazily remembered evening, Phred took us to Ginjōtei. I remember a veritable procession of superb sakes trooping their way along the bar top into our glasses. A couple of highlights that survived the hangover's regrets: an unpasteurized "Dassai" (獺祭) from Asahi brewery with a superb balanced fruitiness, and the overripe melon smell of the rich "Yuuho" *junmai ginjō* (遊穂純米吟醸) from Mioya brewery in Ishikawa prefecture. The *kanji* on the "Yuuho" bottle means "playful rice head" but it is also a pun on the Japanese pronunciation of UFO: Mioya is based in Hakui city, which is known as Japan's UFO sighting capital. Until recently, the brand was itself a bit of a UFO in the sake world. The *kura* did not have a strong reputation until Miho Fujita, a women's college English literature graduate who had been working as an office lady, suddenly found herself in charge of a brewery! In 2004, she met Toshiaki Yokomichi, one of the most exciting young master brewers, at a meeting of sake makers but refused to tell him her name or *kura* because she felt she didn't know enough about the business. They met again the next year and her raw enthusiasm and commitment convinced him to commit his bright future to a *kura* that had, until then, only been making *futsūshu* (sake's equivalent of *vin ordinaire*) for the local market. Mioya has started winning regional and national medals and is now being taken very seriously indeed.

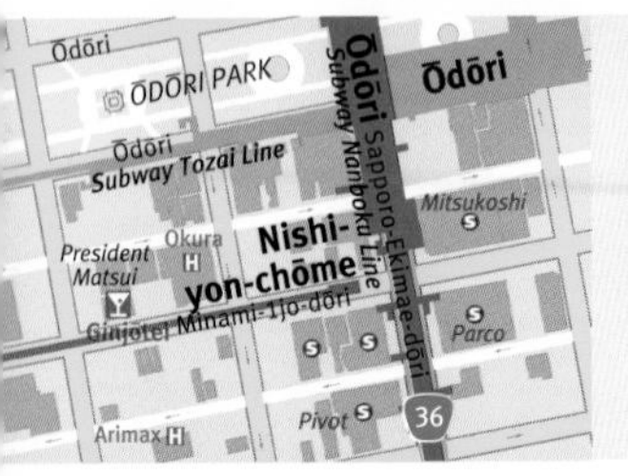

DIRECTIONS: Ōdōri Station (Tozai/Tōhō/Nanboku Lines), Exit 3. Turn left and walk one block. It is in the basement of the President Matsui building, on the same block as the Hotel Okura. It is one block west of the Nishi 4-chōme tram stop.

Hanamori 花守り 082-247-5722 r.gnavi.co.jp/y120000

3F Taira Biru, 10-18 Mikawachō, Naka-ku, Hiroshima-shi, Hiroshima, 730-0029
〒730-0029 広島県広島市中区三川町 10-18 平ビル 3F
Open: 6 pm–1 am Booking recommended? Yes Credit cards? Visa, Master, DC and JCB, not Amex
English menu? No Table charge: 400 yen

Hiroshima has long been admired for its soft and relatively sweet style of sake. Saijo town, to the east of Hiroshima city, has been a center for the industry since 1650, and there are old breweries dotted all over the prefecture. During the 20th century, the area gained a particular reputation for its high quality and was an early leader in the development of the *ginjō* and *daiginjō* techniques. Hanamori is a very good place to sample this rich tradition, with about 50 types of sake available, about a third of which come from the Hiroshima area. The interior is traditionally Japanese in style, with *tatami*-floored rooms threaded along a long and narrow floor plan. The food is strong on local marine specialities, such as *anago* (conger eel, 1,200 yen) and *kawahagi sashimi* (raw kawahagi fish, 2,400 yen). The *sashimi moriawase* (a seasonal selection of five types of *sashimi*, about 950 yen depending on the fish used) is very popular with customers. From the sake menu, I was recommended a "Taketsuru" (竹鶴) *junmaishu*. Taketsuru brewery is the same 300-year-old family enterprise that the founder of Japanese whisky, Masataka Taketsuru, came from (see page 164). Tatetsuru brewery's current *tōji* (master brewer), Tatsuya Ishikawa, was a student at Waseda University in Tōkyō when he got hooked on quality sake and decided to make it his calling. He has significantly changed Taketsuru's style since his arrival, throwing up any effort to make polite, well-behaved *ginjō* in favor of a much more raucous approach. He calls the *junmai* a *junmai bakudan* ("pure rice bomb"). It hits the drinker hard with strong acidity and body, but is rounded enough to end up quite more-ish. Compare and contrast with more typical Hiroshima offerings like the "Shinrai" *junmaishu* (神雷, 630 yen) from Miwa Shuzō.

DIRECTIONS: Walk east along Heiwa-dōri from the Peace Park. It is about 600 yards after the bridge. Take a left at the gasoline station on the corner. Hanamori is in the building next to the gasoline stand, immediately to your right, and is signed using the Roman alphabet.

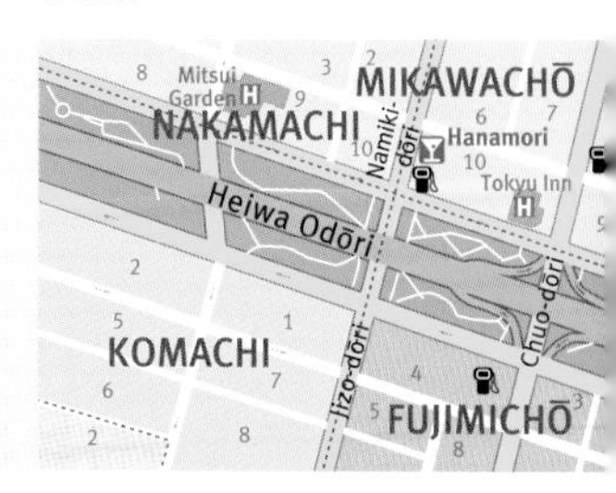

Himonoya ひもの屋 03-3844-8088 e-808.com/himonoya

1F-2F, 1-11-1 Asakusa, Taitō-ku, Tōkyō
東京都台東区浅草 1-11-1 御所第 2 ビル 1・2 階
Open: 5 pm–5 am (but opening times vary between branches) Booking recommended? No
Credit cards? Most major cards English menu? No Table charge: 280 yen

Himono is dried fish. If you drive along the Japanese coast you can still see drying racks lining the roadside, with hundreds of salted fish drying in the open air (and car fumes). It used to be the most reliable way of storing the fisherman's catch for sale, but it also happens to be a great way to prepare a drinking snack. The Himonoya chain, combining cheap and cheerful combinations of *himono* and good-value sake, has expanded quickly since it was set up five years ago. There are now 50 shops across the Kantō area. I was recommended the *kimoiri maruboshi ika* (whole-dried grilled squid, 480 yen) and the *saba ishiru* (fish marinated in soy sauce and dried, 630 yen) with a 180 ml *tokkuri* of "Tōjikan" (杜氏鑑, 600 yen) from the famous Hakutsuru brewery in Nada, Kōbe. Hakutsuru is Japan's biggest sake maker and makes a lot cheaper sake for the mass market. This is a special *honjōzō* made on a smaller scale by their master brewer, Masao Nakazawa. The idea was to make a product that would appeal to the man in the street rather than the sake snob, and the result is an extremely mild, medium-dry sake, with a relatively suppressed fragrance. For someone who is finding it hard to like sake, "Tōjikan" might be worth one final shake of the dice. If it comes up sixes, you could move on to the "Jōzen Mizunogotoshi" (上善如水, 600 yen), a slightly drier but super smooth and clear sake from Niigata. I have heard it described as the Jacob's Creek of sakes. Himonoya is unlikely to be top of the list for experienced sake heads, although there is usually some interesting *jizake* on the menu, but it is a fun and reasonably priced night out.

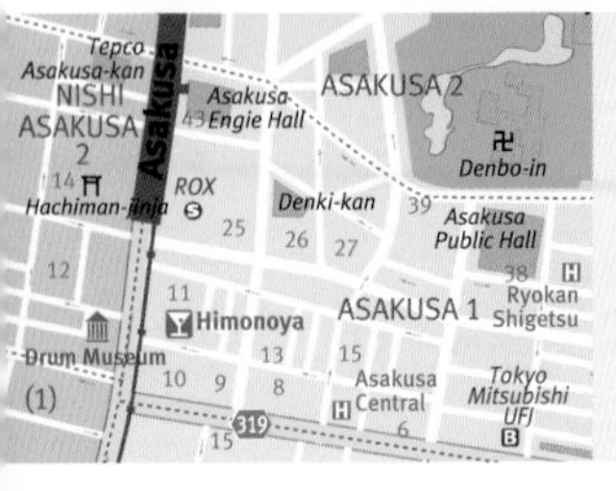

DIRECTIONS: Tsukuba Express Asakusa Station, Exit A1 (for Sensōji Temple, Kokusai-dōri). If you come out on a side road, turn left and left again. If you are on a main road, turn left, then take the fourth left (at the drugstore cosmetics shop sign). There is no Roman alphabet on the sign but the dramatic black and white design is easy to spot. From the Asakusa Tōbu/Metro Station, Exit 1, walk up Kaminarimon-dōri away from Azuma-bashi (and the Asahi Breweries HQ with the golden sperm on its top). Turn right at the T-junction at the top and then right again.

Isshin 一心 022-261-9888/022-261-9889 (for the Kagen Kan)

B1F Jōzenji Hills, 3-3-1, Kokubunchō, Aoba-ku, Sendai
仙台市青葉区国分町 3-3-1 定禅寺ヒルズ B1F
Open: **5 pm–12 pm; closed Sunday** Booking recommended? **Yes** Credit cards? **Most major cards**
English menu? **No** Table charge: **1,500 yen plus 10 percent service charge**

If you find yourself in Sendai, I cannot recommend Isshin highly enough. It is actually two separate establishments, side by side—a general sake bar called simply Isshin and the Isshin Kagen Kan, a sort of sake warmer's heaven. Founder Kōki Yanagisawa says customers who are new to sake might want to start in the general bar and move next door when they are ready for a slightly more connoisseury atmosphere, but the *chirori* heating sets, complete with thermometers for precisely measuring what heat you are drinking your sake at, are such fun that some might want to take a plunge straight into the deep end. The two bars operate separately, so you will need to book a table at the Kagen Kan or Isshin, depending on the destination you have chosen (there are different phone numbers). A note on prices: at first sight, the 1,500 yen entrance charge looks expensive, especially given the extra 10 percent charged for service, but the *otōshi* dish that comes with that is really not so much a snack as a meal in itself. I would advise not ordering too much food beyond the *otōshi* and getting stuck into the real reason for visiting Isshin: extremely interesting sake, such as the big-boned, ricey "Haginotsuru" (萩の鶴, 750 yen for 180 ml), which Yanagisawa-san picked out of the Kagen Kan's sake list for me. Most of the sakes in both bars tend to hover around 750–800 yen for 180 ml and the more expensive drinks (up to 2,000 yen for 180 ml) can be ordered in small 60 ml glasses. In between sips, take the time to seek out the original prints by the famous sake manga writer Akira Oze, who gave them as gifts after featuring the bar in his stories.

DIRECTIONS: Kōtōdai Kōen Station, Exit Kōen 2. Walk about 150 yards straight up Jozenji-dōri away from the park. It is down the stairs next to the Lawson convenience store.

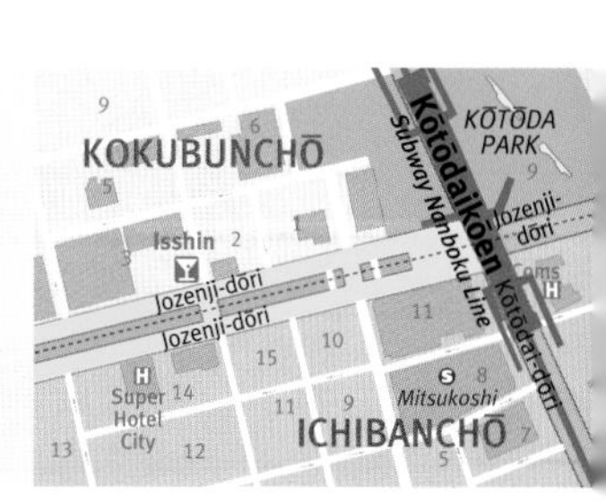

Juttoku 十徳 03-3342-0339 www.juttoku.com

B1, B2, New Sentoraru Biru, 1-5-12 Nishi-Shinjuku, Shinjuku ku, Tōkyō, 160-0023
〒160-0023 東京都新宿区西新宿 1-5-12 ニューセントラルビル B1, B2
Open: **4 pm–12 pm; Friday–Sunday 4 pm–4 am; no holidays except New Year**
Credit cards? **No** English menu? **No** Table charge: **350 yen**

Kimiko Satō features in her *izakaya*'s logo: a cartoon figure of a well-padded motherly type holding a generous jug of sake. In person, she carries off the motherly image with aplomb but you get the definite feeling this is the sort of mother who gets things done. When we met up, she was as interested in finding out about British and American property prices and discussing possible openings for her company abroad as in telling me about her Tōkyō *izakaya*. She set up her original pub in 1982 with the idea of serving properly stored sake at good prices. There are now six shops under the Juttoku banner, including a *shōchū* bar and various restaurant ventures, but the basic philosophy of no-nonsense excellence is still in evidence. The lino-floored, green plastic-seated Shinjuku *izakaya* keeps a seasonally changing selection of more than 80 types of sake, and the reasonable prices, which rarely stray too far from the 400–600 yen range, make it an ideal place to get your sake footing. The three-glass tasting set (*nomi kurabe setto*, 飲み比べセット) varies in price with the sakes featured, but it is usually excellent value at around 550 yen. The food is also pretty cheap for central Tōkyō. Try the selection of five skewers loaded with grilled meat and vegetables (*go shurui kushiyaki moriawase*, 450 yen) or the mountain vegetable *tempura* set (*sansai tempura moriawase*, 650 yen). You might perhaps wash it down with a glass of the classic "Hakkaisan" sake from Niigata prefecture ("Hakkaisan futsū seishu," 八海山普通清酒, 550 yen). The best way to explain Hakkaisan's place in the sake market is to compare it to Moët et Chandon's Champagne brand. Someone looking for a safe bet for a bottle to take along to a swish party is never going to be embarrassed by "Hakkaisan," because these brands build their reputations by consistently producing unimpeachable alcohol. The makers, Hakkai Jōzō, have been producing crisp, well-balanced sakes from the soft waters coming off Hakkaisan Mountain since 1922. The "Hakkaisan futsū seishu" is the least expensive sake in their range.

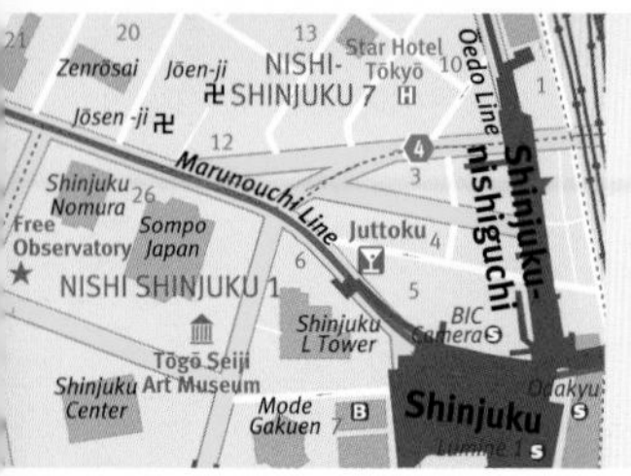

DIRECTIONS: Shinjuku Station, Exit B16. Go up to the street. Turn left down the road between the second-floor McDonald's and the Odakyu store. There is no alphabet used on the Juttoku store front but it is opposite the Arc academy and has a display of sake bottles.

Kaasan かあさん 03-3344-0888 www.kasan.jp

4F Nishi-Shinjuku Kokusai dōri Biru, 1-16-4 Nishi-Shinjuku, Shinjuku-ku, Tōkyō
東京都新宿区西新宿 1-16-4 西新宿国際通ビル 4F
Open: **Weekdays 4 pm–12 pm; Saturday 4 pm–11 pm (varies between branches); many branches closed Sundays**
Credit cards? **Most major cards** English menu? **No** Table charge: **400 yen (some branches cheaper)**

Kaasan means "mom" and they take their name seriously at this cheap and cheerful *izakaya*. It seems (how can I put this and avoid death by rolling pin?) that only women of a "certain maturity" work there. "There is no actual rule on the age," insisted Kōtarō Nanaumi of head office. "I think it is because of the shop's name. We just get a lot of women of that sort of age applying." Kaasan started off in Kawasaki city in 1988, but there are now more than 20 of these unpretentious, Formica-topped establishments dotted around the Tōkyō area. Kaasan's eponymous "mom" seems to be an indulgent sort. She maintains a first-class sake list for her family. There were 40 or 50 sakes available at the Nishi-Shinjuku branch I visited (and 22 *shōchū*). Try the fragrant "Uragasanryū Kōka" sake (裏雅山流 香華, 700 yen) with the *mochimochi pizza* (720 yen) or the *nikujaga* (pork and potato, 580 yen). "Uraga-sanryū Kōka" sake is made by Shindō Shuzō, a long-established *kura* in Yamagata prefecture, using the famous Miyama Nishiki sake rice, a speciality of the region (see page 38). It is a *honjōzō* sake, meaning that a small amount of distilled alcohol is added during the brewing. The technique often lightens the taste and brings out flavors and aromas from the *moromi*. See what you think. Kaasan also recommend the "Denshu" sake (田酒, 800 yen, see page 52).

DIRECTIONS: Kaasan has branches across Tōkyō. For the Nishi Shinjuku branch: Shinjuku JR Station, south entrance. Turn right and follow the yellow signs to the "Skyscraper district" and "Tōkyō Metropolitan Government Office" until you get to an exit pointing you down the stairs to your left. Instead, walk straight ahead. You want to go straight up the alley beside the KFC restaurant that is immediately ahead of you across the large road. Pass Gaia Pachinko on your right. It is on the fourth floor above Ringer Hut.

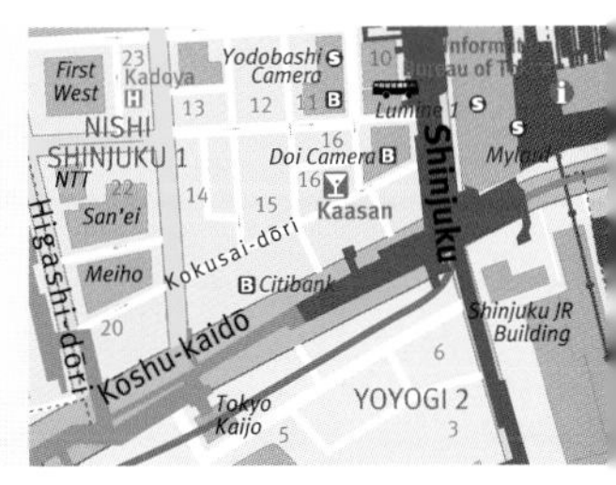

Kōjimachi Japontei 麹町じゃぽん亭 03-3263-3642

2F Kei Biru, 3-4-7 Kōjimachi, Chiyoda ku
千代田区麹町 3-4-7 啓ビル 2F
Open: Weekdays 5.30 pm–12.30 am (last food orders 11 pm); closed Saturday, Sunday and national holidays
Booking recommended? Yes Credit cards? Most major cards
English menu? No Table charge: 400 yen (varies slightly with the *otōshi* dish served)

Kōjimachi, the name of this part of Tōkyō, literally means "mold town" and uses the same *kanji* character as the *kōji* mold used in sake making. One theory has it that this used to be the base for Edo's *kōji* makers. Although booze making has long since been displaced by diplomatic wrangling in what is now a major embassy district, Japontei is doing its best to live up to the district's alcoholic billing with a superb selection of 40 *jizake*. The staff are knowledgeable without being intimidating and, while not English speakers, are quite used to dealing with foreigners: they attract a lot of custom from dipsomanic diplomats, it seems. They specialize in "Jū Yon Dai" (十四代, see page 53) from Takagi Shuzō and their refrigerators normally have at least 15 different bottlings of the famed brand. When I visited they had a very rare "Ryūgetsu" bottling for 3,000 yen a glass. I am afraid I have no idea what it tastes like because it was well beyond my pocket, but it is a measure of the relative cheapness of sake in Japan that they were incredulous when I told them that wines in some Tōkyō bars could reach 10,000 yen and whiskies more than 90,000 yen (see page 180). A selection of three types of *sashimi* (*sashimi moriawase*) will set you back 1,500 yen. More adventurous types might want to try out the ultimate Japanese drinking snack: *chinmi* (pickled unidentifiable seafood bits, 500 yen).

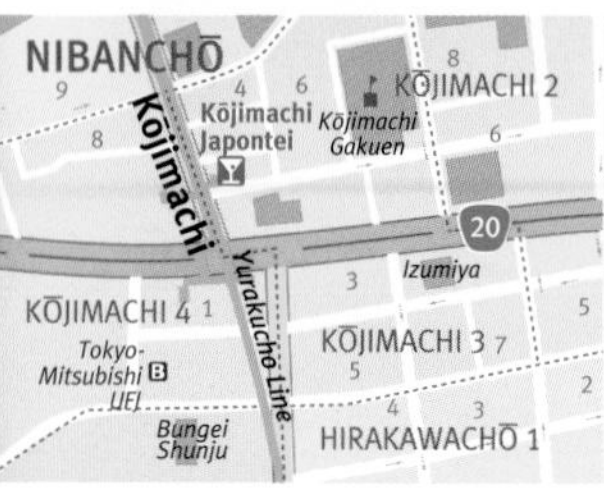

DIRECTIONS: Kōjimachi Station (Yūrakuchō Line), Exit 3. Turn left around the coffee shop, left up the road and it is the next entrance on your left.

Komahachi 駒八 03-3453-2530 www.komahachi.com

Sake annex: 1-2F Ishii biru, 5-16-14 Shiba, Minato-ku, Tōkyō 108-0014
[Main restaurant: 1F Hashimoto Biru 5-16-1 Shiba, Minato-ku, Tōkyō108-0014]
〒108-0014 東京都港区芝 5-16-14 石井ビル 1~2F [Main restaurant: 〒108-0014 東京都港区芝 5-16-1 橋本ビル 1F
Open: 5 pm–1 pm; closed Sunday and national holidays
Booking recommended? No Credit cards? Most major cards English menu? No Table charge: 300 yen

Komahachi is a chain *izakaya* with a commitment to proper sake. The first restaurant was opened in Shiba in 1975 and there are now 20 stores across the Tōkyō area. It is the Bekkan (annex), just round the corner from the original restaurant, that you should seek out if you are interested in sake. Most of the branches offer at least 10 good sakes, but the annex has a choice of about 50. Despite the scale of Komahachi's operation, they are strong on small *kura* sake. They had "Houou Biden" (鳳凰美田, 800 yen) on the menu when I visited in 2008. The makers, Kobayashi Shuzō in Tochigi prefecture, operate on a very small scale and have come up with what must be the ultimate manufacturer's ruse: they actually get their consumers to pay to help them make the sake. Twice a year, at rice planting time, they invite people from all over Japan to come to Tochigi for a "rice planting festival." By all accounts, it is a fun occasion and the payment probably barely covers the cost of the free sake that is laid on in the evenings after hard days spent hand planting rice. They do the same at harvest time. Houou Biden is not heat-treated at bottling (*namazume*, see page 41) and has a pronounced floral, slightly melony aroma with a soft, mild taste. All of Komahachi's sake is priced between 700 and 900 yen. The food is generally reasonably priced too. The *gyū motsu nabe* (beef offal nabe, 980 yen for one person) and *kabocha āmondo age* (pumpkin and almond fry, 580 yen) are favorites with the salarymen who make up much of Komahachi's clientele.

DIRECTIONS: Mita Station (Toei Mita and Asakusa Lines), Exit A3. Turn left away from the larger road and left again. Turn right at the T-junction and take the third road on the right. The main *izakaya* is immediately after the slight kink in the road, about 60 yards after you turn. The annex, which specializes in sake, is a few paces down the road to the right, just before the kink.

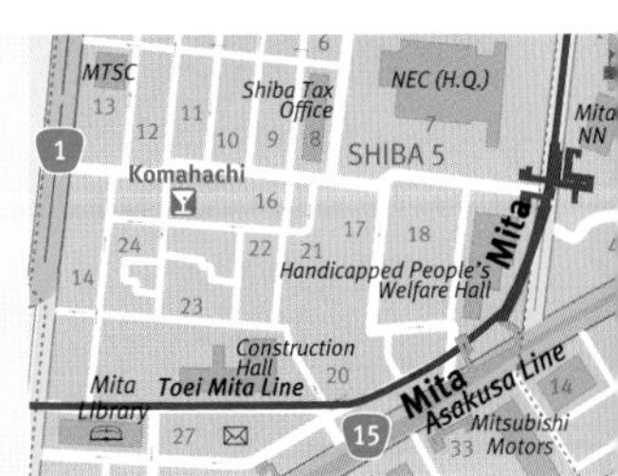

Kushikoma 串駒 03-3917-6657 www.kushikoma.com

1-33-25 Kita Ōtsuka, Toshima ku, Tōkyō
東京都豊島区北大塚 1-33-25
Open: 6 pm–12 pm; closed Sunday Booking recommended? Yes Credit cards? Most major cards
English menu? No Table charge: 1,000 yen

To describe Kushikoma as slightly eccentric would be to do its landlord, Tadashi Ōbayashi, a grave disservice. The man would give Captain Beany from the Planet Beanus (a real Englishman with whom I have had the pleasure of conversing) a run for his eccentric credentials. The first thing Ōbayashi-san did as I entered Kushikoma was to don a Sherlock Holmes deerstalker hat and an Inverness coat and look me steadily in the eye: "You are an Englishman, what do you think?" "Very nice," I said. He immediately whisked off the Inverness to reveal an impeccable Japanese *samue* (monk's outfit) underneath. "I sometimes call myself 'Last Samurai'," he said, and sat down at the *irori* hearth where he holds court every night. It is not going to be everyone's cup of tea, but Kushikoma is like no other sake bar I know and serves excellent sake with *kushiage* (deep fried meat and vegetables on bamboo skewers, 750 yen for five types). Ōbayashi-san is friends with Akitsuna Takagi, maker of the famous "Jū Yon Dai" (Takagi's signature is scrawled on the wall on the second floor) and always has an excellent selection of Takagi's products (starting at 700 yen, see page 53). He also recommends another top-quality *jizake* maker, Sumikawa Shuzō in Yamaguchi prefecture, where they have been experimenting in a most interesting way with the idea of *terroir* in sake (the influence of geography on the taste of the alcohol). The delicately fruity "Tōyō Bijin 437" (東洋美人437, Oriental Beauty 437, 1,000 yen) gets the number in its name from the postal address of the paddy where the rice came from. They have different bottlings called "611" and "372" from paddies with different geographies. I have not had the chance to compare them, but, apparently, they all taste subtly different despite being made from the same Yamada Nishiki rice and being brewed in the same way.

DIRECTIONS: Ōtsuka Station (Yamanote Line/Toden Arakawa Line), North Exit. Walk around to the other side of the Royal Host building, cross the road and the tram tracks. Take the second left after the tracks. Kushikoma is on your right after the Book 8 magazine and comic shop.

Nihonshu Bar Asakura

日本酒BARあさくら 075-212-4417 ameblo.jp/sakebar

Kiyamachi Oike-sagaru, Hitotsu-Sujime Higashi-iru, Oku Biru 2F., Chūō-ku, Kyōto
京都市中京区木屋町御池下がる一筋目東入る大久ビル2F
Open: 7 pm–2 am; closed Tuesday Booking recommended? No Credit cards? No English menu? No
Table charge: 500 yen

Yoshihito Asakura has a deep knowledge not only of sake but of the whole Japanese alcohol scene. I had a fascinating and very informative conversation with him about Japanese whisky, and the good selection of beer in the fridge in his small second-story bar showed he knew his hops too. If you don't fancy discussing booze, mention how lucky his soccer team, Gamba Ōsaka, were on their 2008 Asian Champions league run. Asakura-san's eclectic mind has other benefits: he keeps a good stock of imported cheeses which work very well with some of the sakes. An individual cheese will cost between 400 and 700 yen, and you can get a plate of three varieties for 1,400 yen. Asakura-san speaks a little English, so exploring his stock of more than 80 types of sake is easier than in many bars. If you never thought you would find yourself in the center of Japan's old capital supping a glass of "Shichihonyari" *junmaishu* (七本槍 純米酒), a heavy dry sake from Shiga prefecture, while nibbling a slice of mimolette to the strains of Led Zeppelin's "Whole Lotta Love," then get ready to surprise yourself.

DIRECTIONS: Kyōto Shiyakusho-mae Station (Tozai Line), Exit 1. Walk straight ahead for about 20 yards and turn right. It is on your left, down a narrow alley almost opposite the small bridge over a watercourse.

Sakatomo 酒友 03-5786-3533 www.hasegawasaketen.com/english/restaurant.html

1F, Uchida Biru, 4-12-6 Roppongi, Minato-Ku, Tōkyō
東京都港区六本木 4-12-6 内田ビル 1F
Open: **Weekdays 6 pm–4 am; Saturday 5 pm–11 pm; closed Sunday and national holidays**
Booking recommended? **Yes** Credit cards? **Most major cards**
English menu? **Yes** Table charge: **600 yen**

The earliest drinking shops in old Edo were called *niuri-zakaya*. The name literally meant "sellers of drink and boiled foods." They started out as hawkers with charcoal stoves but gradually developed into roadside stalls and, by the last decade of the 17th century, as the city's nightlife began to roar into life, there were a few permanent shop fronts. Customers, mainly single men, could wander in, sit down on one of the crude benches and and eat a little soy sauce-boiled vegetable dish with their sake. Today, the closest descendants of the *niuri-zakaya* are *oden* restaurants serving vegetables, fish cakes and eggs cooked in a light soy-flavored stew. You can still find rickety *oden* stalls and cheap restaurants across the city, and they are a time-honored place for a quick drink.

Sakatomo could hardly be described as an *oden* store, the range of food is much too wide for that, but they do have excellent *oden* (100–600 yen per type), and the constantly changing line-up of about 12 carefully picked sakes is top rate (they also have about 30 types of *shōchū*). The limited sake menu has a quick turnover (the idea is to have a few excellent sakes rather than dozens of badly kept drinks), but if they have the fruity and smooth "Bessen honjōzō Isojiman" (別撰本醸造磯自慢, 650 yen) on the menu when you visit, I recommend giving it a try. It is an excellent example of why good sake is not always made with traditional techniques. (Otherwise, we would all be drinking chewed sake, wouldn't we? See page 33.) It comes from Shizuoka, a relatively warm part of Japan, but modern technology has allowed Isojiman to turn their whole *kura* into a refrigerator. Steel walls and synthetic floors allow the most efficient temperature control. For more on this and other Shizuoka sakes, look up Robert-Gilles Martineau's excellent Shizuoka sake blog, shizuokasake.wordpress.com.

DIRECTIONS: Roppongi Station, Exit 4a. Take an immediate left. It is about 100 yards up the road on the right, a few steps up a side alley beside a pet shop.

Sake no Ana 酒の穴 03-3567-1133 www.sakenoana.com

B1, Ginza Rangetsu Biru, 3-5-8 Ginza, Tōkyō
東京都中央区銀座 3-5-8 B1 銀座らん月 B1
Open: 11.30 am–11.30 pm Booking recommended? Yes
Credit cards? Most major cards English menu? Yes Table charge: 400 yen

Like a lot of the drinking haunts along the Ginza, Sake no Ana has got used to celebrity customers. It was once a particular favorite among artists, notably the figurative painter Taisei Satō (1913–2004), but probably the most recognizable name for foreigners would be Kevin Costner, who called in here to sample sake when he was promoting the film "The Bodyguard." (He tried two types of sake but unfortunately posterity does not record precisely which ones.) For those of us without baggage trains and a team of translators accompanying us, Sake no Ana's English menu makes it a good a place to start exploring sake. Some 140 types from all over the country are available. Try the fruity, almost white wine-ish "Zaku Honotomo" (作 穂乃智) sake from Mie prefecture (800 yen for 180 ml). The management recently noticed a spike in orders for "Zaku" and the sudden appearance of odd-looking *otaku* (young, obsessive *manga* and *anime* fans) in the bar. There is a very popular robot called Zaku in the famous *anime* "Gundam" and it has become a thing in *otaku* circles to try out "his sake" (the naming is coincidence). For those with no interest in Japanese pop fads, Sake no Ana's own-brand bottling of "Meikyōshisui" (明鏡止水, 900 yen for 180 ml), a gold medal bedecked brew made by Osawa brewery in Nagano prefecture, is elegant and well-balanced. Manager Kōji Sakamoto recommended *kani no sashimi* (crab sashimi, 1,600 yen) with the "Meikyōshisui" and *nikujaga* (Japanese beef and potato stew, 700 yen) with the "Zaku Honotomo." I should mention that the billing system is a little odd: they insist on converting all their prices into their own currency—"Ana"—which is not particularly helpful for foreigners who are already converting between two currencies. Just keep in mind that one "Ana" is 100 yen.

DIRECTIONS: Ginza Metro Station, Exit A13. It is opposite the Matsuya Department Store. There are no Roman characters on the sign, but there are sake bottles in the window and a sign displaying a crescent moon.

Sasagin 笹吟 03-5454-3715

1F Dai Ni Kobayashi Biru, 1-32-15, Uehara, Shibuya-ku, Tōkyō
東京都渋谷区上原 1-32-15 第二小林ビル 1F
Open: Weekdays 5 pm–11.45 pm; Saturday 5 pm–11.15 pm; closed Sunday and national holidays
Booking recommended? Yes Credit cards? No English menu? No Table charge: 350 yen

The owner of Sasagin, Mitsuru Narita, is a leading figure in Tōkyō's sake scene. He once lived in London and speaks some English, so accessing the phenomenal range of sake can be easier here than in some of the capital's other top sake bars. There are about 80 or 90 varieties available, with about a quarter of the menu constantly changing with seasonal production, so repeated visits are as rewarding as the first. Unpasteurized *namazake* make up about a third of the selection. I would recommend letting Narita-san select your sake for you if he is in the house. His selections did more for my sake education than hours of reading and sipping at home. The very dry "Yamatsuru" (山鶴) from Nara prefecture's Nakamoto brewery stands out in my memory. Established in the 1700s (nobody is quite sure exactly when), Nakamoto took a relatively early decision in 1987, when the sake market was awash with adulterated rubbish, to concentrate on premium pure rice sakes and now only make top-quality *junmai* sake. The contrast with Aichi prefecture's "Chōchin" (長珍) *nama-zake*, Narita-san's next selection, said everything about the diversity of the sake world. While the "Yamatsuru" cleans the palate, the unpasteurized "Chōchin" loads it down with heavy, bittersweet flavors, almost like a Chinese Xiaoxing wine. The food at Sasagin tends to be from the standard *izakaya* playbook: *yakitori* (skewered chicken, 260 yen), *tsukune* (meatball, 260 yen), *yuba dōfu* (*tōfu* skin, 630 yen), *kakiage* (mixed *tempura* patties, 950 yen). It is reasonably priced and tasty.

DIRECTIONS: Yoyogi-Uehara Station (Odakyū Odawara and Chiyoda Lines), Exit (South) 1. Turn right. It is less than 100 yards on your left.

Shimbashi Kohju

しんばし光寿 03-3575-0939 [Kanda shop: 03-3253-0044] www.kohju.com

B1F Shimojima Biru, 1-2-17 Higashi Shimbashi, Minato-ku, Tōkyō
[Kanda shop is at: 1F Onuki Biru, 2-9-7 Kajimachi, Chiyoda-ku, Tōkyō]
東京都港区東新橋 1-2-17 下島ビル B1F [Kanda shop is at: 東京都千代田区鍛冶町 2-9-7 大貫ビル 1F]
Open: 5.30 pm–11.30 pm (last order for food 10.30 pm, last order for drinks 11pm)
Booking recommended? Yes Credit cards? Most major cards English menu? No Table charge: 800 yen

Shimbashi Kohju is a sake lover's paradise. The atmosphere is casual and friendly, with old sake labels plastered all over the ceiling, but they take their sake very seriously indeed. The cover charge may seem steep at 800 yen but that includes a dish of six types of food to taste with your sake. Overall, the prices are not excessive considering the location and the excellence of some of the alcohol. The "Kaze no Mori" (風の森, 800 yen for 170 ml), an unpasteurized *namazake* from Nara prefecture, short-circuited my motherboard. It had a lovely thick taste, with lots of rice and starchy flavors. The food changes all the time at Kohju and there is usually something special on the menu. I would advise asking for a recommendation from your waiter. Mine recommended a dish of *ikakimono hoiru yaki* (squid with its liver cooked in foil, 650 yen) to play with the *namazake*'s strong flavors. That was followed by a glass of "Kamoshibito Kuheiji" (醸し人九平次, 780 yen for 170 ml), an acidic, dry drink which contrasted markedly with what had gone before and complemented the creamy *nigaridōfu* well (*tōfu*, 480 yen). Then, another smooth gear change to the fruity, blossoming "Minami" *junmaishu* (南 純米酒) from Minami shuzō in Kōchi prefecture (850 yen for 170 ml), and *namanori no tempura* (seaweed *tempura*, 480 yen). It is experiences like mine at Kohju that make a sake freak out of a perfectly decent member of society.

DIRECTIONS: I found Shimbasi Kohju quite hard to find. Go to JR Shimbashi Station, Shiodome Exit. Don't mess around underground. Get out into the light (or dark) and walk toward the raised Yurikamome light railway station that is just to the east of the JR station. Turn right where the large road (Route 15) goes under the Yurikamome Station. Kohju is on the left of Route 15, almost immediately after it passes under the Yurikamome Station. The sign to the basement is hard to spot but it is just past some soft drink machines.

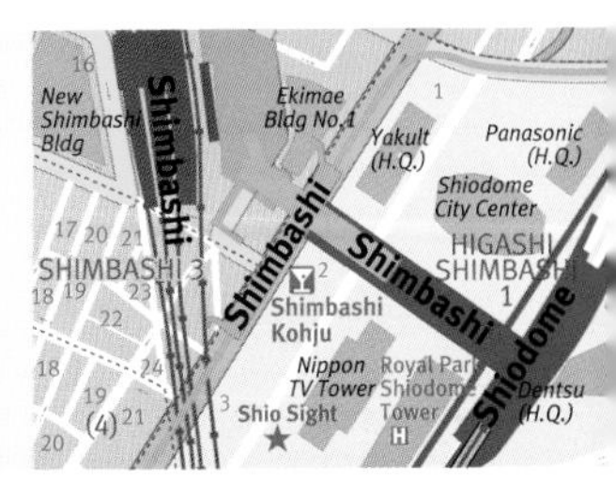

Shusaron 酒茶論 03-5449-4455 koshunavi.com

2F, Keikyu Shopping Plaza Wing Takanawa West, 4-10-18 Takanawa, Minato-ku, Tōkyō, 108-0074
〒108-0074 東京都港区高輪 4-10-18 京急ショッピングプラザ ウィング高輪 WEST 2F
Open: 5 pm–12 pm Booking recommended? Yes Credit cards? All major cards
English menu? No Table charge: 500 yen

This is, quite simply, the best place in the world to drink aged sake (see page 43). The selection of 100 types of *koshu* represents just about everything of significance in the *koshu* world and landlord Nobuhiro Ueno's knowledge is encyclopedic. He has just published the definitive book on *koshu* in Japanese and believes that *koshu* has the potential to revolutionize sake over the next few decades: "There is this high end to the wine market which people hear about, the Romanée-Conti sort of stuff, but this actually raises the general popularity of normal wines as well. What I have been saying to sake makers is that the development of very high-end alcohol like *koshu* will not just lift up the premium end but the whole of sake making." The range of tastes in *koshu* is so diverse that it is probably best to get your bearings with Shusaron's two excellent *nomikurabe seto* (tasting sets, 1,500 yen or 2,400 yen), which offer three different types of aged sake. Ueno-san also offers two-glass tasting sets of differently aged sakes from the same *kura* (1,800 yen). At the risk of oversimplification, the taste of *koshu* tends to be much richer than your average unaged sake and the types of food that partner well with it also differ. Ueno-san serves some delicious assortment plates of cheese (1,200 yen), smoked food (1,500 yen) and the particularly alluring *osusume seto* (chocolate, dry fruits, smoked food and cheeses, 1,800 yen). When you have graduated from Ueno-san's basic courses, there is a virtually endless variety of drinks to be explored elsewhere on the menu.

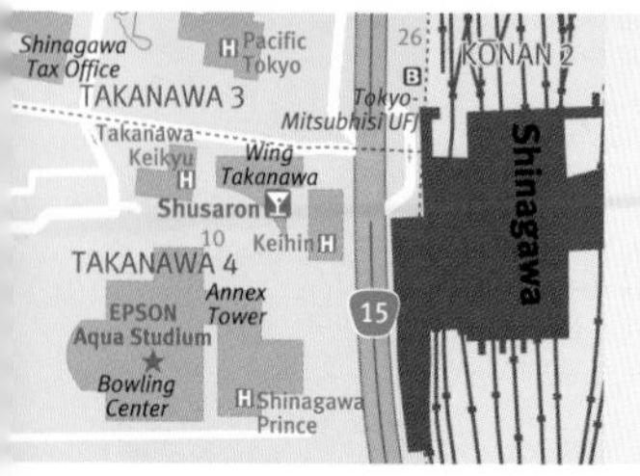

DIRECTIONS: JR Shinagawa Station, Tanakawa Exit (West Entrance). Cross the road to Wing Tanakawa West. Climb the stairs and walk round to your left, to the blue circular bar building.

Takara 宝 03-5223-9888 r.gnavi.co.jp/g107805

B1F Tōkyō International Forum, 3-5-1 Marunouchi, Chiyoda-ku, Tōkyō, 100-0005
〒100-0005 東京都千代田区丸の内 3-5-1 東京国際フォーラム B1
Open: Weekdays lunch 11.30 am–2.30 pm; dinner 5 pm–11 pm; Weekends 11.30 am–3.30 pm; 5 pm–10 pm
Booking recommended? Yes Credit cards? Major credit cards English menu? Yes Table charge: 480 yen

Takara has helped pioneer the opening of sake to foreigners, hosting regular English-language seminars by the famous sake writer John Gauntner, and it is a good place to get acquainted with the drink if you do not speak too much Japanese. They have an English menu, and the sake sommelier Kazuhito Shimizu says there is usually a member of staff on hand who can speak basic English. It is a restaurant rather than a bar, so you will be expected to eat something a little more substantial than a plate of *edamame* (a soya bean snack). The menu features a lot of Japanese food, but also has some fairly approachable Western/fusion dishes. The drink menu is capacious—about 20 *shōchū*, 10 *awamori*, 20 wines, some excellent Japanese single-malt whisky and 10 types of beer (including the yummy Baird craft beer, see pages 143 and 155) as well as the house speciality, sake. "We try to offer a real breadth of choice on the drinks menu. We find that in most groups there is a variety of tastes. Someone will like sake a great deal, but others will not. This is particularly so among non-Japanese," says Shimizu-san. The sake is all sourced from nine specially selected *kura*, covering the full taste range and most styles of the drink. Shimizu-san picked out the red-labeled "Senchū Hassaku" (船中八策, 650 yen), which literally translates as "Eight plans made in a boat" and refers to the assassinated pre-Meiji reformer Ryōma Sakamoto, who reputedly drew up plans for a modernized Japan on the boat ride to the capital. The makers, Tsukasabotan brewery, are based in Sakamoto's home prefecture, Kōchi, on Shikoku Island, and name all of their sakes after him: their general style is quite dry. The "Senchū Hassaku" balances dryness with a more fruity fragrance than usual.

DIRECTIONS: Yūrakuchō Station underground concourse, Exit D5. Go straight ahead into the Tokyo International Forum. Takara is on your left, immediately after the big orange sign to "Hall C."

Taruichi 樽一 たるいち 03-3208-9772 3 taruichi.co.jp

5F Daiichi Asakawa Biru, 1-17-12 Kabukichō, Shinjuku-ku, Tōkyō, 160-0021
〒160-0021 東京都新宿区歌舞伎町 1-17-12 第1浅川ビル 5F
Open: 5 pm–11 pm; closed Sunday and national holidays Credit cards? Most major cards
English menu? Yes. Some English spoken by the owner. Table charge: 500 yen

Taruichi is famous for two things, first, a superb list of 120 delicious and reasonably priced sakes, second, whale meat. The food menu is almost entirely whale and offers the great beasts in their entirety—from succulent deep red back meat through stomachs, hearts, tongues and brains to chewy hides.

This is not going to be everyone's ideal destination but, for those who do not have a problem with eating whale, the sake is superb. The young owner, Shintarō Satō, is an eloquent advocate of whale eating: "A good comparison would be if someone said to an Englishman suddenly, 'Why do you drink tea?' It is the same for us. It is part of our culture. For 4,000 years we have been eating whale. Before beef and pork started coming in from America, this was our meat. It was a food for normal people and we don't waste any part of it. We respect the whale." Taruichi was established in 1968 by Satō-san's father, Takeshi Satō. "My father was born in Miyagi. The idea of the restaurant was to present Miyagi food and drink to Tōkyō people. We have been here ever since," Satō says. For whale eaters, the *kujira sashimi moriawase* (selection of whale *sashimi*, 5,000 yen) can be split between three or four diners.

For those with ethical issues, the *sasakamaboko* (fish cake, 740 yen) does not contain whale, though in truth the menu is so dominated by the forbidden meat that you might want to try somewhere else. Taruichi has been famous for its formidable sake selection for decades. According to the sake guru John Gauntner, the restaurant was one of the first in Japan to provide systematic information to customers on the taste of its sakes and is credited with helping establish the now ubiquitous *Nihonshudo* and acidity measures (see page 41). Taruichi's own-brand "Kin Raberu" (金ラベル, gold label sake, 650 yen) has been a fixture on the menu since the 1960s, long before the current interest in highly refined *ginjō* and *daiginjō* sakes. It has a well-rounded, medium-dry flavor that Satō says goes ideally with whale. Also try the "Kaiun" Hiyazume Junmai sake (開運 ひやづめ純米). Doi Shuzo, the makers of "Kaiun," take a very natural approach to their sake making, avoiding artificial processes and filtering. They only produce one tank of the dry but full-flavored Hiyazume Junmai a year.

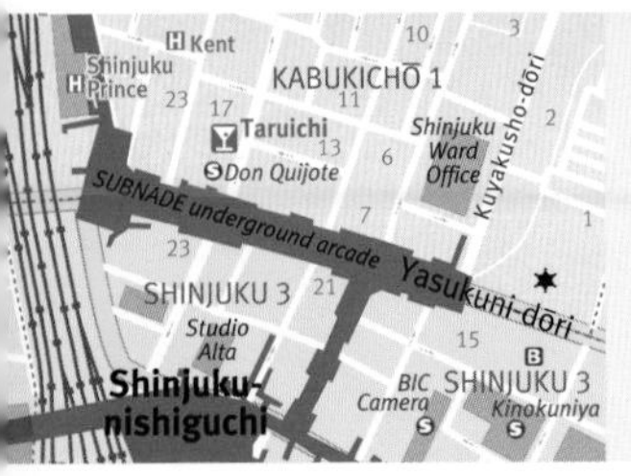

DIRECTIONS: JR Shinjuku Station, East Entrance. Inside the station, follow the yellow "For Kabukichō" sign. Climb the stairs beside the "Promenade to West Exit" sign. Walk straight ahead up the road to the left of the big Alta Vision Mitsubishi television screen. Cross the large road. It is in the second building to your left on the road heading into the Kabukichō entertainment district. There is no English on the sign but look for a whale on a beige background

Tokinoma 時の間 03-5722-8600 r.gnavi.co.jp/tokinoma

2F Conze Ebisu, 2-3-14, Ebisu Minami, Shibuya ku, Tōkyō, 150-0022
〒150-0022 東京都渋谷区恵比寿南 2-3-14 コンツェ恵比寿 2F
Open: 4.30 pm–5 am; Sundays and holidays 4.30 pm–11.30 pm Booking recommended? Yes
Credit cards? All major cards English menu? Yes Table charge: 480 yen

If the commanders of the Starship Enterprise ever decide they need an *izakaya* to help while away all those light years, they could do worse than to approach Tokinoma for a franchise. This late-opening Shibuya bar looks just the thing for intergalactic carousing, but the prices are surprisingly down-to-earth. The constantly changing list of 30 sakes (plus 100 *shōchū*) are priced from a reasonable 530 yen up to about 1,250 yen. The management is keen on promoting some of the smaller breweries, so there is usually something new to try. The elaborate ice buckets and *chirori* for chilling and warming the drink add a sense of occasion. Manager Kazuo Tabukuro recommended the "Ginrei Tateyama" (銀嶺立山) *honjōzō* (580 yen) from Tateyama Shuzō when I visited. Ninety percent of Tateyama's sake is sold locally in Toyama, but the company has a national reputation. It represented Japanese sake at the Paris Exhibition in 1900, and a record of 14 gold medals in 15 years at the New Sake Tasting Competition to 2005 shows it is not trading on past glories. The *honjōzō* method, using a very small amount of distilled alcohol in the fermentation, is not favored by some *junmai* purists but it can bring out delicate flavors in lighter-styled sakes. This is a good example of the genre, with a light clean touch and mild fragrance. The food menu is extensive and the English menu makes things easier for non-Japanese speakers. Tabukuro-san particularly recommended the *taimeshi* (Japanese sea bream and rice served in an earthenware dish, 1,800/2,200 yen) and the *daisen shabushabu* (thinly sliced beef hotpot, 1,800 yen per person).

DIRECTIONS: JR Ebisu Station, Yamanote Line, West Exit (west side) or Ebisu Hibiya Line Station, Exit 1. Across the taxi concourse and diagonally to your left is a road with a decorated entrance topped by colored balls. Follow that street and cross the large road at its end. The Conze building is in the road ahead of you and is signed in the Roman alphabet.

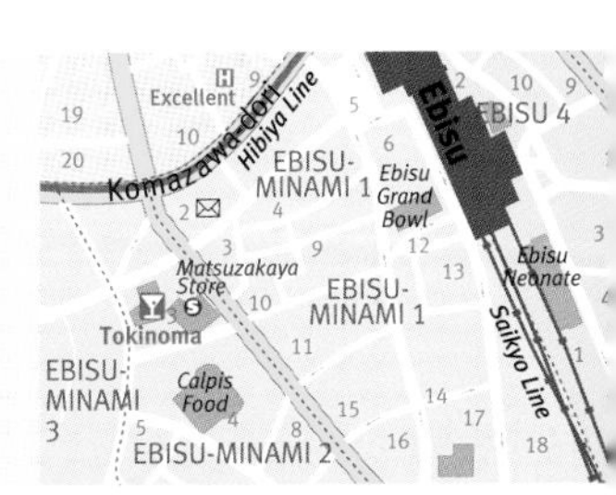

Yoramu よらむ 075-213-1512 www.sakebar-yoramu.com

Nijōdōri Higashinotoin Higashi-iru, Nakagyo-ku, Kyōto
京都市中京区二条通り東洞院東入る南側
Open: Open only Wednesday–Saturday 6 pm–12 pm Booking recommended? Yes
Credit cards? No English menu? Fluent English spoken Table charge: 300 yen

If you really want to get a sake education, there are few better destinations than Yoram Ofer's bar in central Kyōto. He is an Israeli by birth, but his combination of knowledge and uncompromising honesty makes him one of the best teachers I have ever met on the subject. For example, Ofer-san has this to say on why cheap, adulterated sake does not age well: "People will tell you that you cannot age sake, that it will just go bad, but they are talking about bad sake. You cannot age it for the same reason that you cannot age Coca Cola: it is just a chemical, just dead. Then there is real sake. That is something different. It is alive." Yoramu's food is a cosmopolitan mix of influences—*baba ghanoush* (500 yen), spaghetti and *shiitake* mushrooms (1,200 yen), warmed sake-steamed *tōfu* (400 yen)—and the sake selection is also idiosyncratic, with lots of aged *koshu* and sakes from tiny *kura*. Ofer-san speaks fluent English so his bar represents a great opportunity for non-Japanese speakers to start to get their heads around the drink. It is really best just to turn up, without any set ideas about what you are going to drink, and let Ofer-san guide you. He introduced me to an unpasteurized sake that he had aged himself at room temperature. Heresy! It was wonderfully rich and alive.

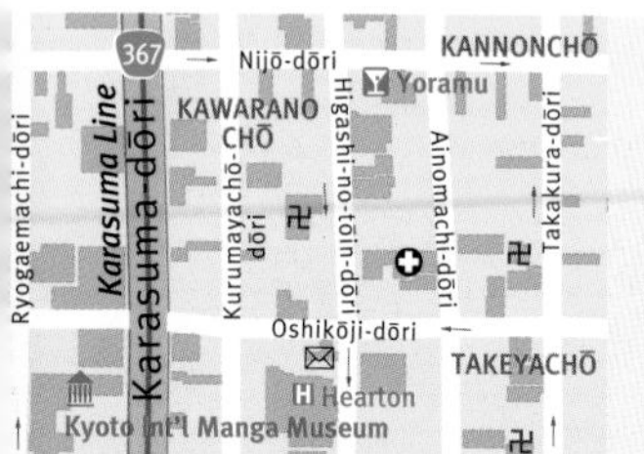

DIRECTIONS: Karasuma Oike Station (Karasuma/Tozai Lines), Exit 1. Walk two blocks north and turn right. Cross two roads and it is on your right. It is quite hard to spot. I have walked past it a few times.

Yorozuya Matsukaze 萬屋松風 03-3986-1047

1-24-5 Nishi Ikebukuro, Toshima-ku, Tōkyō, 171-0021

〒171-0021 東京都豊島区西池袋 1-24-5

Open: 5 pm–11.30 pm; Sunday and national holidays 5 pm–11 pm Booking recommended? No

Credit cards? Most major cards English menu? Yes Table charge: 420 yen

This three-story wood-fronted *izakaya* looks out of place amid the neon bustle of contemporary Ikebukuro, but it will almost certainly outlast the *otaku* stores and dodgy hostess salons that fill the adjoining streets. It has watched all sorts of neighbors come and go since it started business here in 1955, on the cusp of Japan's great post-war revival. The present owner, a lovely, softly smiling man called Yōji Matsumiya, was only eight when the shop opened and has known it as a sweet shop, a coffee shop and a restaurant before they arrived at the current *izakaya* format. Inside, Matsukaze is quite gloomy and can be very noisy, but that only adds to the atmosphere (as, unfortunately, does the cigarette smoke billowing from the older, coal-fired salarymen). There are usually about 30 types of sake on the menu and most cost from 600 yen to 700 yen for a large 170 ml *tokkuri*, which is quite reasonable for Tōkyō. When I visited, they had a *doburoku* from Gifu prefecture (1,180 yen). *Doburoku* is the completely unrefined homebrew sake that, in my experience, charms about 10 percent of its drinkers (see page 42). Much more approachable, but still thoroughly uncompromising, was the "Tengumai" (天狗舞) *junmai* sake from Ishikawa prefecture. Its name means "dancing Tengu demons" and was reputedly inspired by a particularly spooky night in a forest near Shata brewery, where it is made: the *kura* workers were sure they could hear drumming coming from the middle of the forest and concluded it was Tengu demons dancing the night away. This one is made using the old *yamahai* method (see page 41) and carries its distinct acidity well, with a nice balanced fragrance and broad flavor. It can be drunk chilled or slightly warmed. For food, I was recommended the fish. It is a good idea to let Matsukaze know ahead of your visit if you are going to be ordering the *sashimi moriawase* (assorted *sashimi*, 3,150 for three people). Matsumiya-san said the *maguro no kama* (grilled tuna head, 900 yen) was popular with customers and also recommended the *beinasu dengaku* (grilled eggplant with sweet *miso* sauce, 680 yen).

DIRECTIONS: Ikebukuro Station, North Exit. Turn left across the crossing and continue up the road forking to the left. Take the second road to your right, just after the KFC. It is on your right at the end of the block, next to the Iwata building. There is no Roman alphabet on the gold-lettered dark wood sign.

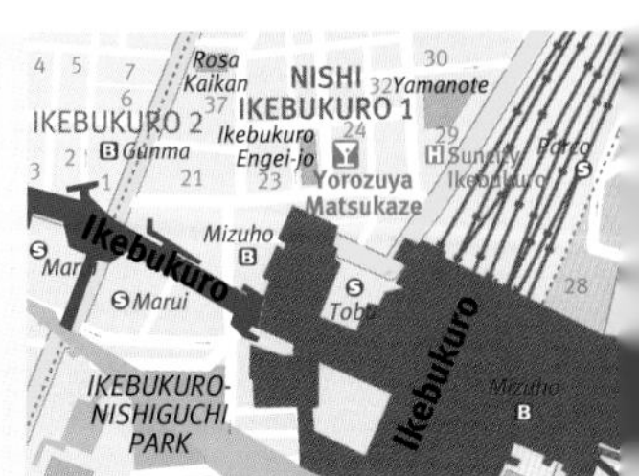

Chapter 2 **Japanese Shōchū and Shōchū Bars**

Japan's Incredible Shōchū Culture

In 1559, two angry carpenters working on the Kōriyama Hachiman shrine in Kyūshū scrawled five lines of graffiti on one of the building's timbers: "The head priest here is such a tightwad! He didn't give us *shōchū* even once. What a nuisance!" They even signed and dated their desecration: "2nd Year of Eiroku. Sakujirō and Suketarō Tsuruta." No one knows if they got lucky on their next job, but their jibe is the earliest reference in Japanese to *shōchū* (焼酎), Japan's homegrown spirit.

Ryūgū kokuto shōchū is a type of sugar shōchū made on the Amami islands north of Okinawa. The distilling process is different from that of rum and it has a distinct taste *(see page 84).*

We also have a slightly earlier report in Portuguese of hard liquor in the area, written thirteen years before the graffiti. The merchant Jorge Alvares said he had seen the people of Yamagawa in Kagoshima drinking "arrack made from rice." Arrack was a term for distilled alcohol common in Southeast Asia.

There are various theories about exactly how distilling arrived in Japan. Some scholars, pointing to records of liquor on boats to Japan from Okinawa in the early 1500s, say it came from those islands. Others argue for a Korean route because of similarities in distilling techniques. What almost everyone agrees is that spirits arrived via the highly developed Indian Ocean and China seas trade in the late 15th or 16th century.

It is a similar story of origin to that of many of the world's distilling traditions. There is some evidence of early distilled drinks in ancient India, China and the Middle East, but the types of spirit we drink now all had their origins in a wildfire spread of technology that came with a growth of international trade from 1200. Distilled alcohols, unlike brewed wines and beers, could be easily stored without spoiling on long voyages, and the techniques seem to have arrived in many

Clockwise from top: Okinawan sugar plantations supply much of the kokuto shōchū industry on the neighboring Amami islands; Manzen sweet potato shōchū; the distilling hall at the Manzen distillery, Kagoshima.

countries in the same way they arrived in Japan: first, as an expensive imported commodity and, then, as a bright idea: "Why the heck are we buying this when we could make it ourselves?" Some of the dates are astonishingly close: the first written record of spirits in Korea (1488), first record of Scottish whisky making (1494), first spirits in Okinawa (1534), first record of *shōchū* drinking (1546), first record of calvados production in France (1554). The name *shōchū* (焼酎) translates as "burned alcohol" or "alcohol that burns," and this too has echoes in traditions across the world: "brandy" (from the German "Branntwein" or "burned wine") has a similar root, as does the Spanish "Aguardiente" (from the Latin "Aqua Ardens" or "fire water") and the southern Chinese "shao-chiu" (焼酒).

And, yet, while drinks such as brandy, whisky and rum (a relative latecomer in the 17th century) have established international reputations, *shōchū* remains obscure outside Japan. There is a very good reason for this, and it has nothing to do with the taste of the alcohol: from the 1630s Japan largely shut itself off from the international trade that had brought distilling to the country and which would spread the reputations of the other traditions. Japan did not become a major trading nation in its own right until the 20th century and did not become a colony of a trading empire either, so *shōchū*, of necessity, stayed local. To this day, it is drunk overwhelmingly by domestic consumers and, until relatively recently, was even more localized: its real heartlands were close to the main areas of production in the south of Japan, on Kyūshū and the small islands trailing off from the Japanese mainlands toward the tropics. The great Japanese alcohol writer Kin'ichirō Sakaguchi called this region the "Scotland of Japan" because of the richness of its distilling culture, and the more I traveled in the area and researched its traditional pot still *honkaku shōchū,* the more I saw his point. (For more on the difference between *honkaku* and *korui shōchū*, see page 80.)

Making honkaku shōchū

Toshihiro Manzen makes *honkaku shōchū* in a tiny distillery high in the backwoods of Kagoshima. He showed me around in the last week in April, with the melodies of *uguisu* birds and

The Manzen distillery in Kagoshima prefecture has a tiny output but a big reputation.

the gentle percussion of the Tekogawa river filling his distilling hall. We did not meet another person during the visit.

It is a special place with a sad history. The original company was set up in 1922, but Manzen-san's father, the third company head, died suddenly in 1969, at the age of 39. Manzen-san was only 10 years old at the time and the stills stayed cold for three decades: "I knew that I had to reopen the distillery, but I had been too young to learn about distilling from my father. It all had to be slowly learned from others," Manzen-san said. It was not until 1999 that he and his uncle eventually managed to reopen the distillery: "I was 39, the same age my father had been when he died."

Manzen-san's methods are resolutely traditional and have served him well in the years since the rebirth of his distillery. He has earned a formidable reputation among the connoisseurs in the big cities for his sweet, aromatic spirits. Most of the tiny production is bought up within days of release, but he has no plans to increase output: "The people who decide to go for big manufacturing have a problem when demand falls. People like me, who have a family perspective, who are making a business for our children and distill the same amount every year, will just keep on going." He uses an old-style wooden still and tuts at the mere idea of modern cooling equipment in his *kōji* room.

A few dozen miles away, there are *shōchū* distilleries on a much larger scale using computer monitored, pressure controlled processes to manufacture thousands of kiloliters a year. However, wherever I went in the *honkaku shōchū* world, I found a similar basic production process:

The harvest *Shōchū* making is often seasonal because fresh ingredients are considered important. Yusaku Takenouchi, president of Shirakane Shuzō, a premium sweet potato *shōchū* maker in Kagoshima, explains that one of the reasons why sweet potatoes originally came to be used for spirit making was their propensity to rot. "Once out of the ground, they go bad very easily," he said. So, production begins as soon as the potato

Toshihiro Manzen tends his wooden distilling equipment at the Manzen distillery. The main still, to Manzen-san's left, is made completely of wood and has to be regularly refurbished to prevent accidents.

harvest starts in late August. (There are more than 40 varieties, but the very starchy "Kogane Sengan" or the slightly less sweet "Joy White" are very popular.) "We are in the fields picking the potatoes. We wash them and peel them by hand and from 5 am the next day the master distiller has them," Takenouchi-san said. *Shōchū* based on other crops have different seasons, and some distilleries will produce more than one type of spirit over the year.

Making the mold (Days 1 and 2) The use of *kōji* (麹) is fundamental to all traditional Japanese alcohol making (see page 38). *Kōji* is not a yeast but a mold. Basically, its job is to break down starches in the main ingredient (potatoes, rice, barley, etc.) into sugars, which can then be turned into alcohol by the yeast (*kōbo*). The *kōji* spores (*kōjikin*, 麹菌) are first propagated on small amounts of steamed rice, barley or sweet potato. At a sweet potato distillery like Manzen-san's, rice is used and the mold is left to grow for about 40 hours in controlled temperatures.

There are three main types of *kōjikin* and each affects the taste of the end product differently. White *kōji* (*shirokōji*, 白麹) is the most commonly used, and has a reputation for producing light and mild spirits. Black *kōji* (*kurokōji*, 黒麹), from the Okinawan *awamori* tradition, is known for adding sweetness and body to the drink. Yellow *kōji* (*kikōji*, 黄麹), the same mold used in sake making, is sensitive to the heat on the southern islands, but can, if used carefully, produce fresh and elegantly aromatic drinks.

First fermentation or Ichijishikomi (Days 3–9) The *kōji* is mixed with water and yeast and left to ferment. At Manzen and at the Shirakane distillery along the Kagoshima coast at Shigetomi, this is done using the traditional *kametsubo jikomi* (甕壷仕込 or simply *kamejikomi* 甕仕込) method, using large pots dug into the ground. The surrounding earth and regular stirring help keep the fermentation temperature down below 30° C. In more modern factories, they use large mechanized steel vats.

Day 9 The main ingredient (sweet potato, rice, barley, etc.) is washed and steamed (or, occasionally, roasted).

Second fermentation or Nijishikomi (Days 9–16) Water and the main ingredient are added to the *moromi* produced in the first fermentation. At Shirakane distillery, one pot of *moromi* is split between five pots and left for about a week. The final brew will usually be between 15 percent and 18 percent alcohol.

Top, left to right:
1 Cleaning kogane sengan sweet potatoes at Ōishi distillery, Kagoshima;
2–4 Shōchū making at Shirakane Shuzō's Shigetomi and Hiramatsu distilleries.
Below: Pouring potato into the fermentation pot at Shigetomi distillery.
Bottom, left to right:
1 Fermentation tanks at Hiramatsu distillery;
2 The wooden still at Shigetomi;
3 Manzen's wooden still;
4 Stainless steel stills at Hiramatsu distillery;
5 The still neck at the Manzen distillery;
6 The jakan (worm tub) at Hiramatsu distillery.

Day 17 Distillation There are almost as many shapes and designs of stills as there are *shōchū* makers in Japan. Usually the stills are made of stainless steel, but I fell in love with the traditional wooden stills at Shirakane and Manzen. Only one man, Tatsuya Tsudome in Kagoshima city, who is now in his seventies, has the skills to repair these pot stills in the traditional way, using bamboo ties to hold the barrels together. "The still has to be repaired regularly because if the ties loosen you could have a dangerous accident. It's not the most convenient way, but it gives a softness to the spirit," said Takenouchi-san at Shirakane. The still is a very simple contraption: a pipe pushes hot steam from a steel tank directly into the fermented *moromi*, from which the alcohol vapor rises into a narrow neck leading to a worm tub or *jakan* (蛇管; literally, snake pipe), where a coiled tin pipe immersed in water condenses the alcohol.

"Every morning, at 5 am the master distiller will begin," said Takenouchi-san. "After about one hour of heating, what we call the *hatsutare* (first drop) starts to emerge, drip by drip. It looks like morning dew. That is why so many *shōchū* have the word *tsuyu* (dew) in their names. Then, it comes like a fountain. That is called the *hondare* (main drop), and finally we get the *suedare* (last drop), which carries the character of the rice and potato most strongly."

Maturing *Shōchū* did not, until recently, have a culture of aging spirits to rival that of Okinawa's *awamori* or Western traditions like whisky or brandy. The spirit was routinely left to sit for between three months and a year before reaching consumers, but longer aging was not very widespread. Even now, there is disagreement about its benefits. Some potato *shōchū* makers, for instance, will tell you that sweet potato *shōchū* can only stand aging up to five years because the aroma so valued by drinkers dissipates. Manzen-san, on the other hand, has an aging cavern built

Toshihiro Manzen ages his sweet potato spirit in a cellar dug into the hillside beside his distillery. Despite resistance from some traditionalists, aging sweet potato shōchū is becoming more common.

into a hillside next to his distillery and plans to age his *shōchū* in large glass bottles for up to 35 years. "The truth is that aging was a bit of a taboo in Kagoshima because the makers were poor. They needed to get their spirit on the market in the same year," he said. Other *shōchū* makers are using wooden casks, pottery jars and stainless steel and enamel tanks to store their spirits. Nobody really knows what is possible, but there is great fun to be had nowadays in exploring the variously aged liquors in the shops. It will be interesting to see how the techniques develop. Aged *shōchū* is called *koshu* (古酒), the same word that is used for aged sake (see page 43).

A crucial distinction

There are two types of *shōchū* and this chapter will concentrate on only one of them—*honkaku shōchū*" (本格 焼酎). The other type—*kōrui shōchū*" (甲類 焼酎)—is definitely the most price-efficient way of buying alcohol in Japan. A plastic gallon bottle of 25 percent alcohol *kōrui shōchū* can cost as little as 1,600 yen. Unfortunately, it is also totally uninteresting. It is a modern innovation that became possible only after the introduction of Western multiple distillation techniques in the 19th century. This distillation method tends to reduce the influence of the base ingredients on the spirit. *Kōrui shōchū* is therefore a neutral spirit which is perfectly good if you want a relatively characterless alcohol to use in a cocktail, but it has very little individuality. In my experience, many Westerners try this stuff once and conclude that *shōchū* in general is merely a cheap vodka substitute. They couldn't be more wrong.

There is also an imported Korean spirit called *soju*, which also falls into the *kōrui* category. It tends to be in green bottles and often has Korean *hangul* characters on its labels. The biggest manufacturer is Jinro. *Soju* is often said to be distinctively sweet, but I have always found it very difficult to tell apart from *kōrui shōchū*. I am sure there is far more variation in Korea itself, but in its current mass-market manifestation in Japan it is of limited interest. Another category that can be safely ignored is *konwashōchū* (混和焼酎), a blend of *korui* and *honkaku shōchū*.

Honkaku shōchū (本格) is the interesting stuff. It is also sometimes called "Otsu" (乙) or "Otsurui" (乙類) *shōchū* and traces its single-distillation pot still method back to the beginnings of *shōchū* making. It is often full of individual character and

Korui shōchū (left) is cheap but relatively characterless. Honkaku shōchū (right) is full of individual character.

some of it is quite superb. The prices can reflect its premium status, reaching more than 30,000 yen for a bottle in some Tōkyō stores (a fact that enrages many of the makers, who only make a fraction of that price), but there are also some very reasonably priced *honkaku*, which represent some of the best value for money of any premium alcohol in Japan.

What are the main types of honkaku shōchū?

The six major types

Unlike, say, rum or whisky, *honkaku shōchū* is defined by its method of production rather than its ingredients. There is very little legal restriction on the ingredients that can be put into *shōchū* and so there is an almost endless variety of types of *honkaku* on the market. There are, however, five or six established traditions:

Sake lees shōchū (kasutori shōchū 粕取り焼酎) Throughout much of the modern era, *shōchū* was regarded as a poor man's drink in Japan, and no *shōchū* had a rougher reputation that *kasutori*, which was made from the lees left after sake making.

It had a long and perfectly respectable history in pre-modern Japan. They produced it all over the country, not just in the traditional heartland of *shōchū* in the south, mainly, it seems, because of its usefulness to farmers. In 1696, an agricultural textbook, *Nōgaku Zensho*, recommended the use of sake *kasu* lees, with all the alcohol removed, as a fertilizer for rice. The best way to remove the alcohol (which damaged roots) was distilling *kasu* (sake lees). It was a wonderfully circular recycling scheme: the waste from the distilling grew the rice that made the sake that left the lees that were distilled. Early on, the spirit seems to have been widely used as an antiseptic, but by the late Edo period working-class drinkers had taken it up.

A quick guide to shōchū

What do you need to know about *shōchū* to get by, without having to get into the technicalities? There are two main types of *shōchū*. *Kōrui* (甲類), which is the stuff sold in big plastic containers in Japanese supermarkets but also in an increasing number of fancily packaged bottles, is just neutral alcohol without much taste. It is okay for cocktails, but that is about as interesting as it gets. *Honkaku shōchū* (本格) is made in pot stills, just like malt whisky and brandy, and its main types (sweet potato, rice, barley, sake lees and buckwheat *shōchū*) all have very individual tastes. If you really want to look like a *shōchū* geek, order a sweet potato *imojōchū* from Kagoshima, a *Kumajōchū* rice spirit from Kumamoto, or an Iki Island *mugijōchū*. For more information on getting by in Japanese shops and bars, see page 248.

In Fukuoka, where they made a famously uncompromising "sanaburi" *kasutori* from rice husks and *kasu* lees, the most enthusiastic drinkers worked as a farm hands, foresters or in the coal mines. The advent of very cheap, multiply-distilled *kōrui shōchū* in the Meiji era challenged *kasutori*'s popularity with the workers, but many continued to mix "sanaburi" with the characterless *kōrui*.

Immediately after Japan's defeat in 1945, however, the reputation of *kasutori* in particular and *shōchū* in general took a nosedive, even among ordinary folk. It became associated with a post-defeat subculture that sprang up around the black markets. People had little money, no hope and horrific memories of the war. They drank, as one black market trader put it, "trying to forget a life that hung suspended like a floating weed" and this dangerous underworld came to be called "*kasutori* culture". The black market liquors often had little to do with real *kasu*. A famous drink at the time was called the *bakudan* ("bomb"), a mixture of methyl alcohol and disguising chemicals. Such cocktails killed at least 384 people in 1946. The bad associations stuck to *shōchū* and *kasutori shōchū*. People turned to more glamorous foreign liquors like whisky for their pleasures when they got more money in their pockets.

Younger drinkers with no experience of the post-war years are now re-exploring *shōchū* and there is much to intrigue them coming out of the *kasutori* tradition. For instance, the aged "Kaitō Otokoyama 1984" (開当男山1984) *kasutori*, which I tried at the Za Enraku bar in Tōkyō (see page 109), was quite unlike any other rice-based spirit I have ever tasted; it was a bit like a very earthy dark sherry. Hakusen Shuzō in Gifu prefecture is another interesting outfit. They are experimenting with a "Ranbiki" *kasutori* made in a reconstructed Meiji-period still and using the same sake lees and rice husk ingredients of the robust drinks of yesteryear. At the other extreme, a growing number of *kura* are making extremely delicate *kasutori* from premium *ginjō* and *daiginjō* sake lees (see page 40). "Amabuki Ginjō kasutori" (天吹吟醸粕取り焼酎) out of Saga prefecture is one of the more interesting examples of the genre, with a strong citrus fruit smell but an elegant, slightly soapy taste.

Sweet potato shōchū (imojōchū 芋焼酎) In 1996, Yūichirō Hamada, the head of a medium-sized *imojōchū* maker in Kagoshima, stood up in front of a crisis meeting of distillery owners and shocked everybody. The meeting had been called because a World Trade Organization (WTO) decision was threatening to destroy the *shōchū* industry, or so most of the distillery owners thought. After years of diplomatic and legal wrangling, the WTO had finally decided that Japan's alcohol taxes discriminated against foreign spirits. The WTO's momentous decision meant that a 1.8 liter bottle of *honkaku shōchū*

Mount Sakurajima, the highly active stratovolcano that looms just 4 km across the bay from Kagoshima City, lies at the heart of Japan's main sweet potato shōchū region.

previously costing 183 yen would rise to 464 yen. The whisky tax would be halved.

What Hamada said next was met with stunned silence, according to an account by the Japanese writer Takashi Nagai. "This is not the end of the world," he breezily told the other Kagoshima makers. "What this means is that the Scotch whisky industry has told the world that it regards Japanese *shōchū* as its equal! This could be one of the greatest opportunities for us to tell the Japanese nation what *imojōchū* is." Many in the room were furious. A number of older men stood up to condemn him. *Imojōchū* was a common man's drink, they said. It should never try to rival whisky.

Koichi Satō, head of another distillery in neighboring Miyazaki prefecture, recalled: "Until then, everybody believed *honkaku shōchū* was for the ordinary people and mostly consumed in Kyūshū. There were some distillery owners who even believed their own product to be a cheaper substitute for *korui shōchū*." The stricter tax regime forced the industry to try to reach more lucrative markets in the big cities and there they found young consumers with few preconceptions about the drink. It helped that, from 2003, there was a series of reports in the media of *honkaku*'s supposed health benefits. Sales grew exponentially and, more importantly, Hamada's prediction that *shōchū* could become a premium product was conclusively proved correct. In 1998, 325,109 kl of *honkaku* were sold, climbing to 450,000 kl in 2003 and 536,856 kl in 2005. The boom has tapered off a little recently, but *imojōchū*, in particular, is now widely regarded as a connoisseur's drink. The once-derided stink of a traditionally

made *imojōchū* is now sniffed intently in hundreds of specialist bars.

Yet, if you visit southern Kyūshū, there is still an abiding sense that sweet potato *shōchū* should never be a posh person's tipple. The volcanic soil is some of the worst in Japan, unsuitable for rice and other grains, but sweet potatoes do grow. The first person known to have planted sweet potatoes in Kyūshū was actually an Englishman called Richard Cocks (in 1615), but tell that to a Kagoshimaite and you will get a blank stare. The real breakthrough came in 1705 when Riemon Maeda, a Yamagawa fisherman, brought sweet potatoes back from Okinawa. Farmers all over the area took them up and when grain crops failed disastrously in 1732, killing more than 12,000 people across southern Japan, Maeda's potatoes saved hundreds of lives. He is still remembered as a local hero and this history makes it difficult for anybody from southern Kyūshū to accept that the potato, and the distilled spirit that is made from it, should ever become merely a plaything for the rich. Yūsaku Takenouchi, whose company makes Ishikura, a craft *imojōchū* highly prized in Tōkyō, says: "I don't like all these ridiculous prices that are being paid. *Imojōchū* is a drink for the working people."

Sugar shōchū (kokutōjōchū 黒糖焼酎)
Another liquor born of the struggles of ordinary people is the sugar *shōchū* of the Amami islands, which trail off from the foot of Kagoshima prefecture toward Okinawa. The spotless white beaches in today's tourist brochures make it look like a tropical paradise, but life has been hard for much of the history of this pit viper-infested typhoon-swept archipelago. Its most famous product, since *samurai* times, has been the back-breaking sugar cane harvest.

The islanders seem to have sought some respite from their labors with millet- and rice-based spirits in the past. They knew early on that the sugar cane also made great alcohol, but their *samurai* overlords came down very hard on anyone who tried to distill it. An oral tradition has it that the *samurai* foremen used to round up all the distilling equipment on the island between January and June, the sugar-producing season, for fear that the valuable commodity would evaporate up the islanders' still necks.

Sugar *shōchū* left its illicit past behind it during World War II, when an American naval blockade made export of the sugar impossible. Production accelerated after the peace. In 1947, with rice distilling banned on Okinawa because of food shortages but surplus stocks of sugar cane available in Amami, total production on Amami's main island reached 180,000 liters.

The islands were returned to Japan by the US in 1953 and, instead of taxing Amami sugar liquor at the exorbitant rates then applied to foreign rums, the Japanese government gave it a special designation as a type of *shōchū*. *Kokuto shōchū* (literally, black sugar *shōchū*) can only be made on the Amami islands and must be made using rice *kōji*, thus distinguishing it from rum. The taste of most of the brands produced by Amami's eighteen distilleries is vaguely reminiscent of rum but is usually less sweet with a distinct savory note added by the *kōji*.

Rice shōchū (komejōchū 米焼酎) Most of the early 16th and 17th century sources talk about *shōchū* as a rice-based alcohol. Today, the best known rice *shōchū* is "Kumajōchū" (球磨焼酎) from Kumamoto prefecture in Kyūshū. As with "Champagne" or "Bordeaux," the WTO has recognized Kumajōchū as having a special "geographic indication." This means that nobody outside Kumamoto's Hitoyoshi city and Kumagun districts can make Kumajōchū. The 28 *kura* in the area must use local underground water, rice *kōji* and pure rice as the main ingredient to get the prestigious designation.

There is also a lot of rice *shōchū* making on Japan's main island of Honshū, with a number of *kura* now making spirit out of the *ginjō* and *daiginjō* polished rice usually associated with sake production. I have tasted some rice *shōchū* with very delicate tastes and smells, not very far removed from sake, while some "Kumajōchū" has a dry sherry-like impact. Generally, the tastes are more restrained and the stinks less aggressive than Kagoshima and Miyazaki's potato *shōchū*. I sometimes think of the difference as a bit like Speyside's delicate single-malt whiskies compared to Islay's big, peaty malts.

Barley shōchū (mugijōchū 麦焼酎) The Japanese word *mugi* can mean either wheat, barley, oats or rye, but most *mugijōchū* is, in fact, made from unmalted barley (*komugi*, 小麦).

Top left: Shirakane Shuzō's Shigetomi distillery steams at distilling time.
Top right and bottom left: Fermentation pots at Shigetomi.
Above: A reproduction of a primitive kabuto still at Nishikinada Shuzō, Kagoshima.

Non-rice grains like millet had been distilled in places such as Akune in Kagoshima since the late 17th century, but the most famous center of *mugijōchū* is on Iki Island, off the north coast of Kyūshū. Unlike the centers of sweet potato distilling, Iki is fertile and has always been a big producer or rice and other grains. Strict surveillance of the rice crop in the 1700s forced the island's enthusiastic distillers to concentrate on barley. By the late 19th century, there were 55 barley *shōchū* distilleries crammed onto the island's 142 square km. That has now shrunk to only seven companies, but the fame of Iki's *mugijōchū* has spread. Like Kumamoto, it has a World Trade Organization "geographic indication" and uses a strictly defined method to produce its famous natural sweetness: rice is used for the *kōji* as well as in the first fermentation. Roughly twice as much barley is then poured in for the second fermentation. The distilling is usually at normal pressure, which tends to lend a richer flavor.

The other major area of *mugijōchū* production is Ōita prefecture in the northeast of Kyūshū. It is a relative newcomer. Historically, Ōita concentrated on sake and rice spirits but, in the mid-1970s, a company called Nikaidō Shuzō released two barley *shōchū*, "Kicchomu" and "Nikaidō." Another Ōita distiller called Sanwashurui followed suit, with the now iconic "Iichiko" brand, in 1979. Iichiko's slogan, "Shitamachi no Napoleon," conveyed the same sort of meaning to the Japanese that boasting of being "Cockney's Cognac" would to the English. It was a refreshing departure from *shōchū*'s old inferiority complex—referring to the drink's unpretentious image, but proudly challenging comparison with any of the much-vaunted foreign alcohols. The new spirit tasted different too. Unlike Iki *shōchū*, barley was used for both the *kōji* and the main ingredient. Low-pressure distilling kept the smell fresh and the taste very smooth. The 1980s and 1990s were the heydey of this style of *mugijōchū*, fueling the first major spike in *honkaku shōchū* consumption since the war. The ultra-light spirit still sells by the bucket load, and distillers all over Ōita prefecture now produce this style.

Buckwheat shōchū and other innovations

The smooth barley *shōchū* draw on an old tradition, but buckwheat *shōchū* (*sobajōchū*, そば焼酎) is entirely new-fangled. In 1973, Unkai distillery in Nishiusuki district in Miyazaki on the island

Saisaidō Magosuke in Kyōto (page 101) champions shōchū in a region more famous for its sake.

of Kyūshū, came up with the idea. It is now produced by a number of makers in Nishiusuki and also in Nagano prefecture on Honshū, which is famous for its buckwheat.

Historically, the main challenge in making buckwheat *shōchū* was suppressing its powerful aromas and tastes, but modern distilling and maturation techniques result in a particularly mild drink. It is more popular in Tōkyō and Ōsaka soba noodle shops than it is among the more traditional Kyūshū drinkers.

The same can probably be said for the dozens of innovative ingredients now being used by *shōchū* makers across the country. Among these are aloe vera, pumpkin, chestnuts, sesame, shisō leaf, corn, carrot, green pepper, tea, peanuts, seaweed, gingko nuts, tomato, devil's tongue and milk. Some of these can be dismissed as gimmicks, but others are definitely worth a try. I like the sesame and refreshing shisō *shōchū*.

How to drink shōchū

There are no rules for drinking *shōchū*. You can drink it exactly how you want to, and most Japanese just follow their own individual preferences. However, there are a number of established ways of drinking with which you can experiment.

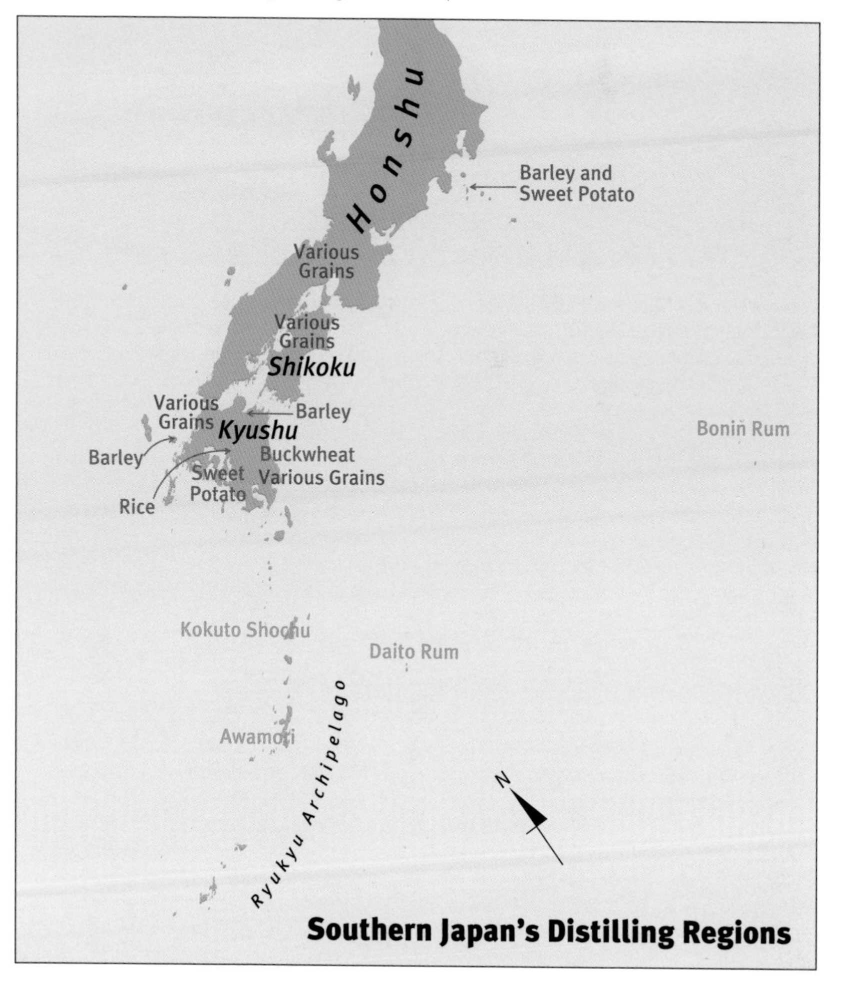

Southern Japan's Distilling Regions

Warm water mix (Oyuwari お湯割) Most of the old stagers I met in Kagoshima drank their sweet potato *shōchū* in an *oyuwari*, a warm mixture of *shōchū* and water. Pour two parts of hot water (about 85° C); shake the *shōchū* and pour in three parts of the spirit. Never pour the *shōchū* in first because it destroys the aromas. Alternatively, you can mix cold water and *shōchū* the day before and then slowly heat your container in a pan of hot water when thirst strikes. It is an old custom in southern Kyūshū to drink things warm. Jorge Alvares, the first recorder of *shōchū*, noted in 1546: "Never in the winter nor in the summer do they drink cold water."

On Iki island, they have a similar way of drinking their barley spirit. The locals dilute it down to about 18–20 percent alcohol and serve it warm. The traditional way of doing this is to warm a glass jug directly over a flame although this risks breaking the glass. Other interesting variations on the *oyuwari* include the mixtures of buckwheat (soba) *shōchū* and the warm water used to make soba noodles sometimes served in soba restaurants, and the classic *umeboshiwari*,

Beware the evils of hard alcohol and tobacco!

An anecdote from the 1840s, recounted by the modern Japanese food historian Hisao Nagayama, told of a stable groom who was a notorious drinker. One day he went to an *izakaya* (Japanese pub) and ordered five *gō* (900 ml) of *shōchū*. He downed it and ordered another five *gō*, to the amazement of the people in the shop. The fifth 900 ml was served personally by an astounded landlord. At last, the man was satisfied. "Thank you," he said, "For the first time I was able to drink my full." He went home and decided to relax with some tobacco. Unfortunately, the account insisted, his body was so soaked with alcohol that he caught fire as he tried to light his pipe, and burned to death.

The nurukan sake at Ramuro in Shinjuku, Tōkyō (page 100), is a gently warmed mixture of 60 percent shōchū and 40 percent water.

Shōchū is often served straight in small choko glasses.

featuring a salty pickled *ume* "plum" added to hot water and *shōchū*.

Straight Most of the premium *shōchū* distillers I have met have served me their alcohol straight. People often use tiny *choko* cups for this style and, as long as you control the refills, these have the great benefit of encouraging moderate drinking. One style of traditional Kyūshū *mizuwari* ("water mix") is actually close to being straight: no ice is used and only one part water is added to nine parts spirit. It is not so far from the old Scottish whisky drinkers' habit of adding a drop or two of water to their single malt, although the alcohol content of the *mizuwari* is often much lower than straight whisky. Although a good number of premium *shōchū* do range up to 40-odd percent alcohol, the mass market brands are usually diluted down to 20 or 25 percent for bottling. This is almost entirely because of Japan's eccentric tax system. The Japanese government currently taxes almost all pure spirits at 10,000 yen per kiloliter for every percentage point of alcohol they contain. However, the last vestiges of protectionism remain: the minimum alcohol content a *shōchū* can be bottled at and still receive tax benefits is a 20 percent alcohol, while other spirits get taxed at a 37 percent rate, even if they contain less alcohol. This encourages the most widely sold *shōchū* to bottle at 20 percent or 25 percent.

Cold water mix (Mizuwari 水割り) Modern *mizuwari* recipes often recommend using more water than the old Kyūshū habits. A typical bar in Tōkyō will put in three parts *shōchū* to two parts cold water, but you can dilute to your own taste. Many people also add ice. My father-in-law and his friends usually share containers of water, *shōchū* and ice at the dinner table. A subtle battle is often waged by some of the wives, who take every opportunity to fill the men's cups with the water and ice, diluting the spirit to nothingness.

On the rocks ("On za rokku") *Shōchū* and ice is one of the most common ways of drinking *shōchū*. It works very well with relatively smooth barley, buckwheat or rice *shōchū*, but I find it can make the more characterful sweet potato and *kasutori* spirits very hard-edged.

Chūhai

The alcohol sections of Japanese supermarkets are usually stacked with hundreds of cans of pre-prepared *chūhai*. The name originally comes from a contraction of "Shōchū Highball," the term given to the soda and *shōchū* cocktails that became popular in Tōkyō's drinking districts immediately after the war. The idea recently got a second wind when Japanese drinks companies found that canned *chūhai* was a good way to sell their cheap *korui shōchū* at rock-bottom tax rates. *Chūhai* is the main competitor with beer in Japan's mass drink market, and *chūhai* cans now contain all sorts of weird and wonderful concoctions (vodka *chūhai* is especially popular with younger women). Of course, you can make tastier *chūhai* at home. Try four parts of any fruit juice, soda or tea that strikes you as promising, and add one part of *shōchū* and some ice.

Hoppy

Almost every cheap drinking joint in Tōkyō (and a good number of the posher *shōchū* bars) seems to have a red "Hoppy" (ホッピー) banner outside at the moment. Hoppy is a carbonated beer-like drink that is made alcoholic by adding one part of cheap *shōchū* to five parts Hoppy. It was first sold immediately after the war to workers who could not afford real beer, and the post-war nostalgia that has swept Japan since 2000 has made it a fashionable drink among trendy 20- and 30-somethings. It is actually quite refreshing in Japan's sultry summers, as long as you don't think of it as beer.

Hoppy is drinkable, as long as you don't think of it as beer.

Umeshu and other fruit liqueurs

Shōchū is also the most common base for various traditional fruit liqueurs (*kajitsushu*), including the heavenly *umeshu* (Japanese plum liqueur, 梅酒). *Kajitsushus* are made by steeping fruits and sugar in *shōchū* for long periods (sometimes many years). These concoctions used to be made by housewives but are now sold widely on the commercial market. They are some of the most approachable Japanese alcohols for the newcomer, usually offering a very sweet taste with a refreshing tang. The most common type is *umeshu* (梅酒), made with the Japanese *ume* fruit (sometimes called Japanese apricot or Chinese plum) but you can get all sorts of *kajitsushu*: *yuzushu* (from the *yuzu* citrus fruit), *momoshu* (from peaches), blueberry-shu, to name but three. There are also experiments with brandy, *awamori*, whisky and sake-based *kajitsushu* on the market. To make your own, experiment around this recipe: layer 1 kg of fruit and 1 kg of rock sugar in a sterilized jar. Pour in seven cups of spirit. Close the lid very tightly. Wait at least six months, occasionally moving the jar to make sure you have a good mix. These liqueurs are good straight or on the rocks but also very nice diluted with hot water, cold water or soda water.

Azabu Kusafue 麻布 草ふえ 03-3498-3181 www.kusafue.com

2F, 2-25-13 Nishi-Azabu, Minato ku, Tōkyō, 106-0031
〒106-0031 東京都港区西麻布 2-25-13 2F
Open: Tuesday–Saturday 7 pm–4 am; Sunday 7 pm–2 am; closed Monday
Booking recommended? Yes, particularly at weekends and for large parties
Credit cards? Major cards Cover charge: 500 yen

As manager of the famous En-Ichi bar, Masahito Komatsu was one of the pioneers of the *shōchū* renaissance of the early 2000s. He opened Kusafue in 2006, just as *shōchū*'s popularity was peaking, but he is convinced that interest in the drink was no passing fad. "At the start it was almost all about
imojōchū, but people are now trying their own paths. *Shōchū* changes with the seasons. Potato *shōchū* comes at the end of the year and there are nouveau styles arriving in the winter, then rice in the spring and barley in summer," he says. His new dining bar is big on food and drink pairings and is not the place to go if you only want to drink. Try the *jikasei sumōku moriawase* (selection of smoked foods, price varies but about 1,500 yen) or the *maguro to shungiku no bainiku ae* (tuna marinated in pickled plum, 800 yen) with the amusingly branded Kagoshima *imojōchū* "Akarui Nōson" (明るい農村). A Japanese friend of mine chuckled as soon as she saw the bottle. I needed the joke explaining to me: apparently, "Akarui Nōson" means "bright farming village" and sounds exactly like the worst kind of World War II government propaganda. A bit like "Dig for Victory" for the British, I think.

The label adopts the same tongue-in-cheek chic. It comes from Kirishimachō distillery, a revived company that, until recently, was just rebottling other distilleries' spirits. They have pulled their socks up and this big blast of potato has been a hit with lovers of the most robust *imojōchū*. They are very good in an *oyuwari* (warm water mix).

DIRECTIONS: A 10-minute walk from Roppongi Station, Exit 4b. Walk straight ahead with the flyover to your left. At the bottom of the hill, cross over Gaien Nishi-dōri. Turn up the second side street on your right after the big junction and take an immediate left. It is in the third building on your left, but the staircase can be a little hard to spot.

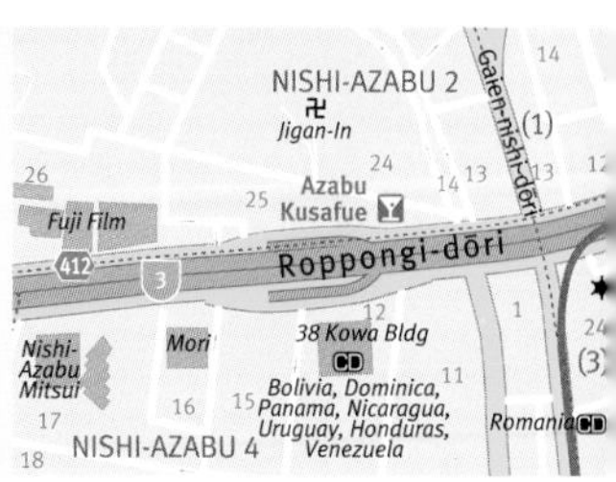

Chūya Shinobu 耐屋しのぶ 078-252-3969 chuyashinobu.blog58.fc2.com

1-20-15 Naka Yamate-dōri, Chūō-ku, Kōbe, Hyōgo 650-0004
650-004 神戸市中央区中山手通 1 丁目 20-15
Open: 5 pm to an indeterminate closing time Booking recommended? No Credit cards? No
English menu? No Cover charge: No

Chūya Shinobu has a nice family atmosphere. There was a toddler walking around the shop when I arrived and everybody seemed to pitch in when I asked what they would recommend from the bewildering array of bottles lining the walls. "We try to emphasize the very small *kura* rather than the very famous ones because there are so many unnoticed places that make great stuff that don't get the attention they deserve," said owner Junko Shimizu. A case in point was the extremely rare "Tsukin'naka" potato *shōchū* (900 yen) from the tiny Iwakura shuzō in Miyazaki prefecture. They have been distilling since 1890 but it has always been a small-scale family operation. Even now, only *kura* head Iwakura-san, his wife, daughter and son work at the distillery. They used to make rice *shōchū*, but they changed to potatoes after the war because of grain shortages and, in the 1970s, dropped their seasonal work as farmers to go full time into *shōchū*. It is the sort of story of part-time distilling that you might have heard among Scottish whisky makers in the 1800s, when whisky was still an extension of agriculture for many people, but it is an era that is only just beginning to fade in the *shōchū* world's memory. "Tsukin'naka" has a sweet but powerful taste. It would work well with the *gobo no karaage* (deep-fried burdock root, 500 yen). The milder, more rounded "Isshō Hanjō" (一生繁盛) potato *shōchū* from Furusawa distillery is recommended with the *mābōdōfu* (spicy *tōfu* and mince, 600 yen), or you could just go with the flow, because there are literally hundreds of reasonably priced *shōchūs* (usually 800–1,200 yen) to be sampled here and you will find few better guides than Shimizu-san.

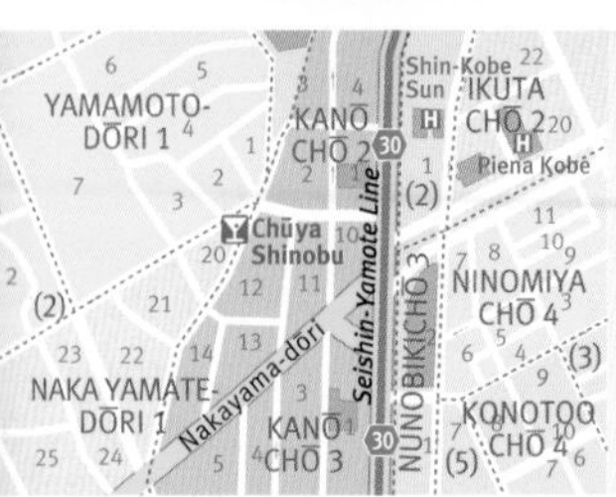

DIRECTIONS: JR Sannomiya Station, north side. Walk up Route 30 (leading off to the right of McDonald's on the main junction to the north of the station). Walk about 400 yards to the major junction straddled by a large footbridge. Continue up Route 30 but take the first left immediately after the footbridge. Chūya Shinobu is on the corner opposite you when you reach a five-road junction.

Garari がらり 03-5786-1820 gala-e.com/galali2.html

2-6-4 Sendagaya, Shibuya, Tōkyō
東京都渋谷区千駄ヶ谷 2-6-4
Open: 11.30 am–2 pm; 6 pm–11.00 pm; closed national holidays Booking recommended? Yes, particularly busy Wednesday–Saturday Credit cards? Most major cards
English menu? No Cover charge: 600 yen

This stylish concept pub is the best place in Tōkyō to explore the Amami islands' sugar *shōchū* (*kokutōjōchū*, 黒糖焼酎, see page 84). They claim to stock every type of *kokutō* currently available (and some that are not): more than 140 bottles in all. The prices are not cheap, but the owners, who also run the nearby Galali sake pub (see page 53), know how to put together a unique drinking experience. At Garari, they have paired the alcohol with the most phenomenal menu of *miso* I have ever encountered. There are 12 different types of the traditional Japanese fermented seasoning to taste with your drink, and the menu relies heavily on *miso* dishes. Try the *kurobuta no misoni* (pork stewed with sweet *miso*, 1,300 yen) or the *tsukune* (grilled chicken, pork and onion meatball, 1,300 yen). They recommended the "Hi no Ryū Asahi" *kokutō shōchū* (飛乃流 朝日, 800 yen) when I visited. It is made by Asahi Shuzō on Kikaijima, sometimes known as Cleopatra Island because of its great beauty, and is unusual because the distillery insists on controlling the entire production, right from farming their own sugar cane. Amami sugar is such a prestigious product in Japan that some Amami distillers cut their costs by shipping in cheaper sugar from Okinawa. "Hi no Ryū Asahi" has a subtle brown sugar flavor and a light aroma. "Amandii" (アマンディー/天孫岳, 800 yen), a *kokutō* from the main island of Amami Ōshima, has more body and an almost brandy-like taste. The makers, Nishihira Honke, are one of a number of *kokutō* makers with roots in the old Nishihara clan of distillers from Okinawa and are also a good example of the growing part women are taking in Japan's previously macho alcohol culture. The previous owner, Moritsune Nishihara, died in 1996, leaving everything in the hands of his wife Chieko Nakamura. She knew absolutely nothing about distilling, but a mixture of determination, enthusiasm and charisma kept the company going. Their alcohol is now highly regarded.

DIRECTIONS: Harajuku JR Station, Takeshita Exit. Turn left and take the right fork at the junction next to the Park Court, Jingūmae building. Walk up the left side of the road for about 500 yards, past Harajuku-gaien High School on your right and Sendagaya Elementary School on your left. It is on the corner of the second turning to your left after the elementary school, about 30 yards beyond the footbridge.

Ishizue 礎 099-227-0125 www.honkakushochu-bar-ishizue.com

Kagoshima daiichi biru 5F, 8-34 Yamanokuchi-chō, Kagoshima-shi, Kagoshima ken, 892-0844
〒892-0844 鹿児島県鹿児島市山之口町 8-34 鹿児島第一ビル 5F
Open: 7.30 pm–4 am (last orders 2.30 am) Booking recommended? Yes
Credit cards? JCB and Visa for bills above 30,000 yen English menu? No Cover charge: 700 yen

It is almost unknown for the *kurabito*, the people who make *shōchū*, to cross over and start selling it to the public, but Ishizue's owner, Yoichi Ikehata, has done just that. He is a young man but has an encyclopaedic knowledge of the industry based on years at the coal face. Perhaps because of his closeness to the industry, he was unwilling to come out and recommend one particular spirit for this guide: "I do not do recommendations like that. What I do is ask people what type of alcohol they want, what sort of drink they normally like, and then I will introduce what best suits the individual." There is certainly a big enough range to choose from: 310 types, mostly sweet potato *shōchū*, from Kagoshima and Miyazaki distilleries. I had just come back from a visit to Shirakane distillery so I went for their famous "Ishikura" (石蔵) *shōchū*, handmade in the wooden still at their Shigetomi distillery. Takamori Saigo, the historical "Last Samurai," used to drink Ishikura and I can see the affinity. Like the old rebel, there is uncompromising but sophisticated power to "Ishikura"—an archetypal old-school *imojōchū*. In marked contrast, "Umi" was a low-pressure distilled spirit from Taikai Shuzō. Umi targets people who want to try *imojōchū* but are not keen on the strong whiffs that often come with it. It is made with the delicate yellow *kōji* usually used by sake makers and has a sweet, fresh flavor. I liked it with ice.

DIRECTIONS: Tenmonkan-dōri tram stop. Walk down Tenmonkan-dōri, which is a side road running southeast from the western end of the Tenmonkan-dōri tram stop. There is a McDonald's on your left as you walk down the road. Take the third right, cross at the traffic lights and it is on your right. The sign is a single and difficult-to-read *kanji* character. Look out for the building between a flower shop and the Lounge Southern Comfort.

Kanayama Johnny 銀山ジョニー 082-247-0426

B1F 1-20 Ebisu-chō, Naka-ku, Hiroshima
広島県広島市中区胡町 1-20 B1F
Open: 5 pm–1 am; closed Sunday Credit cards? JCB, Visa, Mastercard and Amex
English menu? Yes, and some of the staff speak some English Cover charge: 300 yen

The billing system at this friendly, energetic *izakaya* is fun: you serve your own drink. Each of the 250 *shōchū* and 30 *umeshu* (see page 90) bottles lining the walls has a colored tag. You just pull it down from the shelf, pour yourself a glass and note down the color of the tag on the little chit provided.

At the end of the evening, you hand in the chits. The tag prices for *shōchū* on the rocks when I visited were: white (290 yen), blue (390 yen), green (490 yen), black (590 yen), red (690 yen), silver (790 yen) and gold (890 yen). They take off 100 yen for a *mizuwari* (water mix, see page 89) and add 200 yen for a straight shot. The food is, like the drink, reasonably priced. There are 20 types of *kushiyaki* (grilled meat and vegetables on sticks, 60–260 yen per stick) and the *basashi sashimi* (raw horse meat, 1,380 yen) will appeal to the more adventurous. I asked waitress Asaka Kōno if they had problems with drinkers trying to cheat the DIY system. "It is actually quite rare and, remember, the customers are drinking and we are not. We generally know if people are trying it on," she said. "We find the foreigners are really quite religious about writing every last thing down." You will want to find your own way around the vast selection of alcohol at your fingertips here, but Kōno-san recommended "Jaku Umbaku" (釈云麦), a *mugijōchū* from Fukuoka prefecture. The label is written in a mock aggressive style, with words to the effect: "To fight against this invasion of [strong smelling] potato *shōchūs* we have broken a taboo and made this one unfiltered and with black *kōji*." The taste is strongly toasted and has a distinctive grain smell. If you get sick of all the *shōchū*, you could also sample Kanayama Johnny's excellent selection of *umeshu* (traditional Japanese plum liqueurs), such as the *honkaku shōchū*-based "Torotoro no Umeshu" (590 yen) and the brandy-based "Ebisu Fukuume" (590 yen).

DIRECTIONS: Kanayama-chō Hiroden tram stop (Station number M5). It is in a building close to the corner of Yagenbori-dōri (the road with the UCC coffee-sponsored gate). The sign is in Japanese script, but look for the basement entrance immediately to the left of the Honmamon yakiniku restaurant.

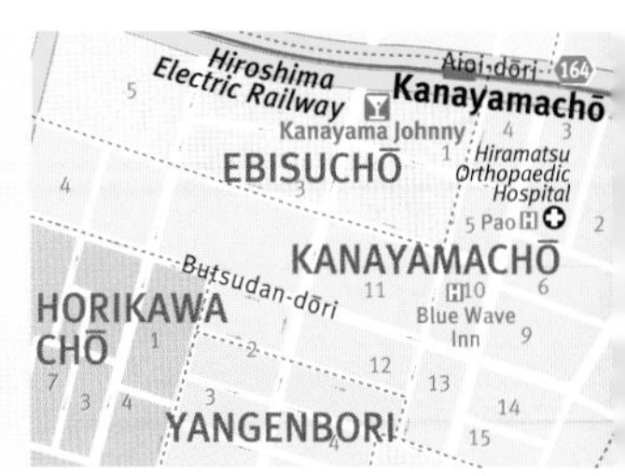

Koten 古典 03-3496-1899 home.c06.itscom.net/koten

7-10 Maruyama-chō, Shibuya, Tōkyō
東京都渋谷区円山町 7-10
Open: 7 pm–2 am; closed Sunday and national holidays
Credit cards? No Cover charge: 1,000 yen

Koten nestles in one of Tōkyō's more hodgepodge districts, a bizarre mix of love hotels, teen gig venues, old *kimono* shops and martial arts emporia. Its name means "classic" and that about sums up this subdued jazz-infused refuge from Shibuya's hard-charging nightlife. The 1,000 yen entrance charge is on the high side, but Nagaya-san's potato *shōchū* tasting sets (*imojōchū kikizake seto*, 1,500 yen each) make it a good place for a spiritual education. There are two different sets available, each offering three small glasses of different styles of *shōchū*, so two drinkers can share up to six samples between them. The owner also recommended the "Mannenboshi" (万年星), a full-bodied barley *shōchū* with a toasted flavor, which is very good in an *oyuwari* (warm water mix, see page 88). Its makers, Watanabe distillery in Miyazaki prefecture, are a unique product of the American dream. The founder of the company, Sugaichi Watanabe, saved up the capital he needed to go into distilling in 1914 by working in forestry in the United States. From the food menu, try the *kakiabura no negiyakisoba* (stir fried noodles with oyster oil and spring onion, 800 yen) or the less filling *mozzarella chiizu no sembe* (800 yen, mozzarella cheese cracker).

DIRECTIONS: A longish walk from Shibuya Station. From the Hachikō statue (dog statue), head west up the road to the right of the building containing L'Occitane en Provence. Bear left past the 109 building. Turn right at the Dōgenzakashita police box, which is just after the 7&i convenience store. Take the second road on your right. Koten is on your right immediately after Club Maruyama 59 and Hotel Two Way and before the 24-hour parking lot. There is no Roman alphabet on the sign, but look for the telephone number.

Kurosawa 黒澤 082-247-7750 www.completecircle.co.jp/kurosawa

Temmaya Ebisu Kurabu 5F, 3-20 Horikawa-chō, Naka-ku, Hiroshima
広島県広島市中区堀川町 3-20 天満屋エビスクラブ 5F
Open: 6 pm–3 am (to 4 am Friday and Saturday and 12 pm Sunday)
Credit cards? Most major cards English menu? Some English on the menu Cover charge: None

The toilet in Kurosawa is quite bizarre. Unusually for the land of toilet seat enemas and internet capable privies, Kurosawa's *benjo* owes none of its oddness to technology. There are just three standard ceramic sit-down bowls. It is in the arrangement that the weirdness is achieved: the three latrines sit within a yard of each other in the same room, with no cubicle or division of any kind, and face each other as though waiting for some sort of defecators' summit. The rest of the bar is more conventional, in a bare concrete-walled, ultramodern way. In such surroundings, the *shōchū* of choice has to be "Hyaku Nen no Kodoku" (百年の孤独, "One Hundred Years of Solitude," 1,270 yen). It is named after the Gabriel García Márquez novel, and is popular among the trendy existentialist brigade. There was once an unconfirmed rumor that Crown Prince Naruhito was partial to the odd glass of "Solitude." The innovativeness of the makers, Kuroki Honten in Miyazaki prefecture, does not stop at inspired branding. They are heavily into sustainability, farming their own ingredients and fertilizing their fields with their by-products, and "Hyaku Nen no Koduku" is one of a new wave of *shōchū* aged using oak barrels. "Kodoku," which retails at anywhere between 8,000 yen and 14,000 yen a bottle, is matured for between three and five years. At 40 percent alcohol, it is comparable to whisky in strength. The taste is much lighter than any whisky I have ever tasted, however: sweet and mellow. Try it with the *ojaga to kinoko age-harumaki* (potato and mushroom fried spring roll, 682 yen) or the *kaki furai* (fried oysters, 788 yen).

DIRECTIONS: Ebisu-chō Hiroden tram stop (Station number M6). With the road behind you and facing Mitsukoshi department store, walk down the road to the left of the store under the entrance saying "Welcome to Nagarekawa." Take the first right into the shopping arcade. It is the fourth shop entrance on your left.

Maruhachi Shōten まるはち商店 03-3348-7540

1-3-10 Nishi Shinjuku, Shinjuku-ku, Tōkyō
東京都区西新宿 1-3-10
Open: Weekdays 5 pm–1.30 am; Saturday 5 pm–10 pm; closed Sunday and national holidays
Credit cards? No English menu? No Cover charge: No

This new standing bar is a good place to try out *shōchū* in central Tōkyō without breaking the bank. The food is unpretentious home-style *kushiage* (fried meats and vegetables on sticks) and is reasonably priced. Try a stick of *kushikatsu* (skewered deep-fried pork, 150 yen), *asupara* (asparagus, 100 yen) or *tamanegi* (onions, 100 yen). The *shōchū* is all from Kagoshima prefecture and therefore the emphasis is on potato spirits. Again, the prices are the main attraction: 400 yen a glass, which is very reasonable for Tōkyō. I was recommended the "Kicchō Hōzan" (吉兆宝山), made from organically farmed sweet potatoes by Nishi Shuzō, a 165-year-old *kura* in Kagoshima. "Hōzan" takes its name from a famous player of the *biwa*, the traditional Japanese lute. It is quite well rounded but the use of black *kōji* brings out rich flavors from the sweet potatoes. "Hōzan" keeps its flavor well in an *oyuwari* (warm water mix, see page 88).

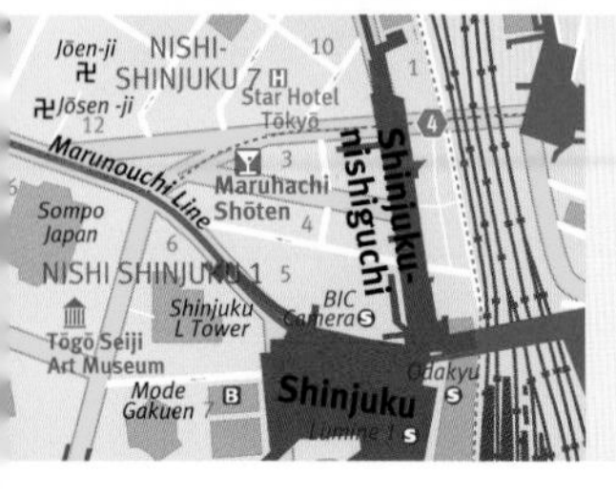

DIRECTIONS: Shinjuku underground station, Exit B1. Turn left down the road between the second-floor McDonald's and the Odakyu store. Take the next right and an immediate left. It is on your right near to the end of the road.

Masamichi 正道 06-6977-4466 masamichi.main.jp

1F, Shinkoh Bldg 1F, 1-1-15 Higashi-Obasi, Higashinari-ku, Ōsaka, 537-0024
〒537-0024 大阪市東成区東小橋 1-1-15 新光ビル 1F
Open: 6 pm–11 pm (last orders 10.30 pm); closed Sunday, national holidays and the first Thursday of each month
Booking recommended? Yes Credit cards? No English menu? No Cover charge: 800 yen

Masamichi is a fixture on the Kansai craft beer scene and its constantly changing selection of three real ales and five kegs on tap is hard to beat. There is also a good range of about 20 craft sakes and six *umeshu* liqueurs. For me, however, the pick of the menu was the range of more than 140 *shōchū* and *awamori*. The owner, Toshio Hashimoto, knows his alcohol inside out and has assembled some of the best brands available. This stylish bar is an excellent place to get your head (and lips) around Japanese domestic spirits, with the added bonus of the other drinking options for uninterested buddies. The food is in a Japanese style. Although I did not get the chance to eat at Masamichi, the *Kawachi dori no aburi yaki* (grilled Kawachi chicken, 1,360 yen), *otsukuri* (*sashimi* plate, 1,200 yen), and the 35 types of *ippin ryōri* (Japanese tapas) had my mouth watering. Hashimoto-san picked out a "Manzen" *imojōchū* (900 yen for a 90 ml glass, see page 100) and a "Cangoxina" (カンゴシナ, 1,200 yen for 60 ml) potato *shōchū* from Sata Sōji Shōten distillery. The name "Cangoxina" is taken from 16th-century European maps of Kagoshima. and this is an *imojōchū* in the old style by a company with a reputation for ignoring the whims and fancies of current fashion. At 44 percent alcohol, it is an unusually strong *genshu* (undiluted spirit) and is best served straight or on the rocks.

DIRECTIONS: Tamatsukuri Station (Ōsaka loop line). Turn right out of the gates and right out of the exit (Exit 2). Masamichi is over the crossroads on your left.

Ramuro 羅無櫓 03-3358-9515

Nana Ban Chi, Araki-chō, Shinjuku-ku, Tōkyō, 160-007
〒160-0007 東京都新宿区荒木町 7 番地
Open: Weekdays 6 pm–12 pm; closed Saturday, Sunday and national holidays Booking recommended? Yes
Credit cards? Most major cards English menu? No Cover charge: 1,000 yen

Makoto Suematsu has married the two passions of his life, *shōchū* and mountaineering, in this stylish backstreet bar. A mountaineer since his college days, Suematsu-san took Ramuro's name from *raamro*, the Nepalese word for "good," when he set himself up here in 1999. Antique ice picks, snow shoes and backpacks are displayed around the walls, but the real business here is the *shōchū*. Suematsu-san has more than 200 types, mostly priced between 500 and 600 yen a glass. About 80 percent is potato *shōchū*. The "Manzen" (萬膳) and "Manzenan" (萬膳庵) potato spirits from Manzen Shuzō (see page 76) are both excellent. "Manzen" is made with black *kōji* mold, which produces a strong and rich spirit, while "Manzenan" uses yellow *kōji*. The traditional wisdom has it that yellow *kōji* potato *shōchū* is best drunk cold, but this mild and delicate *shōchū* tastes wonderful gently warmed. Talking of warmed sake, a star attraction at Ramuro is the *nurukan shōchū* (800 yen for a pot), a traditional mix of 60 percent *shōchū* and 40 percent water (taken from Takao Mountain near Tōkyō). It is put in large earthenware pots up to four days before serving and then gently warmed for the customer. At about 16 percent alcohol, it is more like sake in strength. "In nine years here, I have never had a problem with a rowdy or argumentative customer. It gives everyone a good feeling," says Suematsu. Try the *gyōza* dumplings (ギョーザ, 600 yen) or the dried fish (Himono, 干物, 600–800 yen) with the *nurukan*. This place is popular with players from Suntory Sun Goliaths, one of Japan's big rugby teams.

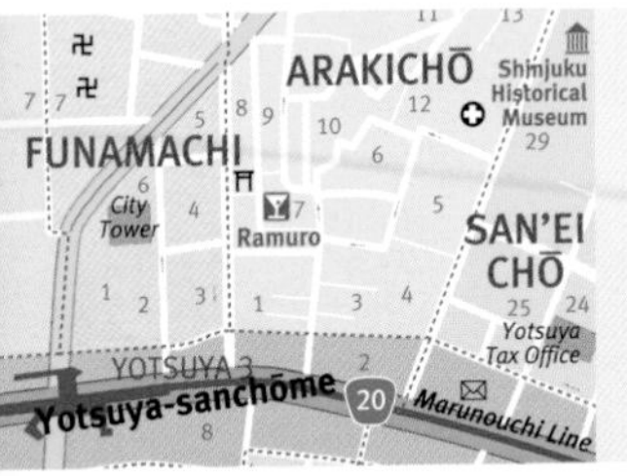

DIRECTIONS: Ramuro is very difficult to find. From Exit 4 of the Yotsuya-sanchōme Station on the Marunouchi underground line, continue walking down Shinjuku-dōri in the same direction you climbed the stairs. Take the third road to your left, just past the Mizuho bank. Pass the Dali piano bar on your right. Take a left down the paved alley which has Bar Marutan on it. Walk toward a bar called Deep. Take a right at the end of the alley. Ramuro is the sixth shop on your right, opposite a faceless yellow-tiled building. There is no Roman alphabet on the frontage, but look out for the picture of two mountain climbers on a small white sign. Two large urns flank the entrance.

Saisaidō Magosuke 菜菜堂孫助 075-255-0899

87 Tsuchiya-chō, Yanagino Bamba-dōri, Sanjō kudaru, Chukyo-ku, Kyōto-shi, Kyōto
京都府京都市中京区柳馬場三条下ル槌屋町 87
Open: 5.30 pm–11 pm; closed Tuesday Booking recommended? Not necessary
Credit cards? Visa English menu? No Cover charge: 400 yen

On any map of *shōchū* consumption in Japan, Kyūshū is usually painted in a proud scarlet. Hokkaido and Tōkyō have a nice salmon pink hue (both prefectures excel in the consumption of almost any type of booze) but the Kansai region is in a chilling blue. Few places are less enthusiastic about *shōchū* than Kyōto, which came 42nd out of 47 prefectures in average consumption in 2004. They will tell you there that it is all because of loyalty to their traditional sake but Kyōtoites are actually some of the nation's most enthusiastic wine, beer and cocktail drinkers. Spirits just don't seem to ring their bell, which makes for a challenging environment for a specialist *honkaku shōchū* bar like Saisaidō Magosuke. They stock about 200 types of *shōchū*, 50 types of *kajitsushu* (fruit liqueur, see page 90) and a changing line-up of 20 sakes. Most of the *shōchū* cost 550 yen a glass. Teruo Motomura, Magosuke's resident *shōchū* (and tea) expert, was keen to point out to me that the old capital actually produces some very good spirits. The local sake industry is well known for its rice and sake lees distilling. He recommended "Kyō no Hikari" (京のひかり, 550 yen) from the famous Kyōto sake makers Tama no Hikari.

While many rice *shōchū* are made with cheap table rice, Kyō uses premium sake rice and a *moromi* fermented from the lees of *junmai ginjō* sake. It is strong but the taste and smell are reminiscent of *ginjō* sake.

Try it straight or on the rocks with the *obanzai moriawase* (assorted side dishes, 800 yen) or the *akajidori to brocori no Kamogawadare* (Kamogawa-style chicken and broccoli, 750 yen). You could finish the evening off with a sweet "Kyō no Hikari"-based *umeshu* plum liqueur ("Kyō no umeshu," 650 yen).

DIRECTIONS: At the Shijō-Karasuma crossing looking north, turn right and walk past the front of the Daimaru building. Turn left at the Starbucks coffee shop. It is four blocks up on your left and is a little difficult to spot. You need to find a small door that leads up steep stairs to the second floor. Look for the building beside the *kimono* shop and opposite the southern end of the YMCA.

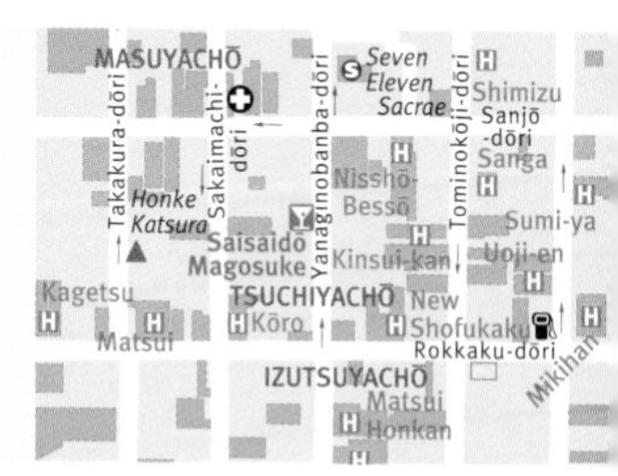

Sakatomo 酒友 06-6821-2985 www.sakatomo.jp

1F Hōyū Manshon, 2-20-103 Enoki-chō, Suita-shi, Ōsaka, 564-0053
〒564-0053 大阪府吹田市江の木町 2-20-103 豊友マンション 1F
Open: 5.30 pm–4 am (last orders 3 am); closed Sunday
Booking recommended? Yes Credit cards? No English menu? No Cover charge: 500 yen

Sakatomo could easily have justified a place in this guide's sake chapter. Owner Yorihisa Satō offers a constantly changing list of about 90 brands of sake and 200 types of *shōchū*. He believes that Japan's brewing and distilling traditions can only be understood together and has been making it his business to blur the boundaries even further. In 2009, he released his own sake, called "Shiro Oni" (550 yen), made with the white *kōjikin* usually only used by *shōchū* makers. It is unlike any sake I have ever encountered: a sharp acidic taste, almost like a Chablis wine. Experiments aside, Satō's excellent contacts with the *shōchū* distilleries, built up over nearly two decades in business here, mean his drink list features some of the biggest names at very good prices. The three most iconic Kagoshima potato *shōchūs*—"Maō" (魔王), "Murao" (村尾) and "Mori Izō" (森伊蔵), nicknamed the "3Ms" by *shōchū* buffs—are all available at 500 yen for a 100 cc glass and the three-year matured "Mori Izō" can be tasted for 600 yen in a 50 cc taster glass. Maō's name, incidentally, literally means "Devil King," and is part of a tradition of diabolic branding among Japanese alcohol makers. Satō's "Shiro Oni" means "White Demon," and there are a number of sakes and *shōchū* called "Oni Koroshi" or (Demon Killer). The best explanation I have heard for the "demon killer" theme comes from the sake writer John Gauntner: "Oni koroshi" used to refer to an alcohol that was so bad that it would kill a demon. Some confident *kura* caught everybody's attention and turned the meaning around, boasting that their product was so good it would help kill a demon. The other fiendish references—to variously colored demons and devil monarchs—are unclear. Perhaps the makers just like the excitement of a Hellish brand?

DIRECTIONS: Esaka Station (Midosuji/Namboku lines), Exit 8. Cross to the Royal Esaka building and continue walking in the same direction. Take the next right, at Tina's Cafe. Cross one junction and it is on your right with a blue sign.

Shōchū Tengoku 焼酎天国 099-224-9750

1F, Daini Edokichi Blru, 9-33 Yamanokuchi-chō, Kagoshima, Kagoshima
鹿児島県鹿児島市山之口町 9-33 第 2 江戸吉ビル 1F
Open: 5 pm–12 pm Credit cards? No English menu? No
Cover charge: 300 yen

There is a charming touch of the regal about Sachiko Hamazono, the mistress of this famous *izakaya*. She is not the sort of person who gives interviews. Rather, the writer is granted an audience which lasts for as long as they can hold the interest of the mistress of "Shōchū Heaven". In my case, that was about five minutes but, in that short time, I was given a compelling exposition of a powerful strand of opinion in Kagoshima toward their local spirit. Put bluntly, Hamazono-san feels a significant part of the *shōchū* industry has "gone to the dogs": too many makers are chasing a quick buck with highly priced products aimed at supposed "connoisseurs" in Tōkyō and forgetting *shōchū*'s real identity as a drink for normal Kagoshima folk. Mention of several well-known Kagoshima *imojōchū* makers drew tuts of disapproval. Hamazono-san said she simply refuses to deal with them. On the approved list, however, was "Wakamatsu" *shōchū* (わか松, 500 yen), from Wakamatsu Shuzō, a *kura* with over 290 years of history. It would go down well with the *kibinago sashimi* (raw Kibinago herring, 420 yen) or the *satsuma age* (fried fish cake, 325 yen).

DIRECTIONS: Tenmonkan-dōri tram stop. Walk down Tenmonkan-dōri, which is a side road running southeast from the western end of the Tenmonkan-dōri tram stop. There is a McDonald's on your left as you walk down the road. Take the second right, then a left and an immediate right at the crossroads. It is on your right.

Tachinomi Fukuichi 立呑み 福市 075-221-0004

Nishikiyamachi, Takoyoakushi noboru, Chukyō-ku, Kyōto-shi, Kyōto
京都府京都市中京区西木屋町通蛸薬師上ル
Open: 6 pm–3 am; closed Wednesday; Sunday and national holidays 5 pm–12 am
Booking recommended? No Credit cards? No English menu? No Cover charge: No

Kuniomi Katao has a simple philosophy: he doesn't make the *shōchū* he sells so he shouldn't be trying to make a huge profit from it. He does prepare the excellent fish dishes that are served with the *shōchū*, but there must be another strand of his self-denying creed dealing with that, because they too are very reasonably priced. The *saba no kizushi* (mackerel sushi, 480 yen) and *tako no umani* (stewed octopus, 500 yen) were delicious. For my money, this is one of the best *tachinomiya* (standing bars) in Japan. Unlike some of the new breed of *tachinomi* in Tōkyō, it retains an unmannered, traditional look and an intimate atmosphere. The *shōchū* list emphasizes small craft distilleries, and there are some very sought-after spirits being sold at ridiculously cheap prices. The rare "Manzen" *imojōchū* (see page 100) was only 500 yen a glass! I tried the craft-produced barley *shōchū* "Sei Ippatsu" (青一髪, 500 yen) from Kubo distillery in Nagasaki, which is only sold in about 30 establishments nationwide. The name roughly translates as "one blue hair" and refers to a description by the Edo-period poet Sanyō Rai of the thin blue line that marks the horizon, between a blue sky and a blue ocean. I enjoyed its strong character, more like a traditional potato *shōchū* in the complexity of its tastes and aromas than a smooth barley *shōchū* in the modern style.

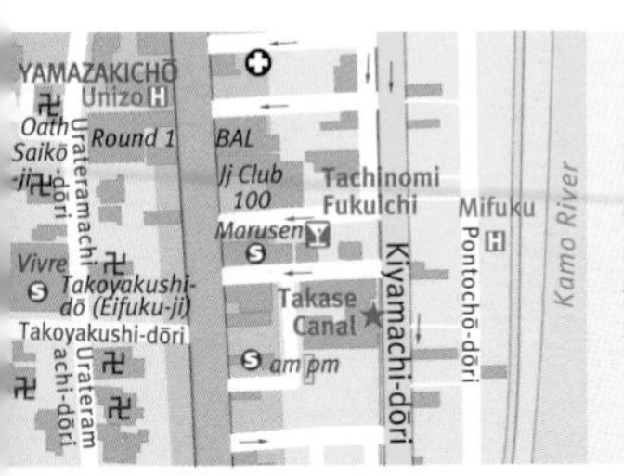

DIRECTIONS: Hankyu Kawaramachi Station, Exit 3a (east gates). Turn right and walk north up Kawaramachi-dōri for about 300 yards. Turn right at the Häagen-Dazs shop. It is about 100 yards down the road on the right, with Kirin beer signs outside (and a second-floor sign saying "Getto" when I visited).

Tetsugen Nikushō 鐵玄 肉匠 03-5774-4533

1F La Collina Shibuya, 1-5-6 Shibuya, Shibuya-ku, Tōkyō
東京都渋谷区渋谷 1-5-6 ラ・コリーナ渋谷 1F
Open: **Weekdays 11.30 am–3 pm/6 pm–2 am (4 am on Friday); Saturday 6 pm–2 am; Sunday 5 pm–11 pm**
Credit cards? **Most major cards** Cover charge: **500 yen**

Tetsugen is a restaurant specializing in unusual meats, including boar, frog and deer. They have a good drinks menu, with wine, beer, 20 types of sake, numerous *umeshu* and other Japanese fruit liqueurs (see page 90). However, the 50 varieties of *shōchū* are their strong point. The food menu varies with the season, but I was recommended the *inoshishi no karamisoyaki* (spicy *miso* and boar, 1,200 yen) and the *kaeru no honetsuki age* (fried frog on the bone, 1,200 yen) when I visited. I drew the line at the *Haruna Jidori no sashimi* (raw chicken!, 1,000 yen). Perhaps predictably, Tetsugen's *shōchū* selection features a number of eccentric choices. "Kurogohō" (黒胡宝) black sesame *shōchū* is made in Kumamoto prefecture by the huge Kirin conglomerate. The taste is quite clean, with just a hint of sesame and a sweet finish. It is good on the rocks. They also had a rare chestnut and barley *shōchū* called "Dabada Hiburi" (ダバダ火振) on their list when I visited. It is made on the island of Shikoku using locally grown chestnuts and is very hard to get hold of. Tetsugen is a place to consider if you are in the mood for something a little different.

DIRECTIONS: From the Hachikō statue (dog statue) and looking at the Starbucks, turn right under the tracks and walk straight up the hill (Miyamasu-zaka). Take a left at the junction at the top of the hill (before the footbridge) and a right at the AM/PM convenience store. It is about 40 yards up the road on your left.

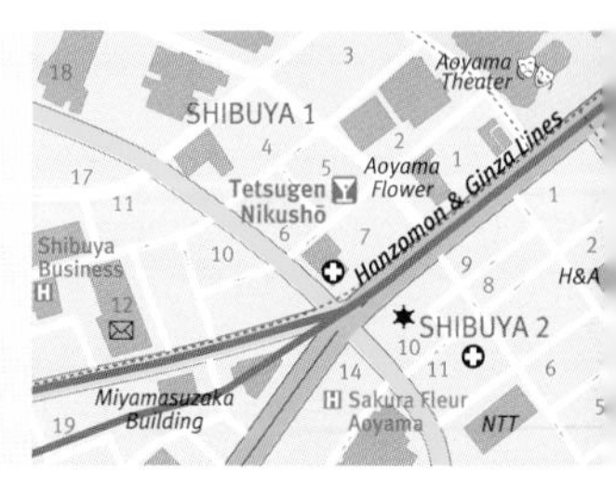

The Zen ザゼン 03-6717-0925 www.thezen.jp

Atré Shinagawa 4F, 2-18-1 Kaigan, Minato-ku, Tōkyō, 108-0075
〒108-0075 東京都港区港南 2-18-1 アトレ品川 4F
Open: 11 am–midnight daily (last order 10.45 pm) Credit cards? Most major cards
English menu? A food menu, but only a few roman characters on the drink list Cover charge: 500 yen

The Zen was introduced to me by Nicholas Coldicott, *The Japan Times* drinks columnist and general Japanese alcohol boffin, and I left myself in his very capable hands when ordering my drinks here. It has a fairly relaxed atmosphere and is a great place to explore *shōchū* since it lacks the rather connoisseury feel of some bars in Tokyo. I sat at a table near the window, with a not particularly inspiring view of a clearing in the concrete jungle, but Coldicott correctly recommends grabbing a counter seat. As he says: "With a staggering 350 *shōchū* to choose from, you might need the bartenders' help." Drinks are grouped by ingredient in the menu and color-coded (yellow dots signify drinks best served over ice, blue dots recommend *mizuwari* (see page 89), red for *oyuwari* (page 88) and green for straight up). I tried the "Hanajōjō" (華上々) barley *hatsutare shōchū* from Fujii distillery in Oita prefecture (1,100 yen). Only the first 1–3 percent of *shōchū* dripping out of the still can be classified as *hatsutare* (see page 79). This is the strongest spirit and is usually bottled at a little under 45 percent alcohol, which Coldicott pointed out means it can be stored in the freezer and served straight and ice cold. I really enjoyed the clean but sweet taste of "Hanajōjō," a classic Oita barley *shōchū*, with the firm white flesh of the *shirobaigai* (ivory sea snail) provided with the 500 yen table charge. For a bit of a contrast, try the "Tenshi no Yūwaku" (天使の誘惑, 1,100 yen), a potato *shōchū* from Nishi distillery in Kagoshima prefecture. The name literally means "Temptation of Angels," and it contains a blend of spirits matured in tanks and oak barrels for at least three years. It has a mellow, nutty character but packs a punch at 40 percent alcohol. I would advise asking for it straight, rather than on the rocks.

DIRECTIONS: Shimbashi JR Station, North Exit. Follow the signs to the Kōnan Exit. It is on the fourth floor of the Atré Shinagawa building, through which you pass to get to the Kōnan Exit.

Tōkyō Shōchū Bar Gen

東京焼酎 Bar GEN 03-5485-8316 shochu-crazy.jugem.jp

B1F Aoyama Biru, 2-9-10 Shibuya, Shibuya-ku, Tōkyō
東京都渋谷区渋谷 2-9-10 青山ビル B1F
Open: 5 pm–5 am; closed Monday Booking recommended? No English menu? No
Cover charge: 500 yen

Bar Gen claims to have more types of *shōchū* on its shelves than any other bar in the world. There were 5,000 bottles at the last count, plus about 100 Japanese fruit liqueurs for good measure. There was something about the heavily laden jerry-built shelves, worn green carpet and the quiet manager that reminded me a little of a musty secondhand bookshop on London's Charing Cross Road. Prices are reasonable. Yamaguchi-san recommended an "Okoge" *mugijōchū* (600 yen) from Ōita prefecture. It comes from a very old stable: the Oimatsu distillery was founded in the same year as the storming of the Bastille, 1789, and the current president is the eleventh generation. Okoge has only 25 percent alcohol but, unlike many Oita barley *shōchū*, has a quite assertive taste. They roast the barley before distilling and this adds strong toasted barley flavors. This is another *shōchū* that really goes well in an *oyuwari* (hot water mix, see page 88). If you are visiting in winter, you may want to check out Bar Gen's *oden* (500 yen for five pieces). *Oden* is a bit difficult to explain to the uninitiated; it is basically a lot of vegetables, processed fish and other sometimes unidentifiable objects stewed in a broth (see page 64). Not every foreigner likes it, but it is classic Japanese drinking food.

DIRECTIONS: From the Hachikō statue (the famous statue of a dog) and looking at the Starbucks, turn right under the tracks and walk straight up the hill (Miyamasu-zaka). Cross the road using the footbridge at the top of the hill and continue walking up Route 246. It is about 20 yards after a turning to your right.

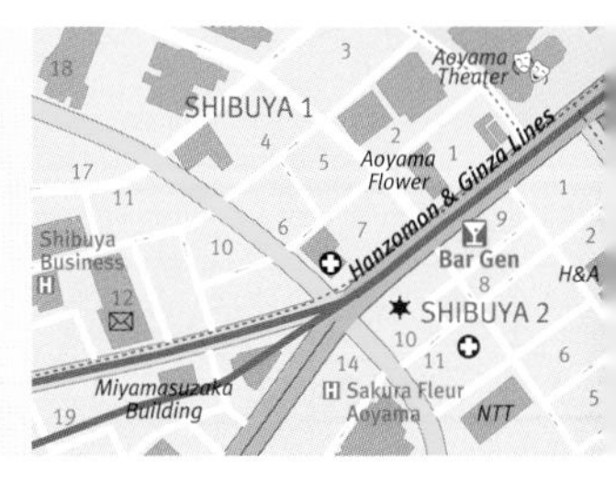

Washoku T 和食T 03-5777-5557 www.tasaki-shinya.com

1-5-3 Atago, Minato-ku, Tōkyō, 105-0002
〒105-0002 東京都港区愛宕 1-5-3
Open: Lunch 11.30 am–2 pm; dinner 5 pm–9.30 pm; closed Monday
Booking recommended? Yes. For dinner, 1–2 weeks in advance is advised. Specify time of arrival
Credit cards? Most major cards English menu? No Cover charge: No

If you are looking for a drink, or even a light meal and a drink, Washoku T is definitely not for you. This is a proper full-course Japanese restaurant serving set menus of formal *kaiseki* cuisine. It is also one of the best places to try *shōchū* from Izu-shotō, an archipelago stretching out far into the Pacific below Tōkyō. It is owned by Shinya Tasaki, a famous wine sommelier (see page 194) but also a great Izu-shotō *shōchū* enthusiast. Tasaki fell in love with the islands on fishing excursions and at one time ran a specialist *shōchū* bar in Roppongi featuring about 40 examples of the islands' spirits. That bar has since closed, but the unique collection has been inherited by Washoku T, part of a fascinating selection of sakes, beers and *shōchū* all sourced from Tōkyo prefecture. The Izu-shotō *shōchū* tradition traces its roots back to the 1850s, when a Kagoshima merchant called Shōemon Tansō was exiled to Hachijōjima. Making alcohol from grain had been banned on the then prison island for fear of causing famine, but Tansō brought sweet potatoes and techniques for distilling them. The Izu tradition, numbering 10 distilleries on six islands, has since developed differently from the Kyūshū mainstream. Izu's sweet potato distillers, for instance, use barley in the *kōji* instead of rice. The recent trend is toward more barley spirit and blends of barley and potato. This is partly to do with consumer tastes, but "Gojinka" (御神火, 900 yen), a well-known blend from Izu-ōshima Island, has a more interesting tale to tell: a volcanic eruption in 1986 forced an evacuation just when the potatoes were at their sweetest. Wild monkeys had a fine time pulling up the neglected crop and have since developed such a taste for them that sweet potato farming has become a nightmare. In any case, the addition of barley lightens the flavor of "Gojinka" while the potatoes give sweetness. It works well with ice. Alternatively, "Ipponzuri" (一本釣り, 700 yen), a barley *shōchū* from Hachijōjima, has a mellow, toasted flavor. The cheapest set menu at Washoku T, at 5,800 yen, comes with a starter plate, three fish dishes, a *nabe* dish and a grilled food dish. There are more extensive 7,800 yen and 9,800 yen menus, with the dishes included varying from day to day and according to the season. Because there is no choice at the time of serving, it is best to specify allergies when booking.

DIRECTIONS: Washoku T is in the middle of the grounds of the Atago shrine. From Tōkyo Metro Hibiya line, Kamiyachō Station, Exit 3, turn left out of the exit and left again on the large junction, so that you are walking southeast away from Sakurada-dōri (Route 1). Take the second left and walk to the end of the road at the T-junction. Turn right and take the steps up to the shrine to the left of the tunnel. Washoku T is in the precincts of the shrine by the large *torii* gate.

Za Enraku 座◯楽 03-3414-2601

1-19-13 Mishuku, Setagaya-ku, Tōkyō, 154-0005
〒154-0005 東京都世田谷区三宿 1-19-13
Open: 7 pm–4 am; closed Sunday, national holidays and occasional other days (telephone to check)
Booking recommended? Yes Credit cards? No English menu? No Cover charge: 500 yen

Za Enraku's modern exterior gives way to a hushed *tatami*-matted room surrounded on four sides by Nobuo Nakagawa's huge collection of 1,480 *shōchū*, 85 *awamori*, rare whiskies, brandies and a constantly changing line-up of more than a dozen sakes. This is definitely not a place to come for a no-holds-barred knees-up but it is a great place for an all-round education in Japanese alcohol. The drinks menu looks like a phone book and prices range from 500 to 5,000 yen a glass. Nakagawa-san himself has a precise manner and an infectious interest in the history of his subject. I was introduced to so many new drinks at Za Enraku that it is not possible to list them all, but the owner talked so informatively about rice and *kasutori shōchū* that the "Rambiki Kasutori Shōchu Kokoichiban" (らんびき粕取り焼酎 ここいちばん) from Hakusen Shuzō (see section on *kasutori*, page 81, 800 yen) stands out in my memory. Kumamoto's famous rice *shōchū*, "Kumajōchū," is a much more genteel drink and the subtle, almost mannered flavor of the traditionally produced "Toyonagakura" (豊永蔵 800 yen), compared to the rumbustious "Rambiki," left a vivid impression of the diversity of *shōchū*. From the food menu, you could try the *yamauni dōfu* (*miso*-pickled *tōfu*, 600 yen) or the *watairi surume aburi* (grilled whole dried squid, 500 yen). Unfortunately, Nakagawa-san does not speak English, so bringing along a Japanese speaker would be a good idea if you want to get the full benefit of this place.

DIRECTIONS: A 10-minute walk from Ikejiri-Ōhashi Station (Tōkyū Den'entoshi Line), West Gate. Turn right at the top of the stairs. Then turn right between the Daily Yamazaki store and the Ten Temari Asian Chūbō shop. Continue for nearly half a mile (1 kilometer) until you reach a crossroads where the road ahead narrows markedly. Walk up this road. It is the third shop on your left in a modern-looking concrete building, just before a 7-Eleven convenience store on your right.

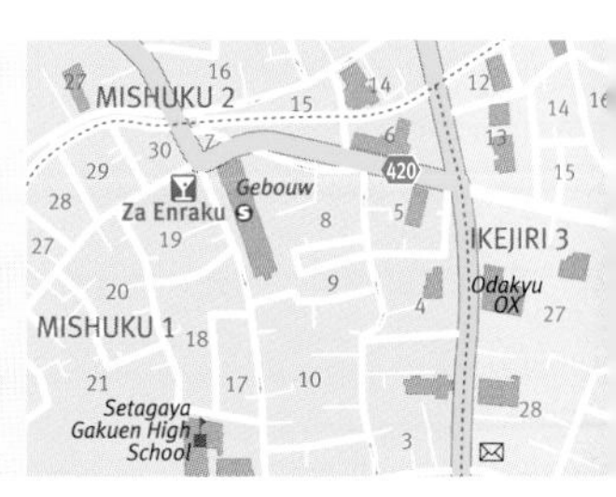

Chapter 3 Okinawan Awamori and Awamori Bars

The Joys of Okinawan Awamori

The Chinese imperial envoy Tung-yen Li visited Okinawa in 1800 for the crowning of the boy king Sho On. He later recalled that two big pots of the local spirit, *awamori*, appeared on his delegation's doorstep every morning. It was good enough stuff, another envoy lavished praise on it, but the locals seemed to expect them to drink at an inhuman rate. The envoys tried to drink their share but each morning two new pots would be waiting for them. Eventually, Tung-yen Li admitted, they had been forced to write to the Okinawan royal family: the alcohol was very nice but they would be obliged if the King could send less of it.

The British captain Frederick William Beechey was also defeated by Okinawan hospitality at a reception held by a local official in 1827: "During the whole time we were closely plied with sackee in small opaque wine glasses, which held about a thimble full, and were compelled to follow the example of our host and [empty our glasses]: but as this spirit was of a very ardent nature, I begged to be allowed to substitute Port and Madeira, which was readily granted, and we became more on a footing with our hosts, who seemed to think that hospitality consisted in making every person take more than they liked."

If these accounts give the impression of a culture lost in mindless drunkenness, they are a little unfair. Okinawa's distilled alcohol, *awamori* (泡盛), was always one of the islanders' finer pleasures, bound up with elaborate social rituals and spirituality. Traditionally, it was aged for years in large earthenware pots by the highest ranking families. It was said that the head of an aristocratic household might let a trusted servant keep the keys to the strong house that held his money but never to his *awamori* store.

A bottle of Kokka awamori photographed at the Tsukayama distillery, Nago city, where it is made by a three-man team.

Clockwise from left: Awamori maturing in pots at Zuisen distillery, Naha city; An Okinawan man holds a bottle of Kumesen awamori aloft; Dust-laden bottles at Urizun, Naha city (page 130).

AWAMORI DISTILLERIES IN OKINAWA
Iheya Island
Iheya
Izena
Izena Island
Yanaha Island
Ie Island
Kōri Island
Takazato
KUNIGAMI VILLAGE
NAKIJIN VILLAGE
Nakijin
Yagaji Island
ŌGIMI VILLAGE
MOTOBU TOWN
Yamakawa
Sesoko Island
Minna Island
HIGASHI VILLAGE
Ryusen
NAGO CITY
Tsukayama
KUNIGAMI DISTRICT
Helios
Onna
ONNA VILLAGE
GINOZA VILLAGE
KIN TOWN
Sakiyama
Kin
Kamimura
Higa
YOMITAN VILLAGE
URUMA CITY
KADENA TOWN
OKINAWA CITY
Shinzato
CHATAN TOWN
NAKAGAMI DISTRICT
Chatan Chōrō
KITANAKAGUSUKU VILLAGE
GINOWAN CITY
NAKAGUSUKU VILLAGE
URASOE CITY
Shikina
Mizuho
NASHIHARA TOWN
NAHA CITY
Sakimoto
Ishikawa
Tsuhako
Zuisen
YONABARU TOWN
Miyazato
Kumesen
HAEBARU TOWN
Chuko
TOMIGUSUKU CITY
Kamiya
NANJO CITY
SHIMAJIRI DISTRICT
Higa
Uehara
YAESE TOWN
ITOMAN CITY
Ojima Island
Kudaka Island
Ikei Island
Miyagi Island
Henza Island
Hamahiga Island
Minamiukihara Island
Tsuken Island
Kumejima no Kumesen
Kume Island
Yoneshima
Ojima Island
Ikema Island
Ohgami Island
Chiyoizumi
Tokuyama
Irabu Island
Ikema
Miyanohana
Oki no Hikari
Kiku no Tsuyu
Miyako Island
Kurima Island
Taragawa
Takamine
Ishigaki Island
Yaesen
Seifuku
Nakama
Taketomi Island
Tamanaha
Ikehara
Irinamihira
Kokusen
Sakimoto
Yonaguni Island
Hateruma
Hateruma Island
N
0 5km
0 10km
● : distillery locations

Matured *awamori*, some of which had reached 150–200 years when the oldest stocks were wiped out in World War II, was a precious thing. There is nobody still alive who actually tasted those ancient pre-war *awamori*, but the American traveler Bayard Taylor got a rare chance to sip some from the Okinawan royal family's cellars in 1853. He wrote: "It was old and mellow with a sharp, sweet unctuous flavour, somewhat like French Liqueur."

Suzume Sakeya

The Okinawan folktale "Suzume Sakeya" (Sparrow Liquor Store) tells the story of a sparrow which made a nest in a tree near a village. After some days, the people noticed the bird was flying about in a strange way. They went to the tree and found that all the millet and rice that the sparrow had dropped from its beak had fallen in a nook in the branches, which had filled with rain water and fermented. From this, the story says, Okinawans first learned how to make alcohol.

The origins of awamori

The exact beginnings of *awamori* making are hard to pinpoint, but we do know that the Okinawans were enthusiastic drinkers long before they learned the art of distillation. A Chinese reference to the islands in AD 636 said the locals drank a type of wine, and the *Omoro Sōshi*, a collection of Okinawan poems written between the 12th and 16th centuries, contains several references to *miki*—a drink made by first chewing grain and spitting it out to promote fermentation. In 1477, we get a priceless snapshot of medieval Okinawan alcohol culture from a group of Korean sailors shipwrecked on the far western island of Yonaguni. They were kept for six months on Yonaguni and only encountered a weak, opaque chewed alcohol, like the *miki* mentioned in the *Omoro Sōshi*. Once transferred to the larger but still remote Miyako island group, the castaways drank more sophisticated but still unfiltered brews. When they reached the center of Ryūkyūan civilization, on the main island of Okinawa, they found clear filtered alcohols and a very strong yellowish alcohol that was highly prized by the Okinawans.

We don't know whether that "yellowish alcohol" is an early report of distilled alcohol in Okinawa, or just of a strong matured wine. The first clear evidence of distilled spirits comes from the Chinese envoy Chin K'an in 1534: "The alcohol the King gave was clear and powerful. It came from Siam and is made the same way as Chinese distilled alcohol." K'an's report has wrongly been taken as definitive evidence that Siamese distilling was the original inspiration for Okinawa's *awamori* tradition. You will see this theory repeated in tourist brochures if you visit Okinawa. But all K'an's report really proves is that Siamese alcohol was among the spirits drunk by the Okinawan royals. In fact, the Okinawans were trading all over the South Seas at the time and were notorious for their interest in all descriptions of alcohol in every port. About 15 years before K'an visited Okinawa, the Portuguese adventurer Tomé Pires noticed Okinawan merchants in Malacca scouring the markets for the strongest booze: "Among [them] Malaccan wine is greatly esteemed. They load up large quantities of one kind which is like brandy, with which the Malays make themselves [so drunk as to] run amuck."

What is clear from the early reports is that distilled alcohol in Okinawa was, from the start, an aristocratic drink. The famous Ryūkyūan courtier and reformer Sai On (1682–1761) felt that distilled alcohol (which by then was being produced domestically) was perfectly acceptable for consumption by the Okinawan elite or export to Japan, but said that commoners should not drink it. During the 18th and early 19th century, distillation was limited to only three villages in the "Sanka" area, immediately southeast of the walls of Shuri castle—Akatachō, Torihorichō and Sakiyamachō. Only forty individuals were given permits and all distilling was done under royal patronage; the stills and the ingredients were owned and loaned out by the kingdom and all of the liquor had to be returned to it, save for 5.4 liters left as payment with each maker. Unlicensed distilling brought the death penalty and transportation of the culprit's family to a prison island.

We have no way of knowing exactly how much *awamori* moonshine went under the noses of the Okinawan authorities. The geography of the archipelago, with hundreds of islands separated by hundreds of miles of ocean, makes it seem unlikely that distilling was limited only to the Sanka district. Many of the outlying islands have their own distilling histories and some activities seem to have been officially tolerated. However, until the late 19th century, the drink of most normal Okinawans was not distilled but brewed and had not advanced much since the days of the chewed *miki* beer encountered by the Korean castaways on Yonaguni. Fumi Miyagi (1891–1990), writing of her childhood on the Yaeyama islands in the early 1900s, recalled a beverage she called *mishi*. During the rice harvest, there would be a big pot of *mishi* in the middle of the field for everyone to drink from, she said. It was the women's job to do the chewing: "They would say, 'Today, it is my *mishi* turn' and they would brush their teeth carefully before they went out.'"

The two worlds sometimes collided. Chewed alcohol was an important part of some island festivals, and in 1756, the Chinese imperial envoys were served it at court. (They stopped drinking as soon as they were told how it was made.) Much of the elite's distilled *awamori*, on the other hand, was doled out in rations to officials and noblemen who would then share it, in the form of gifts and hospitality, with others.

In this way, the spirit seeped down through society. But, generally, the rural brewing and urban distilling continued as two separate traditions until the 1870s, when the formal annexation of Okinawa by Japan, and the fall of the Okinawan royal family brought an end to the old restrictions on making *awamori* outside Sanka. There was an explosion of distilling outside the towns. By 1893, there were 447 distillers across the islands, less than a quarter of them in Sanka. By the early 20th century, *awamori* could genuinely claim to be the "people's drink" for the first time in its history.

The "Nantō Zatsuwa" (Stories from the Southern Islands) revealed exotic scenes from Okinawan life to a mid-19th century Japanese readership. Partying by the islanders was featured prominently.

World War II and the rebirth of awamori

World War II completed the revolution by hammering the old aristocratic tradition almost to extinction. On October 10, 1944, a massive air raid devastated Shuri. The Battle of Okinawa the following year, which killed more than 75,000 local civilians, smashed what little was left. Between May 24 and 26 1945, the huge naval guns of the battleship USS *Mississippi* reduced the old Shuri castle to dust, and the traditional center of *awamori* making, nestled right under the castle's walls, was annihilated. Ancient stores of aged *kusu awamori*, some of it well over 100 years old, were lost forever and the stocks of black *kōji* spores necessary for making *awamori* (see page 117) were destroyed.

After a desperate search, a straw mat with traces of *kōji* on it was found under the rubble of one distillery and, after several failed attempts, the mold was successfully cultured. But such technical issues were the least of the distillers' problems. As soon as the American's established control of Okinawa's main island, they banned *awamori* because of rice shortages. The Okinawans were not easily dissuaded: the US military reported brown sugar, palm, corn, wheat, fruit and even chocolate moonshines being made and, on some of the outlying islands, where distilling had not been stopped, production was in full flow.

In March 1946, locals sent a delegation to the authorities pleading for the ban to be lifted and the Americans eventually relented. Initially, they set up five closely regulated factories making only molasses-based spirits but two years later they tendered for private companies to make *awamori*. They received 229 applications and 79 working distilleries were established. Only 11 of these could trace their roots back to the pre-war industry. The new *awamori* map would have been unrecognizable to an 18th-century Okinawan: there were distilleries on almost every sizeable island, many with roots in village co-operatives.

But if *awamori* had broadened its base in Okinawan society, it had also cheapened its image. "In those days, the drink got a bad reputation," says Akiyoshi Miyagi, owner of the Awamori Kan (see page 239). "It was partly to do with competition from whisky but it was also to do with the image that surrounded *awamori* itself. People here, not just the Americans but the Okinawans too, didn't want to drink the old spirit and, to be honest, it wasn't always that good."

Black kōji breaks down the starches in the rice into sugars.

The advent of bottling and the emergence of bottled brands from the early 1950s brought problems. *Awamori* is rich in rice-derived fatty acids, which are important in lending character and mildness to a matured spirit, but which can also produce off smells and tastes. Traditional earthenware pots naturally disperse these aromas but glass bottles, if not handled properly, shut them in. Many islanders turned to whisky and neutral spirits, such as the popular "Shirasagi" brand, in the 1960s. *Awamori* production dropped from 5,424,000 liters to 3,443,000 liters between 1958 and 1963 and the number of distilleries fell from 118 to 85.

Since 1972, when America returned Okinawa to Japan, the number of active *awamori* distilleries has fallen further, to a current total of only 46, but there has also been a gradual rebuilding of *awamori*'s old pride.

Miyagi-san started buying and maturing the Okinawan spirit in 1987 and says, even then, the spirit was being dismissed by many. A series of initiatives, including a project to document the history of *awamori* and a committee to encourage long maturing of *awamori*, have since helped remind people of the drink's heritage. Although a spike in *awamori*'s popularity across Japan in the early 2000s, which saw sales outside Okinawa growing 50 percent every year at one stage, has not been sustained, *awamori* has regained its place as a key part of Okinawan culture and is

Left: Inside a fermenting tank
Below from top: Yoshimi Oshiro, manager of Tsukayama distillery, shows off his still; Oshiro-san checks the fermenting pots at Tsukayama; Tsukayama's "bottling plant."

sold as such, not only on the islands, but across Japan. Perhaps most significant in the long run, is the emerging consensus among producers that the future of *awamori* lies in producing top-quality spirits. Rules on the labeling of matured *awamori* have been tightened up and an increasing number of premium drinks are reaching the market.

Making awamori

Part of the roof of Tsukayama distillery has fallen in and weeds grow in the mortar between the traditional red tiles. Looking up at the sunlight slanting through the rafters, I couldn't help wondering what would happen in an earthquake. The structure looked one good shake away from total collapse. "Uh, an earthquake?" laughed manager Yoshimi Oshiro. "That's not what worries us. The biggest problem is the rain. It comes straight through."

The old building has seen it all since they started making *awamori* there in 1927. The original owner died in the war and his eldest son,

Shīsā are models of mythical beasts traditionally used to ward away bad spirits in Okinawa. This one guards the Zuisen distillery in Naha city.

Chōyu Tsukayama, a soldier stationed in the Solomon islands, was killed by disease in 1946, before being shipped home. The distillery itself became a shelter for homeless families after the conflict because every other building in the area had been flattened. It was then commandeered by the Americans, who used it as a bakery and a local headquarters. It was only in 1949 that the determination of the old master's wife, Tsuru Tsukayama, brought it back to its original use. She summoned her second daughter Sada and Sada's husband Chishin Zukemura, a classmate of Chōyu's, from Kyūshū to start making *awamori* again. The operation has not changed significantly since then. Three men still do all the distilling (about half of Okinawa's distilleries employ nine or fewer workers). Oshiro-san explained the basic production process to me during a visit to Tsukayama in April 2009:

Making the kōji Oshiro-san uses imported broken Thai rice grains that are unsuitable for eating but very good for making *awamori*. This ingredient is one of the three main features of *awamori* that distinguish it from mainland Japanese *shōchū*. *Awamori* used to be made from all sorts of things, including millet, local rice, sweet potatoes and sugar cane, but nowadays all *awamori* must be made using the long-grained Thai rice, which is less sticky than Japanese rice but easier to convert into sugars and therefore alcohol. The other two distinguishing features are that all *awamori* is made with black *kōji* (*kurokōji*, 黒麹) and, secondly, that all of the rice is cultivated with the *kōji* mold from the start, rather than the two-stage process used in *shōchū*.

Oshiro-san begins by washing all of the rice and then steams it in a large stainless steel drum for about 50 minutes. It is then allowed to cool and black *kōji* mold spores (*kurokōjikin*, 黒麹菌) are mixed into the rice. The purpose of the *kōji* mold is similar to the malting of barley in beer and whisky making—to convert the starches in the rice to sugars which can later be turned into alcohol by the yeasts introduced in the fermentation stage. The rice is usually spread out and left for about 24 hours for the mold to establish itself. However, some traditionalist *awamori* makers still use the *hinekōji* (老麹) method, which leaves a special a type of black mold to propagate for three days. This creates a strong tasting and smelling drink that its makers say is well suited to long maturation. Ryusen distillery (龍泉酒造), down the road from Tsukayama in Nago city, is well known for this method.

Fermentation At Tsukayama, fermentation takes three weeks. All of the mold-covered rice is put into a fermentation tank with yeasts and about 1,300 liters of water. The end product has an alcohol content of about 18 percent alcohol.

Distilling Tsukayama's distilling method is pretty basic. Steam is simply injected from a boiler directly into a small stainless steel still containing the fermented *moromi*. But there are all shapes and sizes of stills on Okinawa. At the modern Helios distillery, a few kilometers south of Tsukayama, they run three large copper stills that reminded me of a Scottish whisky distillery. At the Zuisen distillery in Shuri, one of only four currently operating in the old Sanka *awamori* district, I found a complicated stainless steel device in which the *moromi* was indirectly steam-heated in a side arm before flowing into the main still. Other distilleries use very high-tech low-pressure stills which produce a lighter spirit while, on the other side of the technological coin, there are some old direct-fired stills in operation at distilleries, including Takamine distillery on Ishigakijima (look for the "Omoto Homura" brand, written "於茂登 炎", with the last character for "flame" dominating the label).

The proponents of all these types of equipment claim they improve their end product but, of course, the basic process is the same as any other pot still; the alcohol in the wash turns to vapor, rises through the still neck, and is turned back into liquid in a condenser. Most *awamori* distillers collect a distilled alcohol at about 44 percent alcohol but will often dilute it down to 30 per cent or even lower before bottling. Notable exceptions are the three distilleries on Yonaguni (the island where the Korean sailors found only weak chewed beer in the 15th century), which are now famous for their ferocious 60 percent alcohol *hanazake* spirit (花酒), so strong that it cannot legally be labeled *awamori*. (Check out the "Donan" (どなん), "Maifuna" (舞富名) or "Yonaguni" (与那国) brands.)

Maturing awamori

The best things in life come to those who wait and so it is with *awamori*. Okinawans call their matured spirit *kūsu* (古酒, *koshu* in standard Japanese), which literally means "old alcohol." Many people will tell you that *kūsu* tastes mellower and richer than unaged *awamori* but, in truth, the taste varies markedly with the nature of the original spirit and the methods of maturation. One old categorization described three different types of *kūsu*: the first was characterized by the "aroma of a white plum," the second had an "aroma of cheek" and the third the "smell of a male goat." I can't pretend to know what those classifications meant, though I have definitely detected a little goatishness in the odd *kūsu*, but it gives an idea of the variety of flavors that maturation gives *awamori*.

Okinawans seem to have been aging spirits on the islands for almost as long as they have known how to make them. In fact, they may have been aging brewed alcohols long before distilling arrived. The *Omoro Sōshi* contains references to storage houses that some scholars think may have been used for holding alcoholic beverages of some sort, and a Korean eyewitness in 1461 said he had visited an alcohol warehouse in Naha

The Tsukayama distillery opened in 1927. This pre-war photograph shows workers on a promotion drive.

Maturing awamori at home

If you really get the *awamori* bug, you could try maturing it yourself. You need several bisque-ware pots. Okinawans never wash their pots with soap, only with water. Pour the strongest *awamori* you can find into the pots and cover them. The lids need to be airtight. The Japanese language guide, *The First Book of Tasting Awamori*, published by Nihon Shurui Kenkyūkai, recommends the following for home use: put two layers of cling film under the pot lid, fastened in place with tape, and then two layers of cling film over the lid, tied with a rope. Keep the jars in a cool place where there is no sun and move them gently every two or three months. Once a year, open the pots and follow the *shitsugi* method described below. I have never tried home maturing of *awamori*. My problem would be drinking it all too quickly.

that had three separate sections for one-year-old, two-year-old and three-year-old goods. *Awamori* aging was certainly well established by 1719 when the Japanese scholar and politician Hakuseki Arai came across a seven-year matured *awamori*. Okinawans must have been laying down stocks for much longer aging at about that time because, in 1926, we have a report of *awamori* in Shuri that had been aged for 200 years.

The traditional way of maturing *awamori* is by the *shitsugi* method, which is similar to the *solera* method used for sherry. A series of earthenware pots holding different ages of *awamori* are kept beside each other in a storehouse. When spirit from the oldest jar is drunk, *awamori* from the next oldest pot is used to replace it. What is taken from that pot is, in turn, replaced from the

The three large copper stills at the Helios distillery, Nago, are reminiscent of the pot stills used in single-malt whisky making.

next oldest jar and so on down to the youngest container, which has its liquor replaced by newly distilled spirit. This has the benefit of allowing the *kūsu* to be exposed to the air and to interact with other spirits, promoting changes in the alcohol. The rough earthenware pots also accumulate residues and themselves give flavor to the alcohol over time.

Unfortunately, the *shitsugi* system is also ideally suited to cheating. Any *shitsugi*-aged *kūsu* is actually a blend of *awamori* of different ages. The oldest spirit in a "100-year-old" *awamori* will indeed be a century old, but it will also contain younger spirits. Depending on the speed of the *shitsugi* process, it might actually contain a surprisingly small amount of 100-year-old alcohol and some makers made the most of this when rules were lax. A code of conduct introduced in 2004 has cleared up the ambiguity. It states that any *awamori* labeled *kūsu* has to contain at least 51 percent of alcohol over three years old and that all of the spirit in bottles carrying specific age statements (such as "10-year-old *awamori*") must be at least the stated age.

Awamori drinking customs

People from the island of Miyakojima, to the south of Okinawa's main island, have a reputation for eloquence—for good reason. It is called the *otōri*. Islanders gather in a circle and the first among them, called the Oya, gives a speech. When they have finished, the Oya drinks a shot of *awamori* and sends the glass around the circle, to be filled and emptied by all present. The next person in the circle then becomes the Oya, followed by the obligatory speaking and drinking, and so they continue into sozzled and word-heavy evenings. It is testament to the importance of alcohol in traditional Okinawan society that, according to the Japanese writer Toshiaki Hagio, when one Miyako village decided to abolish the *otōri* because it forced excessive drinking, the villagers elected to hold an *otōri* to celebrate their progressiveness! Not all the drinking customs of Miyakojima encourage overindulgence. Some people still pour the first glass of a newly opened bottle on the earth. They call it "Kami no mono" or "God's property."

Awamori maturing in oak casks at the Helios distillery in Nago.

One of the warehouses at Helios, where awamori is aged in earthenware pots.

Many makers have now discarded the *shitsugi* method. Some, including Tsukayama, retain the jars but do not use the method. Others are using stainless steel or enamel-lined tanks because they want to avoid the earthy notes introduced by the traditional pottery jars. A number of makers, including Helios distillery in Nago, are also aging in oak casks (the result at Helios is so whisky-like in smell and appearance that the Japanese government currently insists that they lighten the color to avoid confusion). In fact, there are now almost as many variations in maturing methods as there are distillers. At Zuisen in the Shuri district, they hold classical music concerts on site, on the theory that the music will affect maturation, and Onna distillery has taken to placing pots 400 meters (1,310 feet) under the sea for a day! They claim it makes their "Shinkai" ("しんかい", "Deep Sea") brand more rounded and fragrant.

How to drink awamori

The classic way to drink *awamori* is straight. Most of the early sources talk of small thimble-like cups called *chibugwā* and, personally, I would recommend these as the best vessels for tasting the spirit. Most bars now use gorgeous chunky Ryūkyū glass tumblers or fancy brandy tasting glasses, but there is something about the feel of a tiny pottery *chibugwā* that helps concentrate the taste buds on the alcohol.

If *awamori* is too much for you straight, don't worry. Most people now drink it on the rocks or in a *mizuwari* (water mix). A room-temperature *mizuwari* is best for bringing out the flavor, but some find it easier to drink with ice. Vary the proportion of water according to taste and the alcoholic strength of the liquor (try four parts *awamori* to six parts water, if you have a standard 30 percent spirit).

Another style, recommended by distiller Hajime Sakimoto for her 60 percent "Yonaguni" *hanazake*, is straight but chilled in the freezer. She says it makes a sweet, thick liquor that goes well with salty foods. You can also drink *awamori* in an *oyuwari* (warm water mix). This custom may have been introduced by Japanese *samurai* from Kagoshima, who turned the Ryūkyūan kingdom into a client state after 1609, and it became quite common in the pre-modern period. Ideally, the water should be about 70–80° C when it is poured into the glass. Shake the bottle and pour it into the water. Okinawans often prefer a stronger mix than they serve on the mainland; about one part water to one part *awamori* mix is common for 30 percent alcohol *awamori*. Finally, unaged *ippanshu* is often drunk in fruit juice mixes. The juice of the native citrus fruit, *shikuwasa*, goes particularly well.

A Sign Bar Aサイン バー 03-3481-5353

1F Biru SS, 2-7-7 Kitazawa, Setagaya-ku, Tōkyō
東京都世田谷区北沢 2-7-7 ビル SS 1F
Open: 7 pm–4 am Booking recommended? No
Credit cards? No English menu? No Cover charge: 500 yen

An "A" sign could mean the difference between ruin and a livelihood in post-war Okinawa. It stood for "US Military Approved" and GIs were forbidden from entering bars which did not have one. Since the Americans were the only people with any money, it was vital for bars to keep on the right side of the inspectors and get the all-important "A" daubed over their entrances (blue for bars, red for restaurants). The sign has come to symbolize more than just a trading license but an entire era. Not all of the associations for the locals were very positive (defeat, destitution, rampant prostitution), but the boom in post-war nostalgia, combined with the trendiness of all things Okinawan, has brought a return of "A" sign bars all over Japan. I like this Setagaya shop because it goes beyond the nostalgic shmaltz that is the norm in these sorts of bars. It has a good selection of *awamori* and tasty food dishes at reasonable prices. The Okinawan *yakisoba* (fried noodles, 700 yen) is a good standby and the *sukugarasu tōfu* (*tōfu* topped with a little beady-eyed fish, 500 yen) is interesting. The spirit pots on the bar top contain some special *awamori*, including a 20-year-old "Kaneyama" *kūsu* (かねやま, 3,600 yen), but, in a bar chock full of references to post-war Okinawa, a ladle full of the eight-year aged, rich-smelling but dry "Sakimoto" (咲元) *kūsu* has a certain resonance. Sakimoto is one of only four distilleries still operating in the old Sanka distilling district and Masayoshi Sakumoto, the second generation head of the company, played a key role in finding the straw mat covered in black *kōji* spores that allowed *awamori* to be reborn in 1945 (see page 115). Sakimoto recommends drinking the eight-year-old *kūsu* straight.

DIRECTIONS: Shimokitazawa Station (Odakyū Odawara/Keiō Inokashira lines), South Exit. Turn left away from the railway bridge and turn right at the Ozaki supermarket. Turn left around the side of the supermarket and right at the end of the block. It is straight ahead on the T-junction in front of you, with a big red "A" sign on top of the door.

Awamori Shōchū Bar Shabon

泡盛焼酎バー Shabon 03-5549-9772
sha-bon.com

1F Sansui Kaikan, 3-6-12 Akasaka, Minato-ku, Tōkyō, 107-0052
〒107-0052 東京都港区赤坂 3-6-12 山翠会館 1F
Open: Mondays–Thursdays 7 pm–5 am; Friday 6 pm–5 am; closed Saturday, Sunday and national holidays
Last orders one hour before closing Booking recommended? No Credit cards? Visa and Mastercard
English menu? No Cover charge: 500 yen

My young son is into blowing *shabon dama* or soap bubbles, which raised the question why a spirits bar would adopt such an apparently childish name. Bar manager Suzuki-san explained that it was down to the literal meaning of *awamori* (泡盛)—"piled up bubbles." There are all sorts of theories about the name, but one of the most convincing points to a primitive technique, found not only on Okinawa but also in mainland Asia, of pouring the very high alcohol liquor that comes out of a still first into the weaker liquor that flows last. If the blend is too alcoholic, no bubbles are seen, but they begin to pile up when it approaches the desired strength. Shabon's name may have a traditional root, but the bar itself is a welcome departure from the folksy "Ye Olde Ryūkyū" style favored in most Okinawan establishments. The interior is ultra modern—white bar top, ivory furniture, moody lighting and dance music on the stereo. There is also something of the modern Tōkyō cocktail bar about the way they serve their drinks, including huge globes of ice hand-chiseled by the barman, but the menu, featuring 180 types of *awamori* and almost as many *shōchū*, would stand up to any traditionalist's scrutiny. Suzuki-san recommended a 20-year-old *kūsu*, "Gyoku Yuu" (玉友, 5,000 yen) from Ishikawa Shuzō. Ishikawa is unusual because they use earthenware pots for both aging and fermenting their rice *moromi* before distillation, a method called *kamejikomi* (甕仕込み, see page 78). For those with shallower pockets, the full-bodied and sweet "Miya no Tsuru" (宮之鶴, 600 yen), from the minute Nakama distillery on Ishigakijima Island, is a worthy alternative. The food menu's no-frills *supamu pōku pizza* (spam pizza, 840 yen) and taco rice (rice and Tex-Mex style meat, 840 yen) seemed a little out of place in Shabon's stylish interior, but both are tasty and filling examples of the American influence on Okinawan food.

DIRECTIONS: From Akasaka Station (Chiyoda line), Exit 1b, cross the road to the Tully's coffee shop. Take the second left after Tully's. Shabon is about 30 yards on your right. From Nagatachō Station (Namboku/Yūrakuchō lines), Gate 8 or Akasaka-Mitsuke Station (Ginza/Marunouchi lines): Walk down the road opposite Akasaka Excel Hotel Tokyu and to the right of McDonald's. Turn left around the back of McDonald's and walk about 400 yards. Shabon is on your left, about 30 yards before the road crosses Route 413.

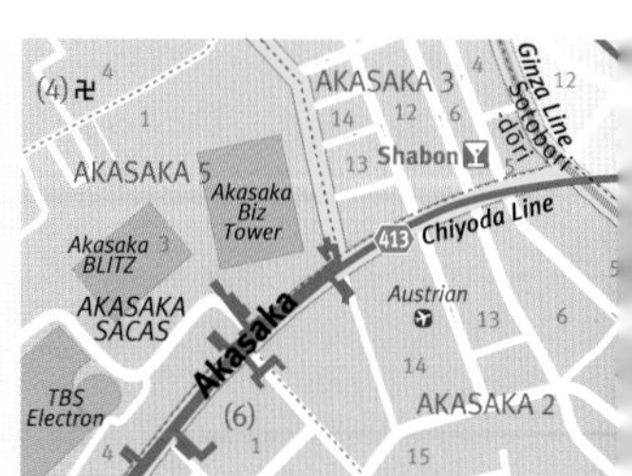

Bashyōfu 芭蕉布 082-879-6353

1-20-28, Ōmachi, Nishi Asaminami-ku, Hiroshima-shi, Hiroshima, 731-0125
〒731-0125 広島県広島市安佐南区大町西 1-20-28

Open: 5:30 pm–11 pm (last orders 10.30 pm); they take irregular holidays so telephoning before a visit is a good idea Booking recommended? Yes Credit cards? No English menu? No, but there are some pictures on the menu Cover charge: A *toriaezu* menu replaces the normal *otōshi*. You can choose from a number of dishes ranging between 380 yen and 630 yen

Do not try to walk to Bashyōfu from the center of Hiroshima. I did, and I was still tramping through the gathering gloom one and a half hours later. I was starting to despair when I finally found this cozy family-run Okinawan restaurant tucked in the dark backstreets behind Furuichibashi Station. Within seconds of sitting down, the journey began to seem worthwhile. The atmosphere was friendly, with gales of laughter from Mutsuko Kajikawa and her family in the kitchen, and the simple home-style menu had my mouth watering. Okinawan food is famously healthy and, though the homeland now has the worst obesity in Japan (all those American hamburgers!), Bashyōfu's vegetable and *tōfu* dishes were a reminder of how it got that reputation. The *Jimami dōfu* (peanut tōfu) was complemented excellently by a fresh, quite sharp-tasting five-year-old "Sakura Ichiban" (さくらいちばん, 580 yen) *awamori* on the rocks. The maker, Yamakawa Shuzō in northern Okinawa, was noted for its stolid commitment to aging high-quality *kūsu* during the spirit's dark days from the 1950s to the 1970s, and is now reaping the rewards with a range of *awamori* aged up to 40 years. In contrast to Sakura Ichiban's refreshing, almost leafy taste, the eight-year-old "Kiku no Tsuyu VIP Gold" (菊之露 VIP Gold) from Miyakojima, Kajikawa-san's home island, was sweet and mellow and perfectly complemented the sharp but creamy flavors of the *gōya champuru* (bitter gourd stir fried with pork and egg).

DIRECTIONS: JR Furuichibashi Station (JR West Kabe line, which starts at Hiroshima Station), east side. Take the second road on the left at the junction outside the station (with the Kakuichi cosmetics store on it). Pass a Lawson convenience store on your left. Cross the tracks and turn left just before the 7-Eleven convenience store. Turn right at the T-junction at the end of this narrow road. Take the next left and walk down to the traffic lights. Bashyōfu is ahead of you in the white building with a tower.

Karakara to Chibugwa カラカラとちぶぐゎ 098-861-1194 www.b-kara.com

1F Daini Yamako bldg. 3-15-15 Kumoji, Naha-shi, Okinawa, 900-0015
〒900-0015 沖縄県那覇市久茂地 3-15-15 第二やまこビル 1F
Open: 6 pm–11 pm; closed Sunday Booking recommended? No Credit cards? Major cards
English menu? No Cover charge: 500 yen

Karakara to Chibugwa's name alone was an education for me. I knew that a *karakara* was the traditional teapot-shaped *awamori* serving vessel used in Okinawan homes, but a *chibugwā*, owner Tetsunari Nagamine explained to me, is an Okinawan word for the tiny thimble-sized cups in which the spirit is served straight. I love drinking out of these tiny receptacles and the tiny quantities they contain mean you can afford to experiment with some very special liquors at Karakara. How about a 1984 "Shurei" (守禮, 800 yen for a thimble)? It is strong, at 43 percent alcohol, but the oily texture with chocolate and maple syrup flavors is beguiling. The maker, Kamimura distillery in Uruma city, was one of the five US government-run distilleries set up immediately after the war, but the company traces its roots back to 1882. Kamimura pioneered the now fairly widespread practice of aging *awamori* in oak barrels way back in 1961 and their oak barrel aged "Danryu" brand (暖流, 700 yen for a glass) is definitely worth a try if you are coming from a whisky background. A word of warning: I remember being told these barrel-aged varieties were "like whisky" before I tried one. Tasting them with that expectation is inevitably going to lead to disappointment. They are *awamori* and are not trying to be anything else, but the barrel sometimes does add interesting flavors to the liquor. Nakamine-san recommended the *soki no jikabiyaki* (pork ribs, 800 yen) with the "Danryu." If that doesn't fill you up, try the intriguing *ika sumi no nigiri* (squid ink *sushi*, 500 yen for three).

DIRECTIONS: Kenchōmae Station (Yui monorail), Exit 1. Cross Route 42 and head down the road forking away from the monorail tracks. Take the sixth turning to your left, just before the bend in the road. It is on your left as you turn the corner.

Katakura 嘉多蔵 03-3260-4504

1F Katakura Biru, 1-3 Ichigayatamachi, Shinjuku-ku, Tōkyō
東京都新宿区市谷田町 1-3 片倉ビル 1F
Open: Weekdays 5 pm–11 pm; Saturday 5 pm–9.30 pm; closed Sunday and national holidays
Booking recommcards? Amex, Visa, Mastercard and JCB
English menu? No Cover charge: 300 yen

Shigenori Katakura's family have been running a shop here since the Meiji period. It used to be an old-fashioned eatery called Ichigaya Shokudō, but Katakura-san turned it into an *izakaya* when he took over 10 years ago. There is house wine and, of course, beer but the emphasis is squarely on Japanese alcohol: 200 types of *shōchū*, 80 kinds of sake, and 90 *awamori*. The food menu, on the other hand, is eclectic. Their Italian pastas are particularly popular with customers and go surprisingly well with the punchy Japanese spirits. Try the *jaga imo to hōrensō no niyokki to kani miso kuriimu* (potato and spinach gnocci with brown crab meat, 980 yen) or the *penne arrabiata* (spicy tomato pasta, 860 yen). Katakura might have been included in either the *shōchū* or sake sections of this guide, but the beautiful collection of old Okinawan drinking containers, and the impromptu lesson Katakura-san gave me on the differences between the teapot-shaped *karakara* (used when entertaining in the home) and the crescent-shaped hip flasks called *dachibin*, mean I will always remember Katakura as a great place to drink *awamori*. The range of "Harusame" (春雨) *awamori* from the tiny Miyazato distillery in Naha was exceptional: a rich, slightly vanilla-influenced "Karii Harusame" (500 yen); an even smoother eight-year-old (700 yen) and a 15-year-old *kūsu* (2,000 yen) that carried its 43 percent alcohol content incredibly lightly. Miyazato's young distilling team use stainless steel tanks to age.their *kūsu*, resulting in a fresh taste that has attracted many admirers.

DIRECTIONS: From JR Ichigaya Station, Main Exit: Turn left out of the gates and cross the bridge. Cross the road and turn right. Katakura is on the corner of the next left turn. From Ichigaya Station (Yūrakuchō line), Exit 7: Walk toward the bridge, cross the road and continue walking in the same direction. It is on the corner of the next left turn.

Kozakura 小桜 098-866-3695

3-12-21 Makishi, Naha-shi, Okinawa, 900-0013
〒900-0013 沖縄県那覇市牧志 3-12-21
Open: 6 pm–11 pm; closed Sunday
Booking recommended? Yes Credit cards? No English menu? No

This small family-run *izakaya* has been operating since 1955. The current landlord, Kōichi Nakayama, inherited the business from his father and has seen great changes in *awamori* since the early days. A key change, he says, was the return of Okinawa to Japanese control in 1972. The Japanese authorities have taken a much more hands-on approach than their American predecessors, disseminating research through the industry, and Nakayama-san believes this has directly affected the taste of the spirit. Kozakura's *awamori* is priced from 800 yen for 180 ml (*ichi-gō*) and their food menu features uncomplicated but tasty Okinawan home cooking. The *misobi* (*miso* peanuts) and *buta mimi* (pig's ears) are very popular. Nakayama-san recommended the "Nankō" (南光) *awamori* made by Kamiya Shuzō on Okinawa's main island. The current head of the distillery, Masaki Kamiya, took over the business in 1995 because of the sudden illness of his predecessor, and knew virtually nothing about distilling at the time. He was forced to go cap in hand to other distillers, and admits, with refreshing honesty, that there were some horrible mistakes along the way. Nowadays, however, "Nankō" has a reputation as one of the softest and easiest to drink of *awamori*. Kamiya-san has said his aim is to produce *awamori* of "brandy-like sweetness."

DIRECTIONS: Makishi Station (Yui monorail), Exit 1. Turn left on to Kokusai-dōri. Pass the Lawson convenience store and take the second left. It is about 20 yards along on your left.

Salon de Awamori Koshuraku

Salon de Awamori 古酒楽 098-951-0123

5F Urban Planet Biru, 2-4-35 Mekaru, Naha-shi, Okinawa, 900-0004
〒900-0004 沖縄県那覇市銘苅 2-4-35 アーバンプラネットビル 5F
Open: 7 pm–3 am (last order 2 am); closed Sunday Booking recommended? No Credit cards? Visa, Master, JCB, Amex and Diners English menu? No Cover charge: 500 yen

Salon de Awamori feels more like a whisky or upmarket cocktail bar than an *awamori* drinking shop. During my travels around Japan, I got used to Okinawan establishments with a chirpy, ethnic feel. Their electricity bills must be higher than in the average Japanese bar, too, because the lights are usually just a bit brighter and the music a tad louder. At Salon de Awamori, the tunes are classical or ice-cold jazz. The atmosphere is more Ginza than Naha, but they know their *awamori* inside out. It was here that I first tasted "Shirayuri" (白百合, "White Lily"; 600 yen), my favorite unaged *awamori*, with a side dish of *tōfuyō* (a fermented cheese-like *tōfu* covered in bitter red *kōji*, 700 yen). Yogi-san, Salon de Awamori's owner, was extremely amused that I liked the *tōfuyō* (he said very few customers finished it) and I have heard similar responses from Japanese people to my enthusiasm for "Shirayuri." One bar owner described it as combining the tastes of "a gutter, a dirty floor cloth, soil and antiseptic." I think Yogi-san came closer when he introduced it as "*awamori*'s Irish whiskey." There are earthy tastes in "Shirayuri" but it is the rich unctuousness of "Shirayuri" that I love. "Shirayuri" and its sister brand "Akauma" (赤馬) are made using traditional techniques by a small family-run distillery, Ikehara Shuzojo, on Ishigaki Island. The name comes from the local wild lilies. If you are not keen on dirty floor cloths or are intent on spending the last of your holiday cash on something really flashy, order some freshly cut *nama hamu* (ham, 1,000 yen) with a glass of Zuisen distillery's "Omoro" *kūsu* (おもろ, 2,000 yen), which has a distinct rice flavor when it hits the mouth, but an elegant, light finish.

DIRECTIONS: Furujima Station (Yui monorail), Exit 3. Walk up the side street to Route 251 and turn left. It is about 200 yards up the road on the right, opposite the Max Valu store.

Shimauta Paradise 島唄楽園 03-3470-2310 homepage1.nifty.com/myers/index.htm

4F Seishidō biru, 7-14-10, Roppongi, Minato-ku, Tōkyō, 106-0032
〒106-0032 東京都港区六本木 7-14-10 誠志堂ビル4F
Open: Monday–Thursday 5 pm–12 pm; Friday and Saturday 5 pm–3 pm; Sunday and national holidays 6 pm–11 pm (last orders an hour before closing) Booking recommended? Yes Credit cards? Most major cards
English menu? No Cover charge: 530 yen

Fusions of rock and Ryūkyūan folk music have enjoyed great popularity among mainland Japanese since the 1990s and have helped fuel a thriving music scene on the islands. Shimauta Paradise is a key Tōkyō venue for both traditional and modern Okinawan styles. There is usually a live band on Saturdays and up to two other days a week. Be warned: the entrance charge is higher on music nights (1,000–2,000 yen) and popular bands will fill the 70 seats (the atmosphere can be fantastic). Shimauta's food is standard Okinawan fare: taco rice (950 yen), *sōki soba* (stewed pork ribs and noodles, 1,030 yen), *shima gyōza* (Okinawan *gyōza* dumplings, 730 yen). There is a bewildering variety of alcohol, including sweet wine made from Okinawa's *shikuwasa* citrus fruit, *awamori*-based *umeshu* (traditional plum wine), *goyawari* (a mix of bitter gourd and *awamori*) and Okinawa's Orion lager on tap (680 yen). There is some very special *awamori*, too, including unique bottlings made for Ishigakijima festivals, which are unavailable anywhere else in Tōkyō. But the "crack" here has nothing to do with pretentious connoisseurship. If you really want to fit in, order the iconic "Zanpa" (残波, 630 yen) from Higa distillery. It was created in the depths of *awamori*'s unpopularity and has a fruity and rounded taste that has made it one of the most popular *awamori* brands. Zanpa advertising has always ignored the macho *awamori* stereotype and instead targeted women and young people. They have hundreds of thousands of gallons of sales to prove the wisdom of their strategy.

DIRECTIONS: Roppongi Station, Exit 4a. It is on the corner immediately to your left.

Urizun (Okinawa) うりずん 098-885-2178 www.urizn.gr.jp

Asato 388-5, Naha-shi, Okinawa
沖縄県那覇市安里 388-5
Open: 5.30pm–12 pm; closed second and fourth Sunday of every month Booking recommended? Yes
Credit cards? Major cards English menu? Yes Cover charge: 525 yen

When Saneyuki Tsuchiya opened Urizun in 1972, the *awamori* scene was very different. The local drink had suffered badly at the hands of beer, cheap *shōchūs* and foreign spirits, and many makers were hunkered down in their fox-holes, hoping only to survive. A sort of unstated, mob-style code had developed, under which the distilleries did not try too actively to seek outlets on each other's turf, as long as their rivals stayed out of their areas. The *awamori* available in Naha city tended to be made in Naha. Tsuchiya-san shook all this up by touring the outlying islands in search of local spirits and badgering the makers to open up. Urizun's tireless championing of *awamori* from all parts of the prefecture played an important part in ushering in the new era. Set up in an age-worn former residential house, the *izakaya*'s dark wood interior, decorated with Okinawan musical instruments and dust-encrusted *awamori* bottles, is an atmospheric place to taste the local spirit. The food is delicious. Specialities include *duru ten* (525 yen), a local variety of potato mixed with mushroom and pork fried in croquettes, and *duru wakashi* (523 yen), the same mixture but not fried. The *rafutei* (*miso*-marinated pork ribs, 735 yen) are very good. Just as I found at Urizun's newly opened Tōkyō shop (see facing page), there was great fun to be had with Urizun's house *awamori*, unique blends of spirits from distilleries across the prefecture (8-year *kūsu*, 1,050 yen for 180 ml; 12-year, 260 yen; 20-year, 2,940 yen). For those who want a named brand, try a flask of "Zuisen" (瑞泉, 840 yen for 180 ml) from Zuisen distillery, which is just down the road in the Sanka district. They have been making *awamori* at Zuisen since 1887, but it is now one of the most forward-looking distilleries, intent on producing very high quality spirits and developing an export market. The aged *awamori*, which make up the bulk of the distillery's output, come in various styles, including quite complex spirits with honeyed, mustardy flavors as well as elegant, lighter finishing *kūsu* (see page 118). This is their cheaper unaged version and works well with ice on a sweaty summer day.

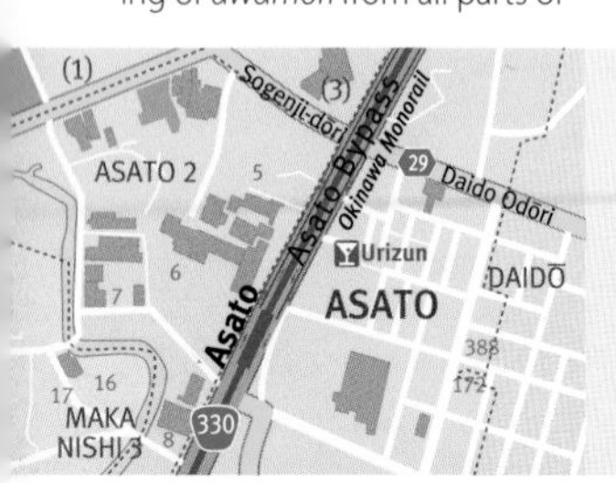

DIRECTIONS: Asato Station (Yui monorail), Exit 1. Walk away from the road junction. Take the second right. It is on your right.

Urizun (Tokyo) うりずん 03-5224-8040 www.urizn.gr.jp

5F Shin Marunouchi biru, 1-5-1 Marunouchi, Chiyoda-ku, Tōkyō
東京都千代田区丸の内 1-5-1 新丸の内ビルディング 5F
Open: **Monday–Saturday 11 am–3 pm/5 pm–4 am; closes 11 pm on Sunday and national holidays**
Booking recommended? **Yes** Credit cards? **Major cards** English menu? **Yes** Cover charge: **525 yen**

Urizun's atmospheric *izakaya* in Naha city, Okinawa (see facing page) is one of the best places to sample *awamori*. For those unable to get to the islands themselves, their Tōkyō branch lacks the patina of the Naha shop but is an excellent place to start exploring *awamori*. A major bonus is the English menu. It is a bit more limited than the Japanese version (which itself has some very helpful photographs), but it covers most of the main points. The food includes all the usual *champurus*, *sobas* and *rafutēs* that you would expect from Okinawan cuisine. The main attractions on Urizun's *awamori* list are the exclusive blends created by the shop itself from the products of various Okinawan distilleries. Branch manager Yosefu Ota picked out the Tōkyō branch's exclusive "Tōkyō awamori" (東京泡盛, 1,260 yen for 180 ml), a fruity blend specially created for the *izakaya's* opening in 2007. The buttery 12-year-old *kūsu* blend (1,575 yen for 180 ml) is also recommended but, if you are feeling flush, you could order the blend of 15-year aged, 60 percent alcohol *hanazake* (3,990 yen for 180 ml) from Yonaguni Island (see page 118). The price may look steep, but 180 ml of spirit at that strength goes a long way.

DIRECTIONS: Ōtemachi Station, Exit B1. Turn right on Route 402. Urizun is in the Shin-Marunouchi building, which occupies the second block on your right. Pass one entrance and enter by the central entrance. Urizun is on the fifth floor. Bear right and turn round one corner of the building. It is straight ahead at the next corner.

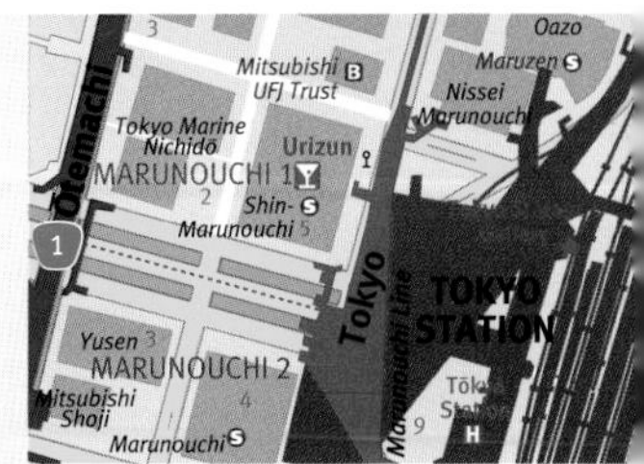

Wasabi 山葵 06-6933-1935

1-8-10 Gamō, Jōtō ku, Ōsaka, 536-0016
〒536-0016 大阪市城東区蒲生 1-8-10
Open: 5 pm–11 pm; closed Sunday and national holidays
Booking recommended? No Credit cards? No English menu? No Cover charge: No

The locals at this standing bar, tucked away beside the Kyōbashi train tracks, are a friendly bunch. The casual design, with circular standing tables dotted around the limited floorspace, makes it almost impossible not to get into conversation when you visit. The food menu is dominated by fish and fresh vegetables prepared in a Japanese style. I came here having already eaten in another bar, but landlady Saori Shiohama's sizzling grill was hard to resist. She recommended the *yakizakana* (grilled fish, price varies with the day's fish but is usually between 350 and 400 yen) as a perfect accompaniment for the 40 types of *awamori* available. For a visitor from Tōkyō, the prices looked very reasonable indeed. I had seen "Kuroshinju" (黒真珠, "Black Pearl", 450 yen) at almost double the price in Tōkyō. It is a big favorite with the clientele—a strong (43 percent) but very smooth-tasting matured *kūsu*. Makers Yaesen Shuzō on Ishigaki Island got into *awamori* by accident.They were originally a sweet shop called Zakimi Kashiten. Business was booming after the war and, in 1955 they took over an old *awamori* factory (an industry in steep decline at the time). Although they had no expertise at making alcohol, they decided it would be a waste not to use the abandoned equipment. In 1989, they moved to a new site, famous for the pure underground water running off the Omoto mountains, and have built a loyal fan base for their amiable and easy to drink brands—"Yaesen" (八重泉) and the aged "Kuroshinju."

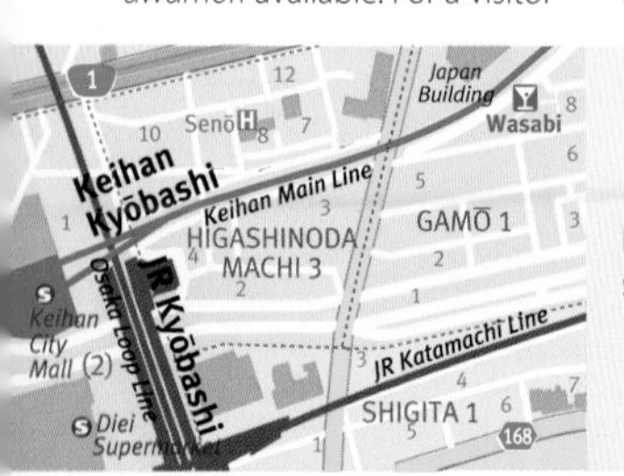

DIRECTIONS: Kyōbashi Station, North Exit. Turn right and walk alongside the tracks for about 300 yards. Wasabi is on your right.

Yamanekoya 山猫屋 098-869-2848

3-11-2 Kumoji, Naha-shi, Okinawa, 900-0015
〒900-0015 沖縄県那覇市久茂地 3-11-2
Open: 6 pm–12 pm (last orders 11 pm); closed Tuesday Booking recommended? No
Credit cards? Visa, Mastercard and JCB, not Amex English menu? No Cover charge: 300 yen

The stare of the pit viper in the bottle of *habushu* was the first thing that caught my eye on entering Yamanekoya. It seemed out of place. Yamanekoya has a nice modern feel—a fresh lime green logo, long tables and *awamori* from all 46 *awamori* distilleries lined up in optics behind the bar. If you find very traditional *izakaya* a bit intimidating, Yamanekoya may be a good alternative. Personally, I would recommend steering clear of the moldy, foul-tasting *habushu* (500 yen), a traditional medicine combining *awamori* and a whole snake stuffed inside a bottle. They either drown the serpent in the bottle or kill it and gut it first. *Habushu* is now sold mainly to tourists, but it actually represents a very important part of the *awamori* tradition. Okinawans used to believe that the smell of alcohol could repel the plague and many folk cures were made by steeping vegetables as well as animals in the spirit. All very interesting, but, instead, I would recommend a refreshing shot of "Kokka" (國華) from Tsukayama distillery (350 yen, see page 116) with the *kamekame dōfu* (fried peanut *tōfu*, 590 yen) or *papaya champuru* (papaya stir fry, 590 yen).

DIRECTIONS: Kenchōmae Station (Yui monorail), Exit 1. Cross Route 42 and head down the road forking away from the monorail tracks. It is a few paces past the first turning to your right.

The Glories of Japanese Beer

The dark amber pint of "Aldgate Ale" bought for me by the beer expert Chris Phillips felt like a home coming. I had spent the greater part of a year traveling around Japan trying to grapple with the intricacies of profoundly foreign drinks: *yamahai* and *ginjō* sakes, *imojōchū*, *habushu* and *kūsu awamori*. The beer's thin off-white head and hoppy, caramel-sweet flavor seemed to recall a thousand other pints downed in warm pubs back in England. Here, at last, was something I knew a little about. The beer chapter would be a breeze.

A pint of Aldgate Ale at The Aldgate, Shibuya, Tōkyō (page 158).

"The Aldgate Ale is from Swan Lake in Niigata prefecture," Chris said, taking a sip from his own burnished black pint of Preston Stout. "Mine is made by a company running some brew pubs in Chiba prefecture and the North."

I took another startled gulp of the "Aldgate Ale" (see page 158). It was delicious, but the thought that there was a beer made in Japan that was not a pallid lager was profoundly unsettling. I had been living in Japan for more than four years and it had never occurred to me that there might be a world beyond the refreshing but incredibly samey light pilsener lagers sold by Japan's big brewers—Asahi, Kirin, Sapporo and Suntory. Chris, the author of the definitive "boozelist.blogspot.com" website (he is affectionately known as "Chuwy" among Tokyo's beer drinkers), had opened a door to a new world.

Ever since my "Aldgate Ale" shock, I have been frantically making up for my years in the Japanese beer wilderness by trying every domestic craft beer I can get my hands on, from turbo-charged 9 percent alcohol brown ales from Hakusekikan brewery in Gifu, through deliciously complex altbiers from Baeren in Iwate prefecture, to deep-piled export stouts from Baird Beer in Shizuoka.

Not all of the sector's 200-odd microbreweries make beers as good as those highlights. In fact, many produce uninspired drinks only discernible from the lagers of the big brewers because they

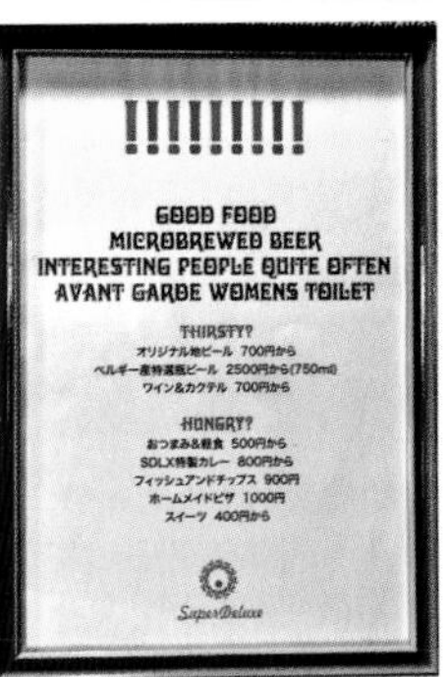

Clockwise from top: Baird Beer at Towers, Tōkyō (page 160); A customer in a steam cabinet cools off with a glass of beer, Tōkyō, 1951; In the late 19th century, Japan had up to 150 breweries. Many of these independent brands were killed off by government rationalization policies; A bar notice in Roppongi, Tōkyō.

are less competently made. But there are between 20 and 25 Japanese breweries making first-class products in a wide range of styles. The delusion that researching the Japanese beer chapter would be a straightforward exercise in visiting a few foreign-themed bars and trying some familiar imported brews, has given way to an (almost) sober realization that Japanese beer making is as diverse and dynamic as any other alcohol sector in Japan. You just have to dig a little to find the good stuff.

Small beginnings

Beer has been in Japan for about 400 years. During the Edo period (1603–1868), Dutch merchants first imported and then started to brew beer themselves at their trading post in Nagasaki. They even presented some to the Shogun in 1724. As far as the average Japanese punter was concerned, however, beer really got its start with the modernization of the country in the late 19th century. Some of the Japanese representatives who dealt with the American "Black Ships" in the

The giant brewing kettle at the Sapporo Beer Museum in Hokkaido.

Sapporo Beer Museum, Hokkaido.

Japan's beer museums

If you want to find out more about the history of beer in Japan, there are several beer museums that are worth visiting. Sapporo brewery's Beer Museum in Yebisu (4-20-1 Ebisu, Shibuya-ku, Tokyo; Tel: 03-5423-7255) or Kirin's Yokohama Beer Village (1-17-1 Namamugi, Yokohama City, Japan 230-0052; Tel: 045-503-8250) will be the most convenient for many visitors, but Sapporo's Beer Museum in Sapporo City, Hokkaido (Kita 7-Jo Higashi 9-chome Higashi-ku, Sapporo; Tel: 011-731-4368) is also well worth a visit. All of these are large facilities run by Japan's big beer conglomerates. They are professionally presented and offer company-biased versions of beer history. Tastings of a company's products are usually a focal point of the experience. For something completely different, go to Ishikawa sake brewery in Fussa city, Tokyo prefecture (1 Kumagawa, Fussa city, Tokyo 197–8623, Japan; 042-553-0100; www.tamajiman.com). It is a tiny little place with more space given over in the very limited museum to their main business of sake making, but they have some interesting beer relics. In the grounds, there is an iron cauldron that was, until recently, being used as the lining of a pond in a local garden. It turned out to be a relic from the company's brief dalliance with beer in the 1880s, one of dozens of forgotten enterprises all over the country. Try the "Tama no Megumi Beer" in the attached beer restaurant.

1850s were treated to beer during the negotiations and, shortly afterwards, the father of Japanese chemistry, Kōmin Kawamoto, became the first Japanese to make his own beer. He used an improvized setup in his back garden. His brewing method was published in a textbook in 1860.

Over the next decade, foreigners started flocking to Japan's newly opened ports and imported beer flooded the rowdy pubs and clubs in the foreign quarters. Bass Pale Ale, still a common sight in Japanese bars, seems to have been the dominant brand, but various other British styles and a few Bavarian lagers were being distributed quite widely by the 1870s.

Beer was expensive, however. In 1871, the Nankaitei restaurant in Tokyo was charging more than three gold coins for one bottle. For the less affluent, there was a substitute—used beer bottles refilled with locally produced ersatz "beer." Nobody knows how it was made, but we can be pretty sure it bore no resemblance to conventional beer making. In 1871, the Tokyo city authorities issued an edict specifically banning fake Bass labeling, but the pirate industry seems to have been in rude health seven years later when the Yokohama *Mainichi* newspaper commented that drinkers were prepared to drink any foul concoction so long as it carried an exotic enough beer label.

Commercial brewing in Japan got under way about the same time as the pirate bottling (and the two industries may have overlapped in some cases). G. Rosenfelt built the Japan Brewery in Yokohama in 1869, about the same time as a Japanese-run operation set up in Shinagawa, Tokyo. The next year, Dutchman J. B. N. Hecht's Hecht Brewery and the Norwegian-American William Copeland's Spring Valley Brewery (later to become Kirin beer) came on stream in Yokohama. Breweries started popping up all over the country: Shibutani beer in Osaka (1872), Mitsu Uroko beer in Kōfu (1873) and a government-run brewery in Hokkaido in 1876 (to become Sapporo beer). At an industrial show in 1890, 83 beer brands from 23 prefectures were exhibited. By the end of the century, there were up to 150 breweries nationwide. This was the first Japanese micro-brewing boom but, sadly, its days were numbered.

The rise of big beer

The 20th century was the long, dark night of Japanese beer's soul. From 1901 to 1994, the Japanese government pursued a consistent policy of turning the industry over to a few huge conglomerates making a product of such uniformity that it was, at most points in the period, almost impossible for even the most discerning of beer tasters to tell the leading brands apart. Japanese beer is still suffering from the hangover from this century-long policy: 99 percent of beer consumed is still made by the same big companies in the same light, fizzy lager style. The average Japanese consumer has become so used to regarding beer as a relatively tasteless and inoffensive thirst quencher that the exciting

Asahi's environmentally friendly Kanagawa Brewery was opened in 2002. The company says modern processes keep emissions to a minimum.

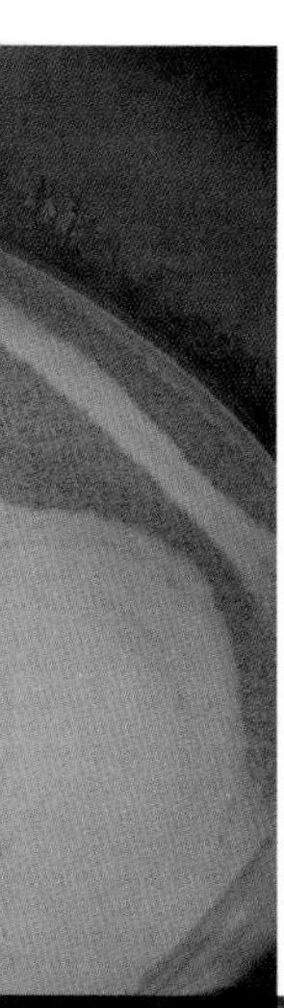

Clockwise from top left: Malted barley; Making the wort at Fujizakura Heights Brewery, Yamanashi; Coedo Brewery in Saitama prefecture.
Below: Hiromichi Miyashita, head brewer at the Fujizakura Heights Brewery.

diversity of styles that is now coming out of the tiny craft beer sector has barely scratched the surface of mass consumption.

The corporatization of beer in Japan started in 1901, when the Japanese taxman, needing to raise money for military aggression in Asia, imposed a beer tax. It immediately closed numerous smaller makers operating on very narrow profit margins. The tax was ramped up over the next decade as the government pursued an aggressive policy of rationalizing the industry to increase tax revenues. It encouraged the merger of three of the largest firms into the Dai Nippon Beer Company in 1906 and, two years later, imposed a minimum annual production volume of 180 kl on companies, effectively ruling out the little men.

The policy of rationalization was extremely successful from the government's point of view.

Beer tax revenues more than doubled in the five years following the introduction of the levy, significantly boosting an Imperial exchequer which relied on alcohol taxes for an astonishing one-third of its income in the early 1900s. In 1923, there was at least some diversity in the industry; in addition to the Dai Nippon company and Kirin Beer, there was also Sakura Beer, Kabuto Beer, Tōyō Beer, the Anglo Japanese Brewing Company and Takasago Brewing. By the 1930s and 1940s, even these medium-sized enterprises were being swallowed up, leaving Kirin and Dai Nippon dominating the field.

If fans of small enterprise thought Japan's defeat in World War II would radically change the situation, they were bitterly disappointed. Dai Nippon was split into two companies in 1949, creating Asahi Beer and Nihon Beer (later to become Sapporo). In the 1960s, the whisky giant Suntory entered the fray, making a total of four large producers (the *shōchū* maker Takara tried and failed at around the same time). However, alcohol taxes still accounted for a staggering one-sixth of government tax revenues in 1955, and alcohol policy was (and still is) run from the tax office. The minimum production volumes were increased as the beer market expanded, and the effect of the government's policies was consistently to foster a few huge conglomerates with fat profits capable of keeping the tax drip flowing.

The market is not uncompetitive. In fact, the

Toriaezu beer

If you listen to groups of Japanese people when they first arrive in a bar, you will often hear the phrase: "Toriaezu zenin biiru de!" It means, "Just to start off with, beer for everybody!" The "toriaezu beer" is an institution in Japan, an easy, refreshing drink that can be ordered quickly on first arrival at a bar before everyone takes a look at the menu. You will not hear the speaker ask, "What types of beer do you have?", "Do you have any bitter? Or an Indian pale ale, perhaps?" It is just beer—a cold, light substance that quenches the thirst, clears the mouth and gets the toasts out of the way as quickly as possible. Sales of beer in Japan far outstrip those of any other alcohol—about two times as much alcohol is consumed in the form of lager as is poured from sake bottles—but a sizeable proportion of this beer is served as a thirst quencher rather than a drink that is expected to have great individual character.

Immediately after Japan's defeat in World War II, few Japanese could afford to drink beer. The Lion Ginza Beer Hall (page 153) became popular with the occupying Allied forces.

Learning to distinguish between happōshu imitation beer (left) and the real stuff (right) is the first lesson for any beer drinker in Japan.

big brewers have fought like cats in a bag. At the top of the heap in the 1950s were Sapporo, with a network of tied bars in the east of Japan, and Asahi, with a lock on much of the west. Kirin, the smallest of the three brewers after the war, was forced to concentrate on the household market, but, as drinking patterns changed and people started consuming more in the home, Kirin rapidly overtook the two Dai Nippon fragments. It had 63.8 percent of beer sales by 1976. Asahi fought back from the late 1980s with the very light "Asahi Super Dry." It replaced Kirin's top brand as the most popular beer in Japan and led the beer market further down the road of light, fizzy lager. Recently, there has been a turn back to slightly richer styles, with many of the big brands, including Kirin, starting to use only malt for their premium beers (instead of the rice/malt mixes used in the 1980s and 1990s). But these are, in the final analysis, only small variations around a single and pervasive light lager style.

The mass-market beer is not bad, per se. Bryan Baird, an American who runs the craft brewery Baird Beer in Numazu, says: "I like industrial beer. It is refreshing and highly drinkable, but it all tastes the same. Less than one percent of what is possible in beer making accounts for perhaps 99 percent of production in Japan and this has been the case for so long that it has become ingrained. When we started selling our real ales to the locals in Numazu, many of them were not prepared for the sort of beer experience we were providing. Beer, to them, was industrial lager, nothing else."

A year of revolution

In 1994, two things happened that started to upset the status quo. The first was a change in the law that allowed small makers like Baird to start up. The second was the invention by a Suntory laboratory scientist of *happōshu* (発泡酒) or "Frankenbeer," as it has been dubbed by Bryan Harrell, the leading foreign writer about Japanese beer.

In terms of its immediate effect on the mass beer market, *happōshu* has been the more significant development. It is basically imitation beer that has a very low malt content, and the reason for its runaway success is familiar—the clodhopping footprints of the Japanese government are all over the scene of the crime. Without getting too bogged down in the technicalities, Japanese tax law defines beer by its malt content and, because beer is punitively taxed compared to other alcohols, there is a large tax benefit to be had by ducking under that minimum and getting your sweet yellow fizzy stuff defined as "sparkling alcohol" (*happōshu*). There are some high-quality craft beers (for instance, some fruit beers) that are also labeled *happōshu* because of their lower malt content but we are talking here about the cheapest cans in the supermarkets. The only reason for their low malt is price;

Many of Japan's most famous beer brands were once under the umbrella of the giant Dai Nippon Brewery Company. Yebisu, Sapporo and Asahi bottles from 1908 are exhibited at the Sapporo Beer Museum in Hokkaido.

40 percent less tax is paid on a can of *happōshu* than on real beer. The beer companies have not stopped there. In 1999, Shūsaku Kashiwada, an engineer at Sapporo beer, came up with the bright idea of making beer with no malt in it whatsoever, which would be taxed at an even lower rate than *happōshu*. The completely maltless "Draft One" was released from its cage in 2003—a "beer" made from caramel and pea protein! Kirin and Asahi responded with no malt brews called "Nodogoshi Nama" and "Shin Nama."

These "Frankenbeers" now account for nearly as many sales as real beer in Japan. (The Japanese consumer usually disappoints beer snobs like myself; a test marketing for "Draft One" in Kyūshū in 2003 aimed to sell 170,000 boxes of the beer in a year. They sold 100,000 in a month.)

In the short term, the *happōshu* catastrophe has been a thoroughly bad thing for Japanese beer quality. However, I have a sneaking suspicion that its consequences have not been fully played out. For a start, by flooding the bottom end of the market with cheap light lager imitations, the beer companies have put themselves under pressure to create something distinctive at the top. In 2009 and 2010, there was a definite shift toward all malt, slightly richer styles from the major makers and it is possible that this trend may eventually see real diversity emerge from the big companies. The brewers at the conglomerates are extremely skilled and whenever they are given the opportunity to make interesting beer they usually prove themselves more than capable. For instance, Asahi recently produced a very good limited-edition strong stout. If senior managements started to move toward more variety in their styles, some very interesting things might happen.

More significantly, perhaps, is the effect the beer companies' gambit might have on government policy. *Happōshu* was a very radical step; its entire purpose was to deprive the Japanese exchequer of billions of yen of beer tax. The basis of 93 years of Japanese alcohol policy making has therefore been challenged by the very companies it was partly responsible for creating. The Finance Ministry and the big alcohol conglomerates have been at loggerheads on the issue ever since 1993, and in 2003 the government took the very limited but intriguing step of giving a temporary 20 percent tax break for very small producers. There has even been vague talk of root-and-branch reform of an alcohol tax system that has systematically discriminated against quality alcohol making in all sectors for decades. We can but hope!

Meanwhile, of much more immediate encouragement to beer lovers was the second major shift of 1994—a lowering of the minimum production requirements for a beer making license. For the first time since the 19th century, small producers could seriously consider brewing and there has been an explosion of activity as a result. Tatsuo Aoki set up the Popeye beer pub (see page 157) in 1985: "Before the changes, you could not stock several types of cask beer. Each company would insist on it all being their stuff. I thought that was strange. From the mid-1990s, it started to free up. I could do what I had always wanted to do, which was to offer real variety to my customers.

"At first, it was a bit crazy. There were too many breweries set up. A lot of the sake makers and tourist attractions were getting involved. At its height, in the late 1990s, there were more than 300 independent breweries operating, just a few years after a situation where there had been none. It was by no means all good stuff. You would find that the first batch was OK, because they would have a US or German expert over and the expert would have taken care of it. After that, the quality tended to decline. But at least it was interesting. People were experimenting and there were a handful of makers who were making very good beer."

There has since been a shake-out of the industry, says Aoki, with only about 230 independent breweries still in business. "Some of it is still basically *omiyage* beer [beer that people buy as a tourist gift when they visit the countryside]. The style of that *omiyage* beer is usually the same sort of lager that the big breweries put out and is often not as well made. But, at the heart of the industry, Japan now has a number of craft beer makers who are making really excellent beer in many different styles," says Aoki-san.

Hunting good beer

The first problem facing any newcomer to the Japanese beer scene is finding the craft beer. The big brewers have a stranglehold on much of the distribution network and the means to maintain that exclusivity. They will sometimes, for instance, offer to give a bar or restaurant state-of-the-art beer systems for free, on the condition that their beer alone is served. It is therefore possible, as happened in my case, to live in Japan for four years without knowing that there is any alternative to the light lagers. I hope this chapter and Chapter 8 (see page 238) will help to unlock the door for some readers.

The second problem, once you have found the independent breweries, is separating the wheat from the chaff. As Aoki-san says, the sector is establishing itself and there is still much mediocrity. To try to get some basic directions, I asked Chris Phillips to put together a list of what he considered his top 10 Japanese craft breweries in terms of the consistent quality and interest of their output. He cheated and gave me 12:

1. **Baird Beer** (Shizuoka)—Great beer in a wide range of styles. See page 155.
2. **Swan Lake Beer** (Niigata)—Rich, balanced ales. See page 158.
3. **Shiga Kōgen** (Nagano)—Also known as "Tamamura Honten," one of the most reliable Japanese craft beer makers. See page 151.
4. **Yahhō Beer** (Nagano)—Often called "Yaho" or "Yoho." Makers of the popular "Yona Yona" and "Tokyo Black" brands and much else besides. See page 149.
5. **Minoh Beer** (Osaka)—Balanced brews, often in British styles. See page 146.
6. **Fujizakura Beer** (Yamanashi)—A strong suit in German beers, particularly the *weizen* and *rauchbier*. See page 152.
7. **Baeren Beer** (Iwate)—More good German-influenced drink. See page 151.
8. **Oze no Yukidoke Beer** (Gunma)—Perhaps most admired for very individual India pale ales. See page 160.
9. **Ise Kadoya Beer** (Mie)—An old *mochi* rice bun making family producing very tasty beer. See page 149.
10. **Yokohama Beer**—See page 156. Hakusekikan Beer (see page 148)/Iwate Kura Beer (www.sekinoichi.co.jp/beer).

As Chris was keen to stress, his "top 10" is merely a personal opinion. Ask any other Japanese craft beer drinkers for their favorites and some of Chris's top choices would probably be echoed, but they would almost certainly be in a different order of preference. There are numerous other good breweries that might have been mentioned.

I encountered and liked beers from Hida Takayama Brewery (see page 157), Preston Ale (see page 148), Coedo Beer (see page 148), Shinano (see page 159), Sankt Gallen (see page 152) and Kiuchi Hitachino Nest (see page 147), and some of those brands might have made it into my top 10. Other names that would certainly make other lists are Atsugi beer, Nasu Kōgen (especially their barley wine), Daisen G (excellent *weizen*), Tazawako in Akita (nice *kolsch*), Harvestmoon (interesting fruit beers), Shōnan, Hideji, Shimono Loco, Hansharo, Ginga Kōgen and Okhotsk. Japanese craft breweries are, by and large, very small operations. A new brewer or fresh ideas can make a measurable difference to the standing of a company. If I were to ask Chris for a top 10 list a year later, it would almost certainly be different.

And isn't that the joy of it? Beer that is not merely differentiated by a new can design or a clever new marketing ruse—"Autumn beer," "the first beer brewed from the seedlings of barley that has traveled in space" (I kid you not)—but by real differences of taste that we can argue over and change our minds about is surely the only stuff worth sacrificing livers to. The late, great beer writer Michael Jackson once said: "The worldwide tide of bland beers will soon have come as far as it can. After that, it can only ebb to reveal the slow brews of lasting character." In Japan, I believe, we are just starting to see the beach.

Bryan and Sayuri Baird, founders of Baird Beer, make some of Japan's best beer at a small brewery in Numazu, Shizuoka (page 155).

Beer bars

Many of the best beer bars in Japan change their beer menus on a weekly basis, which poses a problem for the author of a drinking guide. Brews I encountered in one bar during my research may be long gone by the time you visit. If you do find an unfamiliar range of beers at a bar, however, it is likely that I will have given information on the brewery in another bar review. It is easy to cross reference using the "top 10" breweries list provided in the introduction or using the index at the back of the book. If you are in the Tōkyō and Yokohama areas and want to know what beers are on tap ahead of your visit, Chris Phillips runs a great website at www.boozelist.blogspot.com, which not only carries all of the latest menus, but also background information on Japanese beer and bars in Kantō. Chris provided invaluable help in the writing of this chapter by providing explanations for many of the beers encountered on my bar visits.

Beer and Food Higurashi

ビアアンドフードひぐらし 011-532-8480
vfhigurashi.blog107.fc2.com

3F Shakō Kaikan Biru, 2 Minami 5 Jo Nishi, Chūō-ku, Sapporo-shi, Hokkaido, 064-0805
〒064-0805 札幌市中央区南5条西2丁目社交会館ビル3F
Open: 6 pm–4 am Booking recommended? No Credit cards? No English menu? No
Cover charge: 300 yen

It can't be easy sharing a city with one of the best beer bars in Japan (Mugishutei, page 154), but Yōji Hyōdō and Tomonari Chida's small cafe bar is carving out a niche a few streets from Sapporo's Susukino's crossing. At Mugishutei, it can feel like you have been interned in a sort of beer drinkers' underworld, where the condemned must drink great beer for eternity. At Higurashi (the name refers to a species of cicada but also means "all day long" in Japanese), the atmosphere is more airy. Chef Hyōdo serves a tasty menu of Japanese-inflected Western fare—*naganasu no dengaku miso pizza* (grilled eggplant and *miso* sauce pizza, 680 yen), Higurashi fish and chips (made with flat fish, 900 yen), Caesar salad (700 yen)—while Chida-san oversees the six beers on tap. They had the "Yona Yona" pale ale (see page 149) and a nice "Minoh Beer Double IPA" (India pale ale, also page 146) on tap when I visited but Chida-san was also keen to introduce some local Hokkaido breweries. He recommended the "Coriander Black" (US pint 1,000 yen) from the Canadian Brewery that, despite its name, is just a few kilometers away in Sapporo city (www.2002cb.co.jp). They are also known as the Tezukuri Brewery and have hit on a cunning wheeze for surviving in Japan's seemingly perpetual recession—offering people the chance to brew their own beer using the brewery's equipment, ingredients and advice. Of course, you need to be able to wait 44 days for the results and the minimum batch size—55 small bottles for 40,000 yen—is not tailored to the back-packing visitor. It is good news for couples wanting to add a personal touch to their wedding, though! The beers produced by their professional staff are not well known or distributed outside Hokkaido, but the herb-packed, well-balanced "Coriander Black" is worth a try if you come across it.

DIRECTIONS: From Susukino Crossing, walk east two blocks along Route 36. Turn right at the Susukino Green Hotel and walk south two blocks. Turn right and Higurashi is a few paces on your right.

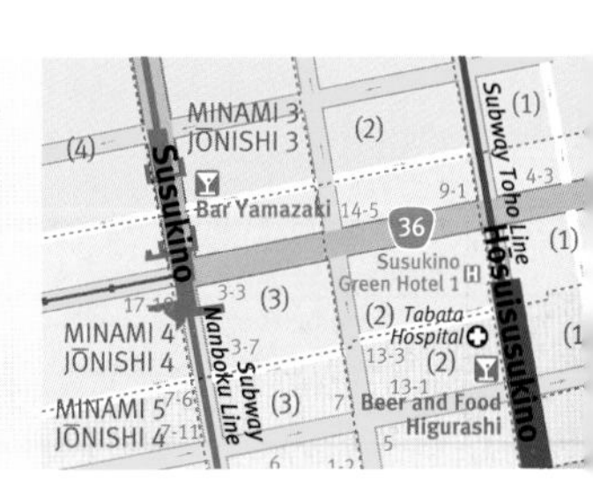

Beer Belly Edobori-ten ビアベリー江戸堀店 06-6445-6366 www.minoh-beer.jp

1F Famiiru Edobori, 2-1-21 Edobori, Nishi-ku, Ōsaka-shi, Ōsaka, 550-0001
〒550-0001 大阪市西区江戸堀 2-1-21 ファミール江戸堀 1F
Open: 5 pm–2 am Booking recommended? No Credit cards? Visa and Mastercard
English menu? No Cover charge: No

I can't help feeling that naming a pub Beer Belly is a bit like calling a casino Poverty or a boxing gym Broken Nose. Mine was hanging over my belt as I entered, but I soon forgot my shame under the reassuring influence of a pint of English bitter from Minoh Beer, the Ōsaka brewery that runs this friendly pub and a sister establishment at Higobashi (Tosabori 1-1-30, Ōsaka River Building 1F). Minoh is run by Masaji Ōshita, a prominent Ōsaka businessmen, but much of the day-to-day work is done by his two daughters, Kaori and Mayuko Oshita. The women have quite a fan club among Japan's craft beer enthusiasts. The emphasis at Beer Belly is heavily, though not exclusively, on Minoh's own products, which tend to be balanced, relatively mild British-style ales (as opposed to the often hoppier North American beers). The "English Bitter" (US pint, 900 yen) was not an attention-grabbing sort of drink (hops firmly in check, underlaid with rich nut, caramel and herbal flavors) but was an ideal accompaniment for a small plate of fish and chips (600 yen). The Minoh that gets most publicity is the "W-IPA" (US pint 1,000 yen), a double India pale ale with far more assertiveness than the bitter but with very good balance. Kaori Oshita, craft beer geekdom's heart throb, simultaneously delighted and disappointed many a beer dweeb when she announced that, if the world were going to end, she would spend her last moments with a pint of "W-IPA."

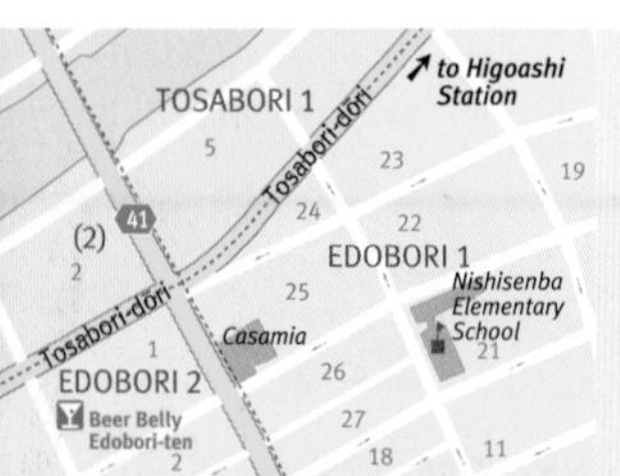

DIRECTIONS: A fairly long walk from Higobashi Station, Exit 8. Turn right out of the exit and reverse the direction you came up the stairs. Walk west away from the junction and continue to the end of the road, where it merges with Tosabori-dōri. Continue in the same direction, crossing Route 41. Beer Belly is down the next turning to your left, after the big junction.

Beer Cafe Barley ビアカフェバーレイ 0798-65-6135 www.beercafe.jp

2F, Liberty 2 Biru, Nagatachō 1-15, Nishinomiya, 663-8034
〒663-8034 兵庫県西宮市長田町 1-15 リバティー2 2F
Open: 1 pm–12 pm (last orders 11.30 pm); closed Tuesday Booking recommended? No Credit cards? No
English menu? No Cover charge: No

Kazuo Hattori offers more than a hundred types of bottled beer and eight beers on tap at this understated but friendly beer cafe. Belgian beer is very well represented among the bottles (about seventy types) but domestic craft beer dominates on the pumps, with "Hoegaarden" and "Yona Yona" always present alongside a rotating line-up of six Japanese brews. The food menu includes pastas, pizzas, sausage dishes and a nice shepherd's pie (850 yen), which would go down well with the "Hitachino Nest Japanese Classic Ale" (bottle 950 yen). The makers of "Nest," Kiuchi Brewery in Ibaraki prefecture, are a bit of an oddity, in that their beer is probably as well known in the United States as it is in Japan. They have put great effort into exporting and have a good English website explaining all about their 180-year sake brewing history (www.kodawari.cc/en/). They seem very keen to bring that heritage to bear on their beer making. The "Classic Ale" (bottle 950 yen) is a good example—an ale matured in the cedar casks traditionally used for storing sake. The result is a complex combination of spiciness, malty sweetness and an overriding bitter taste that seems to come from the cedar wood. Hattori-san also recommended the "Hitachino Nest Red Rice Ale" (bottle 1,000 yen) when I visited, made using a combination of red rice and malt. The rice is prepared with sake-making techniques, and two different types of yeast have to be used to get the rice and malt fermenting. The rice lends an unusual pink color and there are berries, sweet malt and hints of sake in the flavor.

DIRECTIONS: Nishinomiya-Kitaguchi Station (Hankyu Railway), North Exit. Turn right and walk along the raised concourse to the circular dais. Descend the stairs to your right. Walk around the east side of the Acta store. Barley is on the right side of the road at the traffic lights.

Beer Cafe Gambrinus ビアカフェ ガンブリヌス 042-325-0484 gambrinus.jp

6F Dai 46 Tōkyō Biru, 3-16-5 Minamimachi, Kokubunji-shi, Tōkyō, 185-0021
〒185-0021 東京都国分寺市南町 3-16-5 第 46 東京ビル 6F
Open: 5 pm–1 am; closed Sunday and national holidays; open Sundays before national holiday Mondays
Booking recommended? No Credit cards? No English menu? Some English on the menu
Cover charge: No

Gambrinus treads a nice line between a smart, modern feel and a casual beer drinking atmosphere. It is very small—only five tables plus the counter seats—but the no smoking policy keeps the Friday night pub smog at bay. Barman Shin Kadoya offers a changing selection of 13 beers on tap, hovering around a pretty reasonable 900 yen for a US pint, and seems to have his finger on the pulse of the craft beer scene. Last time I looked, for instance, he was serving the "Preston Ale IPA" on tap. Preston Ale is a very small operation connected to a chain of brewpubs in northern Japan and, until recently, hadn't wowed anybody with their standard range of English-style ales. However, their more assertive IPAs (India pale ales) have started to get some notice. Even more uncompromising was the 15 percent alcohol "Hakusekikan Hurricane" (800 yen for a 160 ml glass). Gifu prefecture-based Hakusekikan (www.hakusekikan-beer.jp) make a wide range of beers but are perhaps most valued for their higher alcohol brews ("Hurricane," "Super Vintage," "Crystal Ale"). The "Hurricane" is one to either love or hate—flat, sour, with layers of wine, spice and dried fruit. For those looking for a less challenging beer, Kadoya-san suggested the "Coedo Shikkoku" (US pint 900 yen), one of a range of very approachable beers from Coedo brewery in Saitama prefecture (www.coedobrewery.com). The "Shikkoku" is a German-style black beer (rather than a stout or porter) and has a controlled flavor with a lightly woody finish that Kadoya-san recommended as an ideal accompaniment for his *Berugi biiru stew* (Belgian beer beef stew, 1,350 yen).

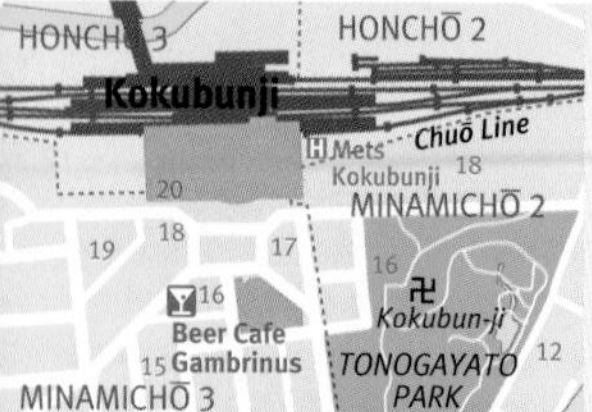

DIRECTIONS: Kokubunji Station, South Exit. Take the road forking off to the right of the Mos Burger. It is on your left, on an upper floor and signed in Roman alphabet.

Beer Pub Bacchus ビアパブ バッカス 03-3231-4666 www.bacchus-yaesu.com

B1F, Dai-ni Yamamoto Biru, 1-7-7 Yaesu, Chūō-ku, Tōkyō, 103-0025
〒103-0025 東京都中央区八重洲 1-7-7 第 2 山本ビル B1F
Open: 5 pm–12 pm; Fridays 5 pm–3 am; closed Sunday and national holidays Booking recommended? No
Credit cards? No English menu? Limited English on the Japanese menu Cover charge: No

Bacchus is not easy to find. It is customary for anyone visiting this small basement bar to spend at least 10 minutes repeatedly walking past the large and (once you have spotted it) perfectly clear, Roman-lettered sign before finally gaining admittance. It is a bit like Platform 9-3/4 at King's Cross Station, only the beer is better when you get through. Landlord Naoki Miura keeps a regularly changing line-up of three Japanese craft beers on tap, plus two regulars: "Yona Yona" (US pint 1,000 yen) and Ise Kadoya brewery's pale ale (US pint 1,000 yen). "Yona Yona" has become a bit of an institution in Japanese craft brewing. "One of the original brewers was Toshi Ishii-san, who is regarded by many as the god of brewers over here," says Chris Phillips. "If any one person is revered, it is him. He started out working for Stone Brewing in San Diego (just taste "Arrogant Bastard" or "Ruination IPA" if you want to know how good they are). Then he came back and landed a job at Yahhō in Karuizawa. He has left Yahhō since and is now in the US but he helped make them into a very good producer of craft beer." Yahhō (sometimes written Yoho or Yaho in English; the name roughly translates as "yee-ha!") have two smash-hit beers—"Yona Yona," a rich, fruity American pale ale, and "Tokyo Black," a strong dark porter, but the breadth of their range of seasonal brews is only matched by Baird Beer (see page 155). Their strong barley wines are particularly well reckoned. Miura-san's other regular beer, from Ise Kadoya in Mie prefecture, is, theoretically, a similar beer to "Yona Yona"—an American pale ale. However, the taste is totally different: where the "Yona Yona" is fruity, almost sweet, the "Ise Kadoya" is quite hoppy, verging on the bitter. Ise Kadoya (which offers a nice English website at www.isekadoya.com) are a four-century-old Japanese *mochi* (sweet pounded rice bun) making family who branched off into brewing in 1997. The pale ale is probably their most famous drink (best in class, Australian International Beer Awards, 2003) but they also have a couple of other styles of pale ale, a well-reckoned stout, a good brown ale and some interesting seasonal brews (anyone for a "Lambic Style White Peach" beer?).

DIRECTIONS: Nihombashi Station, Exit B3. Turn left out of the exit, left again at the junction and left again at the end of the next block, Walk two blocks to the Big Echo karaoke place. Bacchus is facing you at the crossroads, on the road coming from your right. It has a very small entrance three buildings down from the junction.

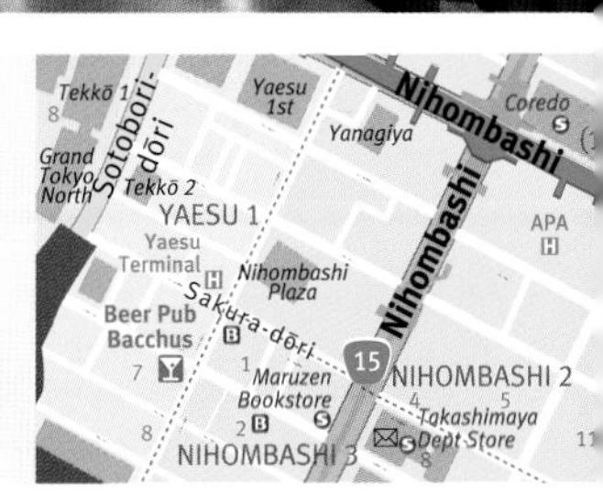

Bulldog ブルドッグ 03-3564-0996 r.gnavi.co.jp/g074200

2F, Ginza Inz 1, 3-1 Ginza Nishi, Chūō-ku, Tōkyō, 104-0061
〒104-0061 東京都中央区銀座西 3-1 銀座インズ 1 2F
Open: 11.30 am–2.30 pm (one hour later on weekends and holidays); 5 pm–11.15 pm Booking recommended? No
Credit cards? Most major cards English menu? Some English on the menu and some staff speak English

Anyone who has stayed in Japan for any length of time will be familiar with the chains of "English Pubs" that replicate everything about the traditional 1970s English local, including the carefree disregard for the quality of their beer. At first sight, the Bulldog looks and sounds like one of the breed. According to Bryan Harrell, the pre-eminent writer in English about Japanese beer, the Bulldog used to offer a cornucopia of "fizzy yellow lagers from several countries" but made a sharp turn toward quality in 2007. I met up with Bryan at the Bulldog and he took me through some of the excellent bottled imports, including a great selection of US brews from Stone, Speakeasy, Green Flash and North Coast (prices from 700 yen). Big brands, including "Asahi Super Dry" (US pint 840 yen), "Hoegaarden" (large 1,400 yen) and "Guinness" (US pint 1,000 yen), are on the pumps, but they usually have some local craft ales on tap as well. When I visited, they were serving a *weizen* from Miyoshi Becken. Unfortunately, a few days later, Becken, a greatly improved maker of German-style beer in Hiroshima, announced they were going out of business. People inside the industry talk of dozens of companies set up during the craft beer boom of the 1990s needing to restructure. A further shake-out will not be all bad, allowing the stronger makers more market share, but some casualties, like Becken, will be missed. Bulldog's food also departs from the 1970s English pub theme, with an interesting and varied menu, including *moule-kai no shiro-wain-mushi* (mussels steamed in white wine, 950 yen), *calamari fritto* (deep fried squid, 680 yen) and *yasai* stick (cucumber and carrot sticks, 680 yen).

DIRECTIONS: Ginza Station, Exit C9. Look for the Ginza Inz 1 shopping mall. Bulldog is on the second floor and signed in the Roman alphabet.

Kurakura 蔵くら 03-6206-8866 j-beer.com

3F Tōkyō Kanda Biru, 1-4-6 Kaji-chō, Chiyoda-ku, Tōkyō, 101-0044
〒101-0044 東京都千代田区鍛冶町 1-4-6 東京神田ビル 3F
Open: Monday–Friday 5 pm–11.30 pm; Saturday 4 pm–11.30 pm; closed Sunday and national holidays
Booking recommended? No Credit cards? Most major cards English menu? No Cover charge: 210 yen

In 2009, Kurakura upped sticks and moved to Kanda from their old shop in Shimokitazawa, which had been just round the corner from the booming Ushitora (see page 161). The new place feels a lot smarter than the old and there are 12 instead of just seven beers on tap. Kurakura has always served its beers in smallish glasses, so it does not represent the best value in Tōkyō, but the quality is good and the slightly more formal, restaurant-like atmosphere will appeal to some. I was recommended the *sausage moriawase* (sausage assortment, 1,100 yen) with the balanced, relatively light "Shiga Kōgen Pale Ale" (780 yen). "Shiga Kōgen," made by the two-century-old sake maker Tamamura Honten in the middle of Nagano prefecture's skiing country, is one of the most reliable Japanese craft beer brands. "They produce what many regard as the best American style IPA [India pale ale] and Double IPA in Japan," says Chris Phillips. It is also worth hunting down their Imperial stout and porter, but the key word with Shiga Kōgen is consistency—pretty much everything they put out is of decent or better quality.

Another beer that caught my eye on the menu at the new Kanda branch was the classic export lager from Baeren Brewery in Iwate prefecture (www.baeren.jp). Baeren were hit by tragedy in January 2008 when a tank exploded in their brewing room, killing a brewer. They are well known for their German-style beers, including one of the best *weizen* in Japan, my favorite altbier (German ale), and this newly released lager. Their seasonal chocolate stout also has many admirers.

DIRECTIONS: Kanda Station (Yamanote Line), South Exit. Walk south over the crossing, with the elevated tracks to your right. Take the left fork in the road ahead of you. Kurakura is facing you on the road to the right at the next crossroads.

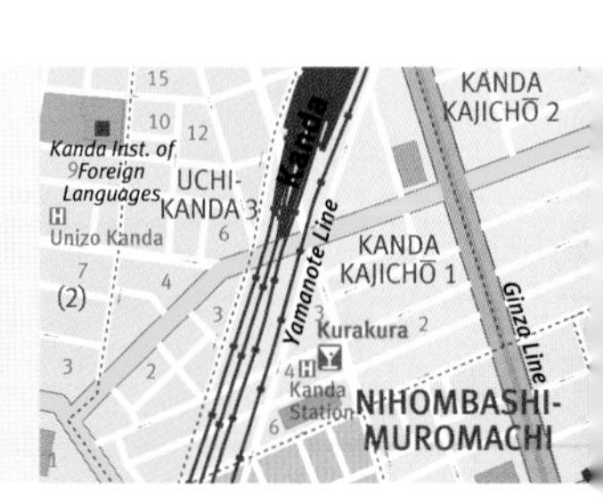

La Cachette ラカシェット 03-3513-0823 la-cachette.jp

3F Sankei Dai 22 Biru, 1-10 Kagurazaka, Shinjuku-ku, Tōkyō, 162-0825
〒162-0825 東京都新宿区神楽坂 1-10 三経第 22 ビル 3F
Open: Monday–Saturday 5 pm–1 am; closed on national holidays if they fall on a Monday
Credit cards? Most major cards English menu? No Cover charge: 500 yen

La Cachette's landlord Noboru Higuchi is a fervent advocate of Japan's craft beer movement. "The big companies deal to the common denominator," he says. "If there is a beer that is full of character, that some people love and one or two people hate, that is not good enough for them. They need everybody to like their stuff and that is how Japanese-style lager evolved. It is a clean, dry taste that doesn't make many enemies. It has its place but it is the lowest common denominator. The craft beer makers, on the other hand, are able to explore those boundaries." Higuchi-san usually has about 20 Japanese craft beers in a constantly changing line-up of seven beers on tap and 50 bottled beers. Higuchi-san recommended the *weizen* (500 ml bottle 892 yen), a refreshing and fruity mouthful from Fujizakura Heights Beer, a small German-style brewery on the north slope of Mount Fuji. In 2008, this beer earned second place in the *hefeweizen* category at the World Beer Cup, ahead of 69 of the best *weizen* in the world. Fujizakura's orange dungaree-wearing chief brewer, Hiromichi Miyashita, is an institution in the Japanese industry (see page 139). "He may look like a strangely dressed Yakuza type but he is gentle as they come. A great guy," says Chris Phillips. Miyashita-san is particularly noted for the *weizen* and an excellent smokey *rauchbier* (another silver medal winner at the World Beer Cup in 2000, just one of a slew of international awards for this brewery). The pilsener is not so highly rated. Miyashita explained to beer writer Glenn Scoggins that the problem was the hard local water—great for *weizen* but not so suited to pils. If you ever find yourself north of Fuji, Fujizakura has a pleasant restaurant and makes a nice stop if you have a designated driver (www.fuji-net.co.jp/beer). Try the *weizen* with La Cachette's *aigamo smoke* (smoked duck, 650 yen) or, alternatively, a dish of fish and chips (850 yen) with "Sankt Gallen's Golden Ale" (892 yen for a 330 ml bottle). Sankt Gallen is run by brothers Kōzō and Nobuhisa Iwamoto, who were among the first on the craft beer scene when they branched out from a family Chinese restaurant business in 1994. They now have a sizeable brewery at Atsugi, Kanagawa, and, although some criticize the inconsistency of their brews, they have earned a solid fan base. Their rich brown porter and this clean, refreshing golden ale are popular. I quite like their "Kokutō Sweet Stout," a new style being taken up by a number of Japanese brewers which uses the strong flavors of Okinawan or Amami Island brown sugar in a way reminiscent of chocolate stout.

DIRECTIONS: Iidabashi Station, Exit B3. It is right in front of you.

Lion Ginza ライオンギンザナナチョウメテン 03-3571-2590 r.gnavi.co.jp/g131800

1F, 7-9-20 Ginza, Chūō-ku, Tōkyō, 104-0061
〒104-0061 東京都中央区銀座 7-9-20 1F
Open: Weekdays 11.30 am–1 pm; weekends and holidays 11.30 am–10.30 pm; last orders 30 minutes before closing
Booking recommended? No Credit cards? Most major ards English menu? No Cover charge: No

Sapporo breweries, one of Japan's corporate brewers, run the Ginza Lion chain of beer restaurants. They serve standard Sapporo lagers in big glasses and lots of sausages. That is about all that can be said about the chain, but this particular Ginza Lion (don't confuse it with the branches down the street) is a bit special. It is a direct descendant of Japan's first proper beer hall, the Yebisu Beer Hall, established a bit to the south of here in 1899. Back then, a 500 ml beer cost one-tenth of a yen, about a quarter of an industrial worker's daily wage. Nowadays, 800 ml of Sapporo Beer's "Black Label" costs 1,050 yen. "Sapporo Black Label" is my favorite of the very light Japanese pilseners because it has a bit of bite to it. It washes down nicely with the sauteed potato and sausages (880 yen). But the real reason to come to this cavernous beer hall is to stare, slack-jawed, at Eizō Sugawara's marble and tile art deco interior or, if that's not your thing, at the large mosaic of scantily clad barley maidens at the head of the room. This successor to the original Yebisu Beer Hall opened in 1934 on the ground floor of Dai Nippon Beer company's headquarters (see page 139). The beer hall has been left pretty much untouched since then. Take a trip to the toilets to understand how untouched: when the time came to fit a women's toilet, they simply chopped the men's toilet in two because they didn't want to harm the building's fabric. The result? A cavernous beer hall serving beer by the kiloliter with a privy fit for a rural train station. Rather wonderful, in my opinion!

DIRECTIONS: Ginza Station, Exit A4. Turn left and walk 250 yards southwest down the main Ginza drag. It is on your left and hard to miss.

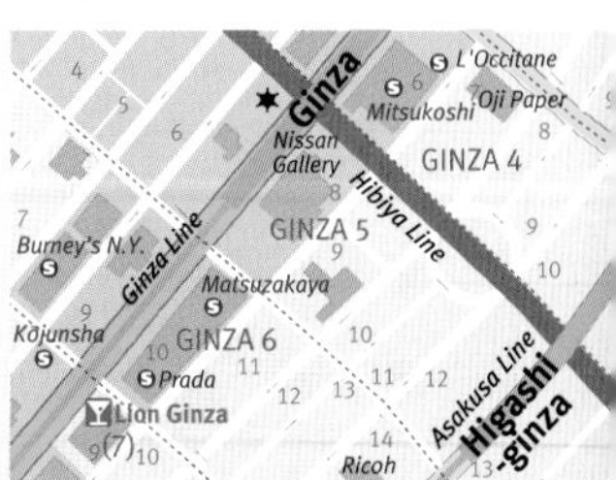

Mugishutei 麦酒亭 011-512-4774 www.ezo-beer.com

B1 Yoshiya Biru, South 9 West 5, Chūō-ku, Sapporo, Hokkaido, 060-0000
〒060-0000 北海道札幌市中央区南 9 条西 5 丁目ヨシヤビル B1
Open: 7 pm–3 am Booking recommended? No Credit cards? Most major cards English menu? Yes Cover charge: 900 yen (foreign travelers or people showing this guidebook will have the entrance charge waived once)

Ebullient, exuberantly bearded Phred Kaufman looks like a sort of ale-drinking Santa. In fact, he looks so like Saint Nick that he once made a pile of cash impersonating him in a Japanese car advert. A long-term resident of Sapporo, who first arrived in Japan avoiding the Vietnam draft, he has become a cherished local celebrity. Almost everybody you talk to knows him. His bar, Mugishutei (beer joint), opened 30 years ago and stocks over 300 types of bottled beers from 50 countries, with six on tap. He claims to have the "largest selection of beer in the Orient" and, judging by the collection of emptied bottles lining every spare inch of wall space, more varieties of beer must have passed through this basement bar than anywhere east of the Urals. It is not all about quantity. Phred, originally from Hollywood, California, is an innovative importer of some of the best craft beers Europe and the US have to offer. On my visit, I bumped into Kjetil Jikiun, a hairy giant of a man who heads the Norwegian brewery Nøgne Ø, whose excellent beer is well stocked at Mugishutei. Phred's longest established collaboration is with Rogue Ale of Newport, Oregon, which brews specially made batches for his import brand, "Ezo Beer." Try the rich, velvety "Rogue Shakespeare Stout" (800 yen), winner of a gold medal in the 2006 World Beer Cup, with one of Mugishutei's LA Burgers ("best hamburgers in Japan," Phred says; 1,300 yen).

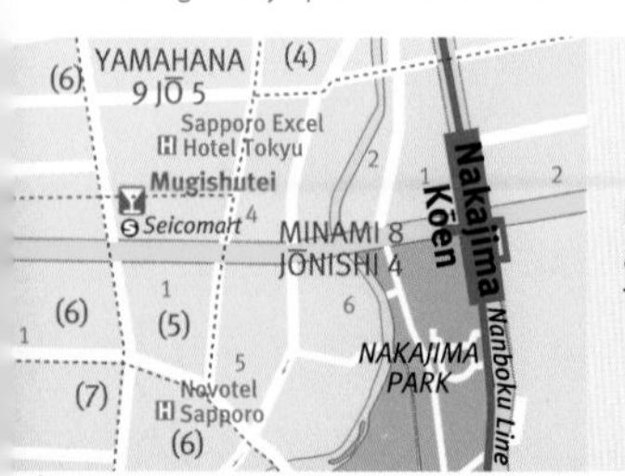

DIRECTIONS: Nakajima Kōen Station (Nanboku line), Exit 2. Turn right and walk west along Kikusui-Asahiyamakōen-dōri for about 200 yards. Take the right after the Seicomart store. Mugishutei is on your right.

Nakameguro Taproom 中目黒タップルーム 03-5768-3025 www.bairdbeer.com

Nakameguro GT Plaza C-Block, 2nd Floor, 2-1-3 Kamimeguro, Meguro-ku, Tōkyō, 153-0051
〒153-0051 東京都目黒区上目黒 2-1-3 中目黒 GT プラザ C 棟 2F
Open: Weekdays 2 pm–12 pm; weekends and holidays 12 am–12 pm Booking recommended? No
Credit cards? Most major cards English menu? Yes Cover charge: No

The Nakameguro Taproom is one of a chain of pubs run by Baird Brewing, a small craft brewery in Numazu on the southern slopes of Mount Fuji. They opened this Nakameguro outlet in 2008 and also have a pub in Harajuku (1-20-13 Jingumae; 03-6438-0450) and a delightful place on the dock-side in Numazu itself. More are planned in the future. All of the beer is Baird, which is no bad thing because it is commonly acknowledged as one of the best craft breweries in Japan. Bryan Baird, who runs the brewery with his wife Sayuri, decided to leave his job in Tōkyō in 1996 and take himself back to California to learn his trade in what was then establishing itself as one of the most creative craft beer industries in the world. A year later, he was back in Japan, having completed the American Brewers' Guild apprenticeship, and began turning out beer in tiny 30-liter batches. "Actually, the only reason we survived was that we started small," says Bryan. "We were selling it all ourselves at the start. What we learned was that Numazu was a great place to brew beer, but the local people we had thought we might sell to were very conservative. The Tōkyō taprooms and wider distribution are vital because it is in the city that we find people who know about beer and want to drink our stuff." Among Baird's flagship beers are the fruity, refreshing "Rising Sun Pale Ale" (US pint 900 yen) and the "Teikoku IPA" (US pint 900 yen), but one of the brewery's strengths is its constant experimentation across a whole range of beer styles—American dry-hopped ales, English milds, German bocks, Belgian fruit beers ... the range goes on and on and the quality is usually excellent. While you are sipping their delicious pints, take note of the beer names. There is usually a pun, or a historical reference or a family joke in there somewhere.

DIRECTIONS: Nakameguro Station. Turn right out of the main exit on to Route 317. Walk down to Tsutaya and take a right. It is in the Nakameguro GT Plaza behind the multistory tower block to your right.

Pivovar Yokohama ピボバル 横浜 045 640 0271 yokohamabeer.com

6-68-1 Sumiyoshi-chō, Naka-ku, Yokohama-shi, Kanagawa, 231-0013
〒231-0013 横浜市中区住吉町 6-68-1
Open: Weekdays 6 pm–11 pm; Saturday 11.30 am–11 pm; Sunday and national holidays 11.30 am–9 pm
Booking recommended? No Credit cards? No English menu? No Cover charge: No

I spent most of my time at this small brew pub resisting a reflex to duck. The brew kettles are a few feet away, and as the workers hosed down the equipment their jets noisily blasted the plastic screen that separated us from the action. The gorgeous smell of beer making filled the bar. There is a very limited food menu, featuring artistically arranged sauerkraut, but if you want proper food, you can go upstairs for some good Italian cuisine and a full list of Yokohama Brewery beers. The brewery owns both establishments. The Pivovar venture was inspired by its 28-year-old brewer Shinya Suzuki's contacts in Czech brewing. They have some very good Czech beer (Pilsener Urquell, Gambrinus, Radegast, Kozel) but also serve some interesting brews of their own at 950 yen for a large glass. I enjoyed the "Pixie Orange Ale," which had a subtle orange taste that avoided making the beer too cloying. They were also selling a fragrant, rounded Bohemian pilsener, a *weizen* and the citrusy "Green-fresh IPA" when I visited.

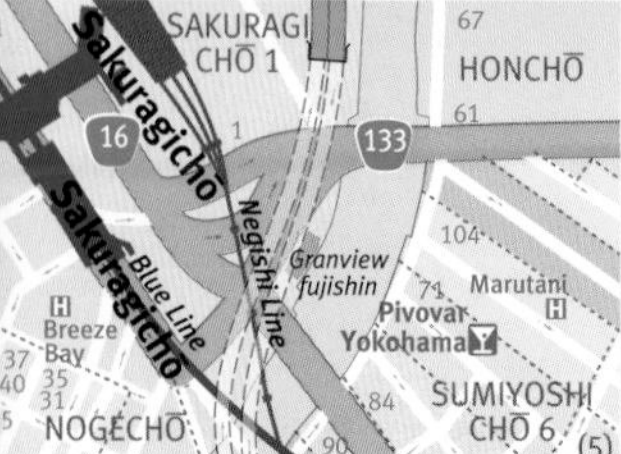

DIRECTIONS: Sakuragichō Station (Keihin-Tōhoku Line, Negishi Line, Blue Line (Line 3)), Exit 2. Turn left out of the exit, cross the road and walk southeast, passing in front of the Jonathan's restaurant. Cross the river using the footbridge and it is down the road immediately ahead of you.

Popeye ポパイ 03-3633-2120 www.40beersontap.com

2-18-7 Ryogoku, Sumida-ku, Tōkyō
東京都墨田区両国 2-18-7
Open: 5 pm–11.30 pm (last orders 11 pm); closed Sunday Booking recommended? No
Credit cards? Most major cards English menu? Yes Cover charge: 300 yen

Popeye is a sort of Lourdes for beer drinkers, except the cures are so much more immediate and hedonistic. Everyone who writes about the place slips into hyperbole, so, here goes: it has by far the biggest range of beer in Japan and the largest range of Japanese beer in the world. Landlord

Tatsuo Aoki gave a hostage to fortune some time ago, when he registered the URL "www.40beersontap.com" for his pub. He now has 70 beers on tap and three hand pumps. You will not find all the good beers in Japan here, but the range verges on being comprehensive. The menu is largely in English, so it is easy to pick and choose. I tried the *weizen* from Hida Takayama Brewery (www.hidatakayamabeer.co.jp) on my last visit. I once lived in Takayama, a beautiful spot in the middle of the Japanese Alps. Much of the city's economy is based on tourism, but the Hida Takayama brewery has gone way beyond the "*omiyage* beer" (poor imitations of mass-market lagers sold as tourist gifts) that sullied the reputation of craft beer in Japan in the 1990s. Their stout and "Karumina" Belgian strong ale (200 ml, 819 yen) also have good reputations. Be sure to check out Aoki-san's "hopulator", a homemade machine that allows him to add extra hops to any beer he chooses! No smoking.

DIRECTIONS: Ryōgoku Station (Sobu Line), West Exit: Turn left away from the taxi rank, cross the small road and walk down the left side of the larger road. Turn left after Petit Rosa. It is about 70 yards on your right. Ryōgoku Station (Ōedo Line), Exit A5: Across the road there is a 7-Eleven convenience store. Popeye is about 500 yards down the road to the left of that store.

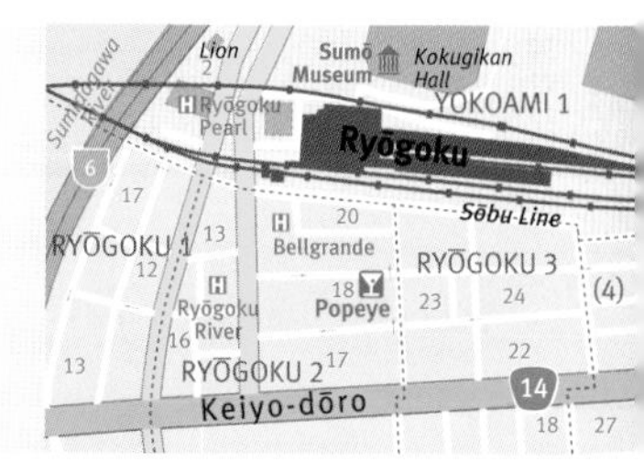

The Aldgate ジオールゲイト 03-3462-2983 www.the-aldgate.com

3F, Shin-iwasaki Building, 30-4 Udagawa-chō, Shibuya-ku, Tōkyō
東京都渋谷区宇田川町 30-4 新岩崎ビル 3F
Open: Weekdays 6 pm–2 am; weekends and national holidays 5 pm–2 am Booking recommended? No
Credit cards? No English menu? Yes Cover charge: No

To think I nearly didn't include the Aldgate in this guide! Chris Phillips introduced me to this superb little pub in Shibuya, and it is now among my favorite bars in Tōkyō. First things first, the Cornish pasties are great big meat bombs of delight—no sogginess or grease about them, just pregnant crusts filled with good-quality meat and potato in a pool of spicy beans. They have some nice meat-free dishes as well. The Aldgate is a British-style pub. They have a large collection of classic British rock and always carry British beers among their 19 draft pints ("Abbot Ale," "Old Speckled Hen"), but it was here that my education in Japanese craft beer began with the "Aldgate Ale" (see page 134), a house ale made for the Aldgate by Swan Lake beer in Niigata prefecture (www.swanlake.co. jp; the brewery itself is called Hyoko Yashiki no Mori). The "Aldgate Ale" seems to be a simple renaming of the "Swan Lake Amber Ale," and its refreshing balance of caramel sweetness and hoppy, citrusy bitterness has made it one of my favorite Japanese pints. The Aldgate's house "Harly Porter" is a rebranding of Swan Lake's porter. Swan Lake is usually near the top of most Japanese craft beer drinkers' favorite breweries. The Aldgate also offer interesting guest ales from other Japanese makers. There is a very small smoking area, well away from the main bar area, but the pub is basically smoke-free.

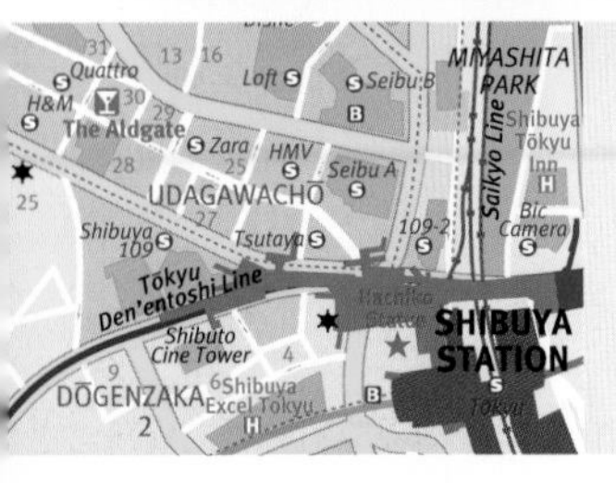

DIRECTIONS: From the Hachikō statue (a statue of a dog used as a landmark in Shibuya's chaos): Walk up to the left of Starbucks; pass the HMV store on your right and McDonald's on your left. It is on your right, one block before the "Book Off" store.

Thrashzone

045-514-9947 www.beerdrinkinginternational.com

2F Paseri bldg, 2-19-8 Tsuruya-chō, Kanagawa-ku, Yokohama, 221-0835
〒221-0835 横浜市神奈川区鶴屋町 2-19-8 パセリビル 2F
Open: 6 pm–2 am; closed Sunday Booking recommended? No Credit cards? No English menu? No
Cover charge: No

When I first heard of Thrashzone, a thrash metal bar which served good beer, I had a vision of a huge sweat-dripping barn of a place filled with angry young men and hormones and pounding music. The music does pound but, in fact, Thrashzone is not a very intimidating place at all. I hesitate to say that it is a very Japanese take on a thrash metal bar (Japan does have sweat-dripping barns of its own), but it is more like a specialist craft beer bar with a thrash metal theme than the other way around. When I visited with Chris Phillips, the pews next to us were taken by an English class in which a group of very polite-looking Japanese people were being taught the language through the medium of thrash: "Now, repeat after me, 'I'm a motherf!@#$ing motherf%!@#$...'" Very Thrashzone! The top West Coast US craft brewers tend to be very well represented on the beer menu (maybe the assertive style goes well with the "Slayer" and "Megadeth"), but Ōsaka's Minoh beer (see page 146), the bitter, yeasty Nagahama Ale and Shinano beer all have regular spots among the nine draft beers. Shinano (www.valley.ne.jp/~beer470/) is a small- to medium-sized craft brewery in Nagano prefecture. They are probably best known for their rounded, roasted "Kurohime" stout that is named after Mount Kurohime from which Shinano's water runs. However, the brew being served at Thrashzone was their "Shinano Dragon Ale," a medium-bodied amber ale with a nice bitter finish. Shinano play "healing music" to their brews while they are fermenting and maturing, which must make the heavy metal at Thrashzone so much more traumatic for the beers as they wait to be poured. No smoking.

DIRECTIONS: JR Yokohama Station, West Exit. The Sheraton Hotel should be ahead of you. Take the road to the right of the Yodobashi store (it is opposite the Sheraton at the far side of the taxi and bus ranks). Continue down that road until you meet a T-junction. Turn right and it is about 20 yards after the first turning to your right.

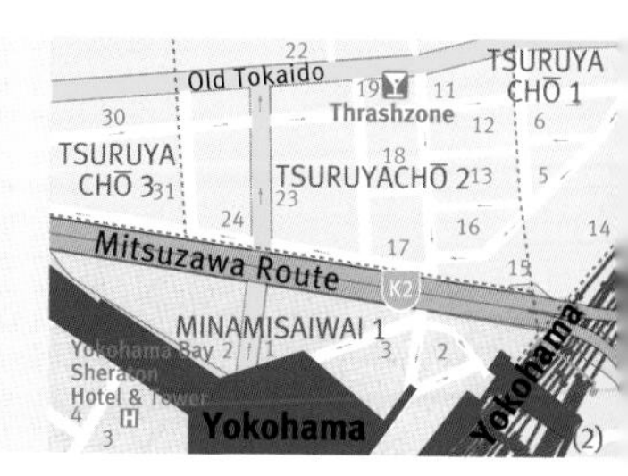

Towers タワーズ 03-3272-8488 www.towers-beer.com

2-8-10 Yaesu, Chūō-ku, Tōkyō, 104-0028
〒104-0028, 東京都中央区八重洲 2-8-10
Open: Monday–Friday 5.30 pm–11 pm; Saturday 2 pm–6 pm; closed Sunday and national holidays
Booking recommended? No Credit cards? No English menu? No Cover charge: No

Yasushi Satō's tiny standing bar serves a limited selection of well-kept beers. There are normally seven types of draft beer on tap, predominantly from Japanese craft brewers. When I visited, Satō-san had "Yona Yona" (see page 155, 900 yen/pint) on a hand pump and Baird's "Rising Sun Pale Ale" at a very cheap 800 yen for a pint (see page 155). The small plates of snacks were not elaborate, but neither were the prices: chips in salsa for 300 yen or Satō-san's homemade pickles for 300 yen.

He is optimistic but level-headed about Japanese craft beer: "The industry has only been around a few years. At the start, 80 percent of it did not taste good. Even now, if you go to a beer festival, your first glass can sometimes be not that great, but people increasingly know who is making the quality beer and they seek them out." When I visited, he was serving an interesting "Oze no Yukidoke" white *weizen* (1,000 yen), with lovely coriander and orange flavors. "Oze no Yuki-doke" is actually a well-known sake brand out of Gunma prefecture (www.ryujin.jp). It literally means "Thaw in Oze." (Oze is a very beautiful stretch of moorland known for its wild flowers and majestic mountain scenery.) The beer brewing sideline started in 1997 and is now well established (it is referred to variously by the Oze brand name or "Ginjō Kura Beer" or "Ryujin beer"). They also make a brown *weizen*, stout and the "Heavy Heavy" barley wine, but their most celebrated style is probably India pale ale (IPA). "They make my favorite IPAs in Japan," says Chris Phillips. "Their beauty is that the young brewer changes his dry hopping each time he makes a special batch for someone. He changes the hops and the bitterness and flavor, but it is always a good IPA."

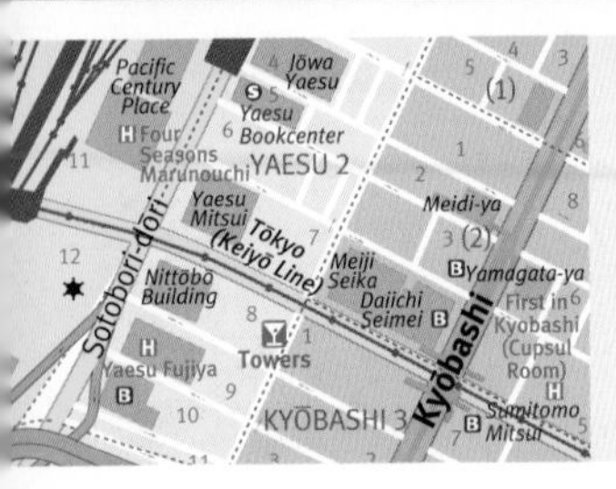

DIRECTIONS: Kyōbashi Station, Exit 3. Carry on walking up Kajibashi-dōri in the same direction you came up the stairs. Turn left at the FedEx Kinkos building. It is on your right—a tiny bar about 20 yards down the road.

Ushitora うしとら 03-3485-9090 www.ushitora.jp

2F Sankyū Biru, 2-9-3 Kitazawa, Setagaya-ku, Tōkyō
東京世田谷区北沢 2-9-3 三久ビル 2F
Open: 5 pm–2 am; closed Tuesday Booking recommended? No Credit cards? All major cards
English menu? No Cover charge: No

Ushitora opened here in March 2006 and was so successful that the two young owners, Akio Terasaki and Shinsuke Yoshida, opened an annex in July 2009. In the original bar, they have 20 beers on tap and three hand pumps, with a good selection of quality beers from Japan and the US, plus a few from Europe. The extension, with 15 more beers on its menu, has given them a quite formidable range. It is not yet enough to seriously rival Popeye, but who can drink 70 beers in a night anyway? The Japanese brews tend to occupy about 80 percent of the taps, except when a big shipment of foreign ales has just come in (about twice yearly), when the ratio drops to about half and half. Terasaki-san said they make a point of not replacing an empty guest beer keg with the same beer, so no two visits to Ushitora are going to be identical. They always have "Yona Yona" on one of the hand pumps (US pint 980 yen, see page 149) and the house ale is specially made for them by Baird beer (see page 155). It changes with the seasons—a hoppy dark ale in winter and something lighter, often with citrus flavors, in summer (US pint 1,260 yen). The clientele tends to be young, but not oppressively trendy. There is no smoking in the smaller standing bar.

DIRECTIONS: Shimokitazawa Station (Odakyū Odawara/Keiō Inokashira lines), South Exit. Turn left away from the railway bridge and right at the Ozaki supermarket. Turn left around the side of the supermarket. It is on the second floor of the building facing you at the end of the road.

Award-winning Japanese Whiskies

The hard spirit and amphetamine-raddled existentialist philosopher Jean-Paul Sartre was an early convert to Japanese whisky. On a visit to Japan in 1966, as Japan's student revolution began to tear the society apart, Sartre pronounced the food inedible but developed a great liking for the country's take on whisky, according to his biographer David Drake. The French philosopher and his partner, the feminist Simone de Beauvoir, swigged through liters of the stuff during their visit. De Beauvoir was also impressed, noting in her memoir *All Said and Done* that on one occasion they had ordered a bottle to their hotel room, and pronounced it "very good."

Ian Fleming advocated the Japanese version in the 1964 James Bond novel *You Only Live Twice*, and the heiress and art collector Peggy Guggenheim was fond of decanting cheap Japanese brands into Scotch bottles for her parties. Some of these early endorsements have a touch of condescension about them ("By Jove, it's actually quite decent!") but nowadays it is possible to say, quite categorically, that no serious whisky critic would challenge the Japanese drink's right to be considered on an equal footing with Scottish, North American and Irish products.

A series of victories in international competitions over the past decade has washed away any tendency to patronize the Japanese distillers. The dam broke in 2001 when a 10-year-old Yoichi whisky won the "Best of the Best" award in an

Nikka Whisky's "Yoichi" 1987 single malt won the 2008 World Whisky Award for the best single-malt whisky in the world. Japan has won a series of top international prizes over the past decade.

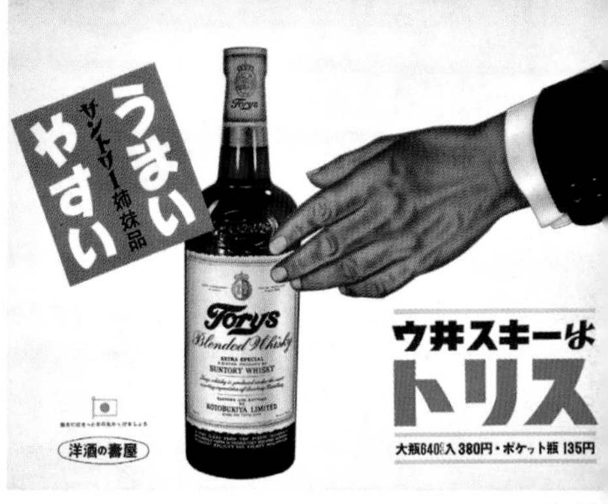

Clockwise from top left: Suntory's "Hibiki 30-year-old" whisky, winner of the 2008 World Whisky Award for the best blended whisky in the world; A pre-war Suntory label featuring naval insignia used on bottles sent to quench the Japanese Imperial Navy's thirst for whisky; Suntory's chief blender, Seiichi Koshimizu; Advertisements for Suntory's "Torys" blend in the 1950 and 1960s took a no-nonsense approach, boasting that it was "cheap and tasty"; Whisky highballs, once drunk in huge quantities by Japan's salarymen, are back in fashion among trendy younger drinkers (see page 184).

international blind tasting organized by the respected *Whisky Magazine*. Since then, the country's two top producers, Nikka (who own the Yoichi and Miyagikyō distilleries) and Suntory (Yamazaki and Hakushū), have become among the most medal-bedecked whisky makers in the world. In 2003, a "Yamazaki 12" captured a gold award at the International Spirits Challenge. The next year, the "Hibiki 30" blended whisky from Suntory won the overall trophy at the same competition and, in 2005, "Yamazaki 18" won a double gold medal at the San Francisco World Spirits Competition. The killer blow to Old World whisky snobs was struck in 2008. At the World Whisky awards in Glasgow, the Japanese not only won the prize for best single-malt whisky in the world (a "Yoichi 1987") but also the award for the world's best blended whisky ("Hibiki 30-year-old"). The rest of the world's top distilleries were left scrabbling for the minor medals.

To list all the competitive achievements of Japanese whisky makers since then would be tedious. It is sufficient to say that an international whisky competition that does not include a Japanese maker among its major awards has become the exception rather than the rule. Gold medals have not only gone to Suntory and Nikka but also to smaller Japanese whisky brands such as "Fuji Gotemba," "Ichiro's Malt" and (the now mothballed) "Karuizawa." It is not too much of a stretch to say that, if a whisky has the words "single malt" and "Made in Japan" on its label, it is almost certainly a quality product from a distillery with a sophisticated understanding of Scottish-style whisky making.

Masataka Taketsuru in 1920, at the time of his historic visit to Scotland, where he learned the secrets of whisky making.

First contacts

To understand why Japanese whisky is generally regarded as being in the Scottish tradition (and hence why it is properly spelled "whisky" rather than "whiskey"), we have to delve a little into its history.

Whisky was actually first introduced to Japan by the Americans. When Commodore Matthew Perry came in his "Black Ships" to negotiate the opening of Japan in 1854, he brought a barrel and 110 additional gallons of American whiskey as a gift for the Emperor and his subjects. By all accounts, a good time was had by all. The *New York Observer* reported that the "toddy flowed" at a meeting of US officers and senior *samurai*, one of whom "became quite merry, hugging the Commodore most affectionately in his happy moments." But, once the Americans had gone home, the smitten Japanese were left with no idea how to make the golden spirit. There was a very limited supply of foreign imports in the early Meiji period, so the slack was taken up by domestically produced imitation "whiskies." These were "whisky" only in the broadest sense of being a bottle with the word "whisky" on it, and they were part of a wider "Western alcohol" (*yōshu*) industry that capitalized on enthusiasm for the new-fangled alcohols by employing trickery in the chemistry lab rather than actually learning how to make them.

Everything about these early Japanese whiskies was fake, and bottles that survive show what might charitably be described as a "playful" relationship with authenticity: "Holy" whisky proclaimed itself a "Special Quality Old Scotch Whisky" but, immediately below that, proudly boasted that it was "distilled and bottled" by the Eigashima company in Japan. "Lady Brand," displaying what looks like a European operatic diva against a backdrop of the hills of lowland Scotland, was also an "Old Scotch Whisky." There is a press account in 1923 of a new "Scotch whisky" being sold in Japan from "Leith, London."

Fortunately for our livers, none of this rotgut survives, but we get a sense of its potency from a bizarre encounter in 1918 in Hakodate, Hokkaido. Japan was not much involved in World War I (then playing out its last macabre act in Europe), but one day in September two troop ships full of 3,700 American soldiers sailed over the horizon and into Hakodate port. The soldiers were destined to spend the next two years in Siberia fighting Bolsheviks, one of the more obscure chapters in US military history, but that night they had only two things on their minds—women and alcohol.

One enterprising bar enlisted a foreigner with a sense of humor to try to pull in the troops, erecting a sign in English to welcome the visitors: "Notice!! Having lately been refitted and preparations have been made to supply those who give us a look-up, with Worst of Liquors and Food at a reasonable price, and served by the Ugliest Female Savants that can be Procured. This establishment cannot boast of a proprietor, but is carried on by a Japanese lady whose ugliness would stand out even in a crowd. The Cook, when his face is washed, is considered the best looking of the company."

Major Samuel L. Johnson, who had been sent ashore with the enlisted men, was soon back on the transports, reporting chaotic scenes to his fellow officers. "All the cheap bars have Scotch whiskey made in Japan," he said. "If you come across any, don't touch it. It's called Queen George, and it's more bitched up than its name. It must be 86 percent corrosive sublimate proof, because 3,500 enlisted men were stinko fifteen minutes after they got ashore. I never saw so many get so drunk so fast."

Captain Kenneth Roberts, who was part of a team sent to round up the paralytic soldiery, described the scene: "Intoxicated soldiers seemed to have the flowing qualities of water, able to seep through doorways, down chimneys, up through floors." It was not just enlisted men; some of the officers also fell victim to Queen George and were later disciplined. Roberts and his men spent hours trying to get the troops back on the boats: "When we slowly edged a score of Khaki-

Suntory's founder Shinjirō Torii (right) and his son Keizo Saji (left) built Suntory into the biggest force in Japanese whisky.

The bottling line at Yamazaki in the 1930s.

clad tosspots from a dive and started them toward the ships, then turned to see if we had overlooked anyone, the room would unbelievably be filled with unsteady doughboys, sprung from God knows where, drunkenly negotiating for the change of American money or the purchase of just one more boll of Queen George."

The ships hurriedly left Hakodate without the coal they had come for. At the next port, Otaru, only a few troops were allowed off. Queen George seems to have had her say there too—an American soldier smashed a bottle over the head of a Japanese policeman.

Stealing Scotland's secrets

The official history of Japanese whisky begins about two months before the debacle in Hakodate. Masataka Taketsuru is now a legendary figure in Japanese whisky—the man whose knowledge helped found the two great rival empires of Japanese whisky, Suntory and Nikka. In July 1918, as he boarded the SS *Tennyo Maru*, with his colleagues and family waving from the dockside, he was just a promising 24-year-old chemist with a reputation for making unexplosive fake spirits. His bosses had decided the time had come to try to find out how whisky was properly made and had picked him out for an audacious mission—to travel to Scotland and bring back the secrets of Scotland's distillers.

After first taking courses at the colleges in Glasgow, to try to improve his English and give himself a basis in the theory of distilling, he began his mission in earnest on Thursday, April 17, 1919, when he boarded the train to Elgin, near the heart of the famous Speyside whisky region. He later recalled singing Japanese traditional songs to calm himself on the journey. At first, he only met with frustration. He was turned away by three hotels because, as he put it with typical understatement, "Some people were afraid of foreigners," and when he approached the famous whisky authority J. A. Nettleton for guidance on learning the whisky trade, Nettleton demanded a prohibitive fee.

Taketsuru was not so easily beaten. He obtained a map of Speyside's distilleries and began knocking on each of their doors. Eventually, at the Longmorn distillery, 5 km south of Elgin, he found someone willing to help. J. R. Grant, Longmorn's general manager, agreed to give him a week's work experience. Taketsuru wrote down everything he learned, from the weekly wage of the cooper to the precise temperatures at which maltose and dextrose were created during mashing. He then spent three weeks working at the Bo'ness distillery in West Lothian in 1919, and secured a five-month stay in the Hazelburn distillery at Campbeltown in 1920. His voluminous notes were to become the bible of Japanese whisky distilling. In the meantime, Taketsuru had fallen in love with the daughter of a local doctor. When Taketsuru set off on the long journey back to Japan in October 1920, he took with him not only a comprehensive record of Scotch distilling but a 23-year-old Scottish wife, Jesse Roberta Cowan, whom he called "Rita." She spent the rest of her life in Japan, a period spanning a world war with her home country.

Upon arriving back in Japan, Taketsuru was frustrated to find his old employers uninterested in putting his ideas into practice. However, the visionary businessman Shinjiro Torii, founder of the empire that would become Suntory, saw the opportunity and employed Taketsuru to set up the first proper whisky distillery in Japan at Yamazaki, near Kyōto, in 1924. Yamazaki's first whisky hit the shelves in 1929 under the brand name "Shirofuda" (White Label), which is still sold in Japan.

Ten years later, Taketsuru set up his own business, which was to become Suntory's great rival Nikka. He bought land at Yoichi on Hokkaido and that distillery's first whisky was released in 1940. Much of the demand in those early days appears to have been from the military and particularly the Japanese Imperial Navy, which drank whisky like the British Navy drank rum. Yoichi was actually designated as an Imperial Navy installation during the war. Hiroyoshi Miyamoto, general manager of Suntory's Yamazaki distillery, says: "When we were at war, every industry had to provide all of their goods to the military. It was only because the Navy wanted whisky to be made that the industry could survive." For the rest of the population, whisky was a complete mystery, according to Tatsurō Yamazaki, the 89-year-old owner of Bar Yamazaki in Sapporo (see page 216): "A tiny minority of the elite—top businessmen and bureaucrats in Marunouchi—seem to have known about whisky before the war. Alcohol meant sake and few people knew that whisky was drunk in the Navy. We were only told about it after the war."

Modern Japanese whisky

By the 1970s, whisky was everywhere. If you were to choose a drink to symbolize the rapid economic growth in the four decades after the war, it would have to be whisky. It started off as an unattainable object of desire, drunk only by the occupation forces and rich businessmen. "Immediately after the war, the Scotch whisky which was most generally known was Johnnie Walker Red and Black. Black was the symbol of luxury," says Yamazaki-san, who at that time was serving American servicemen in Tōkyō clubs. "White Horse was also quite well known and other labels started to come in." But the general poverty and punitive import taxes kept this whisky well out of the reach of most Japanese. The real shift came in 1955, with the opening of a chain of reasonably priced whisky shops—the Torys Bars. "People started to drink whisky mainly because Suntory's Torys whisky was so cheap. It was almost the same price as a cup of coffee at a Torys bar," says Yamazaki-san.

In 1962, only about 50,000 kl of whisky was consumed a year. Thirty years later, 380,000 kl was being drunk, more than three liters of spirit for every person (adult and child) in the population. With protectionist policies limiting foreign imports to the very well-healed, it was the domestic industry, led by Nikka and Suntory, that met much of the demand. The distilleries that are now winning gold medals for their single malts were set up to slake a raging domestic thirst for a more ordinary dram, sold for a few yen a shot. In 1956, the Karuizawa distillery came on line and, between 1969 and 1973, the opening of Miyagikyō distillery by Nikka, Fuji Gotemba by Kirin, and the enormous Hakushū distillery by Suntory increased Japan's production massively. Japan was the fourth biggest producer of whisky in the world, behind Scotland, the US and Canada. It produced three times more whisky than Ireland.

Throughout this development, Japanese whisky stayed remarkably loyal to the Scottish roots put down by Taketsuru. There have been experiments with Japanese Bourbons but, by and large, Japanese whisky has always tried to be Scottish, using Scottish methods and ingredients. The product has not always been as pure as it is now. In the 1960s, Japanese blended whiskies often contained neutral spirit rather than grain whisky, and there are accounts of significant

Clockwise from top: A pre-war photograph of Yamazaki distillery; Yamazaki single malt; The distilling hall at Yamazaki.

amounts of wine being found in some bottles. However, during this period, hundreds of distillery workers were sent in the footsteps of Taketsuru to learn their craft in Scotland, building a reserve of knowledge.

The Japanese mass whisky market has declined precipitously since the early 1980s. Younger generations have looked elsewhere for their drink, notably *shōchū*. The old protectionist rules have gone, allowing extremely high-quality Scotch on to Japan's shop shelves. It is in this hyper competitive environment that the Japanese producers have developed the excellent products that are now receiving international attention. The fourth largest whisky industry in the world is now competing fiercely for an increasingly sophisticated domestic market and a still-nascent export market, which demands the highest quality.

The distilleries

There are seven active single-malt whisky distilleries in Japan.

Yamazaki (Suntory whisky; www.theyamazaki.jp/en/). Yamazaki (山崎) began operations in 1924 and is the oldest Japanese malt whisky distillery. It lies just outside Kyōto at the confluence of the Katsura, Kizu and Uji rivers, nestled up against

Storing whisky during Japan's relatively hot summers raises unique challenges.

forested hills rising out of the Kansai plain. The area has long been famous for its superb water. The 16th-century tea ceremony master Sen no Rikyu had his tea house just down the road because he esteemed it so highly. Yamazaki has 12 pot stills in a variety of designs and, like many of the big Japanese distilleries, can make whisky in a wide range of styles. This is necessary because Japanese distillers, unlike their Scottish counterparts, do not commonly trade whisky between companies to balance their blends. Everything has to be made in-house. However, in general, Yamazaki single malts tend towards a soft and delicate fruitiness, often with sweet spice and incense aromas. There is quite a lot of use of Japanese oak casks (*mizunara*) at the attached Ohmi aging cellar, lending distinctive incense, vanilla and coconut flavors to some of the whisky. Yamazaki's products, as well as those from Hakushū, are used in Suntory's famous "Hibiki" blended whisky, which seems to pick up an international award nearly every year (and is probably best known in the West for its starring role in Sophia Coppola's film *Lost in Translation*).

Yoichi (Nikka whisky; www.nikka.com/eng/distilleries/yoichi.html). Set up 10 years after Yamazaki, Yoichi (余市) is Japan's other iconic pre-war distillery. It is perched on the northern shore of Japan's northern island, Hokkaido. When I visited in February, it was blanketed in several feet of snow. The sight of the silent warehouses, long icicles hanging from their eaves and almost swallowed into the landscape by the snowdrifts, is my abiding memory of Yoichi. The cold climate means that its whiskies mature more slowly than those from the distilleries on the main island. Yoichi still uses old coal-fired pot stills, a method which Taketsuru learned in Scotland but which has now died out in that country. None of Japan's main distilleries produce very peaty whiskies compared to the peat monsters that come out of some parts of Scotland, but Yoichi is perhaps closest to that style. Its whiskies are the most uncompromising and "masculine" of Nikka and

Suntory's products, but there are often also rich stewed fruit, nutty and coffee notes to balance the assertiveness.

Chichibu (Ichiro's Malt/Venture Whisky). At the other end of the scale from the old Yoichi and Yamazaki distilleries is Chichibu (秩父), which was only set up in 2008. Compared to Suntory and Nikka's operations, the Saitama distillery has a tiny production capacity (one-thirtieth of Yamazaki's). At the time of writing, it was only just on the brink of releasing its first properly mature whisky (all whisky must be matured for three years). But the Chichibu experiment is one of the most important things to happen to Japanese whisky in the last decade. We already know that the owner, Ichirō Akuto, makes great whisky. He comes from an old sake brewing family, which started distilling whisky at the Hanyū distillery from about 1980. Unfortunately, the domestic whisky market started to implode during the 1980s, and the firm was forced into bankruptcy in 2000. Akuto-san has led a phoenix-like rebirth, selling whiskies from the old Hanyū stock under the "Ichiro's Malt" brand, with clever playing card names for each whisky ("Queen of Hearts," "Two of Clubs"). The whisky is excellent and Japanese whisky fans are waiting with bated breath for what will come out of Chichibu. So far, the few tastes of unmatured spirit that have been released by the distillery have, according to the experts, shown much promise (see page 189).

Hakushū (Suntory whisky; www.suntory.co.jp/whisky/hakushu/). Nestled in the southern Japanese Alps, Hakushū (白州) is one of the loftiest malt whisky distilleries in the world. At over 2,200 feet above sea level, it is nearly twice as high as Scotland's highest at Braeval. The distillery takes its water from beneath Kai-Komagatake (Pony Mountain), the impressive granite peak on whose forested coattails it sits. During the heady days of the early 1980s, according to the whisky writer Ulf Buxrud, a total of 36 pot stills on two separate sites in the forest at Hakushū were in full production. Only 12 stills at the Hakushū east site are currently working. Like other Japanese distilleries, Hakushū produces whisky in a variety of styles but many of its single malts have a clean, playful taste, with sweet, fruity flavors often balanced by well-controlled peppery or aniseed tastes.

Above: Nikka whisky's Yoichi distillery in Hokkaido is blanketed in snow for much of the winter.
Below: The gatehouse at Yoichi.
Right, clockwise from left: Yoichi's coal-fired pot stills; the coal room; the control room.

NIKKA WHISKY

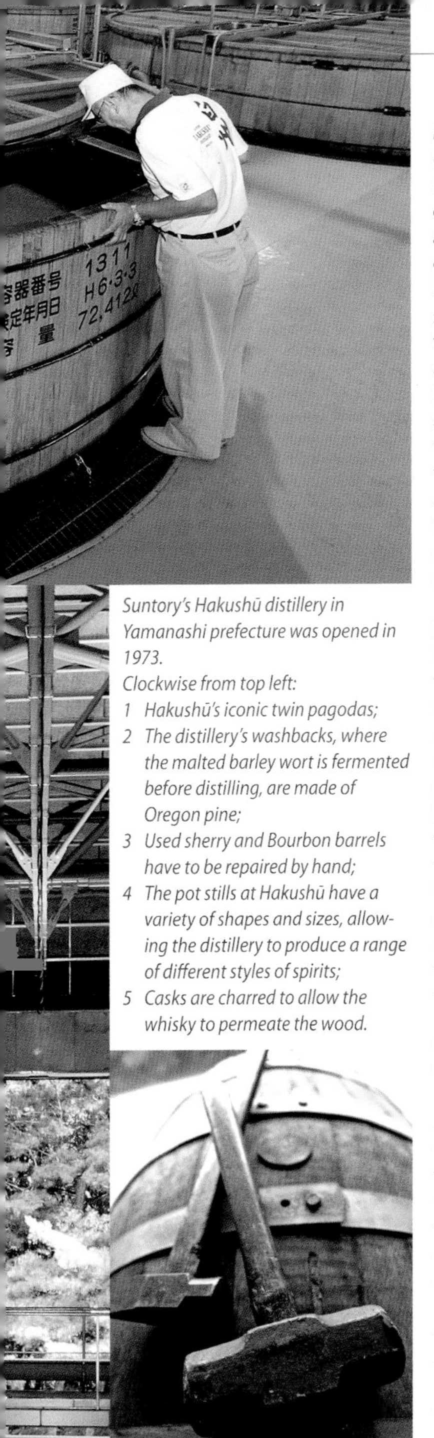

Suntory's Hakushū distillery in Yamanashi prefecture was opened in 1973.
Clockwise from top left:
1. *Hakushū's iconic twin pagodas;*
2. *The distillery's washbacks, where the malted barley wort is fermented before distilling, are made of Oregon pine;*
3. *Used sherry and Bourbon barrels have to be repaired by hand;*
4. *The pot stills at Hakushū have a variety of shapes and sizes, allowing the distillery to produce a range of different styles of spirits;*
5. *Casks are charred to allow the whisky to permeate the wood.*

Miyagikyō
(Nikka whisky; www.nikka.com/eng/distilleries/miyagikyo.html). The Miyagikyō (宮城峡) distillery opened in 1969, just before Suntory's Hakushū, and its pot stills provide much of the malt and grain whisky that goes into Nikka's mass-market blended brands. It also makes some elegant single-malt whisky. Taketsuru chose the site while touring the Miyagi countryside. He was immediately convinced that the location, sandwiched between the Hirosegawa and Nikkawagawa rivers and surrounded by mountains, was perfect for whisky distilling. There is a plaque by the Nikkawagawa where he made the decision. (The coincidence of the name of the river and Nikka's own is just that.) Miyagikyō's whisky is often, though not always, markedly softer and milder than the product from Yoichi.

Fuji Gotemba (Kirin whisky; www.kirin.co.jp/brands/sw/gotemba/index.html). As iconic locations go, it is hard to beat a distillery hidden in forest at the foot of Mount Fuji. At over 610 meters above sea level, Fuji Gotemba's elevation means it is cooler than the great Kantō plain stretching to its east. Down in the flatlands, it is hot and humid in summer but the distillery's temperatures range only a few degrees higher than the Scottish distilleries. Fuji Gotemba takes its water from rain and melted snow running off Mount Fuji itself. Its single malts, sometimes labeled "Fuji Gotemba" (富士御殿場) and sometimes "Fuji Sanroku" (富士山麓), tend to be relatively light and are elegantly balanced.

White Oak (Eigashima Shuzō; www.ei-sake.jp). White Oak is a tiny distillery by the sea in Hyōgo prefecture. Eigashima Shuzō, the sake and *shōchū* company in charge, has a plausible claim to being the second oldest Japanese whisky company. They began selling whisky in 1919, after Suntory's "Torys" whisky was first marketed, but before the Yamazaki distillery was built. (Shinjiro Torii seems to have used imported whisky or whisky imitations before building Yamazaki.) Eigashima (江井ヶ嶋) do not claim to have been making authentic whisky themselves from that date, but their operation certainly has a long history. They also have a fantastic location, right next to the sea. If this were a Scottish distillery, they would have daubed their seaside rooftops with their brand name and be furiously using their charismatic location in their advertising, but the folks at Eigashima seem to prefer an understated public image. For a long time, they produced only cheap blends, but in 2007 they quietly released their first single malt, an eight-year-old spirit branded "Akashi." It had a nice rounded licorice and bread flavor. In January 2010, they followed this up with a five-year-old "Akashi" and released a limited-edition 12-year-old spirit in the spring of 2010. President Mikio Hiraishi says he intends to switch much of their production to premium single-malt whisky in future. Watch this space.

The seven active distilleries above account for the vast majority of Japanese whisky on the market, but there is one prominent name missing: **Karuizawa** (Kirin whisky). Like Fuji Gotemba, Karuizawa distillery (軽井沢) is owned by the Kirin

Below: Some of the whisky in Yamazaki's storehouses dates back to the early 1920s.
Bottom: The White Oak distillery in Hyōgo prefecture is Japan's most maritime distillery.
Right: Mikio Hiraishi, who runs White Oak, recently launched a new range of premium whiskies.

The Karuizawa distillery in Nagano prefecture has been mothballed by the Kirin group, a significant loss to the industry.

group, which acquired it as part of a takeover of Mercian wines in 2006. Unlike Fuji Gotemba, however, it is not currently in regular production. Tours of the distillery can be arranged and there is a small staff keeping it in working order, but what distillation there is seems to be for maintenance or one-off projects. This is a pity because it is fair to say that Karuizawa has a stronger international reputation than Fuji Gotemba. Its malts are still commonly available in good liquor stores in Japan, and also in independent bottlings distributed abroad (for instance, the excellent Number One Drinks Company range at www.one-drinks.com). The distillery, in a populated area to the west of the town, sits somewhat insecurely on the southern slopes of Mount Asama, the island of Honshu's most active volcano. Some of Karuizawa's malts can be very tense and restrained but others are explosive, with tremendously rich and complex flavors. Like Mount Asama, they are unpredictable and rarely boring.

Other distillery names that you might see on shop shelves are Shinshū, owned by Hombō distillers, who own the Mars whisky brand. Shinshū was not operational at the time of writing but Hombō did have a plan to repair the stills and bring it back on stream in 2011; Chita, a Suntory grain whisky distillery south of Nagoya, which occasionally puts out a single-grain whisky; Monde whisky, a Yamanashi wine maker that has been known to dabble, so far unsuccessfully, in single-malt whisky making; Nishinomiya, a defunct Nikka grain whisky distillery in Hyōgo prefecture, which made the Nikka grain whisky currently on the market; Kagoshima, a *shōchū* distillery owned by Hombō whisky, which made small amounts of Mars whisky until 1984; and Hanyū distillery, whose excellent products are still being sold under Chichibu distillery's "Ichiro's Malt" brand (see page 170) and Toa Shuzō's "Golden Horse" brand (www.toashuzo.com).

Bar Argyll バーアーガイル 03-3344-3442 www.wood-river.co.jp/argyll

3rd Floor, Daiichi Hōtoku Biru, 1-4-17 Nishi-Shinjuku, Shinjuku-ku, Tōkyō 160-0023
〒160-0023 東京都新宿区西新宿 1-4-17 第一宝徳ビル 3F
Open: 6 pm–3 am all week; occasional holidays are taken Credit cards? Most major cards
English menu? No Cover charge: 500 yen

Perched in a side street above the ballyhoo and caterwauls of the drunken crowds of Shinjuku, Bar Argyll does one thing very well—quietness. In another city, the range of 250 premium whiskies on offer at Argyll would grab attention but, in Tōkyō, where some bars run to thousands of bottles, it is verging on the understated. Manager Jumpei Oda and his bar staff are friendly but they tend to leave you in peace in this cozy 15-seat bar. As the name indicates, the emphasis is on Scottish single malts, but Bar Argyll also has a well-judged selection of excellent Japanese whiskies, mostly from the Ichiro's Malt range. There are about 16 types of premium Cuban cigars available and a steady stream of Americans from nearby hotels taking the opportunity to smoke them. You can expect to spend in the region of 4,000 yen on the cover charge, two single malts and a side dish of beef jerky (ビーフジャーキー, 750 yen) or smoked oysters (スモークオイスター, 850 yen). This is not cheap but it is not ostentatiously expensive. That would not be the Argyll way. Oda-san recommended the complex, fruity "Springbank" 10-year-old single malt from the famous whisky making area of Campbeltown in Argyll and Bute (from where Bar Argyll takes its name and inspiration). Springbank, established in 1828, is the oldest family-owned independent distillery left in Scotland and carries out every step of the whisky making process on one site, from floor malting the barley to bottling. They never chill filter their whisky or add colorings.

DIRECTIONS: Shinjuku underground station, Exit B16. Walk past the McDonald's and turn left immediately after the Big Echo karaoke parlor. It is about 100 paces past the crossroads. The sign uses the Roman alphabet.

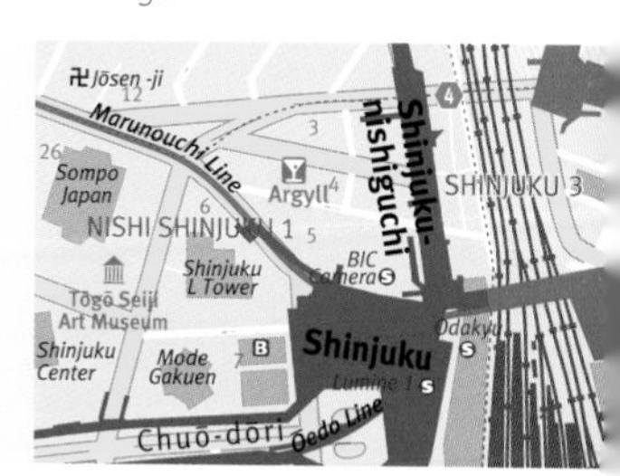

Bar Caol Ila バーカリラ 03-5428-6184 www.caolila.jp

3 MST Dōgenzaka, 1-13-3 Dōgenzaka, Shibuya-ku, Tōkyō, 150-0043 (Ginza branch: 3F Muraki Shigetake Biru, 8-6-4 Ginza, Chuo-ku, Tōkyō, 104-0061) 〒150-0043 東京都渋谷区道玄坂 1-13-3 MST 道玄坂 3 (Ginza branch: 〒104-0061 東京都中央区銀座 8-6-4 村喜・茂竹ビル 3F) Open: 7 pm–6 am; Sunday 7 pm–12 pm
Booking recommended? No Credit cards? Most major cards English menu? No Cover charge: 500 yen

This bar is a sort of Caol Ila library of record, with more than 70 versions of the Scottish whisky distillery's drams making up about half of the stock. "I am not sure whether we have the most Caol Ila in the world or not," says owner Masahide Kobayashi, "but we do have the most available in any bar in Japan and that might mean we have the most in the world." As if one bar devoted to one distillery was not enough, Kobayashi opened a second Caol Ila in Ginza in 2007 (the prices in Ginza are a little higher). Astonishingly, despite devoting his professional life to the Islay distillery, Kobayashi-san has never actually been there: "They know about me, but I haven't been able to go yet." He recommended the *smoke moriawase* (smoked egg, bacon, mushrooms etc., 1,200 yen) with a Caol Ila 12-year-old (1,000 yen), a relatively light take on an Islay whisky, with salty, medicinal notes balanced by a smooth sweetness and a dry finish. He also picked out the independently bottled John Milroy "Provenance" 1981 Caol Ila from his rarer bottlings, which he described as having unusual mango and tropical fruit tastes. I am still kicking myself for being too mean to part with the 2,000 yen for a glass.

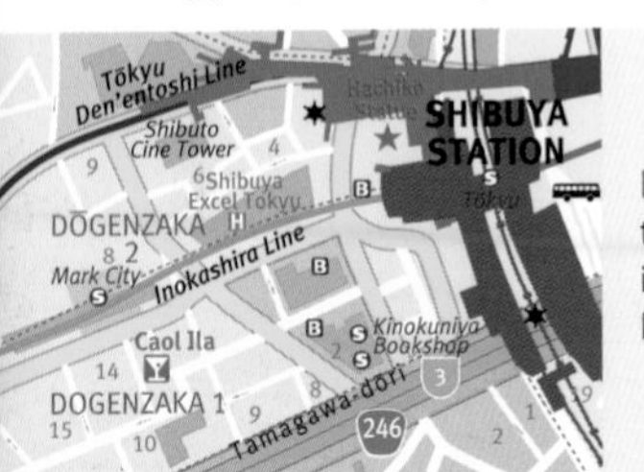

DIRECTIONS: JR Shibuya Station, West Exit. Walk on the left side of the bus station and up the large road with an elevated highway above it. Turn right at the AM/PM convenience store and take the next left. Bar Caol Ila is straight ahead of you.

Bar Main Malt バー メイン モルト 078-331-7372

B1F, No.7 Sharuman Biru, 2-10-11, Kitanagasa-dōri, Chūō-ku, Kōbe-shi, Hyōgo-ken
兵庫県神戸市中央区北長狭通 2丁目 10-11 第7シャルマンビル B1F Open: Weekdays 5 pm–1 am; Saturday 3 pm–12 pm; Sunday and national holidays 3 pm–11 pm; irregular holidays are taken
Booking recommended? No Credit cards? Most major cards English menu? No Cover charge: 500 yen

The whisky I had at Bar Main Malt was pretty foul, but I have only myself to blame. "Are you sure you want to try it? It is not the best," said barman Masahi Gotō, wavering before pouring my glass of "Usuikyō," an independent bottling of whisky bought from Yamanashi prefecture's Monde distillery (see page 176). A customer further down the bar was making jokes about the whisky being *usui*, which means "thin" in Japanese, but I was getting waves of yogurt, cloying caramel and pine needles that could certainly not be described as "thin." "Horrible," yes, but "thin," no. Not every Japanese single malt is a winner. It is part of the beauty of these massively stocked Japanese whisky bars that you can play a few B sides, as well as the disks that went platinum. Gotō-san laughed heartily and got down to the serious business of recommending a sweet, creamy twelve-year-old "Glen Ord" (800 yen). There are 1,000 bottles at Bar Main Malt, including more than 600 single malts, and the atmosphere is comfortably Old School: Gotō-san wears a white tuxedo and slicked-back hair straight out of *Casablanca*.

DIRECTIONS: JR Sannomiya Station, North Side (Central Gate). Take the second left out of the station, not the one following the train tracks, but the next one up. It is the first left after the junction with the Tokyu Hands store. Cross one road. It is on your right.

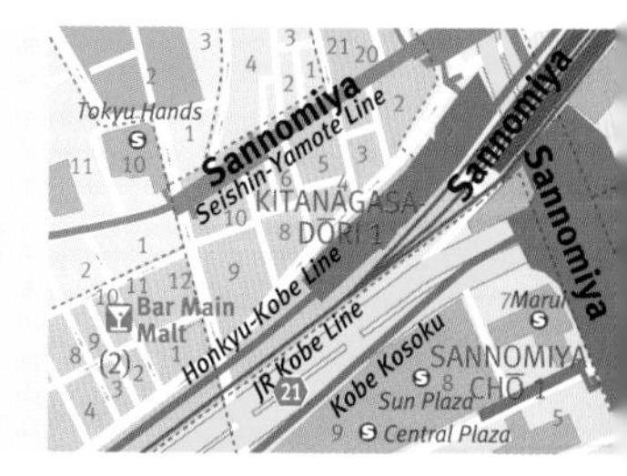

Cask カスク 03-3402-7373 www.cask.jp

B1, Main Stage Roppongi Biru, 3-9-11 Roppongi, Minato-ku, Tōkyō 106-0032
〒106-0032 東京都港区六本木 3-9-11 メインステージ六本木ビル B1
Open: 6 pm–5 am Booking recommended? No Credit cards? All major cards English menu? No
Cover charge: 1,000 yen plus a 10 percent service charge

I have a nightmare about my decision to put Cask in this guide. It goes something like this: It is about 1 am and a reader pitches up, a little the worse for wear, at Kiyoshi Shinozaki's incredibly stylish Roppongi bar. "I'll have one of those Yamshakis, please," slurs the intoxicated customer. "A Yamazaki single malt? We have many different types," replies Shinozaki-san. "Er," says the reader, "what's that one over there? The one with the 50 on. I'll have a glass of that!" "The Yamazaki 50-year-old. Are you sure, Sir? It is a rather rare and expensive whisky?" But my imagined reader is very sure and likes the Yamazaki 50 a lot and orders a couple more shots and, before he knows it, he owes 3,000 dollars! The "Yamazaki 50-year-old" is one of the rarest whiskies in the world and costs 90,000 yen a glass in Cask (at present exchange rates, just over 1,000 dollars). Of course, this is all complete fantasy. Shinozaki-san and his staff would never allow anyone to order these drinks without giving a clear idea of what they cost, but I still feel compelled to emphasize that they have some very expensive drinks among the more than 2,500 bottles of spirits and 1,200 types of whisky in stock here. Just looking at them on the shelves is oddly titillating: the "White Bowmore 1964" (35,000 yen a glass), the "Black Bowmore" (50,000 yen). What would happen in an earthquake? Unless you are an arms dealer or an oil heiress, you might want to settle for something a little more modest, like their "1991 Yoichi single cask whisky," bottled especially for Cask's fifth anniversary (1,600 yen).

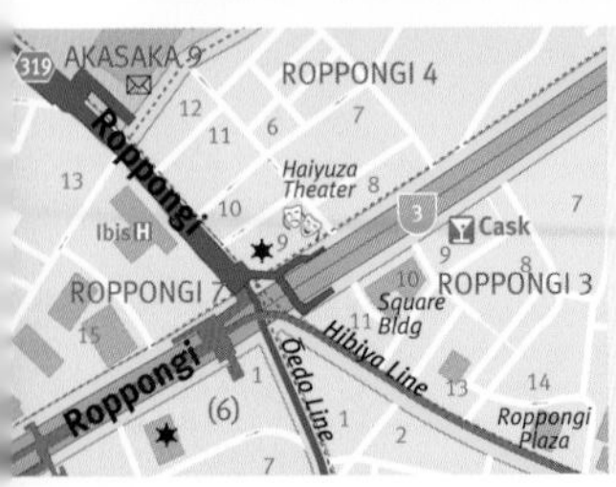

DIRECTIONS: Roppongi Station, Exit 5. Walk straight ahead. Cask is about 30 yards after the second turning to your right, with a sign in the Roman alphabet.

Hayafune バー ハヤフネ 06-7651-8007 scotchmaltwhisky.usukeba.com

B1-1 Yamato Biru No.10, 1-4-1 Higashi-shinsaibashi, Chūō-ku, Ōsaka
大阪府大阪市中央区東心斎橋 1-4-1 大和ビル 10 号館 B1-1
Open: Monday–Saturday 2 pm–11 pm; closed Sunday and national holidays Booking recommended? Yes
Credit cards? No English menu? No, but English spoken Cover charge: 500 yen after 5 pm (even if you enter earlier)

One of the first things that may strike you about Hayafune is the beautiful sound. Owner Kotaro Hayafune has installed hand-built Sonus Faber speakers, imported from Venice. The music is crystal clear (classics until 5 pm but tending toward jazz in the evenings). He invites visitors to bring along their own jazz and classical CDs to experience them in a near-perfect environment. The other great passions at Hayafune are wine (120 bottles) and, of course, single-malt whisky, of which Hayafune-san offers a collection of 300 bottles. He recommended the sardines in oil (700 yen) with a glass of the classic 16-year-old "Lagavulin" (900 yen, 30 ml), a sweet, smoky, peat bog monster of a whisky; or, if you are flush with cash, the complex smoke and dried fruit of the "Ardbeg 1975" (Single Cask 1375, 7,000 yen/glass) with a plate of the smoked oysters (900 yen). There is a nice range of cheaper malts ("Laphroaig 10," "Ardbeg 10," "Macallan 10," "Highland Park 12" and "Talisker 10") and more than 50 kinds of Japanese single malt, including whiskies from Yamazaki, Hakushū, Yoichi, Miyagikyō and Ichiro's Malt.

DIRECTIONS: Nagahoribashi Subway Station, Exit 7. Hayafune is immediately to your right, in the basement of the white-tiled Daiwa 10 building.

Helmsdale ヘルムズデール 03-3486-4220 www.helmsdale-fc.com

2F Minami Aoyama Mori Biru, 7-13-12, Minato-ku, Tōkyō
東京都港区南青山 7-13-12 南青山森ビル 2F
Open: 6 pm–6 am; Sunday and national holidays 6 pm–2 am Booking recommended? No
Credit cards? Most major cards English menu? Some English on the blackboard menus Cover charge: No

After a couple of drinks at Helmsdale, you could be forgiven for looking out of the window and expecting to see a wet, windy street in Dumfriesshire. The atmosphere is very relaxed and recreates the feel of a Scottish local remarkably well. They even have their own Sunday league football team. The food menu is filling and tasty: haggis (1,000 yen), fish and chips (1,200 yen), deep-fried mushrooms (800 yen). In winter, they serve game (wild boar BBQ, 2,500 yen; venison burger, 1,800 yen). While the draft beer departs a little from the Scottish theme ("Yona Yona," "Bass Pale Ale," "Guinness" and "London Pride"), the Scottish single malts are unrealistic only in that you would rarely find such a comprehensive selection in a normal Scottish boozer. There are about 500 bottles of whisky, plus an interesting selection of about 30 types of Japanese malt, including Ichiro's Malt, Nikka and Suntory. The house whisky is the spicy and complex "Talisker 10-year-old" (500 yen a glass), which is a very good drink indeed, and much of the rest of the malt whisky is priced from 1,000 yen. It is interesting to note that Murasawa-san's most expensive dram when I visited was the 1964 "White Bowmore." At 20,000 yen a glass, it was 15,000 yen cheaper than the same whisky being served at Cask in Roppongi, although I did not explore the serving quantities.

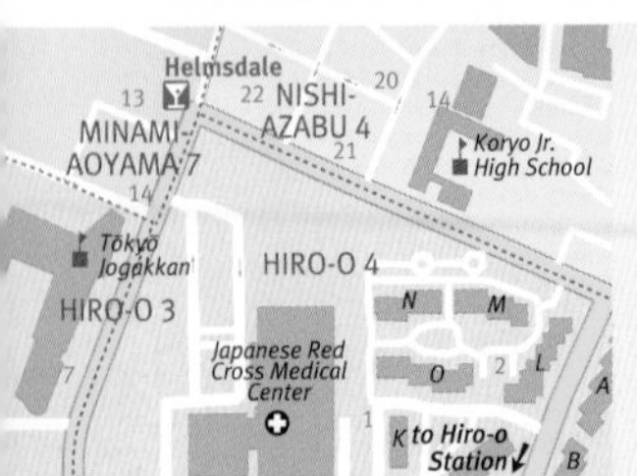

DIRECTIONS: A long walk from Hiroo Station, Exit 3. Cross over the footbridge and turn right. Turn left at the first set of traffic lights between the Claudia building and a hair salon. Take the next right and then a sharp left. Follow this road for at least 500 yards until you get to a T-junction. Helmsdale is on the second floor of the building opposite.

Hibiya Bar Whisky-S 日比谷BAR WHISKY-S 03-5159-8008 www.hibiya-bar.com

B1 Kaneko Biru, 3-3-9 Ginza, Chūō-ku, Tōkyō, 104-0061
〒104-0061 東京都中央区銀座 3-3-9 金子ビル地下 1 階
Open: 5 pm–11.30 pm (last orders 11 pm) Booking recommended? No Credit cards? Most major cards
English menu? No Cover charge: 650 yen

Hibiya Bar Whisky-S is not actually owned by Suntory but the management has a close relationship with the whisky giant, allowing them to stock one of the best ranges of Suntory whisky in Japan. It feels a lot like Suntory's equivalent of the Nikka Blenders' Bar (see page 188). Both are fairly spacious compared to the very intimate independent whisky bars and have a slightly corporate feel. The whisky is all from Suntory, but you will have the chance to drink Suntorys, but the range is priced slightly cheaper than the norm, and includes whiskies that are not available anywhere else. The "Yamazaki 10-year-old" comes in at 780 yen and a slug of Suntory's classic "Kakubin" blended whisky will set you back just 580 yen (the rectangular, tortoiseshell-pattered "Kakubin" bottle is a design icon and has been sold since 1937). They also offer several original whisky-based cocktails, including the popular "Whisky Sonic" (pear, tonic water and whisky, 690 yen). Their habit of adding historical notes to the whisky entries in their voluminous menu adds a bit of fun if you can read Japanese. The rare 1991 "Yamazaki Vintage Malt" (1,100 yen) carries a note about Carl Lewis's phenomenal performances in that year and the entry for "Hakushū 1987" reminds the drinker of the "Black Monday" Stock Exchange crash. Depending on your age, it will remind you of just how old/young these whiskies are.

DIRECTIONS: Ginza Station, Exit A10. Walk straight ahead. Take the second right just before the Tenshodo store. After Gucci, go over the crossroads. It is in the third building on your left.

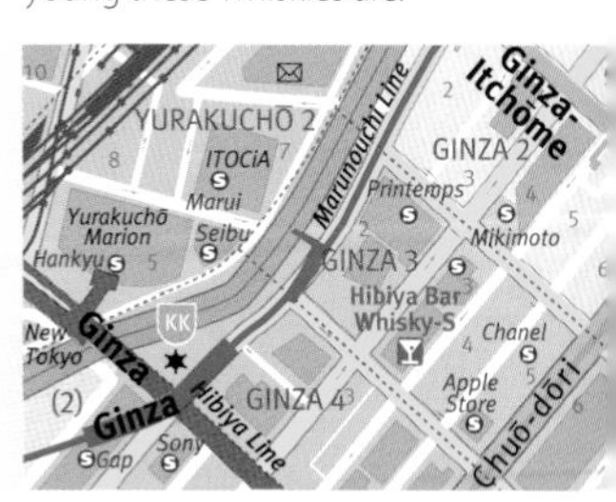

Jūsō Torys Bar 十三 トリスバー 06-6301-4826

1-2-7 Jūsō honchō, Yodogawa-ku, Ōsaka 大阪府大阪市淀川区十三本町 1 丁目 2-7
Open: 5.30 pm–12 pm (last food orders 11.30 pm, last drink orders 11.45 pm); closed Sunday and national holidays
Booking recommended? No Credit cards? Visa, Amex and JCB English menu? No
Cover charge: 200 yen

If you want to learn about Japanese whisky history you could do much worse than starting at Jūsō Torys Bar. The Torys Bar chain was vital in establishing whisky as a popular drink in Japan between the 1950s and 1980s (see page 167). This one was set up in 1956 and has survived virtually unchanged.

Sixty-year-old landlord Eiji Eigawa has been working at Torys for much of its history, having taken over the running of the bar from his father Hiroshi. "Things have changed a lot," said Eigawa-san. "In those days, Johnnie Walker was one month's salary. Japanese whisky was the only whisky people could afford. They used to drink it in a highball.... The boss used to come in and order a highball. Then, everybody with him would order a highball, right down to the newest guy in the office. It's not like that now. The youngest guy will order a single malt." Torys, Suntory's mass-market blended brand, was the ingredient of choice for those highballs (*sodawari*). You can still order a Torys *sodawari* from Eigawa-san now (460 yen). It is extremely refreshing, quite similar in effect to the lager beers now so popular with Japanese drinkers. This is how the mass-market Japanese blends like Torys were intended to be consumed, and Suntory has had success recently with an advertising campaign aimed at reviving the highball. "The taste of the Torys has changed a bit since then, though," said Eigawa-san. "There are different blenders, and the stills themselves have been altered. It used to have a harder edge. Now it is more rounded and mild." Another classic Japanese whisky style is the Suntory "Kakubin" blended whisky in a *mizuwari* (water, ice and whisky mix, 560 yen). For a snack, try the *ikayaki* (squid, 780 yen) or Eigawa-san's homemade *jikasei* corned beef (it takes him three days to make it, 600 yen).

DIRECTIONS: Juso Station, West Exit. Turn right under the covered junction opposite the Sweet Garden cake shop. It is about 50 yards on your right, with a yellow sign and Suntory regalia outside, and opposite a Korean restaurant.

K6 075-255-5009

2F Baruzu Biru, Higashi-iru, Nijo Kiyamachi, Chukyō-ku, Kyōto
京都府京都市中京区木屋町二条東入ル ヴァルズビル 2F
Open: Weekdays 6 pm–3 am; weekends 6 pm–4 am Booking recommended? No Credit cards? Most major cards
English menu? No Cover charge: 300 yen to sit in the counter area

K6 is a bit like the apocryphal story about the Forth Road Bridge in Scotland, which we were told was so large that, as soon as they had finished painting at one end, they had to start again at the other. At K6, they clean the huge stock of more than 1,300 bottles on a continuous fortnightly cycle. I staggered in here at the end of a day trudging around Kyōto. I hadn't planned to put it in this guide, but, as soon as I entered, I knew it had to be included. The stock of 600 single malts is one of the most extensive in Japan (and therefore the world). The feel of the place is smart, without being intimidating. A nice lively chatter fills the room. It is actually quite a large bar compared to most Japanese whisky establishments, but the long counter, snaking around an L-shaped room, and the clever placement of tables in the center of the space gives a feeling of intimacy. I enjoyed an Ichiro's Malt "Uniting Nations pure malt," a unique whisky made by Ichirō Akuto of Chichibu distillery, blending malts from Japan and the United Kingdom, and a conversation with two slightly inebriated women, complaining about their lecherous boss.

DIRECTIONS: Kyōto Shiyakusho-mae Station (Tōzai Line), Exit 2. Walk east along Oike-dōri. Take the second left on to Kiyamachi-dōri. Walk to the traffic lights at the T-junction. K6 is opposite you on the other side of the crossing.

Ken's Bar ケンズ バー 03-3204-2028 kensbar.ojaru.jp

B1 Maruha Biru, 1-1-7 Kabuki-chō, Shinjuku-ku, Tōkyō, 160-0021 〒160-0021 東京都新宿区歌舞伎町 1-1-7 マルハビル B1
Open: 7 pm–5 am; closed Sunday and national holidays Booking recommended? No
Credit cards? Diners, JCB, UC and NICOS English menu? No
Cover charge: 500 yen to 8 pm; 1,000 yen after 8 pm

Ken Matsuyama travels regularly to Kentucky to augment his phenomenal selection of more than 400 American whiskeys. I have visited some specialist Japanese bars where I couldn't help feeling a prick of doubt about the number of bottles they said they stocked. The selection on view does not always obviously support the claimed stock (though, whenever I have raised an eyebrow, I have always been humbled by a trip to the backroom). In this diminutive bar on the edge of the famous Golden Gai drinking district, however, there is no room for doubt. Everywhere you turn, the bottles are poking out at you. They are crammed on to improvized shelves and stand on almost every spare surface. Among the highlights Matsuyama-san picked out for me was a full range of "Maker's Marks" (Red, 700 yen per glass; Black, 1,000 yen; Gold, 1,300 yen) and a very rare bottle of "George T. Stagg" (3,000 yen a glass). He also offers a limited selection of bottled American beers and some simple snacks (ham, 800 yen; sausage, 800 yen; cheese, 700 yen). Unlike some other owners in the Golden Gai district, Matsuyama-san is welcoming to foreign customers (workers from Microsoft Japan's office in Shinjuku are among the regular visitors). The combination of good jazz and great Bourbon is a welcome respite from Tōkyō's 24-hour bustle.

DIRECTIONS: JR Shinjuku Station, East Exit. Inside the station, follow the yellow "For Kabukichō" sign. Climb the stairs beside the "Promenade to West Exit" sign. Walk straight ahead up the road to the left of the big Alta Vision Mitsubishi television screen. Cross over Route 4 and walk up its left side. Ken's Bar is on the western fringe of the Golden Gai drinking district—the second left after the 7-Eleven convenience store on Route 4 (not including the path signed to the Golden Gai). It is on the corner between the fourth and fifth roads to your left.

Malt House Islay モルトハウス アイラ 03-5984-4408 homepage2.nifty.com/islay

2F Kijima Biru, 5-22-16 Toyotama Kita, Nerima-ku, Tōkyō
東京都練馬区豊玉北 5-22-16 キジマビル 2F
Open: 6 pm–4 am; Sunday 6 pm–2 am Booking recommended? No Credit cards? Most major cards
English menu? No Cover charge: 500 yen

Malt House Islay is slightly less formal than uber-suave bars like Cask and The Crane, but marginally more dressed up than the more pub-like end of the whisky bar spectrum (Helmsdale and Speyside Way). It is a comfortable halfway house, but the alcohol doesn't have the whiff of compromize about it—2,000 bottles in total, including 1,500 Scottish single malts, 300 other whiskies and 200 other spirits and fortified wines. Owner Katsuo Suzuki regularly organizes exclusive private bottlings from some of the most famous Scottish distilleries. In 2008, for instance, he bottled "The Islay Malt" (2,500 yen a glass), a unique blend of 14-year-old whiskies from three of the great Islay distilleries: 60 percent Ardbeg whisky, 35 percent Laphroaig, and 5 percent Bowmore. An interesting touch is that every one of Suzuki-san's private bottlings is associated with a ship from the old Japanese Imperial Navy. A photograph, diagram and information about the chosen ship is printed on the bottle. "The Islay Malt" has three whiskies in it, so three ships have been chosen: the *Aoba* heavy cruiser (Ardbeg), sunk in 1945, the *Furutaka* heavy cruiser (Laphroaig), sunk at the Battle of Cape Esperance in 1942, and the destroyer *Fubuki* (Bowmore), another casualty at Cape Esperance. I have no idea how exactly Islay whiskies can be compared to large metal vessels with big guns, but then I don't know anything about the history and cultural resonance of these ships. The pictures on the bottles looked nice though.

DIRECTIONS: Nerima Station (Oedo Line), Exit A2. Walk down the road to the left of Mister Donut. Malt House Islay is near the end of the street on your right and signed Shot Bar Islay.

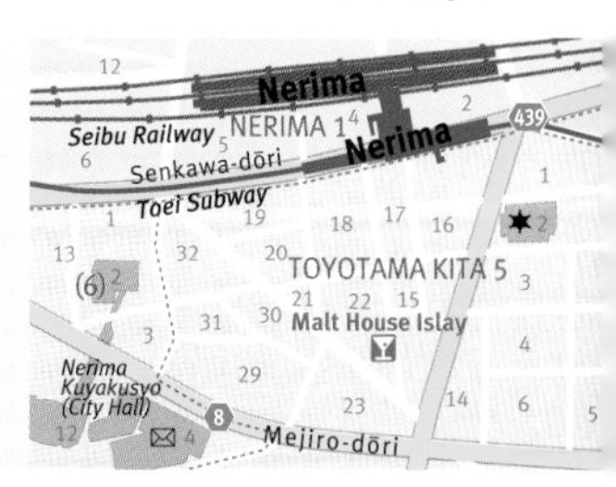

Nikka Blender's Bar

ニッカブレンダーズバー 03-3498-3338
www.nikka.com/start/shop/index.html

B1, 5-4-31, Minami-Aoyama, Minato-ku, Tōkyō, 107-8616
〒107-0062 東京都港区南青山 5-4-31 ニッカウイスキー本社ビル B1
Open: 5 pm–11.30 pm (10.30 pm last food orders, 11 pm last drink orders); closed Sunday and national holidays
Booking recommended? No Credit cards? Most major cards English menu? No Cover charge: 600 yen

The Blender's Bar is owned by Nikka, one of the Big Two Japanese distillers, and is limited to their products. That is not much of a limitation. Some of the whisky they are serving is phenomenal, and you could easily spend a week in here exploring their extensive range. It is a fairly large bar compared to the independent counter bars that are the norm in Japan and, while this means you may miss out on the cheek-by-jowl intimacy of the classic Tōkyō drinking experience, there are advantages to the anonymity afforded, especially if you are not a great whisky buff and prone to being intimidated by small, connoisseury locations. The Blender's Bar is definitely more geared to the non-expert than many of the private bars. There is a "Key malt and Coffey Grain Tasting Set" (3,000 yen), which allows you to taste a range of six of Nikka's whiskies, from a highly sherried "Yoichi" to one of the well-regarded "Nishinomiya" single-grain whiskies. Note that the Blender's Bar shares its front door with Usquebaugh, which is more of an eating establishment and, although also owned by Nikka, is run as a totally separate enterprise. Bear left as you enter to get to the Blender's Bar.

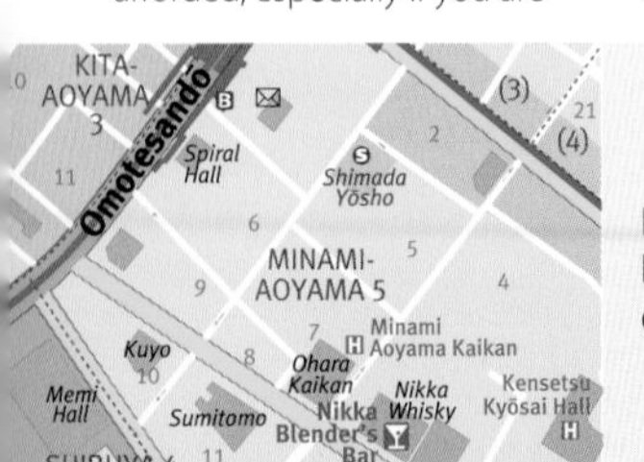

DIRECTIONS: Omotesandō Station, Exit B1. Walk straight ahead. Turn left at the Max Mara shop. The Blender's Bar is a few hundred yards down the road on your left. Watch out for the big "Nikka Whisky" sign.

Quercus Bar クエルクスバー 03-3986-8025

Ōkuma Bld. B1, 1-32-5, Higashi-Ikebukuro, Toshima-ku, Tōkyō, 170-0013
〒170-0013 東京都豊島区東池袋 1-32-5 大熊ビル B1
Open: 5 pm–4 am; Sunday and national holidays 5 pm–2 am Booking recommended? No
Credit cards? Most major cards English menu? No Cover charge: No

This little gem was introduced to me by Dr John Hawkins, a fellow whisky fan who lived in Tōkyō before returning to the UK in 2006. It is not widely known in Japanese whisky circles but, in my opinion, is one of the best whisky bars in Tōkyō. "It is really a great little place, a lot more casual and more reasonably priced than some of the other whisky bars," says Dr Hawkins. Owner Atsushi Watanabe used to work at Malt-ya, another very good Ikebukuro whisky bar (Ikebukuro 1-8-6, DKY12 Biru, 03-5952-9277) and set up here in 2001. He has the Japanese craft beers "Yona Yona" and "Tokyo Black" (see page 149) on tap as well as the English beers "Pedigree" and "London Pride." The whisky includes a formidable selection of the Japanese Ichiro's Malt whiskies. I got my first taste of the brand-new Chichibu distillery, opened in 2008, at Quercus—the "New born New Hogshead" (800 yen) and "Newborn Bourbon Barrel" (800 yen) were less than half a year old and could not be called "whisky" (whisky has to be aged at least three years). Despite the unmellowed spirit taste, Watanabe-san assured me they promised great things for the future. If you are looking for something a bit more proven, try the haggis (1,200 yen) with one of the 200-odd Scottish single malts, ranging from the "Glenfiddich 12-year-old" (400 yen) to a "1970 Oban Unblended Highland Malt Scotch" (8,800 yen per glass).

DIRECTIONS: JR Ikebukuro Station, East Exit (North). Turn to your left as you come out of the station and walk in front of the large white Bic Camera building (be careful, there are a lot of Bic Cameras in the area, but this one is distinctively white, with brand names written on it.) Quercus is on the right side of the road, four roads up, just after the Toshima Ward Office (Toshima Kuyakusho). It is in the basement below a Mos Burger.

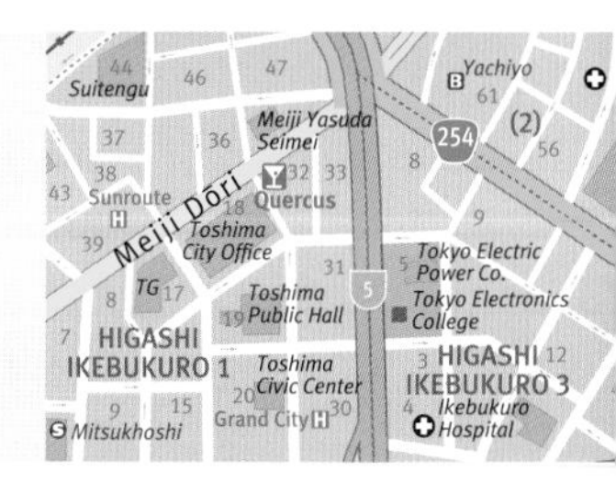

Shot Bar Zoetrope ゾートロープ 03-3363-0162 homepage2.nifty.com/zoetrope

3rd floor, Gaia Biru Number 4, 7-10-14 Nishi Shinjuku, Shinjuku-ku, Tōkyō 160-0023
〒160-0023 東京都新宿区西新宿 7-10-14 ガイアビル 4 3F
Open: 7 pm–4 am; closed Sunday and holidays Credit cards? No
English menu? No (but limited English information is available online) Cover charge: 600 yen

Zoetrope is the best place in the world to drink Japanese whisky. Atsushi Horigami set up his unique bar in 2006 after giving up his job as a salaryman with a video game company. He now has over 250 Japanese whiskies from every distillery in Japan lining his shelves, as well as more than a hundred other weird and wonderful Japanese alcohols, including Japanese rum, Japanese mead, Japanese vodka and even Japanese grappa. The bar has an interesting moving image theme. A large screen shows a continuous loop of silent movies at the end of the bar and the music is selected from modern film tracks. The bar's name is taken from a 19th-century device that prefigured the movies. It is pronounced "Zotrope" rather than the standard English "Zoetrope." Horigami-san explains: "There are two pronunciations in Japanese. One is after Francis Ford Coppola's *American Zoetrope*, the other is after a Japanese *anime*—'Zotrope.' The *anime* is definitely better known, so I went for that." There are so many whiskies available at Zoetrope that it is possible to follow any number of paths through the collection. Last time I was there, I tried the "Yamazaki 12-year-old Plum Liqueur Cask" whisky, matured in barrels that once carried Japanese *umeshu* plum wine. There was a definite hint of *umeshu* on the palate. I asked Horigami-san what he would recommend to a newcomer to Japanese whisky: "If someone came in here who really knew about whisky, I would go for the 'Yoichi 12-year-old single malt'—quite smoky and with a lot of presence—and then on to the Ichiro's Malts. If it was someone who did not have so much experience, I might go for the 'Komagatake 10-year-old' from Mars Whisky's Shinshū distillery. It is quite easy to drink and is graceful."

DIRECTIONS: Shinjuku Subway Station, Exit B16. You emerge next to the Odakyu Halc building. Climb the escalator to the right of the Odakyu Halc entrance and then the stairs to the street. Walk up the street, passing a McDonald's on your left. Cross the large road and take the second small road to your left. It is on your left.

Speyside Way スペイサイドウエイ 03-3723-7807 www.speysideway.co.jp

Mikasa Biru 5F, 1-26-9 Jiyūgaoka, Meguro-ku, Tōkyō, 152-0035
〒152-0035 東京都目黒区自由が丘 1-26-9 三笠ビル 5 階
Open: 6 pm–2 am; closes 3 am on Fridays, Saturdays and the day before national holidays; closed second Tuesday of the month Booking recommended? No Credit cards? Most major cards English menu? No Cover charge: No

As the soft, handmade chocolate melted in my mouth, I took a sip of a rich, rounded 16-year-old "BenRiach" single malt (800 yen/glass) and pondered whether to order the home-made smoked bacon (*jikasei tezukuri bacon*, 600 yen) or the cheese plate (*cheese moriawase*, 1,500 yen). Life as a drink guide writer, I reflected, was not so bad after all. Speyside Way was established in 1996 and is therefore an old stager in Tōkyō bar terms. It is fairly spacious, with an informal pub-like atmosphere and a very good whisky selection: more than 900 types of Scotch at the last count and a decent collection of about 20 Japanese single malts. Even the more expensive whiskies tend not to be wallet busters: the 35-year-old "Gleann Fearann Glas 1971," for instance, is priced at 1,800 yen. If you are interested in Japanese craft beer, Speyside Way has a limited but well-judged selection. The ubiquitous "Yona Yona" and "Tokyo Black" craft beers (see page 149) are always on the hand pumps, plus two guest beers. When I visited, the guests were the excellent "Oze no Yukidoke IPA" (see page 160) and a "Hitachino Nest White Ale" (see page 147).

DIRECTIONS: Jiyūgaoka Station (Tokyu Oimachi/Toyoko lines), Main Exit. Cross to the far right of the junction and turn right down the "No Entry" street. Walk down to the traffic lights at the crossroads and turn right. Speyside Way is about 20 yards on your left.

The Crane ザクレイン 03-5951-0090 www.the-crane.com

1F Akebono Biru, 2-3-3 Ikebukuro, Toshima-ku, Tōkyō, 171-0014
〒171-0014 東京都豊島区池袋 2-3-3 曙ビル 1F
Open: 5.30 pm–5 am Booking recommended? No Credit cards? Most major cards English menu? No
Cover charge: 15 percent service charge

Norimichi Tsurumi was only 24 when he decided to take the plunge and set up his own bar in 1991. "In those days, Japanese banks loaned out money very easily, even to a 24-year-old," he says. Almost immediately, the Japanese bubble economy burst and all the ill-considered loans started to come home to roost. Not all the risks turned out bad. Tsurumi-san's bar is still thriving two decades later and has grown into one of the classiest bars in Tōkyō. His prices are not cheap (budgeting for around 5,000 yen per person would be sensible), but the stock is astounding. Quite apart from the whisky, Tsurumi-san has a stock of 500 bottles of premium grappa made by Romano Levi, the famous artisanal Piedmont maker who died in 2008. Each label was hand-illustrated by Levi. The chance to taste spirits like his "Donna Salvatica" 2006 (3,000 yen) is rare and about to get a lot rarer, according to Tsurumi-san: "The prices have rocketed since he died, but we have been taking his stuff for 10 years. Nowhere else has a range to match ours." The stock of over 700 single-malt whiskies is even more remarkable, not only for its breadth but also for its thoroughness. For instance, Tsurumi-san has a comprehensive range of Macallan single malts from the 1940s onwards, allowing comparison between different decades. "Unfortunately, quality has changed. You can taste back to other eras. For me, the 1950s Macallans are the best, then the 1960s. The 1970s are okay, but now we have something that I don't like so much," said Tsurumi-san. You could even try a glass of "1890 Macallan" (40,000 yen/glass). Or, if you are anything like me, you could dream about doing that sort of thing in another life and content yourself with a "Highland Park 12-year-old" (1,200 yen) and a plate of Tsurumi-san's scrumptious Stilton, Mimolette, and Rochefort cheeses (2,000 yen, four types) and think yourself ridiculously extravagant. The Crane also has a selection of handmade cigars (1,300 yen–9,000 yen).

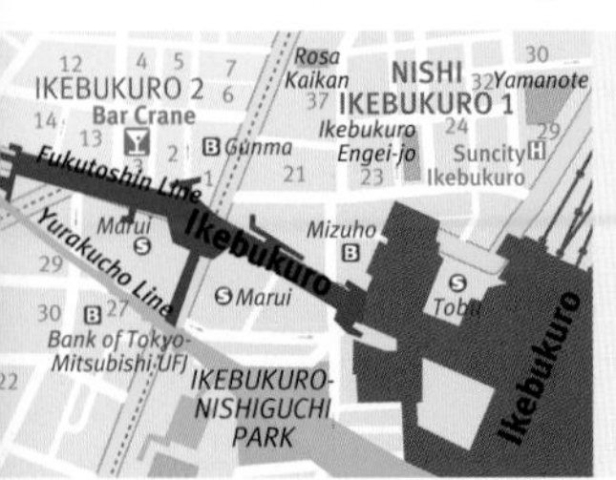

DIRECTIONS: JR Ikebukuro Station, North Exit (West side). Turn left across the crossing and continue up the road forking to the left. Cross the large intersection and continue walking in the same direction. Crane is down the second turn on your right, opposite the OI City building.

The Mash Tun マッシュタン 03-3449-3649 www.themashtun.com

2-14-3 Kami-Ōsaki, Shinagawa-ku, Tōkyō
東京都品川区上大崎 2-14-3 三笠ビル B 棟 2 階
Open: Weekdays 7 pm–3 am; weekends and national holidays 7 pm–2 am; irregular holidays, often Tuesdays
Booking recommended? No Credit cards? Most major cards, not Diners English menu? No Cover charge: 500 yen

I was introduced to the Mash Tun by Taylor Smisson, a long-time resident of Japan and the man who opened my eyes to Tōkyō's world-beating whisky bars. "I can often find more malts I like here than at other bars with larger selections. I find Suzuki-san's tend to have a high 'hit ratio'," says Smisson.

"To increase your ratio, give him some examples of specific malts that you like and do not like so he can choose something appropriate". One of the great strengths of The Mash Tun is owner Toru Suzuki's focus on keeping his stock of about 350 single malts as fresh as possible. Unlike beer or wine, whisky can be kept in an opened bottle for relatively long periods, but it is not completely inert and will react with the air. Leaving dozens of half-empty bottles on a bar shelf over several years will change the flavor. "I try to keep the whisky moving all the time," Suzuki-san told me. "I hold events with cheaper prices every now and then to finish off the older bottles." The discounts can sometimes be significant, so count yourself lucky if your visit coincides with a sell-off (if you understand Japanese, watch the website for details). There are usually 20–30 types of Japanese single malt on the shelves, plus about 150 other types of wines and spirits. The food is basic (nuts, 600 yen; cheese selection, 1,200 yen) but works well with the malts.

DIRECTIONS: Meguro Station, East side. Cross the taxi turning circle to the McDonald's and bear round to your right. Take the second left on the main road, after the Doutor coffee shop. The Mash Tun is in the building on your left after the car park and is quite hard to spot. It is the middle window on the second floor.

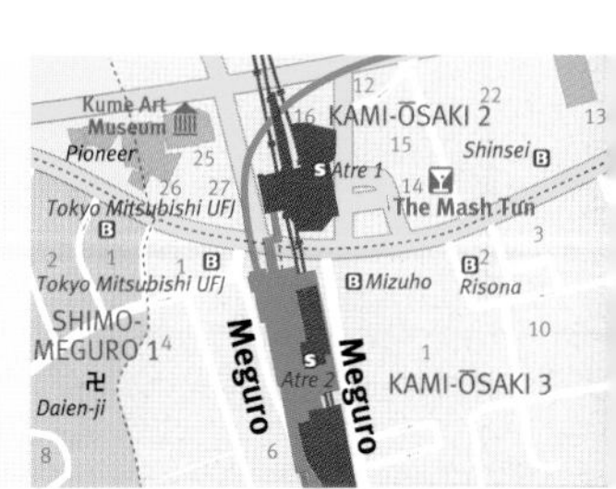

Chapter 6 Japanese Wine and Wine Bars

Japan's Excellent Wine Bars

Before 1995, wine drinking in Japan was largely the preserve of businessmen with fat expense accounts and slick-haired wine waiters in unbearably snotty French restaurants. Wine had no real connection with mainstream Japanese food and drink culture except as a vaguely understood symbol of foreign sophistication. As far as the international wine market was concerned, the country was a forgotten backwater, a place to hawk substandard bottles at inflated prices.

Then, an obscure Japanese wine expert called Shinya Tasaki won the 1995 World Best Sommelier Competition. The victory, in a competition that would merit only passing attention in most countries, had an electrifying effect in Japan. The idea that a Japanese could know more about wine than the best the great wine cultures could offer seemed to open a world of possibilities. The mass-media interest was intense and sustained. For the first time in Japan, there was a popular interest in wine. The next year, a wine *manga* called "Sommelier" was first published in *Ōruman* magazine. For anyone who has never visited Japan, *manga* is a type of comic which sells more than any other type of publication. It is as mainstream as Hollywood and has a comparable cultural influence. A successor to "Sommelier," called "Kami no Shizuku" (the "Drops of God"), arrived in *Shūkan Mōningu* magazine in 2004 and blew the lid off wine's popularity. By 2007, it had a readership of about half a million people. It told the story of a young hero called Shizuku Kanzaki on an international quest to get the keys to his father's wine cellar but, like many *manga* of this sort, it really doubled as a sort of textbook—it featured a real wine in every issue and stuffed its readers full of information about wine while they were being entertained. It became a

Left: Manga comics about wine have sold in their millions and have spread knowledge about wine culture.
Right: Shinya Tasaki's victory in the 1995 World Best Sommelier Competition shocked Japan and helped break down old snobberies.

mover of the wine market, not only in Japan but in many other parts of Asia where *manga* enjoy wide popularity. When the Italian wine "Colli di Conegliano Contrada di Concenigo" appeared in one issue of "Kami no Shizuku", the maker Umberto Cosmo saw sales jump 30 percent overnight. A Taiwanese importer reported selling 50 cases of "Château Mont-Pérat" in two days after the comic compared that wine to a Freddie Mercury rock concert (the comic's descriptions are never boring).

The cumulative effect of Shinya Tasaki's success and of the *manga* that built on it has been profound. There are now more wine manuals than their sake equivalents in most Japanese bookshops. Game console-based wine guides are popular, and a prime-time television adaptation of "Kami no Shizuku" arrived in 2009.

Wine is securely in the mainstream. The key demographic tends to be young and literate, and a new breed of wine bars catering to consumers eager to explore the world of "Kami no Shizuku" on restricted budgets are serving excellent wines by the glass. Modern Japan is no longer a backwater in the international wine market. It is one of its most developed and demanding markets and a great place to explore wines from across the world and from Japan itself.

Japanese wine's beginnings

Despite wine's relatively shallow roots in modern Japan, the country's history of making wine may stretch back 5,000 years, further than any record of wine making in France or of sake brewing in Japan. Excavations at the prehistoric village at Sannai-Maruyama in Aomori prefecture have challenged the idea that Japan's first alcohol arrived with rice farming, some time between 1000 BC and 300 BC. Archaeologists have found waste tips at Sannai full of unexpectedly large quantities of nuts and fruit seeds, including wild *yamabudō* grapes, elderberries, raspberries and mulberries. What has led some experts to suspect something more interesting than large-scale berry eating is the very significant number of dead fruit flies found in the same dumps. Unless the villagers were in the habit of throwing away tonnes of uneaten fruit, the presence of the flies seems to indicate that the grapes and berries were being allowed to ferment before consumption. And why

Grapes have been cultivated at Suntory's 150-hectare Tomi no Oka winery in Yamanashi prefecture since 1909.

would anyone allow fruit to ferment? It is still a matter of scholarly debate but it is an intriguing possibility that the early Japanese, who kept up a fairly large settlement at Sannai-Maruyama for 15 centuries, were getting together for little wine tasting sessions between boar and deer hunts.

Wine almost completely disappears from the Japanese historical record after Sannai-Maruyama. In the late 1500s and early 1600s, it made a brief reappearance with the arrival of Europeans in Japan and, for a time, seems to have been quite easily available to the country's elite. Although the evidence is far from conclusive, some sources claim that the warlord Nobunaga Oda even hosted a tasting party in 1569 to judge wines brought into the country by Jesuit priests. The subsequent closing of the country and banning of Christianity seems to have brought an end to wine's short heyday (its close association with Christian clerics and their sacrament probably did it no favors under the new regime). The early 18th-century botanist Ekken Kaibara writes about *chinta* (from the Portuguese for red, *tinto*) and other types of *budōshu* (grape alcohols) but, by that time, it was a foreign curiosity almost impossible to obtain in Japan.

Viticulture did expand rapidly in Japan during the Edo period (1603–1868) but table grapes, not wines, were the desired items. There are a number of myths about the origins of Japan's *kōshū* grape variety. One has it that, in 718, the famous Buddhist priest Gyōki had a vision of a Buddha holding a vine while praying in Katsunuma in Yamanashi prefecture and planted grapes on the spot. Another story features a monk called Kageyu Amemiya who noticed an unusual vine growing by the roadside in Yamanashi in 1186. But, whatever the precise starting point, we do know that *kōshū* is of a species (*vitis vinifera*) originally native to Europe, North Africa and Western Asia and is probably descended from grape varieties exported along the Silk Road. It is likely to have been brought into Japan along with Buddhism, hence the association with Buddhist priests long before the arrival of the Jesuits.

Cultivation remained on a very small scale until the early 1600s, when a famous medic called Tokuhon Nagata introduced the distinctive *tanajitate* (棚仕立) or *tanashiki-saibai* (棚式栽培) overhead frames that are still a feature of Japanese vineyards. If you visit Japan's grape country in Yamanashi prefecture, you will find grapes hanging down above your head in almost every available space—there are car parks covered in the ubiquitous vine canopy. The method spaces vines much more widely than those in a European vineyard. Each vine produces huge grape yields, with its branches trained across overhead frames allowing bunches of grapes to hang down from the canopy. It is labor intensive but avoids damage in Japan's hot and humid climate and is ideally suited to producing the perfect table grapes that became an expensive luxury item in Edo Japan (but is less suited, some argue, to producing good wine). Between 1601 and 1716, the number of vines in Yamanashi prefecture, which was only a day's journey from the Shogunate's palaces in Edo, grew from 164 to 3,000.

The second coming

The juicy, purple grapes hanging in the Yamanashi vineyards were an object of unimaginable luxury for ordinary 19th-century Japanese but wine seems to have scared the wits out of them. "A boy brought a bottle and a cup at the command of the captain and put it onto the table," reported Renjo Shimōka, a local official sent out in 1846 to tell the American Captain James Biddle that Japan was closed to foreigners. "What was poured from that black bottle was a red blood-like thing. I was taken aback and I started shivering, almost certain that the liquid contained some kind of poison. But I made the decision to give my life to my nation. I closed my eyes and drank it in one go."

When Commodore Matthew Perry arrived with his "Black Ships" seven years after Biddle's failed journey, a Japanese sailor sent on to the foreigner's ships had a very similar experience: "I was given bread which had terribly smelly, hair-oil sort of stuff on it. It was disgusting. Then one person brought a glass containing a very dark red water. Everybody turned pale. What else could it be other than human blood?"

But where the man in the street saw blood, Japan's modernizing leaders and capitalists saw opportunity. Almost immediately after the opening of the country, there were attempts to make wine. At some time between 1870 and 1874,

Hironori Yamada and Norihisa Takuma set up a winery in Kōfu, Yamanashi. Public interest was boosted in 1877 by a gift of wine and beer to soldiers injured fighting the Satsuma rebellion from the Emperor Meiji, and Kōfu-made wine was exhibited at the Ueno industrial fair that year. However, Yamada and Takuma's business, which appears to have been using sake making techniques and tools to make its wine, foundered and the center of Yamanashi's fledgling viniculture shifted east to Katsunuma, where a group of farmers and merchants set up the Iwaimura Winery in 1877. The new company dispatched two young men, Masanari Takano, aged 19, and Ryuken Tsuchiya, aged 25, to France to find out about proper wine making. Neither spoke any French. They learned their trade in a Bordeaux vineyard through sign language and a laborious process of translation by correspondence—sending questions in letters to Masana Maeda, an agricultural expert living in Paris, who would send the French translation by return of post. The French wine maker's answers would then go through the same treatment. Tsuchiya complained to his bosses in Japan: "We work morning to night but, since we can't even speak the language, we are little better than farm animals."

Traditional overhead tanijitate grape frames increase yields from vines but many wine makers have adopted European techniques.

Despite the difficulties, they had learned enough to immediately start throwing out the sake and soy sauce making tools when they returned to Japan in May 1879. Proper wine making machinery was installed at great cost, and the winery was churning out about 40,000 liters of French-style wine a year by 1880. Again, however, the enterprise ended in failure. There are differing accounts. Tsuchiya claimed the market was depressed and consumers were not ready for real wine. Kōtarō Miyazaki, the company's marketing man, thought it was a problem with their product—vinegary, undrinkable and sometimes completely off. Competition was also growing: huge vineyards were opened in Aichi prefecture during the 1880s. There was a government-run winery in Hokkaido from 1879 and the private Banshū vineyard in Hyōgo prefecture had its own wine on the market in 1884. More importantly, a new type of sweetened and spiced wine was proving much more popular than the dry, European-style drinks Iwaimura was trying to make. Dembei Kamiya, founder of the famous Kamiya bar in Tokyo (see page 230), launched the sickly sweet "Hachijirushi" (Bee brand) wine in the mid-1880s. It was a simple formula. Ship in gallons of dirt-cheap imported wine and fill it with flavorings and sugar to appeal to Japanese consumers. Much to the disgust of the "real" wine makers, it sold very well. Iwaimura Winery was wound up only seven years after Tsuchiya and Takano's return from France.

Kamiya's initial tactic of using cheap imported wine might have been the death of Japan's fledgling wine sector were it not for a major cholera epidemic in 1886 which killed more than 100,000 people. In the resulting panic, opportunistic wine sellers mixed wine with quinine and other medicinal additives and sold it as a miracle cure. A year after the epidemic struck, wine consumption had tripled, just in time to soak up the increased capacity from the new Japanese vineyards. In 1883, domestic production was only 4 percent of imported wine, but in 1887 Japanese production was meeting about a quarter of the greatly increased demand. Kōtarō Miyazaki, picking up the pieces from the collapse of Iwaimura, quickly launched a new company. Although he always stayed loyal to the ideal of European wine making, investing large sums in a state-of-the-art vineyard in Yamanashi, Miyazaki also carved out a large part of the sweetened and medicinal wine markets with his own "Ebijirushi" (Prawn brand) and "Marunijirushi" (No. 2 brand). Dembei Kamiya moved in the other direction, starting his own vineyard at Ushiku, Ibaraki prefecture, around the turn of the century with 6,000 seedlings imported from Bordeaux.

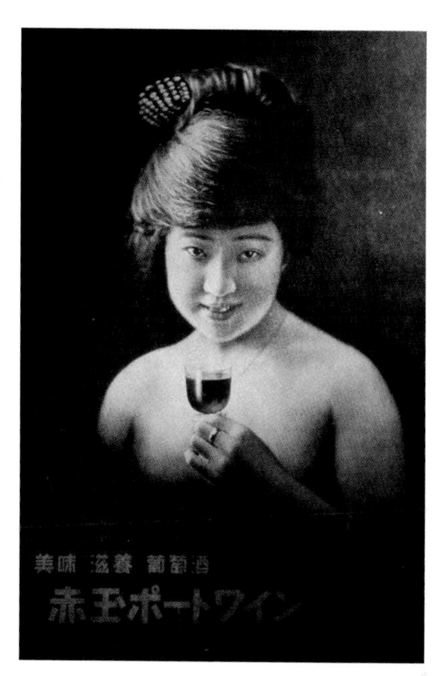

The lack of clothing in this advertisement for Akadama sweet wine shocked Japan in 1922.

In 1907, another major player arrived on the scene with the launch of the famous sweetened brand, "Akadama," by Shinjirō Torii, the founder of the Suntory alcohol empire (Suntory still sells "Akadama Sweet Wine." It is quite nice on ice). Torii had started out selling wine imported from Spain but, like Kamiya and Miyazaki before him, discovered that the dry European taste was unpopular. In 1922, a poster campaign featuring a head-and-shoulders portrait of an unclothed singer, one of the first "nudes" in Japanese advertising, caused a sensation and Akadama took sweetened wine sales to new heights.

The wine makers seem to have been a font of audacious marketing schemes. Miyazaki, maker of the "Prawn brand," even managed to hitch wine to the super-nationalist spirit of the times when he argued in a newspaper column in 1935: "The ingredients for alcohol should never be the rice and grains that are our people's daily food. I am not saying sake is wrong or beer is wrong, but ... what country would waste the nation's staple for anything other than eating? ... It would not be too difficult to replace sake with wine.... Grapes can be cultivated in places where the other crops cannot.... I hope you understand the national benefit of using fruit alcohol instead of grain and support us in our humble business. I will keep working hard at supplying a good, healthy national drink."

This pre-war sweetened wine hardly scaled the heights of quality wine making, but it did help sink sturdy foundations for Japan's viniculture. In 1935, Yamanashi prefecture alone was producing one and a half million liters of wine and had 3,008 wineries. Most were tiny family operations which were to be aggressively rationalized during the war, but the culture of wine had seeped deep into communities. Nowadays, in Yamanashi's wine capital, Katsunuma, they conduct the same Shintō ceremonies to bless the sites of newly built homes that they do all over the country, but they use wine, not sake, for the ceremony. You see the same tobacco-chuffing, wizened "good ol' boys" you meet all over the Japanese countryside, but they shoot the breeze over a carton of cheap red plonk in preference to sake or *shōchū*.

A wide range of grape varieties are cultivated at the Tomi no Oka winery, including cabernet sauvignon, merlot, cabernet franc, petit verdot, black queen, pinot noir, chardonnay, riesling, and the Japanese kōshū grape.

The modern era

The range of the Japanese palate has expanded massively in the post-war period, and the country is now consuming wines in a variety of styles that the pre-war wine makers could not have dreamed of. A key early development came in 1949, with the launch of the "Mercian" wine brand, which used grapes from Yamanashi cultivated on the traditional *tanajitate* vine canopies but aimed for a style much closer to conventional European wine. It was specifically marketed to hotels and restaurants catering to a budding interest in European food, rather than to liquor shops selling direct to consumers, so, for the first time, wine was consistently presented in culinary contexts approximating to those for which it was originally made.

Events like the Tōkyō Olympics in 1964 and the Ōsaka World's Fair in 1970 boosted the number of Western-style hotels in the country, and the number of foreign restaurants increased rapidly after that. Hans Brinckmann, author of *Showa Japan* and a resident in Japan at the time, describes how early *yōshokuya* ("Western food houses"), with very limited and Japanized menus, gave way to eateries representing "virtually every one of the world's major and minor cuisines." Many of these new outlets demanded authentic wines and, as the caterers became more sophisticated, educating their consumers in the process, so wine drinking went through the roof, from 33,000 kl in 1980 to 241,300 kl in 2008.

Unfortunately for the Japanese vineyards, much of this demand, particularly at the upper end of the market, has been met by massively increased imports. In 1970, it was difficult to get a bottle of foreign wine in Japan, but foreign and Japanese labeled wines were sharing the market

about equally in the 1990s. Imports now account for about two-thirds of the market. The domestic production has often gone into very cheap drinks, sometimes costing less than 500 yen a bottle (and tasting like alcoholic grape juice rather than something recognizable as wine). The imported labels are currently making aggressive inroads into this sector too. Very cheap South American, US and French labeled brands are now common in supermarkets. Even a "Made in Japan" label often conceals a largely foreign product; Japan's odd trading laws allow products containing 95 percent imported wine or grape juice to claim the Japanese designation. The government has made some effort to ease the squeeze on domestic producers with localized relaxations of land laws, which prevent wineries from owning more than experimental vineyards themselves, and compel them to subcontract to small farmers. Nevertheless, many in the Japanese wine trade see little long-term hope of competing on price and are instead aiming at a long-term future in quality production.

Mercian's Katsunuma Winery is just one of dozens of wine making operations packed into a few square kilometers of wine-soaked real estate in Japan's viniculture capital Katsunuma, Yamanashi prefecture.

Denis Gastin, the leading English language writer about Asian wine, says he is excited by the willingness to experiment among Japanese wine makers. The traditional grape variety, *kōshū*, has seen a remarkable renaissance and now vies with domestically cultivated chardonnays for the top medal hauls for white wines at the prestigious Japan Wine Competition. "I have a high opinion of the *kōshū* variety," Gastin says. "I have been writing about this for 20 years, and in that time there have been efforts to turn it into something it cannot be: like a rich and flavorsome, barrel-treated chardonnay. However, there is now a very strong reversal in approach by the thinkers in the industry to present the intrinsic characteristics of this shy grape in a fresh and

Left: A bottle of Mercian 1958 at the Museum of Wine in Katsunuma. The brand helped revolutionize Japanese wine drinking after the war.
Center: Patrons of the Buchi standing bar in Shibuya, Tōkyō, sip champagne.
Below: Japanese wine culture still has a few surprises up its sleeve, such as this pint of red wine with ice at a wine bar in Roppongi, Tōkyō.

exciting way. The natural attraction of *kōshū* in Japan is that it complements Japanese food so well. Consumers are rediscovering this too."

New styles of *kōshū* include sparkling versions (e.g. "Katsunuma no Awa Kōshū Brut," "Chateau Mercian," c. 1,800 yen in shops) and a wine fermented and matured in the earthenware pots used for *shōchū* making. Coco Farm and Winery in Tochigi prefecture (www.cocowine.com/english/english.html) has put out a *kōshū* fermented on skins ("Kōshū FOS 2006," 3,600 yen at the time of writing), creating a rusty-colored drink with more body and definition.

Another famous Japanese original is the "Muscat-Bailey A" variety, a red wine cross of the Bailey and Muscat Hamburg types by Zenbei Kawakami (1867–1944), a key figure in building Suntory's wine operations before the war. The variety used to be associated with grape juice-like sweeter wines but has recently been extending its palette: "It also has great Japanese food-matching potential. There is a lot of experimentation, including blends with other varieties, [often merlot]," says Gastin. He picks out Asahi Yōshu's soft and spicy "Soleil Kusakabenne" (1,870 yen) as a good example of the potential of straight Muscat-Bailey A wine. "There are also a lot of interesting ideas being explored with the *yamabudō* grapes and some of them are very good, especially among the hybrid versions and most particularly yama-sauvignon," according to Gastin. Ikeda winery's "Yama-Sauvignon 2006" (2,000 yen), using a cross of the indigenous wild mountain grape with cabernet sauvignon, offers "rich, almost pinotage-like, aromas and flavors." Another interesting cross, "Sawanobori Shokoshi," combining Japanese mountain grapes with Russian and Himalayan strains, is gaining converts, with intense flavors and rich colors.

"Yamanashi is the spiritual headquarters of the industry in Japan but in Nagano and, increasingly, Yamagata prefectures, wineries are also doing very good work with the conventional European varieties, especially cabernet, merlot and chardonnay. Hokkaido is heading out on its own with some very good examples of Central European varieties like Kerner and Sweigeltrebe," Gastin enthuses. "It is very exciting. China is the largest producer in Asia by a long way and has ancient grape growing and wine making traditions, but Japan is indisputably, in my view, the quality leader."

Bongout Noh ボングウノウ 03-5464-0858 www.gatai-psd.co.jp/noh_top.html

2F Miyagi Biru, 1-10-12, Shibuya, Shibuya-ku, Tōkyō
東京都渋谷区渋谷 1-10-12 宮城ビル 2F
Open: **5 pm–3 am (last orders 2 am)** Booking recommended? **No** Credit cards? **Most major cards**
English menu? **Yes** Cover charge: **500 yen for the restaurant**

There are two sections to Bongout Noh: a conventional wine bar at the back and a standing bar next to the large window at the front. The view from the standing bar of Shibuya's gray side streets isn't spectacular by any stretch of the imagination. In the back, you get to watch the apprentice chefs getting bossed around by the chef. You pay an extra 500 yen cover charge for the theater and you also miss out on the free nuts for the plebeians at the counter. There are 12 white wines and 16 reds sold by the glass, priced between 500 and 1,600 yen (plus 150 wines ranging upwards of 2,500 yen a bottle in the seated area). The selection includes a full range of international wines. Unlike some Tokyo wine bars, Bongout does not completely ignore the domestic industry. They had a 2008 "Manriki Delaware Plus" white wine from Caney winery in Yamanashi prefecture on their glass wine list (900 yen/glass) when I visited. Caney (the second syllable pronounced to rhyme with "high") is a small independent producer in Yamanashi prefecture run by Ichirō Kanai, a former construction firm worker who gave up a 9–5 job to work in wine making. His vineyards are full of flowers because he follows *shizen nōhō*, an agricultural philosophy that minimizes fertilizers, pesticides and weeding. Kanai-san also tries to be as natural as possible in his fermentation. His Manriki series of wines are made using only the natural yeasts on grape skins. The "Manriki Delaware" has a nice clean acidity, which the management said would work well with their *shutō pizza* (salted bonito fish guts pizza, 600 yen). *Shutō* literally translates at "sake thief," a name bestowed by the 19th-century Tosa *samurai* clan chief Toyosuke Yamauchi, who felt it went so well with sake that it would cause him to empty his cellar. But does *shutō* work with wine?

DIRECTIONS: From the Hachikō statue (dog statue) and looking at the Starbucks, turn right under the tracks and walk straight up the hill (Miyamasu-zaka). Turn left at the junction at the top of the hill, before the footbridge. Take the second left. It is on your left, nearly opposite the 7-Eleven convenience store.

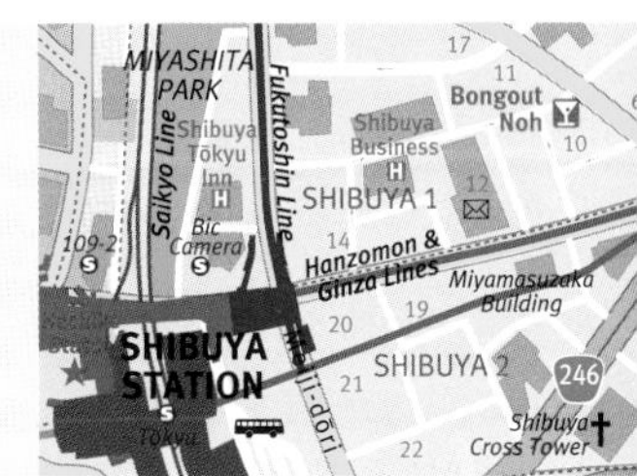

Cheese and Wine Salon Murase

チーズ&ワインサロン 村瀬
03-3575-9100 www.wine-murase.com

COI Ginza 612 Biru, 6-12-15 Ginza, Chūō-ku, Tōkyō
東京都中央区銀座 6-12-15 COI 銀座 612 ビル
Open: 5 pm–12 pm; closed Sunday and national holidays Booking recommended? Yes
Credit cards? Most major cards English menu? No Cover charge: No

There are many rewarding things about living in Japan but cheese is not one of them. The tiny, sweaty bright orange packets of "cheddar" they sell in my local supermarket cost as much as a bottle of wine and have the texture and taste of a pencil eraser. I dream about good cheese and cram myself full of it whenever I fly out of the country. So, controlling myself after walking into Murase and finding a menu stacked with crumbling, oozing cheeses from all over the world and 230 excellent wines to wash them down with, was nearly too much. Ken'ichi Murase has just 14 seats and operates Murase primarily as a restaurant. Visitors who want only to snack and drink, should avoid taking up the seats during the main restaurant hours between 6.30 pm and 9.30 pm. After that, Murase-san is happy to oblige. He has a selection of 30 glass wines (c. 1,200 yen), with a slight bias toward New Zealand and Australian wines. The cheese plate costs 2,150 yen for six types or 1,350 yen for three. Or you could try the cheese fondue (2,900 yen or 1,900 yen for half-size) or the Raclette cheese melted over potatoes and broccoli (1,600 yen) or the oven-baked tomato (tomato to cheese no oven yaki, 950 yen). Murase-san's limited but well-judged menu also offers a nice variety of non-cheese based European meat and fish dishes, but it was the smell of the ripe Stilton that filled my nostrils and drove me half mad as I walked away from this cheese lover's heaven off the Ginza.

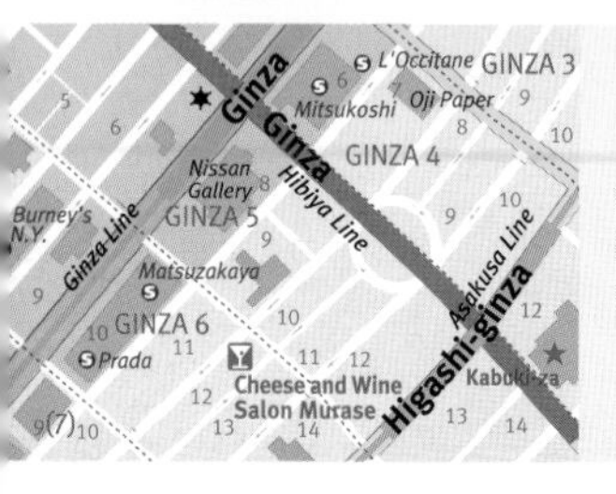

DIRECTIONS: Ginza Station, Exit A4. Turn left and take the next left before the Matsuya department store. Take the second right at the traffic lights. Murase is about 20 yards up on the left.

Goss ゴス 03-3562-8025 www.goss-ginza.com

1F Seiryū Ginza Biru, 3-4-6 Ginza, Chūō-ku, Tōkyō, 104-0061
〒104-0061 東京都中央区銀座 3-4-6 正隆 (せいりゅう) 銀座ビル 1F Open: Weekdays 1 pm–4 pm; 5.30 pm–2 am; Saturday 2 pm–12 pm; Sunday and national holidays 2 pm–10 pm Booking recommended? No
Credit cards? Most major cards English menu? No, but some Roman alphabet is used Cover charge: No

Goss has a machine at its heart. If this sounds a little lacking in soul, that is because it is. However, a machine that allows me to taste 24 wines by the glass, including premium wines that really ought not to be available to oafs like myself, is the sort of mechanism that makes me feel all warm and fuzzy about engineers. I didn't understand every detail of Goss manager's Taizō Tsunaki's technical exposition of the temperature-controlled, glass-fronted "Enomatic" cabinets that line his walls but, basically, inert nitrogen gas is pumped into the bottles, displacing all the oxygen and preventing oxidation. "It allows us to keep lots of bottles open for much longer periods without any spoiling, and that allows us to serve really excellent wines by the glass in a way that hasn't been possible before," he said. "We get young people reading about top wines in a *manga* comic and then coming here to try them out." We are talking top wines—"Château Mouton Rothschild 1994" (3,200 yen for 20 ml); "Clos de Vougeot Lamarche 1991" (1,600 yen for 20 ml). The cheaper wines start at about 600 yen for 50 ml and, if you arrive between 5.30 pm and 7.30 pm, they have a Champagne happy hour—a glass of Bollinger at half price (850 yen). As I say, the serving system does feel a little mechanistic. You buy a plastic card for 500 yen, get it charged up at the bar and then help yourself at the cabinets. The bottles look like museum exhibits behind their glass casings. You can't touch or interact with them in any way. You just stand there waiting for your "Château Mouton Rothschild" to drip out, as if it were a watery cocoa from a service station vending machine. And it is a great feeling.

DIRECTIONS: Ginza Metro Station, Exit A13. Cross the road and walk down the street next to the Apple store. Take the next right. It is on your left with a sign using the Roman alphabet.

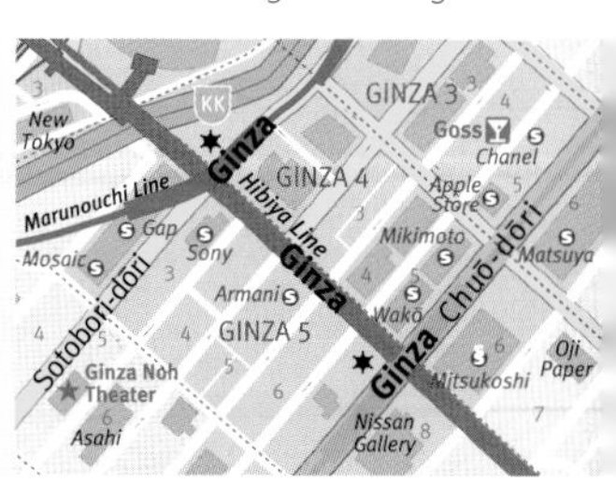

Guapos ガポス 03-5728-4741 r.gnavi.co.jp/b446000

101 Hirota Biru, 1-3-8 Ebisu nishi, Shibuya, Shibuya-ku, Tōkyō, 150-0021
〒150-0021 東京都渋谷区恵比寿西 1-3-8 廣田ビル 101
Open: 5 pm–6 am (last orders 5 am); Sunday and national holidays 5 pm–11.30 pm Booking recommended? No
Credit cards? Most major cards English menu? No, but some English spoken Cover charge: 200 yen

"The idea is that, as soon as you enter, you are in Spain," says Keitaro Nakaya, manager of Guapos. The closest I have ever been to Spain is fish and chips in Gibraltar, so I am in no position to comment, but I do know Guapos is great fun: loud Latin or jazz music drowned out by louder chatter from a crowd that is often spilling on to the pavement by late evening. The prices let you relax and concentrate on the conversation. Budget for between 2,000 and 3,000 yen per person, but for that you will get a couple of drinks, the Grana Padano cheese *otōshi* and couple of dishes of tapas (most in the 500–700 yen range). Nakaya-san says the most popular dishes with Guapos's cosmopolitan clientele are the cow stomach and tomato stew (*hachinosu tomato nikomi*, 500 yen), the sizzling prawns (*koebi no hoiru yaki*, 500 yen) and the moreish anchovy potatoes (500 yen). Most of the tapas is in the 500–700 yen range. All of the glass wines are Spanish, of course, and there are plenty to choose from—six types of sherry, six reds, five whites and a sparkling Cava (450–950 yen). The Guapos management also run the Spain Bar Bodegas Gapa, 10 yards down the road, which, despite the name, is more of a restaurant and has higher prices.

DIRECTIONS: JR Ebisu Station (Yamanote Line), West Exit (west side): Turn right so that the tracks are to your right. Cross the main road and take the road leading north nearest to the rail bridge. Guapos is on your right, about 100 yards up the road. From Ebisu Hibiya line station, Exit 1: Reverse the direction you come out of the exit and follow the instructions above.

Marugo

03-3350-4605 www.bar-maru5.com/pc

3-7-5 Shinjuku, Shinjuku-ku, Tōkyō, 160-0022
〒160-0022 東京都新宿区新宿 3-7-5
Open: 5 pm–2 am Booking recommended? No Credit cards? Most major cards
English menu? No Cover charge: No

Marugo's ultra-modern chrome and glass interior marks it as one of the new wave of wine bars that have done away with the facsimiled "traditional" interiors and stuffed shirts of a previous generation's attempts to recreate European wine culture in Japan. There is no cover charge, just good wine and simple but tasty European food (meat sauce and basil lasagne, 1,200 yen; cream cheese and anchovy canape, 500 yen). Beneath the shiny surfaces, however, a healthy conservatism is evident at Marugo, which takes its name from a Japanese rendition of the French winemaking region Margaux. "We do have wines from lots of places but, in the main, we concentrate on the French," said bar manager Naoto Kubo. There are usually between 100 and 120 wines in stock with more than 15 bottles available by the glass at prices ranging between 500 yen and 1,700 yen. Marugo is very keen on biodynamic wine, made according to a strict set of agricultural principles that differ from organic agriculture but are broadly "ecological".

When I visited, Kubo-san recommended a "Cuvée Carina Coste Longue" red wine. Made by Pierrette and Claude Navare in Languedoc from Carignan grapes, it uses a special method of fermenting the grapes in their skins ("carbonic maceration") to reduce the high acidity and tannins that are often associated with Carignan products. The result was not too heavy, with a satisfying fruity meatiness and a spicy finish. If Marugo is full when you visit, there is a second wine bar, Marugo II, on an adjacent street with a similar menu and slightly more space.

DIRECTIONS: Shinjuku-sanchōme Station (Shinjuku Line, Marunouchi Line, Fukutoshin Line), Exit C3. Turn left and head across the crossroads. Marugo is on your right. The logo is a pun: a number "5" (*go* in Japanese) inside a circle (*maru*). Marugo II is around the corner. Turn right at the next crossroads and then left. It is on your right.

Michel Vin Japonais

ミッシェル・ヴァン・ジャポネ 06-6941-3010
www1.suisui.ne.jp/~michel

REV35 1F, 1-1-9 Tokiwa-machi, Chūō-ku, Ōsaka, 540-0028
〒540-0028 大阪市中央区常盤町 1-1-9 REV35 1F

Open: Weekdays 5.30 pm–11 pm; Saturday and national holidays 2 pm–11 pm; closed Sunday
Booking recommended? Yes Credit cards? Most major cards English menu? No Cover charge: 500 yen

With about 150 Japanese wines in its cellar, Michel Vin Japonais is probably the best place to sample the domestic wine scene. It is owned by Masatoshi Watanabe, alias "Michel," who previously worked as a sommelier at the Ōsaka-based French restaurant Olivier le François, where he acquired the nickname. He is optimistic about Japanese wine's prospects: "Despite what people say, I wouldn't call what we are experiencing now in Japan a 'wine boom' exactly, but it is getting a bit more popular now and what is definitely well under way is a big improvement in the quality of Japanese wines," says Watanabe-san, who has toured Japan picking out 21 of the country's top wineries to supply his restaurant. He recommended the "Petite Grande Polaire Nagano Merlot Cabernet 2006" (800 yen/glass, 5,000 yen/bottle) from Sapporo wine as an example of the broadened horizons of the domestic makers. "We are getting a lot more of these medium to heavy wines now. They tend to be at the more expensive end of the price range and some Japanese people still prefer light tastes, but we are definitely moving in that direction. This one is quite tannic with a little bit of fruit and a good balance." Next came the Chateau Mars Kōshū "Shirane Sur Lie" 2007 (700 yen/glass, 3,900 yen/bottle), a clean, dry white from Yamanashi prefecture, and an example of the growing experimentation in *kōshū* making. It is made using the *sur lie* technique, without taking the wine off the lees before bottling, a method which can produce a livelier taste. The food at Michel Vin Japonais is in a French style and is handled by Watanabe-san's younger brother Hiroyuki, who uses the nom-de-cuisine "Alain."

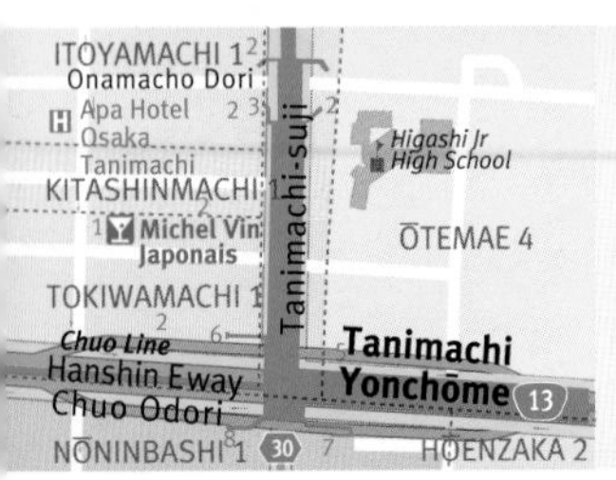

DIRECTIONS: Tanimachi-yonchōme subway Station, Exit 6. Walk straight ahead 30 yards. Take the first right. Turn right again. It is on your left in the Rev 35 building.

Mr Zoogunzoo ミスターズーガンズー 03-3400-1496 www.zoogunzoo.com

B1 Aoyama City Bldg, 2-9-11 Shibuiya, Shibuya-ku, Tōkyō, 150-0002
〒150-0002 東京都渋谷区渋谷 2-9-11 青山シティビル B1
Open: 6 pm–2 am; closed Sunday and national holidays Booking recommended? Yes
Credit cards? Most major cards English menu? English on the menu Cover charge: 500 yen

Despite the great advances made in recent years in informing Japanese people about wine, many consumers in Japan are still quite conservative, says Noroyuki Yokota, owner of Mr Zoogunzoo. "Almost every day, we have somebody in who is blown away that Australian and New Zealand wine can be so good. In Japan, the Old World wines from places like France and Italy still have a grip on people. People don't like to change." To be fair, he says, the suspicion of Australian wine, in particular, is partly based on experience. Some of the Australian wines sold in Japan 15 years ago were not of the highest quality and that has left a mark on some consumers. "The quality has gone up massively in that time. Now we are getting the wines that have been so successful in other places," he says. Mr Zoogunzoo is not really a place to come with a light wallet, and is definitely not a bar for a cheap snack and a glass of plonk. They do have a glass wine selection (two sparkling wines, three whites, three reds, and two dessert wines; all priced 1,050 yen) but the bottles start at about 5,000 yen (including the 10 percent service charge) and range up to 20,000 yen. If you want a fairly free choice of good wines, you need to be budgeting for about 7,000 yen plus per bottle. You will get quality for your money. Yokota-san knows his Antipodean wine inside out. He recommended a bottle of "Pipers Brook Pipers River Chardonnay 2002" (7,491 yen) with some Australian Pacific oysters (490 yen a piece); or a succulent Aussie lamb chop (1,290 yen) with the "Annie's Lane Clare Valley Shiraz 2004" (5,995 yen).

DIRECTIONS: From the Hachikō statue (dog statue) and looking at the Starbucks, turn right under the tracks and walk straight up the hill (Miyamasu-zaka). Cross the road using the foot-bridge at the top of the hill and continue walking in the same direction you have come up Route 246. It is about 100 yards on your right.

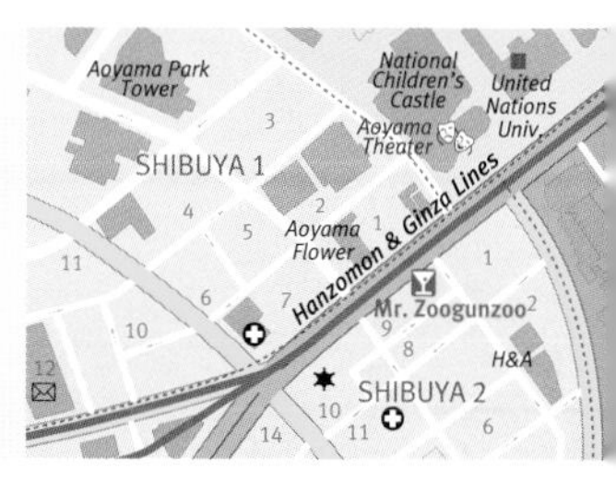

New York Bar

ニューヨーク バー 03-5323-3458
tokyo.park.hyatt.com/hyatt/hotels/entertainment/lounges/index.jsp

Park Hyatt Hotel, 52nd Floor, 3-7-1 Nishi-Shinjuku, Shinjuku-ku, Tōkyō
東京都新宿区西新宿 3-7-1 パークハイアット東京 52F Open: Monday–Saturday 5 pm–1 am; Sunday 5 pm–12 pm
Credit cards? All major cards English menu? Yes. English spoken by all staff Cover charge: 2,000 yen after 8 pm Monday–Saturday and after 7 pm on Sunday. This is levied on anyone still in the bar at that time. It pays for the live entertainment. There is an additional 10 percent service charge. Nobody under the age of 20 is admitted, even if they are drinking soft drinks.

In Sofia Coppola's film *Lost in Translation*, Bob (Bill Murray) and Charlotte (Scarlett Johansson) sit in the New York Bar with a spectacular view of the lights of Tokyo behind them. The young bartender asks Charlotte: "What can I get you?" "Um, I'm not sure." Bob interjects: "For Relaxing Times make it..."

And the bartender finishes the sentence: "Suntory Time!" The bar is the blockbuster's most iconic location and you could re-enact the whole scene here if you wanted to. You could order the Suntory "Hibiki whisky" Bob is advertising or the vodka tonic Charlotte eventually orders, but if you did you would be missing a trick. This place has the best selection of North American wines in Asia. Manager Phillippe Borde enthuses: "We have about 350 different US wines. It is a huge selection. For me, as a Frenchman, I have learned so much working here about the quality and the range of wines that they have to offer." Prices can exceed 300,000 yen for a bottle and most bottles cost north of 8,000 yen, but some wines are available by the glass. Borde recommended the "Wolffer La Ferme Martin Chardonnay" from Long Island (2,000 yen/glass) with the Taraba crab cakes (4,000 yen). The "Vina Robles Cabernet Sauvignon" from Paso Robles (1,800 yen/glass) would work with the veal loin with tuna mayonnaise (3,600 yen). The New York Bar also does good cocktails. Check out their original "L.I.T.," containing sake and Sakura Liqueur (1,700 yen), and just drink in the view of the city. The best time is when daylight is failing and the neon is rising.

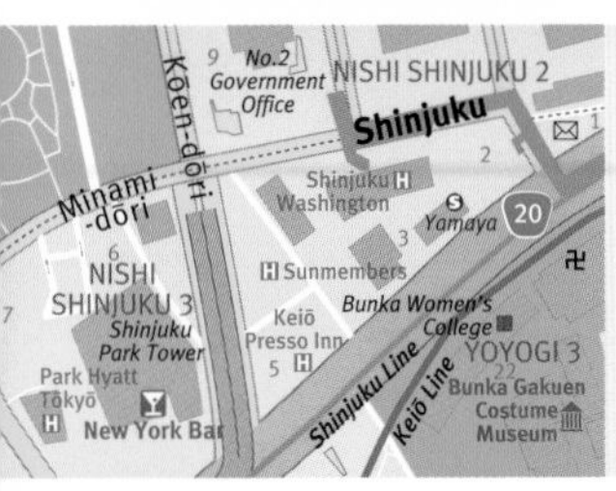

DIRECTIONS: Shinjuku Park Hyatt Hotel, 52nd Floor. From Shinjuku JR Station, South Entrance. Turn right and follow the yellow signs to the "Skyscraper district" and "Tōkyō Metropolitan Government Office" until you get to an exit pointing you down the stairs to your left. Instead, go straight ahead. Cross over to the Akomu shop with the large red clock on its front and walk up Route 20 for about half a mile. The Park Hyatt is on your right.

Pateya パテ屋 03-5439-4330 r.gnavi.co.jp/fl/en/b662300

Twin Ichinohashi Bldg, No. 2 1F, 4-4-1 Azabu Juban, Minato-ku, Tōkyō, 106-0045
〒106-0045 東京都港区麻布十番 4-4-1 ツインーの橋ビル 2 号館 1 Open: Lunch: Tuesday–Friday 11.30 am–3 pm; Dinner: Tuesday–Thursday and Sunday 5 pm–11 pm; Friday and Saturday 5 pm–2 am
Booking recommended? Yes Credit cards? Most major cards English menu? No Cover charge: No

Pork pâté, duck pâté, potato and cod roe pâté, squash and raisin pâté, burdock and red wine pâté, turnip and anchovy pâté, soft salami and tapenade pâté, beef tongue and marscapone pâté, pilchard and shrimp pâté, artichoke and blue cheese pâté, eel pâté, sweetfish and Japanese plum pâté. The list goes on. Pateya is a sort of Ben and Jerry's for the pâté and paste fiend. You can get a selection plate (*pate moriawase*, 1,500–1,800 yen), and they serve individual portions at about 550 yen a slice (with smaller servings available on request). The selection of 12 glass wines (500–1,200 yen) ranges widely and usually includes a Japanese red and white, for those who want to sample what the domestic industry has to offer. The shop is in one of Tokyo's more fashionable districts (I couldn't get through the front door because a model and a seven-strong camera crew were filming a gourmet special for Japanese daytime TV), but Pateya wears its chic lightly. There is a nice simplicity to the design: whitewashed walls, minimal decoration and glass cases displaying the kitchen's latest pâté ruses.

DIRECTIONS: Azabu-Jūban Station (Namboku Line), Exit 2. Pateya is a few steps behind the exit. From the Oedo line tracks, take Exit 5b and walk three blocks south down the left side of Route 415.

Sherry Club しぇりークラブ 03-3572-2527 www.sherry-club.com

2F Yūgen Biru, 6-3-17, Ginza, Chūō-ku, Tōkyō
東京都中央区 銀座 6-3-17 悠玄ビル 2F
Open: Weekdays and Saturday 5.30 pm–12 pm; Friday 5.30 pm–2 am; closed Sunday and national holidays
Booking recommended? No Credit cards? Most major cards English menu? Yes Cover charge: 525 yen

The best-stocked sherry bar in the world. That is official. They have a certificate on the wall from the *Guinness Book of Records* to prove it. The "club" in the title conjured up images of a pompous gentleman's club of sherry. In fact, the atmosphere was very relaxed and not intimidating at all. The objec-tive seemed to be to spread the word about sherry as widely as possible: more automobile club than Bullingdon club. The staff said about half of their customers were newcomers and the inclusivity stretches to foreigners. They have a full English menu and a scrapbook of labels with English explanations of the taste of each sherry. The tasting sets (*kikizake seto*, 2,415 yen) are a good way to get started. They include three glasses of sherry, illustrating ranges of flavor and color in sherry. There is a tasting sheet to help you explore your experiences. Manager Katsuya Masuko noted that, broadly speaking, Americans, French and Spaniards go for the drier sherries, while the English are more wedded to sweet versions. The extensive standard range of sherries are all priced at 945 yen a glass, but they also have some extremely rare drinks under the counter (e.g. a 100-year-old Pedro Ximenez no "Reliquia Barbadillo", 4,000 yen/glass). The food includes a variety of tapas and some lovely cured ham and sausages.

DIRECTIONS: Ginza Metro Station, Exit C2. Reverse the direction you came out of the exit and walk toward the overpass. Take an immediate left down Sukiya Street to the left of the Citizen Clock sculpture. Take the next right, passing the Aux Bacchanales Patisserie, and left up the narrow street. It is about 20 yards on your left.

Stand Bar Maru 丸 03-3552-9210(1F) / 03-3552-4477(2F)

3-22-10 Hacchobori, Chūō-ku, Tōkyō 東京都中央区八丁堀 3-22-10

Open: 1st and 2nd floors: Monday–Friday 5 pm–11 pm; closed weekends and national holidays. 3rd floor: same as 1F and 2F but open Saturday 5 pm–11 pm (food last orders one hour before closing) Booking recommended? No
Credit cards? No (2F and 3F can use major cards for bills over 10,000 yen) English menu? Basic menu
Cover charge: 1F and 2F no charge; 3F 350 yen

Stand Bar Maru serves three types of white wine by the glass and five types of red, but the basic concept in the first floor standing wine bar revolves around the bottle. Customers browse the wines in the attached Miyataya liquor store and, on paying 500 yen corkage, can drink them then and there.

The customer is free to close the bottle and take the rest of it home with them whenever they wish. "We started about 20 years ago. We were one of the first of the new casual places to drink wine but in the last three to five years we have seen more and more casual bars. It is cheap. You don't pay an *otōshi* charge, so you can come in on a whim," explained manager Kōichiro Matsukawa. Maru's three floors offer ascending levels of formality. Downstairs is all standing. On the second floor, courting couples sit around a large circular bar watching the chefs cutting mouth-watering cured hams and grilling *yakitori* on charcoal. On the top floor, it is all a bit more formal, with lots of office parties and groups of older shoppers. The average spend on each floor differs too, according to Matsukawa-san: about 2,400 yen downstairs, 4,500 yen on the second floor and 6,500 yen upstairs. The first floor can get a little crammed and smoky, but there is a tolerant, casual atmosphere. Halfway through my visit, a Scottish actor working with the avant-garde Blue Man Group swung into the bar dressed in a leather jacket and kilt. It is not normal to see men wearing dresses in Japan, but nobody really batted an eyelid at Maru. The sauteed lamb (750 yen) and the plush, fruity Gago red wine from Spain (750 yen/glass, 4,000 yen/bottle) were delicious.

DIRECTIONS: Hatchōbori Station, Exit B1. It is right behind you as you come out of the exit, in the Mitataya building.

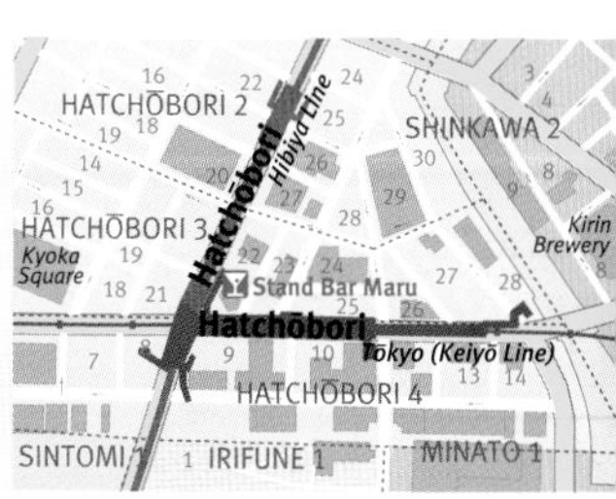

Tasuku たすく 080-1500-8159

1F Yontomikaikan, 615 Nishidaimonji-chō, Tominokōji Shijō Agaru, Chukyo-ku, Kyōto, 604-8054
〒604-8054 京都府京都市中京区富小通四条上ル西大文字町 615 四富会館 1F
Open: 7 pm–12.30 pm; closed Sunday, and second and fourth Wednesdays of the month Booking recommended? Yes Credit cards? No English menu? No Cover charge: 300 yen

A *nano* bar. Living in Japan you get used to undersized bars, but Tasuku is the smallest I have ever come across. There are only five seats and that makes it sound positively spacious compared to the reality. Your back is right up against the door and nobody is much further than an arm's reach away. "I once had a European woman who came in here and she just burst out laughing as soon as she opened the door," says owner Yuka Ikenishi. But Tasuku is not only remarkable for its size, it is also one of very few wine bars in Japan that specialize in domestic wine. Japan's bar districts offer great opportunities to try sake, *shochu*, *awamori*, local beer and whisky but even the best Japanese wine bars still tend to marginalize domestic wine (or *kokusan wain*, as it is called here). Tasuku offers three or four Japanese whites and three or four reds in glasses, plus a much more extensive selection of bottles. Ikenishi-san recommended the *ika no tempura* (squid tempura, 450 yen) with a "Fermier Zweigeltrebe" red wine (800 yen). Fermier (www.fermier.jp) wine is produced by Honda Vineyards, a small producer in Niigata prefecture, who are one of a number of Japanese producers currently experimenting with central European grape varieties. The Austrian Zweigeltrebe and the white Kerner grape, both known for their hardiness in harsh winter conditions, are proving particularly popular in cold spots such as Hokkaido and Niigata. This one was quite fruity with moderate tannins—light and playful, just like the conversation in Tasuku itself.

DIRECTIONS: At the Shijo-Karasuma crossing looking north, turn right and walk past the front of the Daimaru building. Walk past the left turn next to the Starbucks but take the next one (Tominokoji-dōri). Tasuku is in the fifth building on your right, a low, old structure immediately after the modern edifice with the "Calon Hair Design" sign.

Wine Bar Mayu ワインバー繭 03-5453-0301 www.winebar-mayu.jp

B1 Kamiyama Biru, 40-3 Kamiyama-chō, Shibuya-ku, Tōkyō, 150-0047
〒150-0047 東京都渋谷区神山町 40-3 神山ビル B1
Open: 6 pm–3 am; Sunday 6 pm–12 pm; closed Monday and Tuesdayafter Monday national holidays
Booking recommended? Yes, particularly on Friday and Saturday Credit cards? Most major cards
English menu? No Cover charge: 800 yen

Mayu has one of the weirdest bar interiors I have seen. The name means "cocoon" and the owners do not use it merely in the figurative sense of a warm, intimate environment in which to knock back a few glasses: the restaurant area is made up of dimly lit, fiberglass pods accommodating between two and four people. It is the brainchild of Hideo Horikawa, one of a wave of innovative interior designers who are revolutionizing Tokyo's restaurant styling, and is great fun as long as you don't come with a pushy date (far too much privacy). For more Horikawa, see also the wiry design of the Sad Cafe in Suginami (03-3220-7252) and the honeycombed Le Cocon in Shibuya (03-5459-5366). Mayu's food is not as elaborate as the fancy interior might lead you to expect, but nicely judged to bring out the best in a wine list of more than 200 bottles (try the chef's selection of five hors d'œuvre, *chef no yokubari ōdoburu moriawase*, 2,800 yen). There are usually seven types of wine available by the glass, priced between 650 yen and 1,250 yen. Owner Mikiro Tahara was in an Iberian mood when I visited, recommending a dry and fruity "Cavipor Catedral" white wine from Portugal (1,050 yen/glass) and the tempranillo/cabernet-sauvignon "Ramon Roqueta Reserva 2004" (1,250 yen/glass). No smoking in the cocoons! That could get nasty.

DIRECTIONS: From Yoyogi Hachiman Station (Odawara Line), South Gate: Turn left. Keep walking. Cross Route 413 (Inokashira-dōri) and continue for 400 yards. It is on your right, opposite a white building with "Hakuyōsha" on it. If you see the sign, you have probably passed Mayu. Back up a bit. The sign is difficult to spot. From Yoyogi Kōen Station (Chiyoda Line), Exit 3: Turn right. Walk down the hill past the Yoyogi Park police box ("Kōban"). Continue toward the NHK Broadcasting center. Opposite it, take a right down the street next to the traffic island and green tarmac. Follow this winding street to the T-junction. Turn right and look for the "Hakuyōsha" sign (see above).

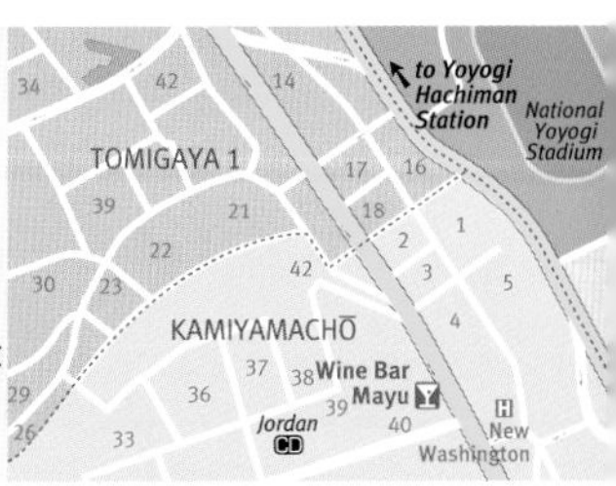

Other Great Bars in Japan

Susukino, Sapporo's legendary drinking district, was in the grip of a blizzard when I arrived there in February. The pavements were covered in treacherous ice. I fell on my back three times on the trudge up from the railway station to the blaze of neon signs at Susukino crossing, but the locals seemed completely oblivious to the conditions. The girls wore the same miniskirts I had got used to in Tōkyō, which I had imagined would be given up for something more practical in a snowstorm. While I buried a shivering chin in my fleece-lined coat, they teetered down the street, making do with a few pom-poms and a fashionable array of loosely knitted hats. They walked on ice and through several inches of snow in five-inch stiletto heels.

Tatsurō Yamazaki at Bar Yamazaki, Sapporo, is a legend among Japanese bartenders.

Bar Yamazaki is on the fourth floor of a side street just behind the restless neon on the main crossing. It is a haven from the raucous merry-making and sleazy pursuits that occupy much of the rest of the quarter. The owner is Tatsurō Yamazaki, a frail but unfailingly courteous 90-year-old who still works behind his bar. He is a legend among Japanese bartenders and, listening to his life story, I felt I learned more about the development of contemporary Japan's extraordinary alcohol culture than in a dozen polished presentations from the big drinks companies.

In 1945, Yamazaki-san was living with two younger sisters in a boiler. Tōkyō had been bombed flat. They had salvaged the boiler from a public bath and furnished it with a rug, an improvised door and a single bare lightbulb

Right: The Susukino Crossing, Sapporo, is at the heart of one of Japan's most lively drinking districts.

- 4°C
KIRIN
KIRIN
すすきのビル
NIKKA

Bar Largo in Shibuya, Tōkyō (page 224) specializes in calvados.

powered by electricity borrowed from a nearby pole. He was a bright and ambitious 25-year-old, but he had no parents, no proper home, no job and no prospects. He was not unusual in this. He was like millions of other Japanese people struggling to survive in a wrecked society.

Before the war, he had taught himself English and dreamed of a career as an artist. The fighting had smashed those hopes but he had applied himself so diligently to his work as an army medic that, in August 1945, a professor of medicine in Tōkyō was recommending him for transfer to Manchuria, where he might have trained as a doctor. The day after receiving the professor's recommendation, "I stood in front of Kashiwa Station and listened to the Emperor's surrender broadcast, and the dream of becoming a medical doctor disappeared. Manchuria disappeared."

His big break after the surrender was getting a job cleaning toilets and mopping floors at the Tōkyō Kaikan, a popular entertainment spot for the occupying forces. He worked his way on to the bar at the Kaikan and then to the prestigious Mitsui Club, another favored location for the Americans. After nearly getting himself killed in a confrontation with a knife-wielding American sergeant who had been pestering a female colleague, he moved through a series of bars in the Tōkyō and Yokohama area, each time in a more senior role, until, in 1953, his old boss asked if he would take a job from a contact in Hokkaido. Yamazaki-san moved north, intending only to stay for a year or so, but stayed the rest of his working life.

His first job in Sapporo was at the Montana, a two-story wooden building with two barmen and more than a dozen hostesses. Susukino was a chaotic and lawless place in those days. Gangsters and pimps ran much of the quarter. It had some of the most dangerous streets in Japan. The owner of Montana and his wife just disappeared one day. Yamazaki-san heard later that they had run off to Sao Paulo.

In 1957, he opened his own bar, called Silo, or at least he thought he had. A woman, whom he will now only identify as Mrs H., helped him organize the opening. Later in the year, she too disappeared with more than 200,000 yen of Yamazaki-san's savings, a very large sum in the 1950s. The extent of the betrayal only became apparent when it emerged that the owners of the property actually regarded him as an employee rather than an independent bar owner. They claimed Mrs H. had told them that Yamazaki-san was their bartender. He stuck it out for two months and still had a large debt for the alcohol he had bought to start up Silo when, with the help of customers and a liquor shop, he set up the first Bar Yamazaki in 1958, recruiting 15 women as hostesses (most bars had hostesses in those days). He paid off his debts in two years, but more setbacks followed. His chief hostess left, taking half of his money and most of his hostesses with her, and then, on December 15, 1975, the bar burned to the ground. One of his customers later told him that the fire burned an extremely beautiful blue. The color was from the stock of alcohol Yamazaki-san had spent years building up.

Yamazaki-san seems to have had an ability to turn misfortune into new opportunity. At the suggestion of a friend, he took the brave step of reopening his bar without hostesses. The decision was well ahead of its time but presaged a change that is now transforming Japan's drinking districts.

"It was taken for granted that no bar could run without hostesses, but, at the same time, they had given us so much trouble I thought that if we could do a bar without them, that would be great," Yamazaki-san said. Contrary to the received ideas, it was a great hit, possibly, he said, because a growing number of young people preferred to go out with friends to a bar with cheaper prices, just enjoying the alcohol together rather than paying money to be served by women.

He said the decision also fundamentally changed his role as a bartender: "Before the fire, I did not have much contact with the people. With no hostesses, I came into the spotlight and had far more opportunity to meet and talk to customers." If you go to Bar Yamazaki now, and indeed many of the bars in this book, the barman or woman is the key personality.

This transition, from hostess bars to establishments in which the bar person is the center of the experience, explains a lot about contemporary Japan drinking culture. In important ways, the hostesses shaped what we have now. For a start, they built the physical environment; hostessing generally requires small, intimate environments rather than the vast barn-like pubs that are typical in many other countries. With the decline of the hostess bars, the drinking quarters in Japan have been left with thousands of tiny bar units. You will often hear overgeneralized stereotypes about the Japanese having a peculiarly corporate culture, but Japanese drinking districts are actually very individualistic, partly because of the physical environment and also, I think, because of the determination of pioneers like Yamazaki-san to

Norimichi Tsurumi at The Crane in Ikebukuro, Tōkyō (page 192), shows off the ice cutting and carving skills for which Japanese bartenders are renowned.

build their own independent enterprises and make running a bar a rewarding and respectable career. There are chain bars in Japan, but they are far less pervasive than in many other countries. In the small units, built to accommodate the hostesses of the 1960s and 1970s, you will find all sorts of odd and sometimes not very savory enterprises (including some giving an entirely different meaning to the name "hostess bar"), but there are also thousands of new specialist bars run by individuals chasing their dreams.

The hostesses also seem to have shaped the expectations of drinkers in Japan. Yamazaki-san was one of the first to realize that changing times and increasing numbers of women drinkers were making the hostesses an anachronism, but many customers continue to expect a very personal experience from a bar. Of course, knowledgeable and engaging bar people are a necessity for the best bars everywhere in the world, but nowhere is the expectation of conversation and interaction as ingrained as it is in Japan's small bars. In a sense, the man or woman behind the bar has replaced the hostess. Instead of flattering conversation (which, in most cases, was all that hostesses provided their customers), the bar offers a very intimate environment in which the customer can take his or her mind off the troubles of the day with the conversation at the bar (always the most sought-after seats in Japan) and in an education in the glittering array of drinks behind it.

Which brings up the second thing that really jumps out at you if you visit a good Japanese bar—the professionalism and sense of vocation of the people who run them. Again, I have entertained all sorts of theories about this. Perhaps the relentless grind of parts of the corporate world in Japan means that Japanese bars get more than their fair share of highly able people unwilling to spend their lives on late-night spreadsheets? Certainly, you meet a lot of former salarymen running Japanese bars.

But again, Yamazaki-san's generation put in the groundwork. "[After the war] bar staff had a really bad image. Newspaper crime pages often carried the description 'ex-bartender' in them. Bar workers could not be proud," said Yamazaki-san.

One of the first things he did when he arrived in Sapporo, was to help set up a bartenders' association and, by the late 1960s, he had a school, offering lectures from invited specialists and developing clear guidelines for professional conduct. There are now hundreds of bar owners across Japan trained by Yamazaki-san and people like him. "My dream used to be to visit all the bars that my employees would have opened after my retirement at 70. Unfortunately, most of my employees have already retired, and, at the age of 90 I have still not managed to do so," he said.

Yamazaki-san was not alone. In fact, throughout the post-war period, the Japanese entertainment districts were rife with conflicts between rival schools of bartending. They would not even join the same associations until the late 1980s. These rival traditions zealously looked after their own, but also developed a great sense of pride and professionalism in their ranks. Yamazaki-san, and others like him worked hard to make their career, which had in many cases been forced on them by circumstance, respectable and rewarding.

Visitors to Japan can now reap the rewards of their devotion. Not every bar is run by a graduate of professional training. As I have mentioned, there are a lot of ex-salarymen and independent-minded young people running bars, but the determination of people like Yamazaki-san to make bar work a vocation was important in setting the foundations for today's exciting bar culture.

My purpose in writing this guide was not to try to chisel out an authoritative list of all the best bars in Japan. The level of activity is just too great for that. Each time I turned a corner I would find a new gem offering a drinking experience that I had not even dreamed of. I am sure there were hundreds of others down the alleys I did not explore. I have organized my book around six main types alcohol—sake, *shōchū*, *awamori*, whisky, wine and beer—but Japanese drinking culture ranges much more widely than that. There are thousands of small bars that would not fit into my categorization. Indeed, the deeper I ventured into the drinking districts the more convinced I became that no way of organizing my book could do justice to the variety I encountered. This chapter is just a taster of some of the bars that did not fit—a quiet backstreet bar offering 400 different types of rum, a mind-blowing tequila bar, world-class cocktail bars, a floating bar, an establishment made entirely of ice, bars thick with the patina of Japanese history. It is just a start, but hopefully it will inspire you to do a little exploring of your own.

Peter at The Peninsula hotel, Yurakuchō, Tōkyō.

Is Tokyo the cocktail capital of the world?

In September 2008, the influential US gourmet magazine *Bon Appétit* declared Tōkyō to be the "cocktail capital of the world" and devoted a richly illustrated feature to explaining how the city was "besting New York and London at the cocktail game." The article caused a minor sensation, prompting follow-up features by other publishers and broadcasters and a shiver of excitement in the blogosphere, but Tōkyō's excellence was already well known among cocktail professionals. About ten months before the *Bon Appétit* article, I met two bartenders from two very prestigious Paris hotels in a Tōkyō bar who were on a "pilgrimage" to learn about the city's famed techniques. They talked in hushed awe about the ice cutting and shaking prowess of their Japanese peers.

But is Tōkyō really the "cocktail capital of the world?" It really depends on what you are looking for, says Nicholas Coldicott, drink columnist for *The Japan Times*. Coldicott is, in fact, as responsible as anyone for Tōkyō's current celebrity. The *Bon Appétit* article seems to have drawn on his coverage of the Tōkyō scene, which had pointed out the Tōkyō bartenders' claims to superiority. But Coldicott himself has always maintained a nuanced detachment from the claims. "Japanese bars aren't the most inventive places. If you want to taste something unique, innovative or quirky, you're much better off in London or New York," he says. "A bartender from one of the most famous Ginza bars once told me that he attended an international cocktail contest and overheard other bartenders describing his shake technique as boring. He told me that it puzzled him, because he couldn't believe their shakes would circulate the ice quickly and efficiently enough to cool and blend the ingredients without watering them down. Every movement, every ingredient and every technique has been perfected over decades and passed down."

"There's nowhere like Tōkyō for perfectionism and obsessive attention to detail. In Ginza, which locals consider the center of bartending, bartenders talk of the optimum temperature and shape of their ice, and they will debate whether or not it's appropriate to stir a carbonated drink, and if so, precisely how. Many top bartenders around the world pour by eye, but in some places in Ginza they produce a perfect bulging meniscus in the glass with the last drop every time. And even if they have award-winning cocktails to their name, they are more likely to suggest a gimlet, a sidecar or a daiquiri. You might not find cocktails with bacon fat or celery bitters, but you'll get the classics done better than anywhere in the world."

The only way to come to your own conclusion is to try out the Tōkyō scene for yourself. In addition to bars like Lupin (page 225) and Tender (page 236), leading Tōkyō cocktail establishments include Y&M Kisling (7F, 7-5-4 Ginza, Chūō-ku; 03-3573-2071), which has a similar Old School feel to Tender's; Koji Ozaki's Radio Bar (3-10-34 Minami Aoyama, Minato-ku; 03-3402-2668; www.bar-radio.com), providing great food as well as exquisite cocktails; Star Bar Ginza (Kazama Building B1F, 37-12 Udagawacho, Shibuya-ku; 03-3465-1932); Bar High Five (4F, No. 26 Polestar Building, 7-2-14 Ginza, Chūō-ku; 03-3571-5815); Park Hyatt Tokyo's Peak Bar (41F Park Hyatt Tokyo, 3-7-1-2 Nishi-Shinjuku, Shinjuku-ku; 03-5323-3461; tokyo.park.hyatt.com); the Shoto Club (Kazama Building B1F, 37-12 Udagawacho, Shibuya-ku; 03-3465-1932); Polestar at the Keio Plaza Hotel (45F Keio Plaza Hotel, 2-2-1 Nishi-Shinjuku, Shinjuku; 03-3344 0111; www.keioplaza.com/restaurants/skybar.html) and Peter at The Peninsula Hotel (1-8-1 Yurakucho, Chiyoda-ku; 03-6270-2763). Not all of these bars cleave closely to the conservative values of the mainstream Japanese tradition. Athough they are separated by less than 400 yards, the contrast between the deadly serious precision with which my gimlet was prepared at Tender and the swagger with which Peter served up its original Tokyo Joe cocktail was striking. I didn't ask, but my guess was that the fellow at Peter called himself a "mixologist."

Agave アガヴェ 03-3497-0229 www.agave.jp

B1F Clover Biru, 7-15-10 Roppongi, Minato-ku, Tōkyō, 106-0032
〒106-0032 港区六本木 7-15-10 クローバービル B1F Open: Monday–Thursday 6.30 pm–2 am; Friday and Saturday 6.30 pm–4 am; closed Sunday and national holiday Mondays Booking recommended? No
Credit cards? All major cards English menu? Yes, and English is spoken Cover charge: No

Faramarz Khadem, the Iranian manager of Agave, said: "We are not in the *Guinness Book of Records* just yet. This year they found a bar in Cancún which says it has 600 types of tequila available, but with our shipment this year we should be up to about 500." Khadem-san (known as Ferri) regularly travels to Mexico to bring back new spirits and says they sometimes get Mexicans in the bar who are astounded by their selection. "There are more than 1,000 tequilas in Mexico but to see all this in one bar impresses people." Agave has a nice, moodily lit intimacy, but the space is much larger than most Tōkyō specialist bars. About 60 percent of the clientele are foreign. My previous encounters with tequila had been mainly of the "I'm so so crazy I'm drinking a tequila slammer" sort, but Agave offered a thorough re-education, with a range of three glass tasting sets to help introduce the beginner to the *blanco* (non-aged), *repostado* (matured for up to a year) and *añejo* (longer-aged) versions of the spirit (seven different tasting sets, 1,500–3,900 yen). Agave also stocks 20 types of the smokier Mezcal spirit and they make their own *sangrita* (200 yen), the spicy tomato drink often consumed as a side drink with *blanco* tequila. Khadem-san recommended the "Margarita Don Agave" (1,200 yen) and the "Fruits Frozen Daiquiri" (1,500 yen) from the extensive cocktail list.

DIRECTIONS: Roppongi Station, Exit 4b. Walk straight ahead. It is clearly signed in the Roman alphabet on your right.

Akitaya 秋田屋 03-3432-0020

2-1-2, Hamamatsucho, Minato-ku, Tōkyō.
東京都港区浜松町 2-1-2
Open: Weekdays 3.30 pm–9.30 pm; Saturdays 3.30 pm–8.30 pm Booking recommended? No Credit cards? No
English menu? No Cover charge: No

Sophisticated bars are all very well, but sometimes a simple pub is hard to beat. In Japan, the Western-style pubs that I would normally gravitate to in such moods are usually not the cheapest places to drink and not always the most down-to-earth either. Places like Akitaya are a much better analog for the local boozer back home. Prices are cheap, the company is unpretentious and the food and drink are hearty but rarely fancy. Akitaya is a *tachinomiya* (standing bar) with just a hint of retro trendiness because of its Tōkyō location, but the fare is essentially the same as a thousand other unadorned *izakaya* around the country. I had two sticks of grilled meat giblets from the grease-encrusted charcoal grill (*motsuyaki nihon*, 340–360 yen), a big bottle of beer ("Dai biiru", 550 yen), and a conversation with a scarlet-faced drunken salaryman who parked himself at my upturned beer crate table (priceless).

DIRECTIONS: Daimon Station, Toei Subway. Turn left out of Exit B4. Akitaya is on the next corner.

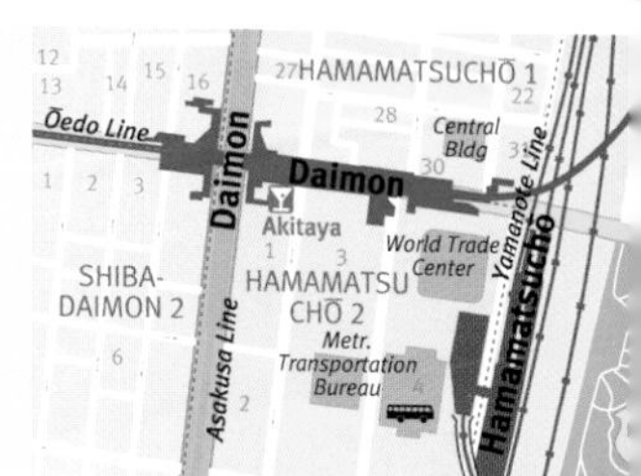

Bar Largo バーラルゴ 03-3400-5594

B1F Takatori Biru, 1-6-3 Shibuya, Shibuya-ku, Tōkyō, 150-0002
〒150-0002 東京都渋谷区渋谷 1-6-3 タカトリビル B1F
Open: 7 pm–4 am; Saturday 7 pm–3 am; Sunday and national holidays 7 pm–1 am
Booking recommended? No Credit cards? All major cards
English menu? No Cover charge: 500 yen (no snack)

Bar Largo specializes in the apple brandy calvados from Normandy in France. I didn't know much about the drink before I visited Largo but I learned enough on my brief stop to want to go back to explore these fine spirits. Calvados has more than four centuries of history. The first recorded distilla-tion in the region was in 1554, just eight years after our first record of *shōchū*, 20 years after the first record of distilled alcohol on Okinawa and 60 years after Scotland's first record of whisky. It is fascinating how all these different spirits seem to have cropped up in such a short time period across the world. Largo keeps about 40 types of calvados, ranging in price from 1,300 yen to about 4,000 yen a glass. It doesn't quite have the obsessive focus of some of the other Tōkyō specialist bars. Manager Tomii-san told me the aim was to be a general bar with a good selection of calvados, rather than devoting the place exclusively to apple brandy. There are a wide range of other spirits and a nice cocktail list, but it would be a shame not to try the fresh apple taste of the "V.S.O.P. Coeur de Lion Calvados pay d'Auge" (1,600 yen) or, if your pockets are deep enough, the rich, flavorful sweetness of the "Calvados Fermicalva 1962" (2,800 yen). Largo's food is a cut above standard bar fare and the prices have a slightly less severe look than the steepish alcohol tabs (shepherd's pie, 1,200 yen; marscapone gratin, 1,000 yen).

DIRECTIONS: From the Hachikō statue (dog statue) and looking at the Starbucks, turn right under the tracks and walk straight up the hill (Miyamasu-zaka). Take a left at the junction at the top of the hill (before the footbridge) and a right at the AM/PM convenience store on your left. It is the second building after AM/PM.

Bar Lupin バールパン 03-3571-0750 www.lupin.co.jp

B1F Tsukamoto Fudosan Biru, 5-5-11 Ginza, Chūō-ku, Tōkyō, 104-0061
〒104-0061 東京都中央区銀座 5 丁目 5 番 11 号 塚本不動産ビル地階
Open: 5 pm–11.30 pm Booking recommended? No, but it fills up quickly so come early Credit cards? No
English menu? No Cover charge: 700 yen

The ghosts of some of Japan's greatest modern writers haunt the richly patinaed bar at Lupin. One of the most famous photographs of the novelist Osamu Dazai was taken at the end of the bar here in 1946. Little has changed since then. You almost feel he might walk in, lift his worn boots up on a second stool and engage Ango Sakaguchi, another literary great who was a Lupin regular, with his dark wit. The bar was set up in 1928 by the beautiful Yukiko Takasaki, who had earned a loyal group of literary admirers while working as a cafe waitress. The original idea was to call it The Gloucester after the Duke of Gloucester, who was due to visit Japan the next year. The Japanese police (presumably unfamiliar with British pub names) banned it, saying it was disrespectful to name a bar after the third son of the British King. The cheeky clique at Lupin, including the famous novelists Ton Satomi, Kyoka Izumi and Kan Kikuchi, came up instead with Maurice Leblanc's fictional gentleman thief, Arsène Lupin. During the war, the bar was again forced to change its name because it sounded foreign. It adopted the sardonic title Pan-tei, meaning "Mansion Bread," to suit those straitened times. Defeat brought Lupin's heyday. It was officially supposed to be a coffee shop, but it became a favorite haunt of the Buraiha group ("the school of irresponsibility and decadence"), selling liquor under the counter to Sakaguchi, Dazai and friends. It was not until 1981 that Yukiko Takasaki, the 1920s muse, was forced at the age of 74 to give up the bar. Her brother Takeshi was still occasionally present until his death in 2008. If you order Ango's favorite cocktail—the "Golden Fizz" (gin fizz and egg yolk, 1,365 yen)—try to get the fifth stool from the left of the long counter. That was his regular pew. Lupin's properly made "Moscow Mule" is also delicious (1,260 yen).

DIRECTIONS: Ginza Station, Exit B3. You emerge beside Emporio Armani. Turn right. At the end of the block, turn right. Turn right again after about 15 yards down a small alley. The sign is in the Roman alphabet.

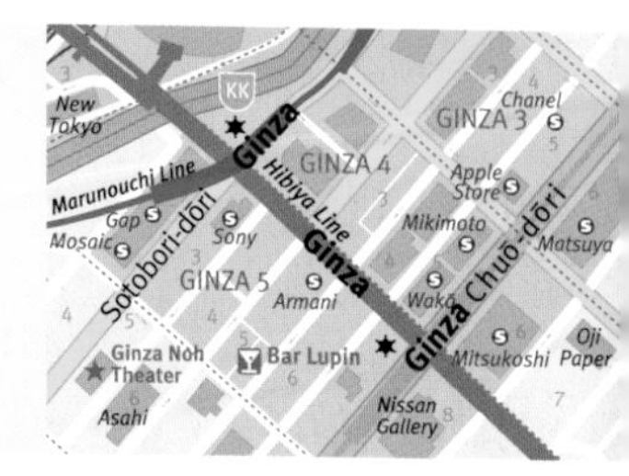

Bar Yamazaki やまざき 011-221-7363 www.bar-yamazaki.com

4F Katsumi Biru, 3 Minami 3 Jo Nishi, Chūō-ku, Sapporo-shi, Hokkaido, 060-0063
〒060-0063 札幌市中央区南3条西3丁目 克美ビル4階
Open: 6 pm–12.30 pm (last orders 12 pm); closed Sunday Booking recommended? No
Credit cards? Most major cards English menu? No Cover charge: 1,000 yen

Tatsurō Yamazaki has spent more than 60 years as a bartender (see page 216) and a visit to his bar in Susukino is a master class in that art. I have been in some excellent cocktail bars where everything seems to be about the bartender and contents of the shaker. The customer's role is limited to watch-ing and appreciating. At Bar Yamazaki, there is a laser-like focus on the customer. Over the years, Yamazaki-san has created more than 200 original cocktail recipes for visitors (about one-third of them carry the name of a woman). The recipe emerges out of a conversation, and reflects a feeling for the drinker's personality, life and interests. For instance, the former chief prosecutor in Sapporo, Michio Satō, once asked for a cocktail called "Prosecutor." He got a cocktail containing brandy, aquavit, anisette, dry vermouth and lemon juice, served in a salted glass and with a maraschino cherry. Powerful stuff! Bar Yamazaki's junior bartenders regularly win national competitions, so whether you are served by the maestro himself or one of his students, you will be in good hands. The bar's classics include Yamazaki-san's original "Sapporo" (vodka, Amaretto, dry Vermouth, green Chartreuse; 1,400 yen) and his "Freiheit." He is also a talented artist (look at the walls) and the world's most prolific cut silhouette portraitist, with a letter from the Guinness book to prove it. He has cut more than 43,000 silhouettes of his customers. If you are lucky, he may make one of you too.

DIRECTIONS: Susukino Crossing. Walking north from the crossing (toward the JR Station), take the first right, next to the KFC. It is the third building on your left. "Yamazaki" is written in *hiragana* characters. Look for the big brown sign on the fourth floor.

Golf and Bar Grip

03-6277-0522 golfbar.jp

B1 Akasaka Tomoe Biru, 3-12-1 Akasaka, Minato-ku, Tōkyō, 107-0052
〒107-0052 東京都港区赤坂 3-12-1 赤坂ともえビル B1
Open: 2 pm–5 am Booking recommended? Yes Credit cards? Most major cards English menu? Yes
Cover charge: After 6 pm, 500 yen (plus the cost of the golf simulators)

Mark Twain once said, "Golf is a good walk spoiled." Golf Bar and Grip is there to remove all that pesky walking and leave only the hair-tearing frustration. Looked at another way, this golf simulation bar is just taking the best bits about the game—the drinks in the clubhouse afterwards, the con-vivial company and the gear fetishism—and rolling them into a good night's drinking. Masochists can still hook their tee shots into the burn and enjoy hacking their ball five feet at a time through the tall grass, but the rest of us never have to leave the bar and always have a glass of draft St. Andrew's beer (700 yen for a small glass) and a plate of fish and chips (600 yen) at our elbows between lackadaisical swishes of the three wood. The system is a bit complex. Basically, there are three booths running the 3DCO computerized golf simulator. It costs 3,000 yen per booth (rather than per person) for 30 minutes, plus 1,500 yen for every additional 15 minutes. At busy times, a maximum of 75 minutes per party is imposed. Gloves and club rental are free. Bring a relaxed attitude, because computer golf can be even more frustrating than the real thing. Good players can find it particularly irritating because shots that would have come off on the turf go skew-whiff on the screen. And don't even look at the course record board opposite the bar: one regular has managed to get five under par on one of the harder courses. If you enjoy Golf and Bar Grip, activity bars like this are present in almost every drinking district, not just golf but computerized darts bars, billiards halls, and, of course, the grandparent of the genre, karaoke.

DIRECTIONS: Nagatachō Station (Namboku/Yūrakuchō lines), Gate 8 or Akasaka-Mitsuke Station (Ginza/Marunouchi Lines): Walk down the road opposite the Akasaka Excel Hotel Tōkyū and to the right of the McDonald's. Turn left around the back of McDonald's. When you get to a big yellow and purple-colored Pachinko parlor called Oriental Passage, continue over the junction and look for the building beside the 82 Ale House. From Akasaka Station (Chiyoda Line), Exit 1b: Cross the road to Tully's coffee. Take the second left after Tully's. It is about 100 yards on your left.

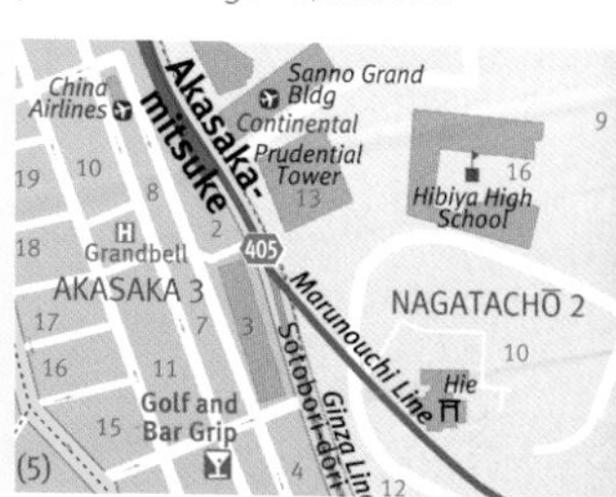

Ice Bar Tokyo アイスバー東京 03-6228-5022 www.icebartokyo.com

SVAX GINZA 1F, 8-5-15 Ginza, Chūō-ku, Tōkyō 東京都中央区銀座8丁目5-15 スバックスギンザビル1F
Open: 1 pm–4 am; Friday and Saturday 6 pm–2 am; occasionally closed for renewal of ice or events
Booking recommended? Yes, you can book online Credit cards? Most major cards
English menu? Yes Cover charge: 3,500 yen

Ice Bar Tokyo is not just "ice-themed," it is actually made out of ice. Temperatures are close to freezing inside, which makes the toasty warm cape and gloves that come with your entrance fee essential. You also get a shot glass made out of ice and one cocktail (or non-alcoholic drink) with the cover price. Refills cost 800 yen. As you drink your warmed sake or the signature vodka-based "Ice Bar" cocktail, take time to notice some of the details in the ice carving. You are standing inside a work of art. The ice has to be renewed every six months because it gets thin. Ice carvers travel to Japan to work for nine days building a completely new design for the interior. You will find the names of the designers of the latest creation carved somewhere in the ice. Note that when the bar is full, the management operates a 45-minute turnover policy, asking patrons to leave to make way for the next bookings. When it is not full, you can, as manager Mitsuhara Kaneda put it, "stay as long as you can stand [the cold]."

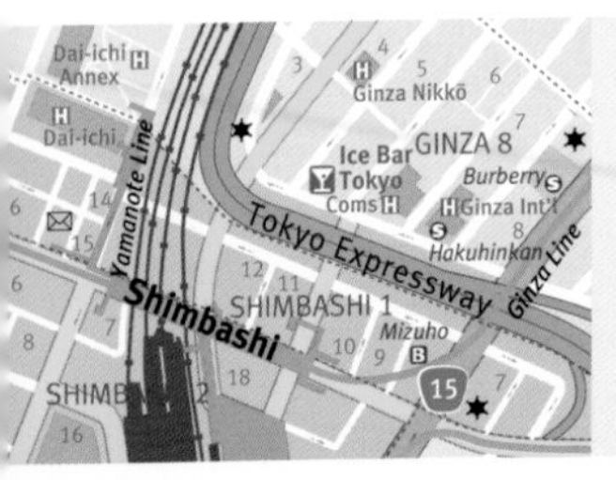

DIRECTIONS: Shimbashi Station (Ginza/Asakusa lines), Exit 5. Walk straight ahead (don't cross the road). Take the first right after the elevated road. It is in the corner building of the first turning to the left.

Jicoo the Floating Bar

ジクーフローティングバー 0120-049-490
www.jicoofloatingbar.com

2-7-104, Kaigan, Minato-ku, Tōkyō, 105-0022
東京都港区海岸 2-7-104 小型船ターミナル
Open: Thursday–Saturday only 8–11 pm Booking recommended? No Credit cards? Yes
English menu? Yes, and lots of foreign staff Cover charge: 2,500 yen (includes one drink)

The good ship *Himiko* looks like an aquatic woodlouse. She was designed by the famous *manga* and *anime* writer Leiji Matsumoto, author of such hits as *Space Battleship Yamato* and *Galaxy Express 999*, and now plies her daytime trade as a humble tour boat at the mouth of the Sumida River. By night, though, she is transformed into the infinitely more sexy Jicoo, a sophisticated music and cocktail bar, floating back and forth under the illuminated Rainbow Bridge. "We call ourselves the Floating Bar. We are the only one of our kind that I know of," says manager Gō Motomura. "I've been to Paris and Amsterdam and looked for places like this and there you see boats for sitting and eating, boats you can hire for parties, and boats which are moored up, but this is a bar that you can just walk into like any other bar, with the difference that it is also always sailing." It is not necessary to book. You just pay your boarding fee when Jicoo docks at Hinode or Daiba and can stay until the end of the evening. Boarding times at Hinode are 8, 9 and 10 pm, Thursday to Saturday. At Daiba, they are 8.30, 9.30 and 10.30 pm. Jicoo offers a variety of live entertainment, ranging from lounge pianists to dancers to dance DJs, so it is a good idea to call ahead for information.

DIRECTIONS: Hinode Station (Yurikamome Line), Exit 1. The pier is behind you and to your left as you emerge from the exit. You can also board at the Odaiba end of the journey, which is at Odaiba Seaside Park (Odaiba Kaihin Koen) and is accessibile from the Odaiba Kaihin Koen Station (Yurikamome Line).

Kamiya Bar 神谷バー 03-3841-5400 www.kamiya-bar.com

1-1-1 Asakusa, Taitō-ku, Tōkyō
東京都台東区浅草 1-1-1
Open: 11.30 am–10 pm Booking recommended? No Credit cards? Visa and Mastercard English menu? No
Cover charge: No

Despite what some guidebooks tell you, the Kamiya Bar was not the first Western-style bar in Japan (or indeed Tōkyō). There were dozens of them in the foreign ports within a few years of the opening of the country by Admiral Perry. One American businessman sublet at least 17 taverns on the Yokohama dock front in the 1860s, including four French, one American, one Dutch, five Portuguese and two British-run establishments. There were even Japanese language guidebooks for people wanting to try these weird and wonderful new drinking holes. Not everybody was in wide-eyed ignorance when Denbei Kamiya started dabbling in importing and remixing foreign alcohol in the 1880s. It was not until 1912, long after the opening of the Yebisu Beer Hall on the Ginza, that Dembei first unveiled this Western-themed Kamiya Bar. The bar does, however, have a special place in Japanese alcohol history. Its founder was the first great popularizer and adapter of Western-style booze for the Japanese market (see page 198). You can still get a taste of his weird adaptations in the shape of the classic brandy, "Denki Bran," a mix of gin, wine, brandy, curaçao liqueur, herbs and spices. The name means "Electric Brandy" and was not applied due to any alarming effects on the human body, but rather because electricity was a modern and funky thing in Meiji Japan. You can choose between the lower voltage, the 30 percent alcohol "Denki Bran" (260 yen) or the 40 percent alcohol "Denki Bran Old" (360 yen). Also, be sure to try the *hachi budōshu* (bee brand wine, 260 yen, available in white (*shiro*) or red (*aka*) versions). This was the sweet wine brand that revolutionized the Meiji wine industry (see page 198). The Kamiya Bar retains the old practice of asking customers to buy tickets for their food and drink at a machine near the door as they enter. There are labeled plastic models of the food in a case near the machine, which makes the whole process a little easier for non-Japanese speakers. Hand the tickets to your waiter once you have found your seat.

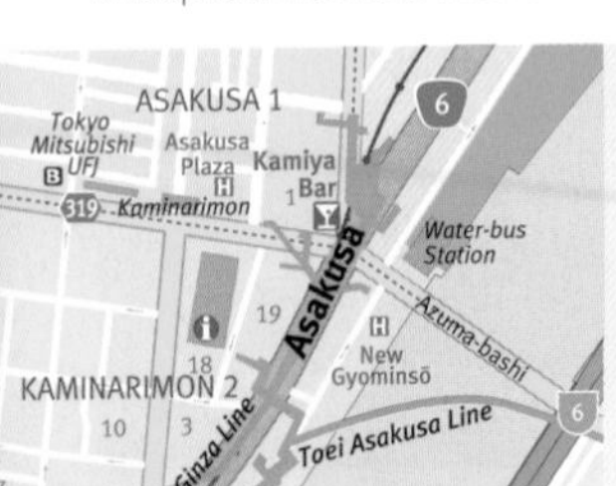

DIRECTIONS: Asakusa Station (Ginza line), Exit 3. It is on the corner facing the bridge.

Leach Bar リーチバー 06-6441-0983 www.rihga.com

Rihga Royal Hotel, 5-3-68 Nakanoshima, Kita-ku, Ōsaka, 530-0005
〒530-0005 大阪市北区中之島 5-3-68 リーガロイヤルホテル
Open: 11 am–12 pm Booking recommended? No Credit cards? All major cards English menu? English on the menu
Cover charge: 10 percent service charge

I like hotel bars. There is something about the polished impersonality you find in the best of them—the dispassionate attentiveness of the staff, the leather muffled hush—that helps draw the sting out of the usually traumatic prices. The Leach Bar at Ōsaka's Rihga Hotel still has a touch of hotel bar cool, but it has been warmed for more than 40 years by a beautiful and timeless interior designed by the famous British potter Bernard Leach and the Japanese architect Isoya Yoshida. Dotted around the room are works by Leach himself, the Japanese potter Kanjirō Kawai and the textile designer and artist Keisuke Serizawa. The bamboo, brick and oak somehow create a very English atmosphere, but I have never been in a bar like it in England. Leach himself was a sort of hybrid of the typically English and the ineffably Oriental (born in Hong Kong, he spent his formative years in Japan), so it would be fitting to toast his memory with a gin and tonic (in a mug, 1,733 yen) and *tatami iwashi* (dried baby sardine biscuit, 900 yen). Or try a martini (1,733 yen) and the fresh chocolate (*nama chocolate*, 1,386 yen).

DIRECTIONS: In the Rihga Royal Hotel, Ōsaka. Nakanoshima Station (Keihan Nakanoshima Line), Exit 3. There is also a free shuttle bus to the hotel from the west side of JR Ōsaka Station.

Makkori Bar Tejimaul マッコリバーてじまぅる 03-5348-5535 www.tejimaul.com

B1 Nishimura Biru, 7-10-10 Nishi Shinjuku, Shinjuku-ku, Tōkyō
〒160-0023 東京都新宿区西新宿 7-10-10 西村ビル B1
Open: Lunch: Monday–Friday 11.30 pm–2.30 pm; Evening: Monday–Saturday 5 pm–12 pm; Sunday and national holidays 5 pm–11 pm Booking recommended? Yes Credit cards? Most major cards English menu? No Cover charge: 500 yen

There is so much for Westerners to find out about Asian alcohol that it is intimidating. Every door you open leads to new, unexplored chambers. This fascinating bar and restaurant is devoted to the unrefined Korean rice beer *makkori* (not to be confused with the distilled Korean *soju* that has become very popular as a neutral alcohol in Japan in recent years, see page 80). *Makkori*, unlike sake, tends to be a white opaque color and has similarities with the unrefined Japanese *doburoku* and *nigori* sakes (see page 42). As soon as you look down the drink list at the Makkori Bar, however, you realize that there is a completely different alcohol culture to be explored. Some *makkori* are sweet, some are bitter, some are flavored with fruit, some with vegetables, and some have a slight fizz to them. There are hundreds of variations. I felt I didn't even scratch the surface on my first visit. I was recommended the "Kansan nama makkori," which had a nice balance between sweetness and acidity. In my complete ignorance of *makkori*, I found myself comparing it to a nicely balanced, fairly sweet amber ale. My next glass was the "Tora nama makkori" (800 yen/glass). If the "Kansan" was an amber ale, then this was a very aggressive, hoppy American craft beer, very acidic but, once I got used to it, the most interesting of the three drinks I tried. Finally, the extremely sweet and approachable "kuromame makkori" (black soy bean-flavored, 600 yen), was just one of a vast range of flavored *makkori*. Most diners at the Makkori Bar seemed to order the Korean barbecue dishes.

DIRECTIONS: Shinjuku Subway Station, Exit B16. You emerge next to the Odakyū Halc building. Climb the escalator to the right of the Odakyū Halc entrance and then the stairs to the street. Walk up the street, passing a McDonald's on your left. Cross the large road and take the second small road to your left. It is on your left, four buildings after the crossroads.

Nakano Bōzu Bar

or Nakano Vows Bar 坊主バー 03-3385-5530 vowsbar.web.fc2.com

2F World Kaikan, 5-55-6 Nakano, Nakano-ku, Tōkyō
東京都中野区中野 5-55-6 (55番街) ワールド会館 2F
Open: 7.30 pm–3 am; Sunday and national holidays 7.30 pm–12 pm; Tuesday non-smoking
Booking recommended? No Credit cards? No English menu? No Cover charge: 500 yen

Maybe it is my Irish heritage, but the idea of a priest running a bar just had me in stitches. It sounded like the punch line to a joke. I had visions of Jack Hackett from the comedy series "Father Ted." Once I had overcome my amusement, my second thought was that this could be some sort of sly way of indoctrinating people with the tenets of one of the numerous cults that prosper on the fringes of Japanese religion. In fact, the Bōzu Bar (literally, "Buddhist Priest Bar," sometimes written as "Vows" in English) is a respectable establishment. Fifty-six year old Genko Shaku is an ordained Jōdo Shinshū Buddhist priest who believes the bar is a way to reach lonely city dwellers with whom established Buddhism fails to make contact. "The idea is that people can relax and talk. I only talk about Buddhism if people have questions," he says. The bar is not devoted to any particular sect. Jōdo Shinshū has been around since the 12th century and is one of the most widely practiced Buddhist traditions in Japan, but Shaku-san's assistant is from the Shingon sect. "We have customers who don't believe in anything. We have Christians and Islamic people. We don't push doctrine at them. The historical Buddha told us not to hide ourselves away in sects. The truth is general," he says. I asked him if he thought it was justifiable for an ordained Buddhist priest to be mixing Bloody Marys (800 yen) and Last Kisses (900 yen) for late-night drinkers. "Buddhism is the opposite of fundamentalism. The rule is to be broken. It is about moderation," Shaku-san responded. Try his original green tea liqueur-based "Gokuraku Jōdo" cocktail ("Heaven", 1,000 yen). It almost lives up to the billing.

DIRECTIONS: Nakano Station (Chūō Mainline, Tōzai Line), North Exit. Walk north under the covered shopping arcade to a T-junction in front of Nakano Broadway. Turn right, then turn left after the DVD shop. The Nakano Bōzu Bar is in the World Kaikan building.

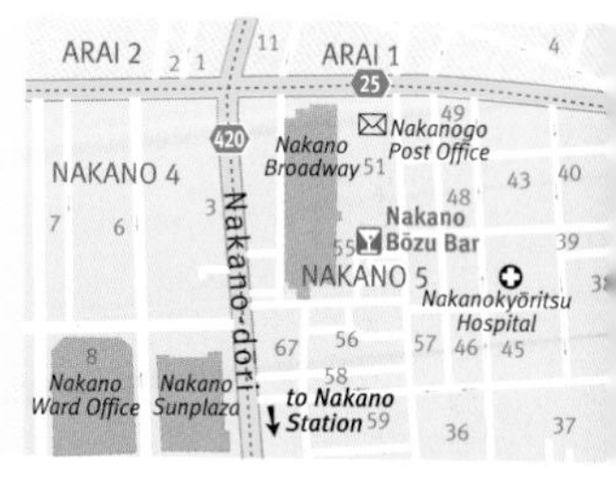

Pub Red Hill パブレッドヒル 0577-33-8139

2-4 Sowa-cho, Takayama, Gifu
岐阜県 高山市 総和町 2-4
Open: 7 pm–12 pm (irregular holidays)
Booking recommended? No Credit cards? No English menu? Yes Cover charge: No

My favorite bar in Japan. Unlike most of the establishments included in this guide, Red Hill does not serve a phenomenal range of alcohol. Neither does it have a particularly long history or an elaborate interior, but since when was a good bar defined by such things? Hisayo Miyakoshi's backstreet pub is filled to overflowing with another quality—warmth. It is popular with Takayama's small foreign community and is probably the closest thing to a *gaijin* bar that I have included in this guide. Most of the big cities have numerous bars aimed at the foreign community. Some are great fun to visit, but I have tended to ignore them because they are, by their nature, the easiest bars to find for English speakers. Red Hill is a bit harder to locate, but there is a friendly welcome for everyone who successfully navigates Asahimachi's maze of alleyways (I walked around for 20 minutes before finding the fairy well-lit doorway.) The interior is ethnic and the music, like the food is, eclectic. For a drinking snack, try the handmade smoked cheese (500 yen) or the pickles (500 yen), but Hisayo-san also turns out more substantial nosh from the ridiculously tiny kitchen at the end of the bar (*nasi goreng* rice, pitta bread sandwiches and green curry, each 700 yen). Drinks include local sake, *shōchū*, wine, whisky, tequila, rum and original cocktails. The beer list features Heineken on tap (600 yen), Corona (600 yen), Bass Pale Ale (650 yen), Guinness (600 yen), Japanese lagers (600–700 yen), and the locally brewed "Cori Cori no Kuni" beer (950 yen).

DIRECTIONS: JR Takayama Station. Turn left out of the station and walk about 200 yards to the traffic lights at the bottom of Kokubunji-dōri, which is the main east–west street in Takayama. Turn right on to Kokubunji-dōri. Pass two more traffic lights. Take the left after the second traffic light and walk about 250 yards.

Tafia タフィア 03-3407-2219

1F Westpoint Biru, 2-15-14 Nishi Asabu, Minato-ku, Tōkyō
東京都港区西麻布 2-15-14 ウエストポイントビル 1F
Open: 5 pm–4.30 am, closed Sunday
Booking recommended? No Credit cards? Most major cards English menu? No Cover charge: No

I liked Chie Tatō's rum bar in Nishi Azabu so much that I was back with my wife the next day. Tafia is intimate and quiet. There is a feeling of intelligence about the place. Tatō-san taught me the difference between *rhum agricole*, drinks from the French Caribbean produced exclusively from pure sugar cane juice, and the molasses-based rums from the English Caribbean (often dark and heavy) and the Spanish Caribbean (generally lighter in style). "The taste is totally different," said Tatō-san. "The agricoles are usually much richer than the molasses-based rums, with very complex tastes. Another variable is the aging. Like whisky, some rum gets a lot of its taste from storage in barrels," she said. More than 400 rums of all types are available at Tafia, including those made on Japan's remote southern islands (see map, page 87). Tafia also offers a good cocktail list (try the "Mojito," 1,000 yen) and quality cigars. I had the "La Favorite" rhum agricole from Martinique (1,500 yen), a rich, powerful drink with a flavor of prunes and a long, rounded sweet finish that forever shattered my idea that God intended rum for daiquirís (lovely though they are). If you like Tafia, the Tōkyō area has a whole rum drinking subculture to explore: Screw Driver in Musashino city, offering more than 400 rums and some great US whiskey (0422-20-5112; www.screw-driver.com); Bar Julep in Setagaya (03-3422-7650 www.julep.jp); Bar King Rum in Ikebukuro (03-3980-2903; www.kingrum.jp), and Bar Lamp in Ginza (03-3561-2666). There are lots of these sorts of specialist bars in Japan. This guide offers a few hints to get readers into the swing of things, but it is impossible to cover all the bars. For almost any type of alcohol you can think of, you will find at least one specialist bar.

DIRECTIONS: A longish walk from Roppongi Station, Exit 4b. Walk straight ahead with the flyover to your left. At the bottom of the hill, turn right on to Gaien Nishi-dōri (Route 418). Follow Route 418 as it turns toward Sendagaya. Take an immediate left beside the shop with the sign "Artworks of Kajimasu." Cross to the furthest of the two parallel roads at the bottom of this lane and turn right. Tafia is about 50 yards along on your right.

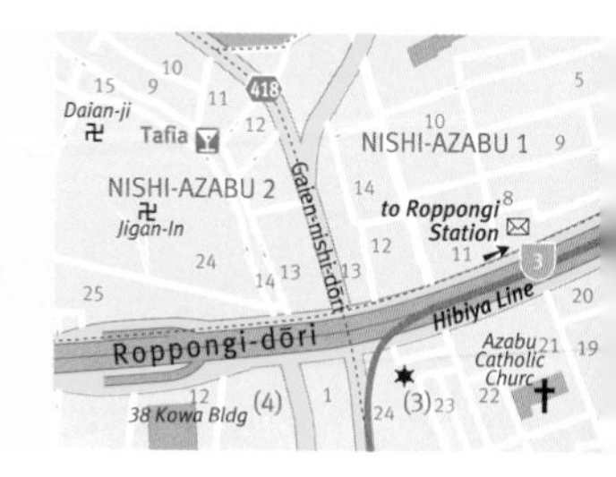

Tender テンダー 03-3571-8343 www.cocktail-academy.co.jp

5F Noh Gakudō, 6-5-15 Ginza, Chūō-ku, Tōkyō
東京都中央区銀座 6-5-15 能楽堂ビル 5F
Open: 5 pm–1 am; closed Sunday and national holidays. Credit cards? Yes English menu? Yes
Cover charge: 1,600 yen

To be honest, I was extremely skeptical when the leading European mixologist Stanislav Vadrna explained the unique ethic of Japanese bartending to me. He said: "A bar in the Japanese understanding means a unique world of details, precise service, thousands of shaking styles, ice diamonds served in cocktails, different techniques of drink preparation, and dedication to this trade.... But it is not only a question of the result, the most important thing is the way that leads to it. Therefore, in Japanese bartending there is an obvious relation to 'The Way of Tea.' The way of the cocktail includes all the principles of this way, naturally adapted to working behind the bar." The alarm bells started going off with those words—"the way of...." Anybody staying in Japan for any length of time hears a lot of explanations for Japanese customs that mention the words "Zen," "tea ceremony," "samurai" or "group-ethic," and they are almost always complete tosh. However, a week after hearing Vadrna's explanation and heeding his advice to visit Tender, I sat in Kazuo Uyeda's legendary bar watching my gimlet (1,600 yen) being painstakingly prepared and began to see precisely what he had meant. Vadrna, who trained at Tender and describes Uyeda-san as his "master," was not indulging in over-vague social theorizing but was instead trying to explain to me how he had been trained. Everything about the experience at Tender, from the extremely precise and practiced movements with which every cocktail is made to the way in which the welcoming of the guest is made central to the art of the cocktail, seems to be self-consciously drawing on Japan's older drink preparing tradition. Uyeda-san, who himself explicitly references the tea ceremony, has won international prizes and is most famous internationally for inventing the "Hard Shake", a complex multi-step shaking method that involves snapping of the wrists and twisting the shaker. Some bartenders in the US and Europe have become enthusiastic devotees of the technique, while others have dismissed it as having no significant influence on the drink produced, but my visit to Tender convinced me that something more than mere technique set the bar apart. There really is a Japanese "Way of the Cocktail" and Tender is one of the best places to see it. Please note the very high cover charge. Dropping into Tender for a single drink is not cheap.

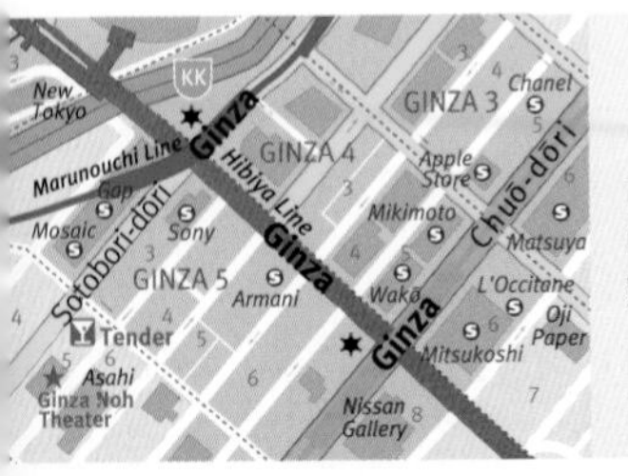

DIRECTIONS: Ginza Station, Exit B7. Turn left. Turn right at the crossroads and left at the junction with Route 405. It is on the fifth floor on your left, opposite Pizza Salvatore and next to a kimono shop.

Yakushu Bar 薬酒バー 03-3421-7229

2-13-7 Sangenjaya, Setagaya, Tōkyō
東京都世田谷区三軒茶屋 2 丁目 13-7
Open: 7 pm–5 am Booking recommended? Yes Credit cards? Yes English menu? No
Cover charge: No

Yakushu literally translates as "medicinal alcohol." The use of alcoholic drinks as cures has a long history in Japan. Both *shōchū* and *awamori* have very long medicinal traditions, and when Western-style wine was trying to find a market in Japan in the late 19th century, it quickly found itself repackaged as a medicine (see page 199). I stepped into this tiny bar in Sangenjaya with some trepidation, because the most famous *yakushu* are spirit bottles containing dead snakes, iguanas and the like. Barman "Hikari" put my mind at rest: "There is *dōbutsukei*, which is the snakes and iguanas and turtles and what not, and there is the *shokubutsukei*, which is just vegetables." Although some lizards do stare out at you from jars in the Yakushu Bar, most of the drink actually consumed is made solely from vegetables by Hikari himself. His Brazilian footballer-style single-word name gives a sense of the New Age feel of the place. They have "live painting" and ecological candle making sessions in the tiny second floor *tatami* room. The music is mostly R and B, chill-out, and dance styles. "We get people coming after the clubs to relax," said Hikari, serving up a sweet "kukonomi yuzuwari" (wolfsberry and citrus mix, 800 yen) which was supposed to be very good for my mind and body. I am not sure whether it was Hikari's engaging laughter or the wolfsberry but I did feel better after a pit stop at the Yakushu Bar.

DIRECTIONS: Sangenjaya Station (Tōkyū Den-en-toshi Line/Tōkyū Setagaya Line). Go out of the central gates and then North Exit A. Walk straight ahead across the side road and then cross the main road to Big Echo karaoke. Bear right toward the Carrot Tower. Turn left after the Stage music bar and before the Farmer's store. Continue down the featureless alley beside the drink machines and, at the fork in the alley, turn to the right of the Sula wine bar. The Yakushu Bar is on the left under a Sapporo sign in an orange building, just after the Sugar Bar Michi.

Buying Japanese Wines, Beers and Spirits

Every neighborhood in Japan seems to have an independent liquor store. The big supermarkets have yet to deal a death blow to these places but, judging by the state of the stock in some of them, the end cannot be too far off.

You often find a refrigerator full of the standard beer and *happōshu* brands (see page 141), an aisle groaning with multi-gallon bottles of cheap neutral spirits (see page 80) and an eccentric selection of dust-covered spirit, wine and liqueur bottles that are clearly intended more as decorations than as items for sale. The proprietors often look about as well-preserved as their stale, boiled booze, hanging on into late semi-retirement, trying to squeeze the last few drops out of a way of doing business that last worked 30 years ago.

But it is not all gloom. There are lots of other shops that have responded to the rise of the supermarkets in innovative and exciting ways. Some of the stores featured in this chapter are run by large businesses, but others are thriving in a viciously competitive and contracting alcohol market by specializing in particular types of alcohol and offering jaw-dropping selections of their chosen liquids. The owners and staff are usually keen to pass on their knowledge and enthusiasm.

Tanakaya in Toshima, Tōkyō (page 246), is the best general foreign alcohol store in Japan. It also offers small ranges of Japanese whisky and craft beer.

Awamori Kan

泡盛館 098 885-5681 www.awamori.co.jp/index-e.html

Recommended for: *Awamori*
1-81 Shuri Samukawa, Naha, Okinawa, 903-0826
〒903-0826 沖縄県那覇市首里寒川町 1-81
Open: 10 am–7.30 pm; closed national holidays
Credit cards? Most major cards

Not just a shop, but a sort of shrine to all things *awamori*. There are are more than 1,000 different *awamori* on sale here from all of Okinawa's distilleries as well as exclusive bottlings of *kūsu awamori* aged by owner Akiyoshi Miyagi. Miyagi-san is a highly respected figure in the *awamori* world, and has helped lead the push to rediscover *awamori*'s traditions since the 1980s.

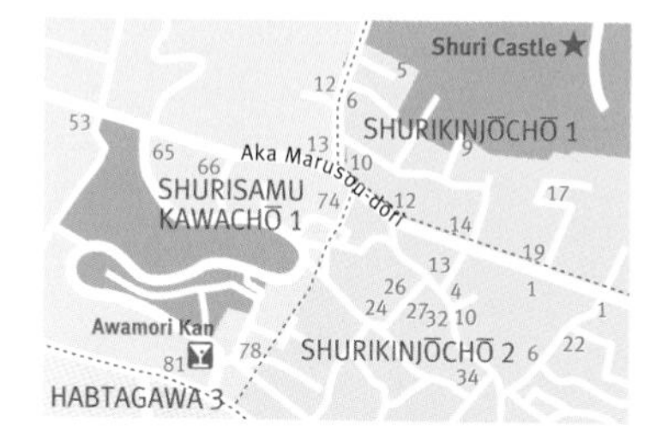

DIRECTIONS: A three-minute drive southwest of Shuri Castle, but not very easy to find. My taxi driver struggled. It is at the bottom of a sharply winding road climbing from Kinjo Dam Street (Kinjo Dam-dōri) to Aka Marusō Street.

Enoteca

エノテカ 03-3280-3634 www.enoteca.co.jp/en

Recommended for: Wine
Arisugawa West 1F, 5-14-15 Minami-azabu, Minato-ku, Tōkyō, 106-0047 (and other locations)
〒106-0047 東京都港区南麻布 5-14-15 アリスガワウエスト 1F
Open: 11 am–9 pm Credit cards? Yes

Enoteca is a major wine retailer and has shops all over Japan (see their website for a list of stores in English). Their flagship shop in Hiroo has an extensive range of imported wine (no Japanese wine) ranging from good-value cut-priced deals to the extremely pricey bottles in the glass cases at the back. They have a standing bar where you can taste some of the wines (last orders 8.30 pm).

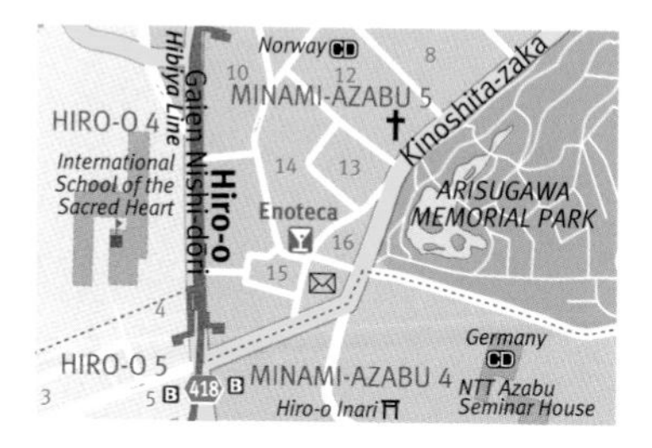

DIRECTIONS: A three-minute walk from Tōkyō Metro Hibiya Line Hiroo Station, Exit 1. Turn left around the corner, left again after the McDonald's.

Hasegawa Saketen

はせがわ酒店 03-5439-9498
www.hasegawasaketen.com/english

Recommended for: Sake, wine
2-3-3 Azabujuban Minato-ku, Tōkyō, 106-0045
〒106-0045 東京都港区麻布十番 2-3-3
Open: 11 am–9 pm
Credit cards? Yes

Hasegawa have three shops—a small tasting bar at the Omotesando Hills development (Harajuku JR Station), their head shop in Kameido and this great new store in Azabu Jūban. They have full details of all of the stores on their English language website (see URL above). I found the staff knowledgeable and helpful, and the small standing bar allows you to taste a few glasses before deciding what to buy. As you would expect from one of Tōkyō's top sake retailers, the sake selection is very good but they also have some interesting wines, including, unlike most of the imported wine stores, a few Japanese products.

DIRECTIONS: Azabu Jūban, Namboku Line, Exit 4. Facing Route 415, take the road behind you to your left. Hasegawa Saketen is in the third block on your left.

Isekane

いせかね 03-3203-2171 www.isekane.jp/store

Recommended for: Sake (some good *awamori*, *shōchū* and wine)
3-19-1 Nishi Waseda, Shinjuku-ku, Tōkyō, 109-0051
〒109-0051 東京都新宿区西早稲田 3-19-1
Open: Monday–Saturday 9 am–10 pm; Sunday and national holidays 2 pm–9 pm Credit Cards? No

My favorite sake store. Owner Shirō Hashiba stocks a good general range of alcohol, but his real passion is sake. He is extremely helpful to newcomers to the drink, and while the range is by no means exhaustive, the quality is very good. Hashiba-san is a mine of information and it is all communicated with a friendly informality, completely devoid of any feeling of precious connoisseurship.

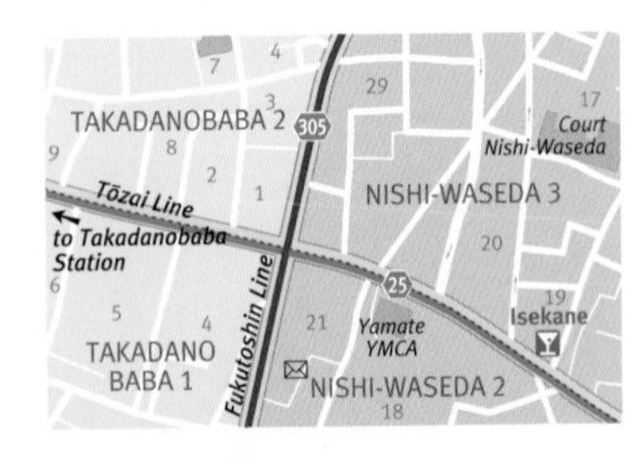

DIRECTIONS: Isekane is about equidistant from the Waseda and Takadanobaba Stations on the Tozai Line. The closest underground station is the new Nishiwaseda Station on the Fukutoshin Line. Turn right out of Exit 1 and right at the crossroads with Route 25. It is on the left-hand side of the road as you walk toward Waseda, two blocks before the 7-Eleven convenience store.

Kinokuniya Liquor Store

紀伊国屋酒店 03-3713-2857

Recommended for: Whisky, wine

1-4-2 Kinokuniya, Ebisu-Minami, Shibuya-ku, Tōkyō

東京都渋谷区恵比寿南 〒1 〒丁目 〒4-2

Open: 10 am–10 pm

A very good selection of Japanese whiskies, particularly the Ichiro's Malt whiskies from Chichibu distillery. They also offer a nice variety of wine and sake. The prices are not as steep as the stylish interior may lead you to believe.

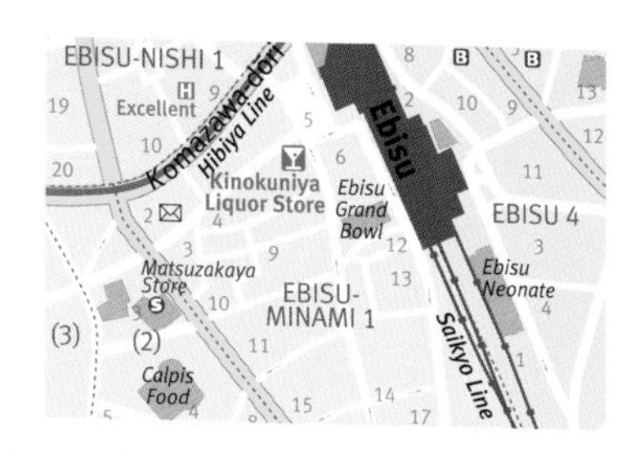

DIRECTIONS: Out of the west side of Ebisu Station, on the left side of the taxi/bus concourse.

Masutoh

升藤 03-3351-1087 www.masutoh.com

Recommended for: Sake, wine

6-29 Yochomachi, Shinjuku-ku, Tōkyō

東京都新宿区余丁町 6-29

Open: 11 am–12 am; Sunday 6 pm–11 pm; closed 2nd Wednesday of every month.

Credit cards? Mastercard and Visa. Only for orders exceeding 10,000 yen

Stuart and Emiko Ablett's Shinjuku shop looks like a thousand other small Japanese liquor stores from the street, but the selection of more than 500 imported wines marks it out. There is also an impressive selection of cigars, and sake fans will want to have a look at the *koshu* sakes, some of which are aged by the Abletts themselves.

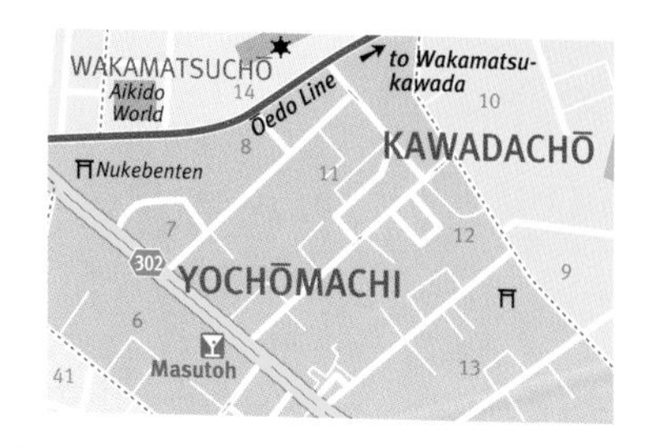

DIRECTIONS: Wakamatsu-Kawada Station, Kawada Exit. Turn left and take the third left. It is on the right side of the street, with Roman alphabet on the sign.

Meishu Center

名酒センター 03-5405-4441 www.bimy.co.jp

Recommended for: Sake
2-3-29 Hamamatsu-chō, Minato-ku, Tōkyō
東京都港区浜松町 2-3-29
Open: 11 am–9 pm; closed weekends
Credit cards? No

The Meishu Center is not a place to come for an anonymous shop. It is all about tasting before you buy and learning from the very knowledgeable staff. If you have enough Japanese or are persistent enough with your sign language, you can have a very rewarding experience finding your ideal sake. Tasting sets cost 500 yen for three samples and there is a wide range to choose from. All sakes are available in bottles to take away.

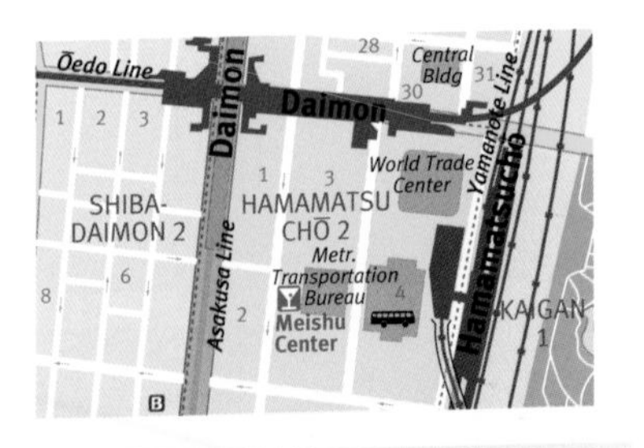

DIRECTIONS: Daimon Station, Toei Subway. Turn left out of Exit B4 and left again up the side road. It is about 150 yards on your left. The Meishu Center is also accessible from JR Hamamatsuchō Station on the Yamanote and Keihin-Tōhoku Lines.

Narita Duty Free

成田空港免税店 0476 322 802 www.narita-airport.jp/en

Recommended for: Last-minute shoppers; limited selections of *awamori*, liqueurs, sake, *shōchū*, whisky, etc.
Narita Airport, Narita-shi, Chiba 282-8601
〒282-8601 千葉県成田市成田国際空港
Credit cards? Yes

The duty-free shops at Narita airport (and some larger regional airports) stock some *awamori*, sake, *shōchū*, Japanese whisky and other domestic liquors. The range is not comparable to the specialist stores, but usually includes some high quality products of each type. A number of shops in the terminal sell different selections of alcohol. The Fa-So-La is Narita's largest chain and the outlet at Terminal 1 offers tastings. Unfortunately, the new rules about liquid items in hand luggage mean that many travelers must forgo shopping for duty-free alcohol. Passengers transiting through locations including (but not limited to) the US, Europe and Japan, where liquid items in hand luggage are limited to very small bottles, may find the alcohol they bought at Narita confiscated when they transfer planes for the second leg of their journey.

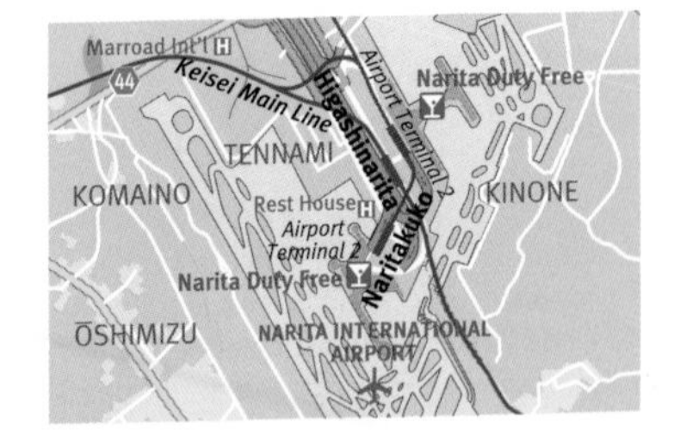

Nissin World Delicatessan

日進ワールドデリカテッセン 03-3583-4586
www.nissinham.co.jp

Recommended for: Beer, wine
2-34-2, Higashi-Azabu, Minato-ku, Tōkyō, 106-0044
〒106-0044 東京都港区東麻布 2-34-2
Open: 9 am–9 pm
Credit cards? Yes

Nissin claims to have the "world's largest wine shop located in the center of a major city." I can think of a few wine stores in a few big cities that felt quite a lot bigger than this single-floor shop but I won't quibble—it is large enough for anyone's needs. Nissin offers a very good selection of imported wines, a reasonable range of foreign beers and one or two Japanese craft brews. Car parking space is available.

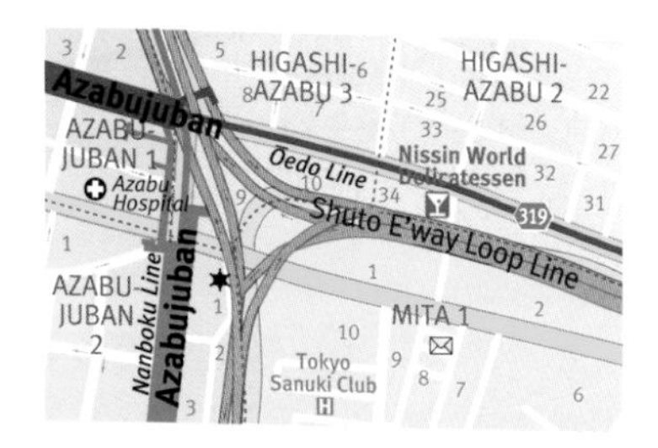

DIRECTIONS: From Azabu Jūban Subway Station Namboku Line, Exit 3, take a right on to Highway 319 and under the overpasses. From Azabu Jūban Oedo Line, Exit 6, walk down 319 away from the overpasses. It is on your right and clearly signed.

Osakaya

大阪屋 03-3354-2202 osaka-ya.net

Recommended for: Beer, wine
Shinjuku Lumine Est B1, Shinjuku 3-38-1, Shinjuku-ku, Tōkyō
東京新宿区新宿 3-38-1 新宿ルミネエスト B1
Open: Weekdays 11 am–9.30 pm; Saturday 10.30 am–9.30 pm Credit cards? Most major cards

Osakaya stocks a good selection of about 150 beers, mainly from Belgium, but also including a small selection of domestic craft brews from makers such as Hitachino Nest (see page 147) and Baird Beer (see page 155). The other half of this tiny shop is devoted to imported wines. If you are shopping for craft beer around Shinjuku, it may be worth your while popping over to the Isetan department store, which is a couple of minutes down the road. Isetan's basement sake and beer shop usually has a limited but interesting selection.

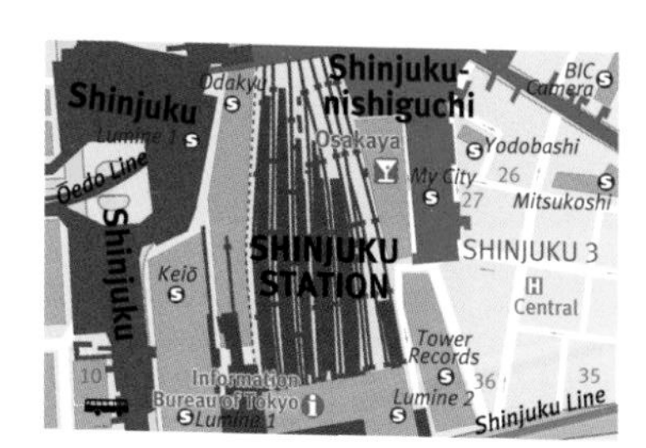

DIRECTIONS: On the B1 floor of Lumine Est, a gaggle of concessions next to JR Shinjuku's East Exit.

Sakaya Kurihara

さかや栗原 03-3408-5379 www.sakaya-kurihara.jp

Recommended for: **Sake**
3-6-17 Moto-Azabu, Minato-ku, Tōkyō, 106-0046
〒106-0046 東京都港区元麻布 3-6-17
Open: **10 am–8 pm; closed Sunday**
Credit cards? **Most major cards**

Another great sake shop that disguises itself as a Mom and Pop store. A refrigerated walk-in cellar stacked full of great sake is hidden in an adjoining room. They also have a small selection of good-quality *shōchū*. I had filled my bag with sake at Hasegawa before arriving at Kurihara so, instead, I bought a Kumamoto rice *shōchū* with a rich, sherry-like flavor.

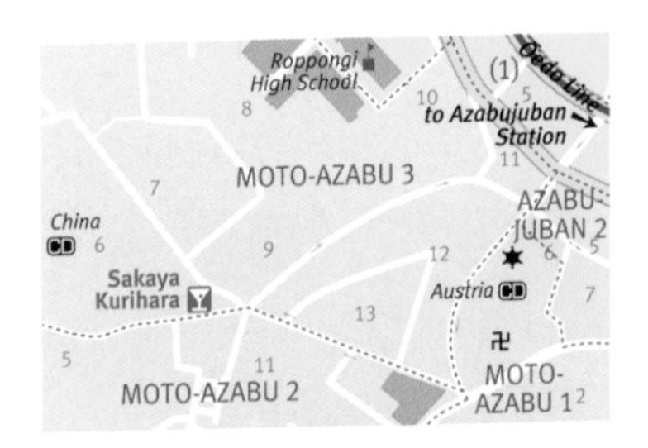

DIRECTIONS: A little hard to find. Azabu Jūban Station, Namboku Line, Exit 4. Facing Route 415, take the road behind you to your right. Keep walking straight ahead for about 500 yards until the road forks into three. Take the middle of the three. Turn left at the next junction. It is about 20 yards on your right.

Shinanoya Liquor Store

信濃屋 03-6439-4708 www.shinanoya.co.jp

Recommended for: **Whisky, wine**
3-2-1 Nishi-Azabu, Minato-ku, Tōkyō, 106-0031
〒106-0031 東京都港区西麻布 3-2-1
Open: **Monday–Saturday 4 pm–1 am; Sunday and national holidays 4 pm–12 pm**
Credit cards? **Yes**

Shinanoya is a specialist liquor store with some rare bottlings of Japanese whiskies, including the sought-after but sometimes hard to find Ichiro's Malt range. I have found Ichiro's Malts here that were not available anywhere else. Their imported wines and other spirits are also very good. I tend to visit the Roppongi store but Shinanoya has another good store in Shinjuku (1-12-9 Kabuki-chō, Shinjuku-ku, Tōkyō. Tel: 03-3204-2365) and a number of other stores in and around Tōkyō (see www.shinanoya.co.jp/shop.htm for a Japanese language map).

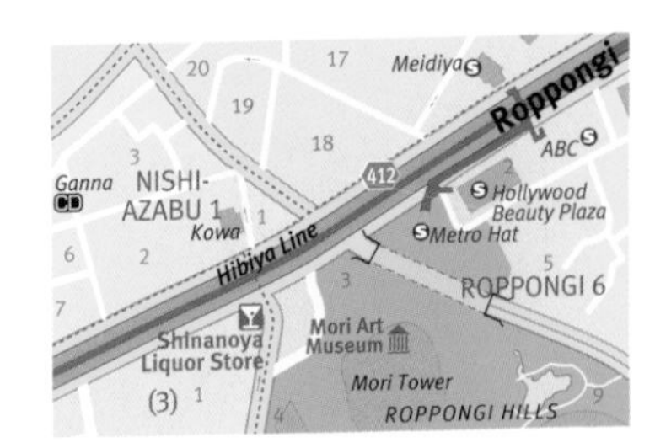

DIRECTIONS: From Roppongi underground station, walk toward Roppongi Hills. It is on your left, about 100 yards after Roppongi Hills.

Sho-chu Authority

焼酎オーソリティ 03-5208-5157
www.authority-online.jp

Recommended for: ***Awamori, shōchū***
1F Tōkyō Station, 1-9-1 Marunouchi, Chiyoda-ku, Tōkyō
東京都千代田区丸の内 1-9-1 東京駅 1F
Open: **10 am–9 pm** Credit cards? **Yes**

This is the best place in Tōkyō for *awamori* and *shōchū*. I was surprised to find two shelving units full of Iki barley *shōchū*, for instance. There is a similar coverage for all other types of *shōchū*. The staff are friendly and are used to explaining things from scratch. (They get a steady stream of foreigners looking for sake, not knowing that *shōchū* is different.) I usually go to the Tōkyō Station store but they now have a chain of shops, including Shiodome Station, Tōkyō (B2F Caretta Shiodome, 1-8-2 Higashi-Shimbashi, Minato-ku. Tel: 03-5537-2105) and Ōsaka (2F, Nanba Parks, 2-10-70 Nanbanaka, Ōsaka. Tel: 06-4397-9711).

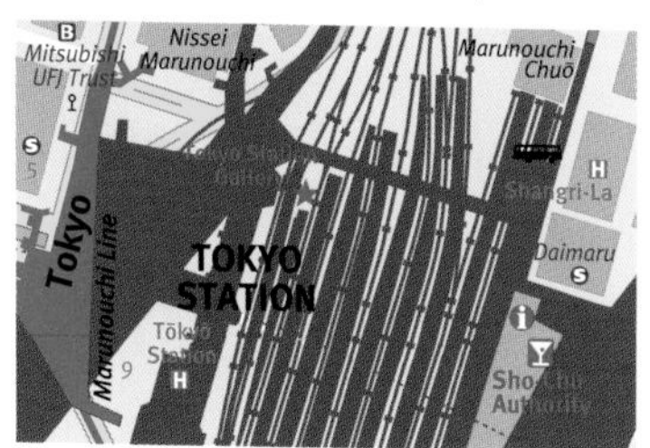

DIRECTIONS: In Tōkyō JR station, go to Marunouchi North Exit and follow the signs for Yaesu North Exit. It is in the connecting walkway on your right.

Suzuden

鈴伝 03-3351-1777 www6.ocn.ne.jp/~suzuden

Recommended for: **Sake**
Yotsuya 1-10, Shinjuku-ku, Tōkyō
東京都新宿区四谷 1-10
Open: **Weekdays 9 am–9 pm; Saturday 9 am–6 pm; closed Sunday and national holidays**
Credit cards? **No**

On first entering this famous store you might be forgiven for thinking that its stock is a little slight. Downstairs, in the refrigerated cellars, however, the range is quite overwhelming. This is not necessarily the easiest place to go as a sake beginner. The price of each sake is not always clear and you are left to fend for yourself by the polite but slightly standoffish staff. If you can navigate those chilly rooms, however, Suzuden will reward you. They have a small standing bar.

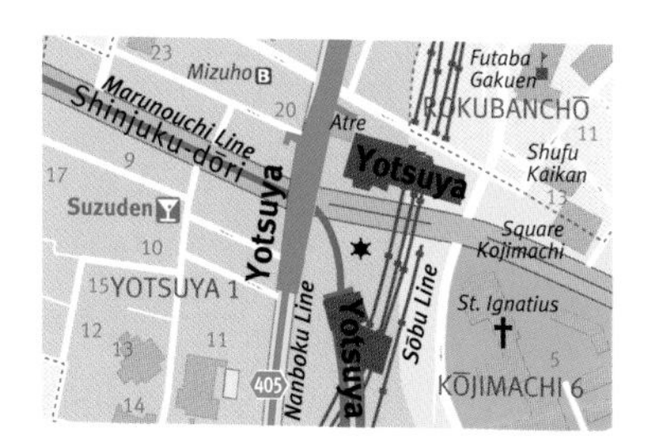

DIRECTIONS: Two minutes walk from Yotsuya station's Yotsuya and Akasaka exits. Take the road between the Rising Sun pub and the Family Mart convenience store. It is tucked on a street corner just off the main road.

Tanakaya

田中屋 03-3953-8888 tanakaya.cognacfan.com

Recommended for: *Awamori*, beer, whisky, wine
Mejiro 3-4-14, Toshima-ku, Tōkyō
東京都豊島区目白 3-4-14
Open: 11 am–8 pm; closed Sunday
Credit cards? No

The best imported alcohol shop in Japan. There are excellent *awamori*, brandy, grappa, rum, port, sherry and wine sections, plus a wall of very good craft beers (mostly imported but some Japanese products). There is a small amount of good quality sake and *shōchū*. The formidable range of whisky is mainly Scottish, Irish and North American, but there is also a nice selection of the hard to find Ichiro's Malt Japanese whisky. Look elsewhere for Suntory and Nikka whiskies.

DIRECTIONS: Mejiro Station, Yamanote Line. Turn left. Walk about 20 yards. It is in a basement on your left, right beside McDonald's.

Wine Yamazaki

ヴィノスやまざき 03-5789-7701 www.v-yamazaki.jp

Recommended for: Wine
5-4-14 Hiroo, Shibuya-ku ,Tōkyō, 150-0012 (and other locations)
〒150-0012 東京都渋谷区広尾 5-4-14
Open: 11 am–11 pm
Credit cards? Yes

Wine Yamazaki have a chain of shops in several locations in Tōkyō and their home prefecture Shizuoka (an English language list of the stores is on their website). The Hiroo store I visited had very friendly English speaking staff and labeling in the Roman alphabet. Sadly, like so many of the best Japanese wine stores, they seem to be ignoring Japanese wine, but the imported wines are first rate.

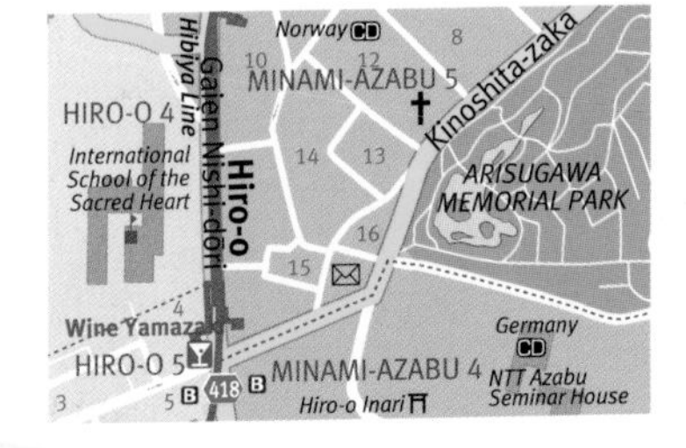

DIRECTIONS: Tōkyō Metro Hibiya Line, Hiroo Station, Exits 1 and 2. The bright pink building is hard to miss.

Other Stores

The stores listed below all have good reputations. In putting together this list, I have relied heavily on the ww.bento.com internet guides to eating and drinking in Tōkyō and Kansai; Bryan Harrell's "Brews News" newsletters (www.bento.com/brews.html); John Gauntner's www.sake-world.com website; *Metropolis* (Tōkyō's top English language magazine); the features pages of *The Japan Times*; and the international beer reviews site www.beeradvocate.com.

Aji no Machida
Recommeded for: Sake (cup sake)
1-49-12 Kamitakada, Nakano-ku, Tōkyō
www.ajinomachidaya. com
03-3389-4551

Beer House Ken
Recommeded for: Beer
2-3-8 Miya-chō, Fuchu-shi, Tōkyō
www.bhken.com
042-369-7710

Cave de Re-Lax
Recommended for: Wine (including some Japanese)
1-6-11 Nishi-shimbashi, Minato-ku, Tōkyō, 105-0003
www.caverelax.com/english/HOME.html
03-3595-3697

Fujikonishi
Recommended for: Wine (fairly strong ranges of most types of alcohol)
1F Daisan Toya Biru, 2-2-9 Chūō, Nagano-ku, Tōkyō. 164-0011
www.fujikonishi.co.jp
03-3365-2244

Hikariya
Recommended for: Sake
5-45-5, Kamata, Ōta-ku, Tōkyō
www.hikariya.com
03-3739-4141

Kanoya
Recommended for: Wine (strong on Japanese wine)
2-44-8 Minami-kamonomiya, Odawara, Kanagawa
0465-47-2826

Koyama Shoten
Recommended for: Sake, *shōchū*
5-15-17 Sekido, Tama-shi, Tōkyō, 206-0011
0423-75-7026

Marche Dix Jours
Recommended for: Wine (including some Japanese)
58 Banchi, Nihonodōri, Naka-ku, Yokohama
045-662-5260

Meishu no Yutaka
Recommended for: Sake (also stock interesting Japanese wines)
4-13 Nishi 15-chōme, Kita 25-jo, Kita-ku, Sapporo, 001-0025
www.yutaka1.com/eindex.html or the very informative blog of American staff member Carlin at www.meishu-no-yutaka.blogspot.com
011-716-5174

Picasso
Recommended for: Wine
1F Space Shimbashi, 15 Benzaitenchō, Higashiyama-ku, Kyōto www.winepicasso.jp
075-525-6052

Rote Rose Wine Shop
Recommended for: Wine (German)
4-9-14 Kitanochō, Chūō-ku, Kōbe
www.roterose-kobe.co.jp
078-222-3200

Sake Haus Shiro
Recommended for: Whisky
5-11, Ebisu-chō, Naka-ku, Hiroshima
www.sake-sumida.co.jp/shiro.html
082-246-9602

Seijio Ishii
Recommended for: Wine
B2F Minamikan, Hankyu Sanbangai, 1-1-3 Shibata, Kita-ku, Ōsaka (and other locations)
www.seijoishii.co.jp
06-6486-2960

Shimada Shoten
Recommended for: Sake
3-5-1 Itachibori, Nishi-ku, Ōsaka
www.sake-shimada.co.jp
06-6531-8119

Sugaya Beer
Recommended for: Beer
5-2-16 Shiboku-honchō, Miyamae-ku, Kawasaki-shi, Kanagawa-ken, 216-0031
sugaya-beer.com
044-877-3946

Tobu Department store
Recommended for: Beer
1-1-25 Nishi-ikebukuro, Toshima-ku (and other locations) Tōkyō, 171-8512
www.tobu-dept.jp/ikebukuro
03-3981-2211

Wine Crazy
Nishigawa Agaru Nishioji Sanjo, Nakagyo-Ku, Kyōto, 604-8435
www.wine-crazy.jp
075-821-1208

Yamatoya
Recommended for: Sake, *shōchū*, wine
4-3 Ebisu-chō, Naka-ku, Hiroshima
www.piconet.co.jp/yamatoya
082-241-5660

APPENDIX

Speaking "Bar Japanese"

Taking the plunge into Japanese alcohol culture can take a little bit of courage, especially for those who do not speak Japanese fluently. It is always going to be easier to play it safe and order a Budweiser from the hotel bar than to venture out into the back streets and start pushing your nose into unfamiliar drinking holes serving unfamiliar drinks. In many moods, I go for the Budweiser and the quiet life, and there are hotel bars and bars catering specifically to foreigners in this guide. Some of them are great. Nevertheless, it is nice at least to have the option of doing something different, and I am convinced that even someone who is completely ignorant of the Japanese language can enjoy the best of Japan's bars and drinks with relative ease.

Learning Japanese is a bit like climbing Mount Fuji. The higher you go, the steeper it gets. This is good news for the beginner, because basic Japanese pronunciation is not difficult and beginners' grammar is also fairly straightforward. The third big factor in the novice's favor is that the majority of Japanese people are very supportive of people giving their language a try.

That's the good news. The bad news is that Japanese is one of the hardest written languages in the world to master. There are two phonetic syllabaries with 45 characters each—*hiragana* and *katakana* (often used for foreign words)—and much of the meaning in any sentence (or on any bottle label) is carried by fiendishly difficult *kanji* ideograms. There are thousands of these to be learned by rote and no prospect of teaching this writing system for the purposes of this book. But who cares? Whoever said you needed to be able to understand everything around you to enjoy a drink at a bar? I have divided this chapter into two sections—"Visiting Japanese bars" and "Shopping for alcohol." They provide some basic spoken phrases and written language that should take you a surprisingly long way into Japanese alcohol culture. But first, two important preliminaries—Japanese pronunciation and counting.

Pronunciation

Basic Japanese pronunciation is not very complicated. It is a good general principle to try to pronounce all syllables with equal stress. English speakers tend to put stress on particular parts of words. Japanese speakers tend to give each syllable equal stress.

There are five basic vowel sounds. There is a difficulty in trying to find reliable analogues in English, because English dialects differ so greatly in their pronunciation, but here is my best shot:

a—to rhyme with the first syllable of "cattle" for an Englishman. Many North Americans might describe this as somewhere between the **a** in father and the **a** in Dad. (International Phonetic Alphabet (IPA): (**a**)

i—to rhyme with the first syllable of "fiddle" or "feet." (International Phonetic Alphabet (IPA): (**i**)

u—to rhyme with "who," or "true" or the first syllable of "cruel." (International Phonetic Alphabet (IPA): (**ω**)

e—as in "pen" or "bed." (International Phonetic Alphabet (IPA): (**e**)

o—as in "not" for an Englishman. Many English speakers lengthen the pronunciation of **o**. The Japanese **o** is pronounced with minimal mouth movement. (International Phonetic Alphabet (IPA): (**o**)

These are combined with consonants—**ka**, **ki**, **ku**, **ke**, **ko** or **na**, **ni**, **nu**, **ne**, **no**, etc.—but the pronunciation of the vowel component remains constant. Japanese has a strict syllable system similar to Italian and, indeed, the five basic Japanese vowel sounds are quite close to their basic Italian equivalents. There are also some elongated vowel sounds, which I have transcribed in this book with an accent (**ō**, **ū**). These are best regarded by the beginner as slightly longer pronunciations of the basic vowel sound (for instance, **ō** to rhyme with "flow" or "hoe" or "oh" in my British English.) There are, of course, plenty of complications (many language teachers will be pulling their hair out at my oversimplifications) but the only ones I am going to mention here are three additional long vowel sounds:

ei—as in "day"

ai—as in "lie" or "fly"

au—as in "out" or "Ow!"

And, finally, one important irregularity in standard Japanese pronunciation: try to leave off the final **u** of words ending in **su**: **desu** ("dess"), **shimasu** ("shimas") and **arimasu** ("arimas").

Counting

In bars and shops, you generally only need to count to five and tell the time after noon. Japanese counting is a very complex business, with all sorts of systems for different types of object, but here is a very basic guide:

Counting things, dishes, etc.

One—**hitotsu** ひとつ 一つ
Two—**futatsu** ふたつ 二つ
Three—**mittsu** みっつ 三つ
Four—**yottsu** よっつ 四つ
Five—**itsutsu** いつつ 五つ

Counting people
one person—**hitori** ひとり 一人
two people—**futari** ふたり 二人
three people—**san-nin** さんにん 三人
More people—replace the **ji** on the times below with **nin** to make that number of people

Telling the time
1 o'clock—**ichi-ji** いちじ 一時
2 o'clock—**ni-ji** にじ 二時
3 o'clock—**san-ji** さんじ 三時
4 o'clock—**yo-ji** よじ 四時
5 o'clock—**go-ji** ごじ 五時
6 o'clock—**roku-ji** ろくじ 六時
7 o'clock—**shichi-ji** しちじ 七時
8 o'clock—**hachi-ji** はちじ 八時
9 o'clock—**ku-ji** くじ 九時
10 o'clock—**jū-ji** じゅうじ 十時
11 o'clock—**jū-ichi-ji** じゅういちじ 十一時
12 o'clock—**jū-ni-ji** じゅうにじ 十二時

Visiting Japanese bars

My fallback patter when visiting any new bar is:

What is your recommendation?
Osusume wa nan desu ka?
お勧めはなんですか？

That phrase and two other words—**daijōbu**, meaning "ok," and **sumimasen**, meaning "excuse me"—will get you a surprisingly long way in Japan. **Sumimasen** can be used, like its English equivalent, to get attention as well as to say sorry. **Daijōbu** is the Swiss Army Knife of Japanese words:

Credit card, ok? **Kurejitto kaado daijōbu?**

Two people, ok? **Futari daijōbu?**

Raw fish, ok! (I can eat raw fish) **Sashimi daijōbu!**

Can I smoke here? **Tabako daijōbu desu ka?**

Just like "ok" in English, a **daijōbu desu** ("it's ok"), combined with skilful enough shaking or nodding of the head, can be used to say you don't want anything more from the overly attentive waiter or that you are perfectly happy to go along with whatever they are suggesting, if only you knew what that was.

Making a reservation on the telephone

Some of the bars featured in this guide are very busy indeed and, in many of the reviews, I have recommended making a reservation. If you are staying at a hotel with English speaking staff, a good ruse is to go to reception and get them to make a reservation for you. If you have a Japanese friend or a good Japanese speaker in your party, get them to do the dirty work but, if all else fails, making a reservation is not the hardest thing in the world:

Is that (repeat the name of the bar)?
(The name of the bar) desu ka?
(店名)ですか？

Could you make a reservation (for two people) from (8 pm) today?
Kyō, (yoru hachi ji) ni (futari) yoyaku o onegai shimasu.
今日、(夜八時)に(二人)予約をお願いします。

Just substitute in the time and number of people from the lists in the section above. Just for clarification, **Kyō** means "today," **yoru** means "evening," **hachi ji** means "8 o'clock" and **yoyaku** means "to reserve." The last bit is just politely asking them to do it for you. If you are happy to cut the formalities completely, you could just say **yoyaku shitai** (to rhyme with "fly") instead of **yoyaku o onegai shimasu**. That would mean "I want to make a reservation...." It would sound a bit abrupt, but it would be understood.

My name is ... (say your name slowly)
Watashi no namae wa ... desu.
私の名前は ... です。

Again, if you are getting tongue-tied, you could cut that back to (very slow pronunciation of name) **desu**, meaning "I'm (name)."

Getting a seat when you arrive

Two people. Are there any seats?
Futari desu. Seki wa arimasu ka?
二人です。席はありますか？

Ordering

Menu **Menu** メニュー

Snacks normally eaten while drinking
Otsumami おつまみ

Recommendation **Osusume** お勧め

Drink **Nomimono** 飲み物

Food **Tabemono** 食べ物

What is your recommended drink?
Osusume no nomimono wa nan desu ka?
お勧めの飲み物は何ですか？

What is your recommended sake/wine/*shōchū*/whisky/beer/*awamori*?
Osusume no (nihonshu/wine/shōchū/whisky/beer(biiru)/awamori) wa nan desu ka?
お勧めの(日本酒/ワイン/焼酎/ウィスキー/ビール/泡盛)はなんですか？

Note that sake is most clearly referred to as **nihonshu** and not "sake," which merely means "alcohol."

I will have one of those.
Sore onegai shimasu
それ　お願いします。

Could you recommend me some food?
Ryōri no osusume arimasu ka?
料理のお勧め　ありますか

Could you recommend me one drink and an inexpensive side order of food?
Nomimono no osusume to nanika yasui otsumami arimasu ka?
飲み物のお勧めと、何か安いおつまみありますか。

Could you recommend me something else?
Hokani osusume wa arimasu ka?
他にお勧めはありますか。

Do you have any...?
... wa arimasu ka?
... は、ありますか？

Just insert what you are interested in. For example, **Nihon no curafuto biiru wa arimasu ka?** ("Do you have any Japanese craft beer?") or **Yamahai no osake wa arimasu ka?** ("Do you have any *yamahai* sake?").

I would like the ... (insert name of alcohol/food)
... o kudasai
... をください

I would like this
Kore o kudasai
これをください

How much does it cost?
Ikura desu ka?
いくらですか

I would like something dry.
Karakuchi no mono ga ii desu
辛口のものがいいです。

I would like something sweet.
Amakuchi no mono ga ii desu
甘口のものがいいです。

I would like something with (a bit of/a lot of) body.
(Chotto/kanari) shikkari shita mono ga ii desu.
(ちょっと/かなり)しっかりしたものがいいです。

Reading the menu

Beer—**biiru** (ビール)
Types of beer:
Craft beer: **ji biiru**" (地ビール)
Nama beer—**nama biiru** (生ビール). Please note that, although **nama biiru** is sometimes translated as "draft beer," the word **nama** has been stretched to near meaninglessness by the big beer companies. It is often not proper draft beer and certainly not real ale. They even sell **nama** in cans but, in general, you should expect something poured into a glass from a tap.

Quantities

Medium glass: **chū nama** (中生); **chū jokki**" (中ジョッキ)
Large glass: **dai nama** (大生); **dai jokki** (大ジョッキ)
Bottle of beer: **bin biiru**" (瓶ビール)
If a glass of beer is offered (**garasu**" グラス), it is usually smaller than a *jokki*.

Wine—ワイン ("wine")
Types of wine:
White: **shiro wine** (白ワイン)
Red: **aka wine** (赤ワイン)
Rose: **roze wine** (ロゼワイン)
Dry: **kara kuchi** (辛口)
Sweet: **ama kuchi** (甘口)
Kōshū grape: 甲州
Countries of origin: Japan (**nihon wine** 日本ワイン, **nihon no wine** 日本のワイン or **kokusan wine** 国産ワイン); France (**Furansu** フランス); Italy (**Italia**" イタリア); Spain (**Spain** スペイン); Germany (**Doitsu** ドイツ); America (**America**アメリカ), Australia (**Ōsutoraria** オーストラリア); New Zealand (**Nyū Jiirando** ニュージーランド); Chile (**Chiri** チリ); Argentina (**Aruzenchin** アルゼンチン); Bulgaria (**Burugaria** ブルガリア); Austria (**Ōsutoria** オーストリア)
Quantities:
Glass: **garasu** (グラス)
Bottle: **botoru** (ボトル)

Whisky—**whisky** (ウイスキー)
Single malt: **shinguru moruto** (シングルモルト)
Blended whisky: **burendeddo** (ブレンデッド) or **burendo** (ブレンド)

Japanese alcohols

Sake:日本 (**nihonshu**) /清酒 (**seishu**)
Shōchū: 焼酎
Awamori: 泡盛
Quantities:
Glass: グラス
Ichi-go: 一合 (about 180 ml. In some bars, the flask will be irregular and the quantity therefore varies from the strict standard. Predictably, this "irregularity" tends towards parsimony.)

Other drinks

Japanese plum liqueur: **umeshu** (梅酒; see page 90)
Sour: **sawā** (サワー), a fruit juice and spirit mix. The meaning of **chūhai** below overlaps.
Chūhai: チューハイ/ 酎ハイ, a mix of spirits and juice, soda or tea
Cocktail: **kakuteru** (カクテル)
Liqueur: **rikyūru** (リキュール)
Rum: **ramu** (ラム)
Brandy: **Burandē** (ブランデー)
Vodka: **Wokka** (ウォッカ)
Port Wine: ポートワイン
Sherry: シェリー
Gin: ジン

Pleasantries

Hello
Konnichiwa (in day) or **Konbanwa** (in evening)
こんにちわ/こんばんわ

Excuse me **Sumimasen** すみません

... please **... onegai shimasu** おねがいします
Thank you **Arigatō gozaimasu** ありがとうございます

That was delicious! **Oishikatta desu** おいしかったです

It is customary to say a word of appreciation when leaving a bar/restaurant. **Oishikatta desu** or **Gochisōsama** ("It was a treat!") would both do the job.

Paying

I would like to pay.
Okaikei onegai shimasu.
お会計お願いします

How much does it cost?
Ikura desu ka?
いくらですか

Do you take credit cards?
Kurejitto kaado daijōbu desu ka?
クレジットカード　大丈夫ですか

Toasts, exclamations, etc.

Cheers! **Kampai** 乾杯

An appreciative sound made when someone else is pouring your drink and the liquor is flowing into your cup
O-to-to-to-to-to.... お-と-と-と- と

Tipsy/slightly drunk **Horoyoi** ほろ酔い

Drunk **Yopparai** 酔っ払い

A drunkard (just like its English equivalent; this word could be taken to be offensive)
Nombei のんべい

Hangover **Futsukayoi** 二日酔い

Finding the facilities

Excuse me, where is the rest room?
Sumimasen ga toire wa doko desu ka?
すみませんがトイレはどこですか

Important written characters when visiting bars

There are a variety of characters that might appear on advertising for drinking establishments (please see page 20 for a discussion of the differences between the various types of bars):

Izakaya: 居酒屋 (Japanese pub)
Sakaba: 酒場
Nomiya: 飲み屋 (sometimes written 呑み屋)
Bar バー
Pub パブ
Snack スナック

"All you can drink" option: **nomi hōdai** (飲み放題 or 呑み放題). Some bars and restaurants advertise "all you can drink" deals. You pay a set fee for a certain period of drinking. There are also all you can eat deals (**tabe hōdai** 食べ放題).

Toilet **toire** (トイレ) or **te arai** (手洗い)
Men's toilet 男性 (**Dansei**—gentlemen); alternatively, **Shinshi**" (紳士)
Women's toilet 女性 (**Josei**—Ladies); alternatively **Fujin** (婦人)

Shopping for alcohol

The first time I walked into a Japanese liquor store, I walked straight back out again. It can be quite bewildering, and the feeling is particularly strong in the *awamori*, sake and *shōchū* sections, where most bottles are covered only with Japanese characters. It can even be hard to tell the difference between an *awamori*, a sake, and a *shōchū*. While bottles of whisky or wine are often identifiable simply by their shape, all three types of Japanese indigenous alcohols use interchangeable bottles, plus a broad array of completely unstandardized pots, weirdly shaped bottles and boxes.

Don't despair! I know from personal experience that even someone with little or no knowledge of the language can find their way around these liquor stores. The key is not to panic. You are not going to understand everything or even a small fraction of what is written but by looking out for a few key characters you can start to narrow down your choices to some excellent alcohols.

Spoken Japanese for shoppers

Where is the (sake/wine/shōchū/whisky/beer/awamori) section?
(Nihonshu/wine/shōchū/whisky/biiru/awamori) wa doko desu ka?
(日本酒/ワイン/焼酎/ウィスキー/ビール/泡盛)はどこですか？

Do you take this credit card?
Kono kurejitto kaado daijōbu desu ka?
このクレジットカード　大丈夫ですか

How much is this?
Kore wa ikura desu ka?
これはいくらですか

Could you write that down?
Kami ni kaite kudasai.
紙に書いてください

Thank you.
Arigatō gozaimasu
ありがとうございます

Buying sake

Most bottles of sake or *nihonshu*, as it is most commonly called in spoken Japanese, carry the characters **seishu** (清酒) somewhere on the label. Occasionally, they will just say 日本酒, **Nihonshu**. But if you see either sets of characters you are dealing with sake. Getting beyond that basic fact can take a little perseverance. If you are lucky, there will be a fairly clearly printed white sticker on the back of the bottle carrying the key bits of information you are looking for. If you are unlucky, however, the vital clues will be written in cursive scripts on the front label. Sometimes it is best just to give up on the most obtuse bottles.

The key characters to look out for are:

Types of premium sake:

Junmai (pure rice sake) 純米

Honjōzō (premium sake with a small amount of distilled alcohol added in production) 本醸造

Ginjō (premium sake made of finely milled or polished rice) 吟醸

Daiginjō (*ginjō*'s even more polished sibling) 大吟醸

Other important words on the label:

Nihonshudo (sometimes called SMV or "sake meter value"—3 is sweet, 0 is sweetish and anything above 4 is getting dry.) 日本酒度
Alcohol-bun (alcoholic content) アルコール分
Genzairyō or **Genzairyōmei** (ingredients) 原材料 or 原材料名

In his excellent book, *The Insider's Guide to Sake*, Philip Harper suggests a fairly good rule of thumb for judging the quality of a sake: count the number of ingredients. The fewer the ingredients, the better the sake generally is. The *kanji* for ingredients is 原材料 (**genzairyō**). A bottle that simply lists 米, 米麹 (**kome**, **komekōji**; rice and rice *kōji*) is a *junmai* sake and is likely to be of good quality. A bottle that lists 米, 米麹, 醸造アルコール (**kome**, **komekōji**, **jōzō arucōru**; rice, rice *kōji*, distilled alcohol) may be a high quality *honjōzō*. However, if the list is adding all sorts of other ingredients 米, 米麹, 醸造アルコール, 糖類, 酸味料 (**kome**, **komekōji**, **jōzō arucōru**, **tōrui**, **sanmiryō**; rice, rice *kōji*, distilled alcohol, sugars, acids), you are likely to be dealing with a cheap mass-market sake. Labels often list the alcoholic content of a sake (アルコール分) immediately after the ingredients. Don't mistake it for an ingredient.

These tips are only the most basic of introductions to sake shopping. I think it is best to start with just a few basic concepts in mind and, once you have found your footing, start to explore in more detail. You will want to start trying to remember and recognize some of your favorite *kura* and investigating the myriad of styles that enrich sake making. The introduction to this book's chapter on sake has much more detail on *yamahai*, *namazake* and suchlike. Philip Harper's *The Insider's Guide to Sake* and John Gauntner's many excellent publications, including the comprehensive *The Sake Handbook*, will take you further into this fascinating world.

Buying shōchū

The characters for *shōchū* are (焼酎). However, there is one bit of vocabulary that you must get your head around before entering the *shōchū* section of a liquor store—the difference between *korui shōchū* and *honkaku shōchū*. *Korui shōchū* is a neutral alcohol. *Honkaku shōchū* is totally different—as different as single-malt whisky is different from cheap vodka—and is the only stuff worth spending any time pondering over in a liquor store. The most popular brands of *soju*, the big green bottles of Korean sweet, neutral spirit, that have become very popular in Japan recently are *korui shōchū* (see page 80).

So, if you find the characters 甲類 (**korui**), you are on the boring side of the *shōchū* aisle. There are usually four-gallon plastic containers, but there are also more elaborately presented bottles of *korui*, so packaging is not a reliable guide to quality. They all, in my opinion, taste very similar to each other.

Honkaku *shōchū* (本格, **honkaku**) is the interesting stuff. It usually displays those two characters—本格—somewhere on the label. Once you have identified it as *honkaku*, you need to start looking for the ingredients because a sweet potato *shōchū* from Kagoshima, a barley *shōchū* from Iki Island and a rice *shōchū* from Kumamoto are totally different from one another. There are dozens of ingredients for *shōchū* but the main types are **imojōchū** 芋焼酎 (sweet potato *shōchū*); **mugijōchū** 麦焼酎 (barley *shōchū*); **komejōchū** 米焼酎 (rice *shōchū*); **kokutōjōchū** 黒糖焼酎 (sugar *shōchū*); **kasutori shōchū** 粕取り焼酎 (sake lees *shōchū*) and **sobajōchū** そば焼酎 (buckwheat *shōchū*). It is often easiest to look for the ingredients list: 原材料 (**genzairyō**). Look out for these characters: sweet potato (芋 or さつま芋 or 薩摩芋 or いも); barley/wheat (麦 or むぎ); rice (米 or こめ); brown sugar (黒糖); *kasu* sake lees (粕 or かす) and soba (そば). You will often find combinations of these ingredients and all sorts of other bases for distillation, including chestnuts, sesame and *shisō* leaf. The other main entry on the ingredients list will also usually specify the ingredient on which the *kōji* rice mold was cultivated (e.g. 麦麹, barley *kōji* or 米麹, rice *kōji*) and/or the type of mold that was used (黒麹, black *kōji*; 黄麹, yellow *kōji*; 白麹, white *kōji*). As I explain in the *shōchū* chapter (see page 78), each type of mold has different taste characteristics. Occasionally, the *kōji* character is written in *hiragana* characters instead: こうじ.

If you see the characters 古酒 (**koshu**), it means that the spirit has been aged. Usually there will be a 年 (*nen*, year) character nearby and the character preceding that will often tell you how long the spirit was aged for.

Buying awamori

The biggest challenge in finding *awamori* in a shop is usually finding the *awamori* section. It often merges in with the *korui* and *honkaku shōchū* areas. Almost all shops have at least some *awamori*. The characters you are looking for are 泡盛 (**awamori**). Finding your way around the best of this spirit is really a matter of getting to know the best distilleries (see the brand index to the *awamori* chapter, page 257), but perhaps the most important variable you will be able to decipher from the label is whether it is an aged **kūsu** (古酒) or not. *Kūsu* has to contain at least 51 percent of alcohol over three years old. If a specific age is stated (look out for the year character, 年), that means that all of the spirit must be at least that age.

Buying beer

Buying beer, wine and Western spirits like whisky tends to be a lot easier than dabbling in the indigenous alcohols because the labels often use the Roman alphabet for much of their lettering. There is one vital distinction to be learned for your visit to the beer section—the difference between beer (ビール, **biiru**) and *happōshu* beer substitutes, which often use beerish English vocabulary phrases to give the feel of beer ("draft", "brew," etc.) but are never actually allowed to call themselves "beer" or use the Japanese characters ビール. These substitutes will usually carry the characters 発泡酒 (**happōshu**) or 発泡性 (**happōsei**) somewhere on the can. In very crude terms, if the *happōshu* is cheaper than the price of the standard Japanese beers, then it is to be avoided because it is a cheap, low-tax beer substitute. There are some very good craft beers and imported beers (e.g. Belgian fruit beers) that have to call themselves *happōshu* because their recipe calls for them to have a relatively low malt content. However, the general advice stands—if you want real beer and you have just picked up a cheap can labeled *happōshu*, put it down again.

Buying wine and other types of alcohol

For useful vocabulary for other foreign alcohol aisles, please refer to the "Reading the menu" section above.

Where to Find Alcohol Brands

There are more than 200 brands of alcohol mentioned in this guide. This index is designed to give easy access to information about those drinks.

The first word in each entry is the name of the brand, followed by that name in the Japanese characters often used on bottles and menus. The company that makes the alcohol, and where it is made, are enclosed in brackets. For *shōchū*, the type of ingredient used to make the spirit is included inside the brackets, before the company name and location.

I have given page references to specific mentions of the brands and also to background information on the breweries and distilleries that make them.

SAKE

SHŌCHŪ

AWAMORI

BEER

WHISKY

WINE

OTHER ALCOHOLS

Index

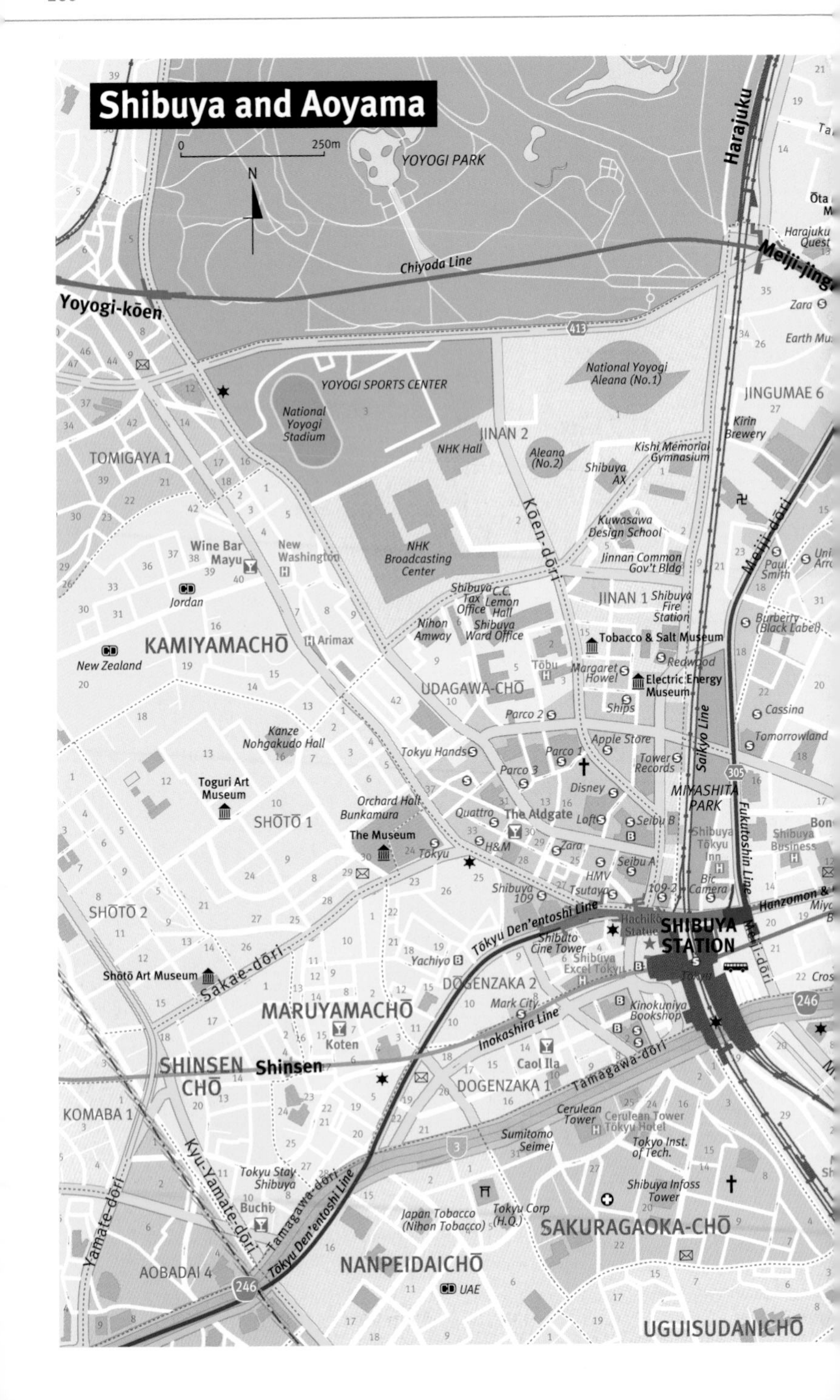
Shibuya and Aoyama
0
250m
N
YOYOGI PARK
Chiyoda Line
Yoyogi-kōen
Harajuku
Meiji-jing
Harajuku Quest
Zara
Earth Mu
YOYOGI SPORTS CENTER
National Yoyogi Stadium
National Yoyogi Aleana (No.1)
JINGUMAE 6
Kirin Brewery
NHK Hall
JINAN 2
Aleana (No.2)
Kishi Memorial Gymnasium
Shibuya AX
TOMIGAYA 1
Kōen-dōri
Kuwasawa Design School
NHK Broadcasting Center
Jinnan Common Gov't Bldg
Wine Bar Mayu
New Washington
Meiji-dōri
Paul Smith
Jordan
Shibuya Tax Office
C.C. Lemon Hall
Shibuya Ward Office
JINAN 1
Shibuya Fire Station
Burberry (Black Label)
KAMIYAMACHŌ
Arimax
Nihon Amway
Tobacco & Salt Museum
New Zealand
Redwood
Tōbu
Margaret Howel
Electric Energy Museum
UDAGAWA-CHŌ
Ships
Cassina
Parco 2
Kanze Nohgakudo Hall
Apple Store
Tomorrowland
Tokyu Hands
Parco 1
Tower Records
Saikyo Line
Parco 3
Toguri Art Museum
Disney
MIYASHITA PARK
Orchard Hall
Bunkamura
Quattro
The Aldgate
Loft
Seibu B
Fukutoshin Line
SHŌTŌ 1
The Museum
H&M
Zara
Shibuya Tōkyu Inn
Shibuya Business
Tokyu
Seibu A
HMV
Bic Camera
Shibuya 109
Tsutaya
109-2
SHŌTŌ 2
Hanzomon &
Tōkyu Den'entoshi Line
Hachikō Statue
SHIBUYA STATION
Shibuto Cine Tower
Shibuya Excel Tokyu
Yachiyo
Sakae-dōri
Shōtō Art Museum
DOGENZAKA 2
Mark City
Kinokuniya Bookshop
MARUYAMACHŌ
Inokashira Line
Koten
Caol Ila
SHINSEN CHŌ
Shinsen
Tamagawa-dōri
DOGENZAKA 1
KOMABA 1
Cerulean Tower
Cerulean Tower Tokyu Hotel
Sumitomo Seimei
Tokyo Inst. of Tech.
Kyu-Yamate-dōri
Tokyu Stay Shibuya
Shibuya Infoss Tower
Yamate-dōri
Buchi
Tamagawa-dōri
Tōkyu Den'entoshi Line
Japan Tobacco (Nihon Tobacco)
Tokyu Corp (H.Q.)
SAKURAGAOKA-CHŌ
AOBADAI 4
NANPEIDAICHŌ
UAE
UGUISUDANICHŌ

Shibuya Ward Central Library
United Arrows
Beams T
Beams F
Beams +
Tōgō Kinenkan
Welfare Centre
JINGUMAE 3
Harajuku Apts
Gaien Nishi-dōri
SHIBUYA-KU
MINATO-KU
Kōtoku-ji
Sompo Japan
Prince Chichibu Memorial Rugby Stadium
KITA-AOYAMA 2
Itōchu
Aoyama Plaza
Tokyo Joshi-Idai Aoyama Hospital
Myōen-ji
Watari Museum of Contemporary Art
Brazil
Gaiemmae
Aoyama Tower Bldg
Dept
Galali
Aoyama Bell Commons
Baisō-in
Aoyama Elem. School
KDDI
Hanzomon & Ginza Line
MINAMI-AOYAMA 2
Japan Int'l School
Tōkyu Store
Daimaru Peacock
JINGUMAE 4
Metr. Aoyama-Kitamachi Apts
Ralph Lauren
Natsuno
Avex
Omotesandō Hills
Dōjunkai Apts
KITA-AOYAMA 3
Oriental Bazaar
Aoyama-dōri
Kinokuniya Int'l
Louis Vuitton
Itō Hospital
Seinan Welfare Hall
Tōkyō Union Church
Zenkō-ji
Anniversaire
Adelaide
One Furula
Hanae Mori
MINAMI-AOYAMA 3
Omotesandō
Floracion Aoyama
Bapy
Aoyama Palacio Tower
MINAMI-AOYAMA 4
JINGUMAE 5
Kita Aoyama Hospital
Ōji Green Hill Apartments
Chiyoda Line
Seinan Elem. School
Spiral Hall
Shimada Yōsho
Vivienne Westwood
Tokyo Women Plaza
MINAMI-AOYAMA 5
Aoyama Book Ctr
Cosmos Aoyama
JBP Oval
Minami Aoyama Kaikan
La Collezione
National Children's Castle
Kuyo
Ohara Kaikan
Nikka Whisky
Kensetsu Kyōsai Hall
Aoyama Theater
United Nations Univ.
Hanzomon & Ginza Lines
Memi Hall
Sumitomo
Nikka Blender's Bar
Nezu Art Museum
Okamoto Tarō Memorial Museum
Aoyama Gakuin University
Hase-dera
Daian-ji
Aoyama Flower
Mr. Zoogunzoo
Blue Note Tokyo
Bar Gen
SHIBUYA 4
NISHI-AZABU 2
H&A
Chapel
Aoyama Gakuin Women's Jr. College
Paul Smith
Kenzo
MINAMI-AOYAMA 6
Sakura Fleur Aoyama
NTT
Fuji Film
Aoyama Gakuin High School
Nishi-Azabu Mitsui
Mori
Roppongi-dōri
Odakyu Minami-Aoyama
Coca-Cola
MINAMI-AOYAMA 7
NISHI-AZABU 4
Tōfuku-ji
Gym
Japan Productivity Ctr for Socio-Economic Dev.
Residence of Prince Hitachi
Jissen Joshi Gakuen
Helmsdale
Koryo Jr. High School
Shibuya Library
Peru
Shibuya Ward Museum
Episcopal Church of Japan
WINS Shibuya
Tsurusawa Apts
Tōkyō Jogakkan
HIGASHI 4
HIRO-O 4
HIGASHI 1
Tokiwamatsu Elementary School
Kokugakuin University
Burkina Faso
Croatia
Japanese Red Cross Medical Center
HIRO-O 3
HIGASHI 2
Hiro-o Jr. High School
Japanese Red Cross Coll.of Nursing
Yamatane Museum of Art
Hiro-o High School

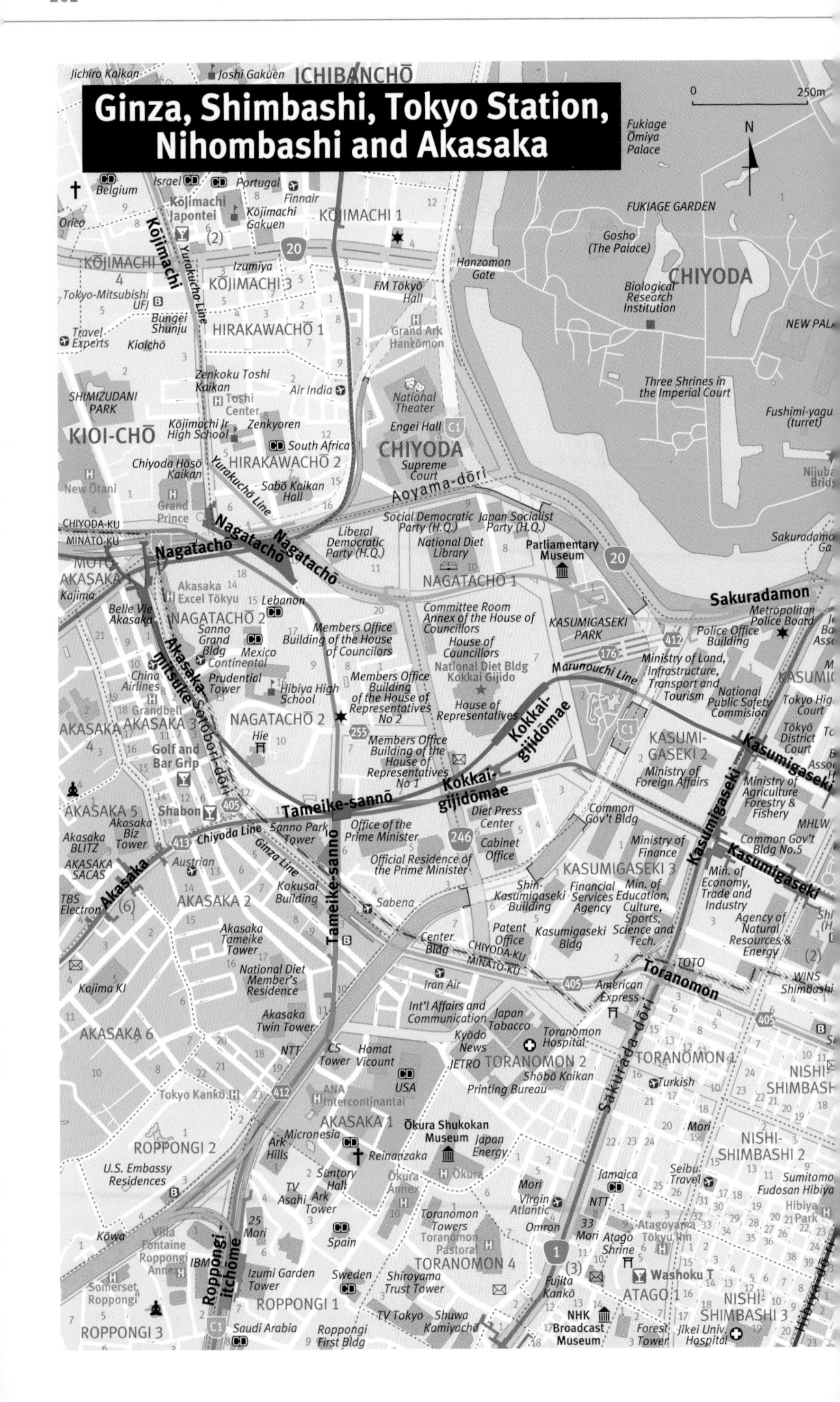
Ginza, Shimbashi, Tokyo Station, Nihombashi and Akasaka
0
250m
N
ICHIBANCHŌ
Jichiro Kaikan
Joshi Gakuen
Fukiage Ōmiya Palace
FUKIAGE GARDEN
Gosho (The Palace)
CHIYODA
Biological Research Institution
NEW PAL
Three Shrines in the Imperial Court
Fushimi-yagu (turret)
Belgium
Israel
Portugal
Finnair
Kōjimachi Japontei
Kōjimachi Gakuen
KŌJIMACHI 1
Kōjimachi
Yūrakuchō Line
KŌJIMACHI 4
Izumiya
KŌJIMACHI 3
Hanzomon Gate
FM Tōkyō Hall
Tokyo-Mitsubishi UFJ
Bungei Shunju
HIRAKAWACHŌ 1
Grand Ark Hanzōmon
Travel Experts
Kioichō
Zenkoku Toshi Kaikan
Toshi Center
Air India
National Theater
SHIMIZUDANI PARK
KIOI-CHŌ
Kōjimachi Jr High School
Zenkyoren
South Africa
Engei Hall
CHIYODA
Supreme Court
Chiyoda Hōsō Kaikan
HIRAKAWACHŌ 2
Sabō Kaikan Hall
New Ōtani
Grand Prince
Aoyama-dōri
CHIYODA-KU
MINATO-KU
Nagatachō
Liberal Democratic Party (H.Q.)
Social Democratic Party (H.Q.)
Japan Socialist Party (H.Q.)
National Diet Library
Parliamentary Museum
NAGATACHŌ 1
Sakuradamon
Metropolitan Police Board
Akasaka Excel Tōkyu
Lebanon
Belle Vie Akasaka
NAGATACHŌ 2
Sanno Grand Bldg
Mexico
Continental
Members Office Building of the House of Councilors
Committee Room Annex of the House of Councillors
House of Councillors
KASUMIGASEKI PARK
Police Office Building
Ministry of Land, Infrastructure, Transport and Tourism
National Public Safety Commision
Tokyo High Court
Tōkyō District Court
Marunouchi Line
China Airlines
Prudential Tower
Hibiya High School
Members Office Building of the House of Representatives No 2
National Diet Bldg Kokkai Gijido
House of Representatives
Kokkai-gijidōmae
Akasaka-mitsuke
Sotobori-dōri
AKASAKA 3
AKASAKA 4
Golf and Bar Grip
Hie
NAGATACHŌ 2
Members Office Building of the House of Representatives No 1
KASUMI-GASEKI 2
Ministry of Foreign Affairs
Kasumigaseki
Ministry of Agriculture Forestry & Fishery
AKASAKA 5
Shabon
Tameike-sannō
Diet Press Center
Common Gov't Bldg
Ministry of Finance
MHLW
Common Gov't Bldg No.5
Akasaka Biz Tower
Akasaka BLITZ
AKASAKA SACAS
Chiyoda Line
Sanno Park Tower
Ginza Line
Office of the Prime Minister
Official Residence of the Prime Minister
Cabinet Office
KASUMIGASEKI 3
Min. of Economy, Trade and Industry
Austrian
TBS Electron
Akasaka
AKASAKA 2
Kokusai Building
Sabena
Shin-Kasumigaseki Building
Financial Services Agency
Min. of Education, Culture, Sports, Science and Tech.
Agency of Natural Resources & Energy
Akasaka Tameike Tower
Center Bldg
Patent Office
Kasumigaseki Bldg
CHIYODA-KU
MINATO-KU
TOTO
Toranomon
WINS Shimbashi
National Diet Member's Residence
Kajima KI
Iran Air
American Express
Akasaka Twin Tower
Int'l Affairs and Communication
Japan Tobacco
Toranomon Hospital
AKASAKA 6
Sakurada-dōri
TORANOMON 1
NISHI-SHIMBASHI
NTT
CS Tower
Homat Vicount
Kyōdo News
JETRO
TORANOMON 2
Shōbō Kaikan
USA
Printing Bureau
Turkish
Tokyo Kankō
ANA Intercontinental
AKASAKA 1
Ōkura Shukokan Museum
Japan Energy
Mori
NISHI-SHIMBASHI 2
Micronesia
ROPPONGI 2
Ark Hills
Reinanzaka
U.S. Embassy Residences
Suntory Hall
Ōkura
Ōkura Annex
Jamaica
Seibu Travel
Sumitomo Fudosan Hibiya
TV Asahi
Ark Tower
Mori
Virgin Atlantic
NTT
Hibiya Park
25 Mori
Toranomon Towers
Omron
33 Mori
Atago Shrine
Atagoyama Tōkyū Inn
Kōwa
Villa Fontaine Roppongi Annex
IBM
Spain
Toranomon Pastoral
TORANOMON 4
Somerset Roppongi
Izumi Garden Tower
Sweden
Shiroyama Trust Tower
Washoku T
Fujita Kankō
ATAGO 1
NISHI-SHIMBASHI 3
Roppongi-itchōme
ROPPONGI 1
TV Tokyo
Shuwa Kamiyachō
NHK Broadcast Museum
Forest Tower
Jikei Univ. Hospital
ROPPONGI 3
Saudi Arabia
Roppongi First Bldg

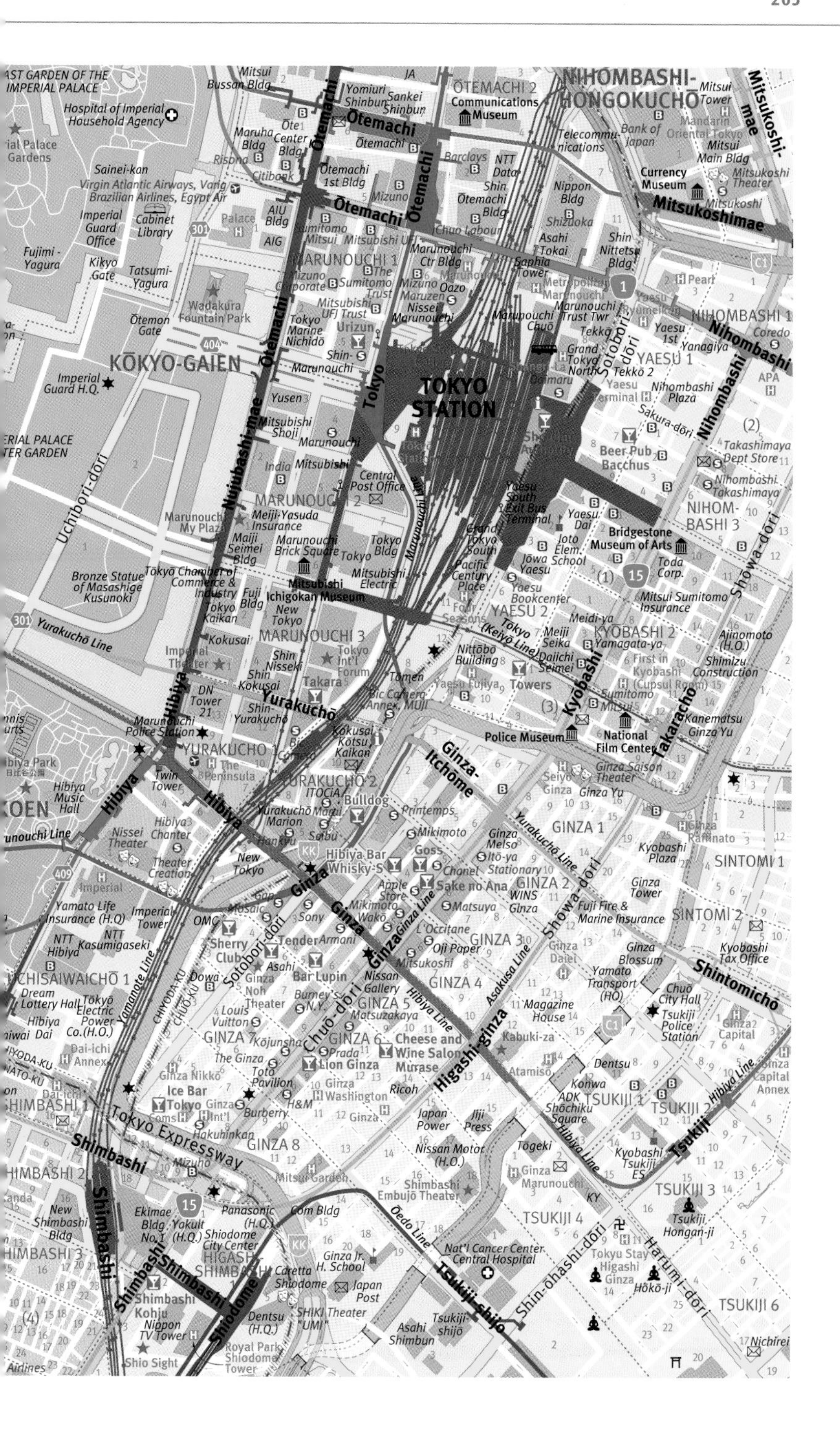
EAST GARDEN OF THE IMPERIAL PALACE
Hospital of Imperial Household Agency
Imperial Palace Gardens
Sainei-kan
Virgin Atlantic Airways, Varig, Brazilian Airlines, Egypt Air
Imperial Guard Office
Cabinet Library
Fujimi-Yagura
Kikyo Gate
Tatsumi-Yagura
Wadakura Fountain Park
Ōtemon Gate
KŌKYO-GAIEN
Imperial Guard H.Q.
IMPERIAL PALACE OUTER GARDEN
Uchibori-dōri
Bronze Statue of Masashige Kusunoki
Yurakuchō Line
Mitsui Bussan Bldg
Yomiuri Shinbun
Sankei Shinbun
JA
ŌTEMACHI 2
Communications Museum
NIHOMBASHI-HONGOKUCHŌ
Mitsui Tower
Mitsukoshi-mae
Ōtemachi
Maruha Bldg
Ōte Center Bldg
Risona
Citibank
Ōtemachi 1st Bldg
Mizuno
Barclays
NTT Data
Shin Ōtemachi Bldg
Telecommunications
Bank of Japan
Mandarin Oriental Tokyo
Mitsui Main Bldg
Currency Museum
Mitsukoshi Theater
Mitsukoshi
Mitsukoshimae
Palace
AIU Bldg
AIG
Sumitomo Mitsui
Mitsubishi UFJ
Chuo Labour
Nippon Bldg
Shizuoka
Asahi Tokai
Shin Nittetsu Bldg
MARUNOUCHI 1
Mizuno Corporate
Sumitomo
The Trust
Marunouchi Ctr Bldg
Oazo
Maruzen
Sapia Tower
Metropolitan Marunouchi
Yaesu Ryumeikan
Pearl
NIHOMBASHI 1
Nihombashi
Coredo
Mitsubishi UFJ Trust
Tokyo Marine Nichidō
Urizun
Shin-Marunouchi
Nissei Marunouchi
Marunouchi Chuō
Marunouchi Trust Twr
Tekkō
Grand Tokyo North
Sotobori-dōri
Yaesu 1st
Yanagiya
YAESU 1
Tekkō 2
Daimaru
Yaesu Terminal
Nihombashi Plaza
APA
Ōtemachi
Nijubashi-mae
Tokyo
TOKYO STATION
Yusen
Mitsubishi Shoji
Marunouchi
Sakura-dōri
Takashimaya Dept Store
Nihombashi Takashimaya
India
Mitsubishi
Central Post Office
Marunouchi Line
Beer Pub Bacchus
MARUNOUCHI 2
Meiji-Yasuda Insurance
Marunouchi My Plaza
Maiji Seimei Bldg
Marunouchi Brick Square
Tokyo Bldg
Yaesu South Exit Bus Terminal
Grand Tokyo South
Yaesu Dai
Joto Elem. School
Bridgestone Museum of Arts
NIHOMBASHI 3
Shōwa-dōri
Tokyo Chamber of Commerce & Industry
Fuji Bldg
Mitsubishi Ichigokan Museum
Mitsubishi Electric
Pacific Century Place
Jōwa Yaesu
Toda Corp.
Tokyo Kaikan
New Tokyo
Yaesu Bookcenter
Mitsui Sumitomo Insurance
YAESU 2
Four Seasons
Meidi-ya
Kokusai
MARUNOUCHI 3
Tokyo Int'l Forum
Tōkyō (Keiyō Line)
Meiji Seika
KYOBASHI 2
Ajinomoto (H.Q.)
Imperial Theater
Shin Nisseki
Nittōbō Building
Daiichi Seimei
Yamagata-ya
First in Kyobashi (Cupsul Room)
Shimizu Construction
Shin Kokusai
Takara
Tōmen
Yaesu Fujiya
Towers
Kyobashi
Sumitomo
DN Tower 21
Yurakuchō
Bic Camera Annex, MUJI
Shin-Yurakuchō
Kokusai Kōtsu Kaikan
National Film Center
Takaracho
Kanematsu Ginza Yu
Marunouchi Police Station
Police Museum
YURAKUCHO 1
The Peninsula
Bic Camera
Ginza-Itchōme
Seiyo Ginza
Ginza Saison Theater
Ginza Yu
Hibiya Park
Hibiya Music Hall
Hibiya
Twin Tower
YURAKUCHO 2
ITOCiA
Bulldog
Printemps
Yurakuchō Line
Yurakuchō Marui
Marion
Hankyu
Seibu
Mikimoto
GINZA 1
Kyobashi Plaza
Ginza Raffinato
SINTOMI 1
Hibiya Chanter
Nissei Theater
Theater Creation
New Tokyo
Hibiya Bar Whisky-S
Goss
Chanel
Itō-ya Stationary
Ginza Melsa
Imperial
Apple Store
Sake no Ana
GINZA 2
WINS Ginza
Ginza Tower
Yamato Life Insurance (H.Q)
Imperial Tower
OMC
Mosaic
Sony
Mikimoto
Wakō
Ginza Line
Matsuya
Fuji Fire & Marine Insurance
SINTOMI 2
NTT Hibiya
NTT Kasumigaseki
Sherry Club
Tender
Armani
L'Occitane
Oji Paper
GINZA 3
Ginza Dai-ei
Ginza Blossom
Kyobashi Tax Office
Yamanote Line
Sotobori-dōri
Asahi
Bar Lupin
Ginza
Mitsukoshi
Nissan Gallery
GINZA 4
Yamato Transport (HQ)
Shintomichō
UCHISAIWAICHŌ 1
Dōwa
Ginza Noh Theater
Burney's N.Y.
GINZA 5
Asakusa Line
Chuō City Hall
Dream Lottery Hall
Tōkyō Electric Power Co.(H.O.)
Louis Vuitton
Matsuzakaya
Magazine House
Tsukiji Police Station
Ginza 2 Capital
Hibiya Dai
CHIYODA-KU
CHŪŌ-KU
Chuō-dōri
Hibiya Line
Dai-ichi Annex
GINZA 7
Kōjunsha
GINZA 6
Cheese and Wine Salon Murase
Kabuki-za
Prada
Lion Ginza
Higashi-ginza
The Ginza
Ginza Nikkō
Toto Pavilion
Atamiso
Dentsu
Ginza Capital Annex
Konwa
Ice Bar Tokyo
Ginza Int'l
Ginza Washington
Ricoh
ADK Shōchiku Square
TSUKIJI 1
TSUKIJI 2
Tsukiji
SHIMBASHI 1
Tokyo Expressway
Burberry
H&M
Japan Power
Jiji Press
Hakuhinkan
Shimbashi
GINZA 8
Nissan Motor (H.O.)
Tōgeki
Kyobashi Tsukiji ES
Mizuho
SHIMBASHI 2
Mitsui Garden
Shimbashi Embujō Theater
Ginza Marunouchi
TSUKIJI 3
New Shimbashi Bldg
Ekimae Bldg No.1
Yokult (H.Q.)
Panasonic (H.Q.)
Shiodome City Center
Com Bldg
Ōedo Line
TSUKIJI 4
Tsukiji Hongan-ji
SHIMBASHI 3
HIGASHI SHIMBASHI
Ginza Jr. H. School
Nat'l Cancer Center Central Hospital
Tokyu Stay Higashi Ginza
Harumi-dōri
Shin-ōhashi-dōri
Caretta Shiodome
Japan Post
Hōkō-ji
Shimbashi Kohju
Shiodome
Tsukiji-shijō
Dentsu (H.Q.)
SHIKI Theater "UMI"
Asahi Shimbun
Tsukiji-shijō
TSUKIJI 6
Nippon TV Tower
Royal Park Shiodome Tower
Shio Sight
Airlines
Nichirei

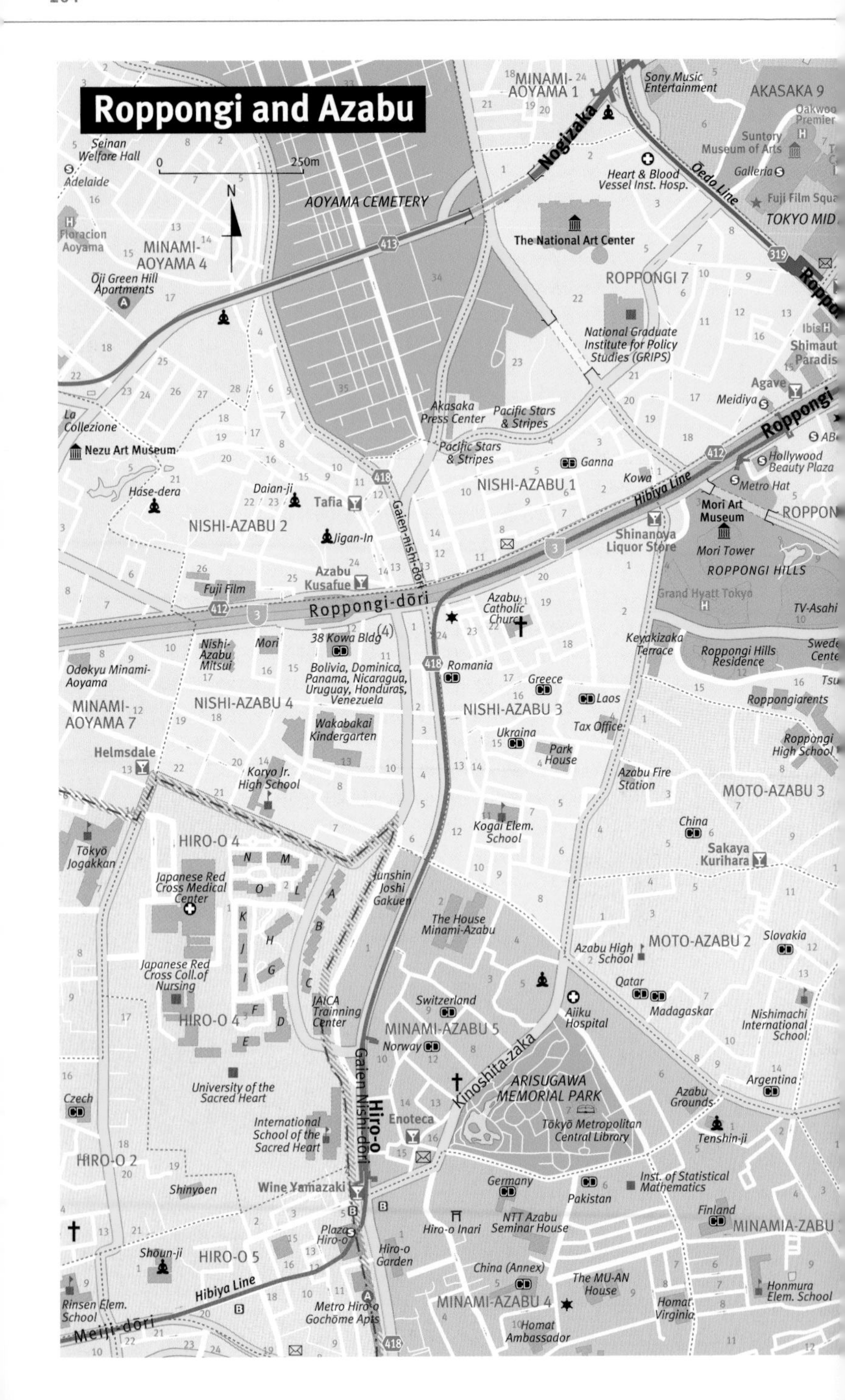

Roppongi and Azabu
0
250m
N
AOYAMA CEMETERY
MINAMI-AOYAMA 1
Sony Music Entertainment
AKASAKA 9
Nogizaka
Heart & Blood Vessel Inst. Hosp.
Ōedo Line
Suntory Museum of Arts
Galleria
Fuji Film Square
TOKYO MID
The National Art Center
ROPPONGI 7
National Graduate Institute for Policy Studies (GRIPS)
Seinan Welfare Hall
Adelaide
Floracion Aoyama
MINAMI-AOYAMA 4
Oji Green Hill Apartments
Ibis
Shimaute Paradis
Agave
Meidiya
Roppongi
Akasaka Press Center
Pacific Stars & Stripes
Pacific Stars & Stripes
La Collezione
Nezu Art Museum
Ganna
NISHI-AZABU 1
Kowa
Hibiya Line
Hollywood Beauty Plaza
Metro Hat
Mori Art Museum
ROPPON
Hase-dera
Daian-ji
Tafia
NISHI-AZABU 2
Jigan-In
Gaien-nishi-dōri
Shinanoya Liquor Store
Mori Tower
ROPPONGI HILLS
Azabu Kusafue
Fuji Film
Grand Hyatt Tokyo
Roppongi-dōri
Azabu Catholic Church
TV-Asahi
Nishi-Azabu Mitsui
Mori
38 Kowa Bldg (4)
Romania
Keyakizaka Terrace
Roppongi Hills Residence
Odakyu Minami-Aoyama
Bolivia, Dominica, Panama, Nicaragua, Uruguay, Honduras, Venezuela
Greece
Laos
Roppongiarents
MINAMI-AOYAMA 7
NISHI-AZABU 4
NISHI-AZABU 3
Tax Office
Wakabakai Kindergarten
Ukraina
Roppongi High School
Helmsdale
Park House
Koryo Jr. High School
Azabu Fire Station
MOTO-AZABU 3
Kogai Elem. School
China
HIRO-O 4
Tōkyō Jogakkan
Sakaya Kurihara
Japanese Red Cross Medical Center
Junshin Joshi Gakuen
The House Minami-Azabu
MOTO-AZABU 2
Slovakia
Azabu High School
Japanese Red Cross Coll.of Nursing
Qatar
JAICA Trainning Center
Switzerland
Aiiku Hospital
Madagaskar
Nishimachi International School
HIRO-O 4
MINAMI-AZABU 5
Norway
Kinoshita-zaka
ARISUGAWA MEMORIAL PARK
Argentina
University of the Sacred Heart
Gaien Nishi-dōri
Hiro-o
Azabu Grounds
Czech
International School of the Sacred Heart
Enoteca
Tōkyō Metropolitan Central Library
Tenshin-ji
HIRO-O 2
Shinyoen
Wine Yamazaki
Germany
Pakistan
Inst. of Statistical Mathematics
Finland
MINAMIA-ZABU
Plaza Hiro-o
Hiro-o Inari
NTT Azabu Seminar House
Shoun-ji
HIRO-O 5
Hiro-o Garden
China (Annex)
The MU-AN House
Hibiya Line
Rinsen Elem. School
Metro Hiro-o Gochōme Apts
MINAMI-AZABU 4
Homat Virginia
Honmura Elem. School
Meiji-dōri
Homat Ambassador

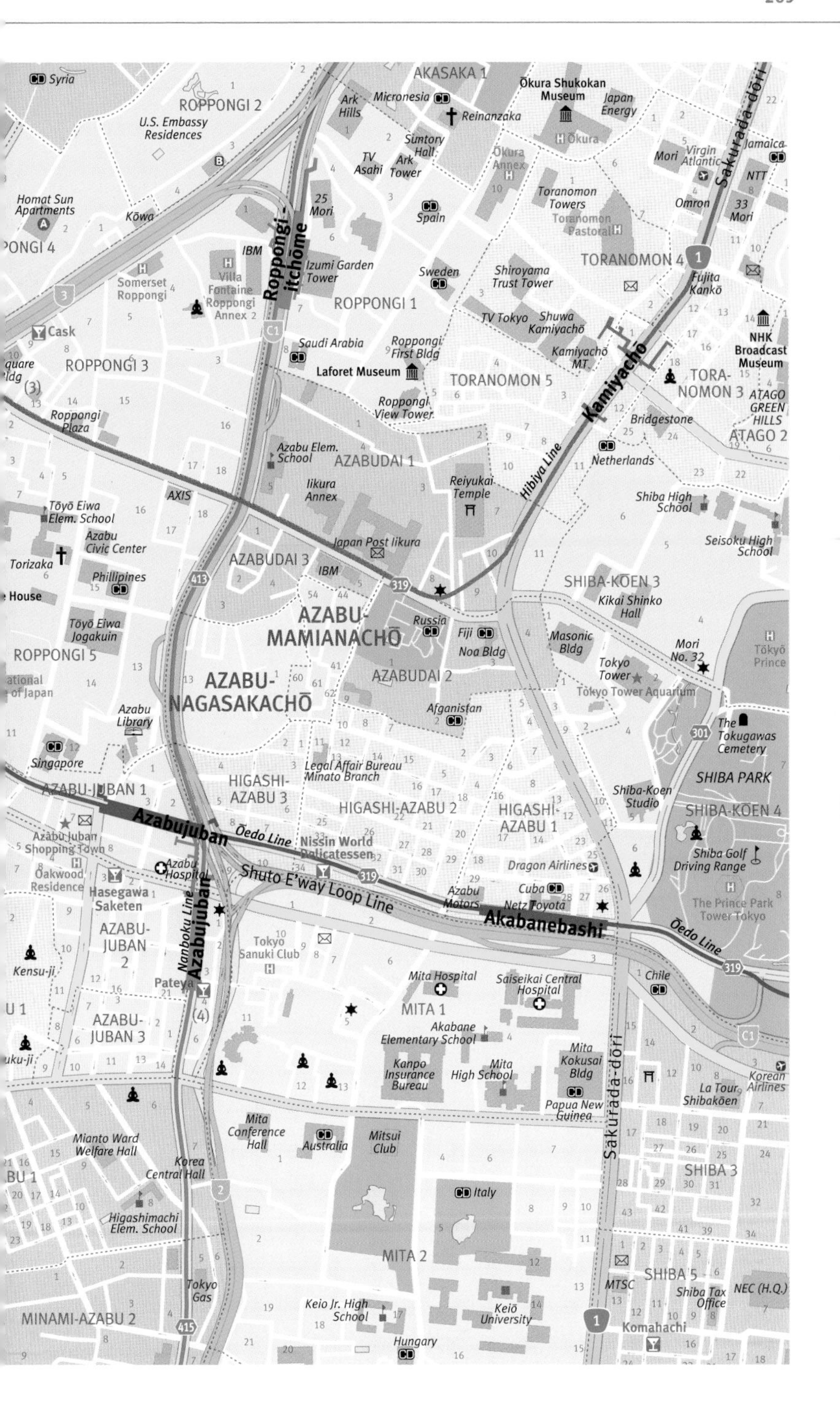
Syria
ROPPONGI 2
U.S. Embassy Residences
AKASAKA 1
Ark Hills
Micronesia
Reinanzaka
Ōkura Shukokan Museum
Japan Energy
Ōkura
Suntory Hall
TV Asahi
Ark Tower
Ōkura Annex
Mori
Virgin Atlantic
Jamaica
Sakurada-dōri
NTT
Homat Sun Apartments
Kōwa
25 Mori
Spain
Toranomon Towers
Toranomon Pastoral
Omron
33 Mori
ROPPONGI 4
IBM
Roppongi-itchōme
Izumi Garden Tower
Sweden
Shiroyama Trust Tower
TORANOMON 4
Fujita Kankō
Somerset Roppongi
Villa Fontaine Roppongi Annex
ROPPONGI 1
TV Tokyo
Shuwa Kamiyachō
Cask
Saudi Arabia
Roppongi First Bldg
Kamiyachō MT
Kamiyachō
NHK Broadcast Museum
ROPPONGI 3
Laforet Museum
TORANOMON 5
TORA-NOMON 3
ATAGO GREEN HILLS
Roppongi Plaza
Roppongi View Tower
Bridgestone
ATAGO 2
Azabu Elem. School
AZABUDAI 1
Hibiya Line
Netherlands
Iikura Annex
Reiyukai Temple
AXIS
Shiba High School
Tōyō Eiwa Elem. School
Azabu Civic Center
Torizaka
Japan Post Iikura
Seisoku High School
AZABUDAI 3
IBM
Phillipines
SHIBA-KŌEN 3
House
AZABU-MAMIANACHŌ
Kikai Shinko Hall
Tōyō Eiwa Jogakuin
Russia
Fiji
Masonic Bldg
Mori No. 32
Noa Bldg
Tōkyō Prince
ROPPONGI 5
Tokyo Tower
AZABUDAI 2
AZABU-NAGASAKACHŌ
Tokyo Tower Aquarium
Afganistan
The Tokugawas Cemetery
Azabu Library
Singapore
Legal Affair Bureau Minato Branch
SHIBA PARK
AZABU-JUBAN 1
HIGASHI-AZABU 3
Shiba-Koen Studio
HIGASHI-AZABU 2
HIGASHI-AZABU 1
SHIBA-KŌEN 4
Azabujuban
Ōedo Line
Azabu Juban Shopping Town
Nissin World Delicatessen
Shiba Golf Driving Range
Oakwood Residence
Azabu Hospital
Dragon Airlines
Hasegawa Saketen
Shuto E'way Loop Line
Azabu Motors
Cuba
Netz Toyota
The Prince Park Tower Tokyo
Akabanebashi
AZABU-JUBAN 2
Nanboku Line
Azabujuban
Tokyo Sanuki Club
Kensu-ji
Pateya
Mita Hospital
Saiseikai Central Hospital
Chile
AZABU-JUBAN 3
MITA 1
Akabane Elementary School
Kanpo Insurance Bureau
Mita High School
Mita Kokusai Bldg
Korean Airlines
La Tour Shibakōen
Papua New Guinea
Mianto Ward Welfare Hall
Mita Conference Hall
Australia
Mitsui Club
Korea Central Hall
SHIBA 3
Italy
Higashimachi Elem. School
MITA 2
SHIBA 5
MTSC
Shiba Tax Office
NEC (H.Q.)
Tokyo Gas
Keio Jr. High School
Keiō University
MINAMI-AZABU 2
Komahachi
Hungary

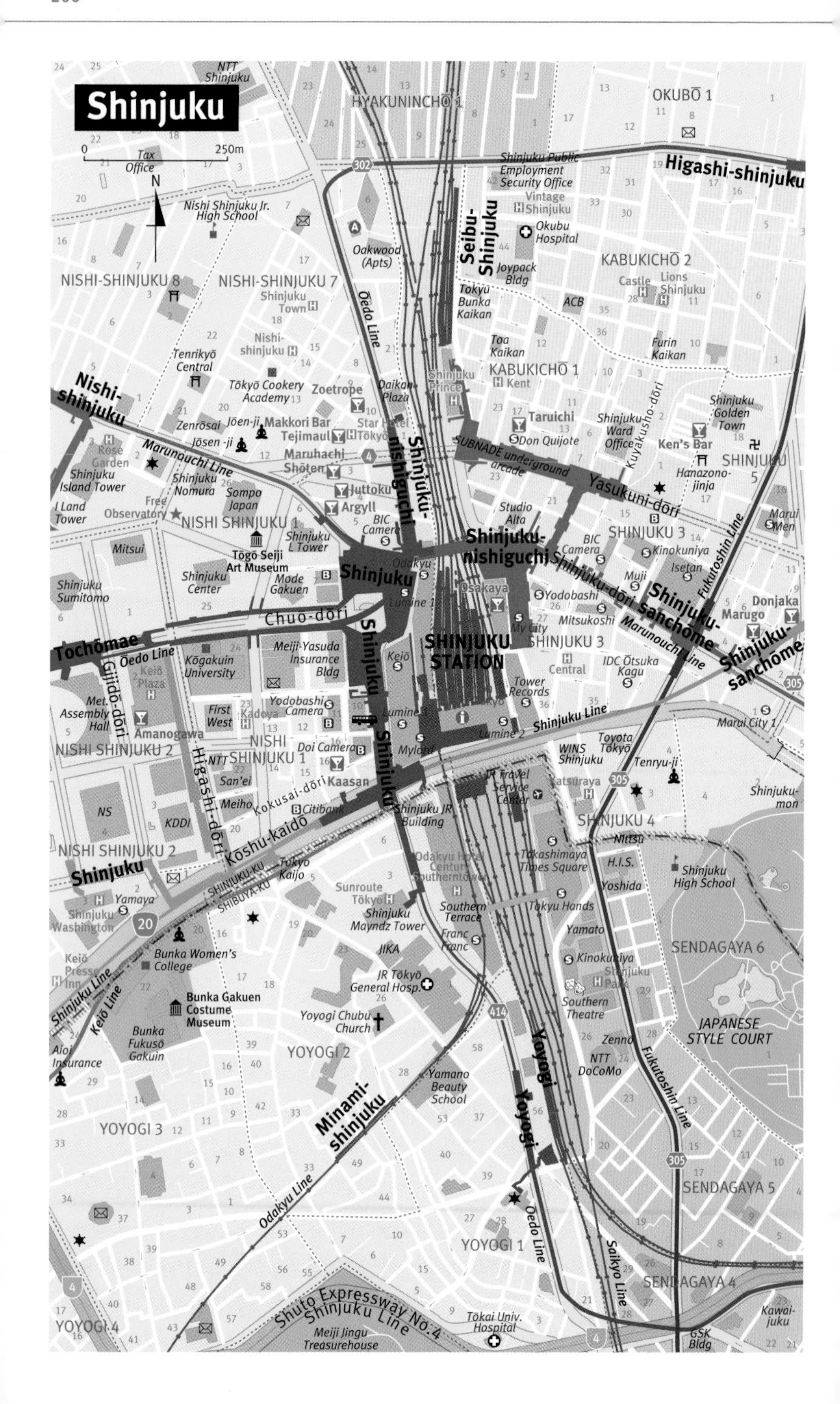
Shinjuku
0
250m
N
NTT Shinjuku
HYAKUNINCHŌ 1
OKUBŌ 1
Higashi-shinjuku
Shinjuku Public Employment Security Office
Vintage Shinjuku
Okubu Hospital
Seibu-Shinjuku
Tax Office
Nishi Shinjuku Jr. High School
Oakwood (Apts)
Joypack Bldg
KABUKICHŌ 2
Castle
Lions Shinjuku
NISHI-SHINJUKU 8
NISHI-SHINJUKU 7
Shinjuku Town
Ōedo Line
Tōkyū Bunka Kaikan
ACB
Toa Kaikan
Furin Kaikan
Tenrikyō Central
Nishi-shinjuku
KABUKICHŌ 1
Kent
Tōkyō Cookery Academy
Zoetrope
Daikan Plaza
Shinjuku Prince
Shinjuku Golden Town
Nishi-shinjuku
Jōen-ji
Makkori Bar
Star Hotel Tōkyō
Taruichi
Shinjuku Ward Office
Kuyakusho-dōri
Zenrōsai
Tejimaul
Jōsen-ji
Don Quijote
Ken's Bar
Rose Garden
Marunouchi Line
Maruhachi Shōten
SUBNADE underground arcade
Hanazono-jinja
SHINJUKU 5
Shinjuku Island Tower
Shinjuku Nomura
Sompo Japan
Juttoku
Argyll
Shinjuku-nishiguchi
Yasukuni-dōri
I Land Tower
Free Observatory
NISHI SHINJUKU 1
BIC Camera
Studio Alta
SHINJUKU 3
Marui Men
Fukutoshin Line
Mitsui
Tōgō Seiji Art Museum
Shinjuku L Tower
Shinjuku-nishiguchi
BIC Camera
Kinokuniya
Isetan
Shinjuku Sumitomo
Shinjuku Center
Mode Gakuen
Shinjuku
Odakyu
Shinjuku-dōri
Muji
Shinjuku-sanchōme
Donjaka
Marugo
Lumine 1
Osakaya
Yodobashi
Chuo-dōri
My City
Mitsukoshi
Marunouchi Line
Tochōmae
Ōedo Line
Meiji-Yasuda Insurance Bldg
Shinjuku
SHINJUKU STATION
SHINJUKU 3
Shinjuku-sanchōme
Gijidō-dōri
Kōgakuin University
Keiō
Central
IDC Ōtsuka Kagu
Keiō Plaza
Tower Records
Met. Assembly Hall
First West
Yodobashi Camera
Kadoya
Lumine 1
Shinjuku Line
Marui City 1
Amanogawa
NISHI SHINJUKU 1
Doi Camera
Lumine 2
Toyota Tōkyō
NISHI SHINJUKU 2
Higashi-dōri
NTT
Shinjuku
Mylord
WINS Shinjuku
Tenryu-ji
San'ei
Kaasan
JR Travel Service Center
Katsuraya
Shinjuku-mon
NS
Meiho
Kokusai-dōri
Citibank
Shinjuku JR Building
KDDI
SHINJUKU 4
Kōshu-kaidō
Nittsu
NISHI SHINJUKU 2
Odakyu Hotel Century Southern Tower
Takashimaya Times Square
H.I.S.
Shinjuku
SHINJUKU-KU
SHIBUYA-KU
Tokyo Kaijo
Yoshida
Shinjuku High School
Yamaya
Sunroute Tōkyō
Southern Terrace
Tokyu Hands
Shinjuku Washington
Shinjuku Mayndz Tower
Yamato
Franc Franc
SENDAGAYA 6
Keiō Presso Inn
Bunka Women's College
JIKA
Kinokuniya
Shinjuku Park
Shinjuku Line
Keiō Line
JR Tōkyō General Hosp.
Southern Theatre
Bunka Gakuen Costume Museum
Yoyogi Chubu Church
JAPANESE STYLE COURT
Bunka Fukusō Gakuin
Zennō
Yoyogi
Aioi Insurance
YOYOGI 2
NTT DoCoMo
Fukutoshin Line
Yamano Beauty School
Minami-shinjuku
Yoyogi
YOYOGI 3
SENDAGAYA 5
Odakyu Line
Ōedo Line
YOYOGI 1
Saikyo Line
SENDAGAYA 4
Shuto Expressway No.4 Shinjuku Line
Tōkai Univ. Hospital
Kawai-juku
YOYOGI 4
Meiji Jingu Treasurehouse
GSK Bldg

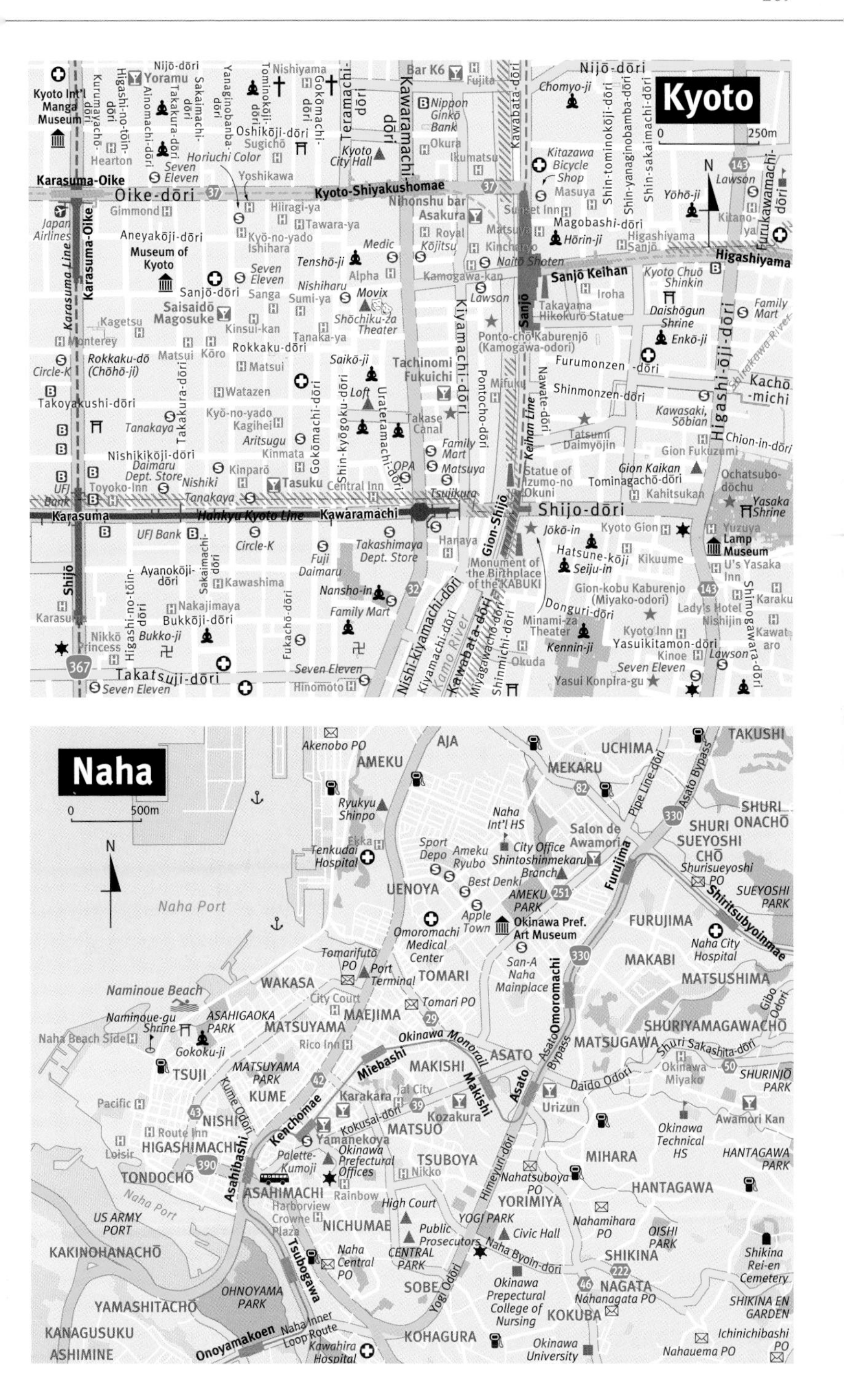
Kyoto
0
250m
N
Nijō-dōri
Kyoto Int'l Manga Museum
Kurumayachō-dōri
Higashi-no-tōin-dōri
Yoramu
Ainomachi-dōri
Takakura-dōri
Sakaimachi-dōri
Yanaginobanba-dōri
Tominokōji-dōri
Nishiyama
Gokōmachi-dōri
Teramachi-dōri
Kawaramachi-dōri
Bar K6
Fujita
Kawabata-dōri
Chomyo-ji
Shin-tominokōji-dōri
Shin-yanaginobanba-dōri
Shin-sakaimachi-dōri
Nippon Ginkō Bank
Oshikōji-dōri
Sugichō
Okura
Ikumatsu
Hearton
Horiuchi Color
Kyoto City Hall
Kitazawa Bicycle Shop
Seven Eleven
Yoshikawa
Karasuma-Oike
Oike-dōri
Kyoto-Shiyakushomae
Masuya
Yōhō-ji
Lawson
Furukawamachi-dōri
Gimmond
Hiiragi-ya
Nihonshu bar Asakura
Sunset Inn
Kitano-ya
Japan Airlines
Karasuma Line
Karasuma-Oike
Tawara-ya
Royal Kōjitsu
Matsuya
Magobashi-dōri
Aneyakōji-dōri
Kyō-no-yado Ishihara
Medic
Kincharyo
Hōrin-ji
Higashiyama Sanjō
Museum of Kyoto
Tenshō-ji
Naitō Shoten
Higashiyama
Seven Eleven
Alpha
Kamogawa-kan
Sanjō Keihan
Kyoto Chuō Shinkin
Sanjō-dōri
Sanga
Nishiharu Sumi-ya
Movix
Lawson
Iroha
Saisaidō Magosuke
Kinsui-kan
Shōchiku-za Theater
Kiyamachi-dōri
Sanjo
Takayama Hikokurō Statue
Daishōgun Shrine
Family Mart
Kagetsu
Tanaka-ya
Ponto-chō Kaburenjō (Kamogawa-odori)
Enkō-ji
Shirakawa River
Monterey
Rokkaku-dōri
Higashi-ōji-dōri
Rokkaku-dō (Chōhō-ji)
Matsui
Kōro
Matsui
Saikō-ji
Tachinomi Fukuichi
Furumonzen-dōri
Circle-K
Pontocho-dōri
Mifuku
Nawate-dōri
Kachō-michi
Watazen
Loft
Shinmonzen-dōri
Takoyakushi-dōri
Gokōmachi-dōri
Shin-kyōgoku-dōri
Urateramachi-dōri
Keihan Line
Kawasaki, Sōbian
Kyō-no-yado Kagihei
Takase Canal
Tanakaya
Takakura-dōri
Aritsugu
Tatsumi Daimyōjin
Chion-in-dōri
Family Mart
Gion Fukuzumi
Nishikikōji-dōri
Kinmata
Daimaru Dept. Store
Kinparō
Matsuya
Gion Kaikan
Ochatsubo-dōchu
Statue of Izumo-no Okuni
Tominagachō-dōri
OPA
Toyoko-Inn
Nishiki Tanakaya
Tasuku
Central Inn
Tsujikura
Kahitsukan
Yasaka Shrine
UFJ Bank
Shijo-dōri
Karasuma
Hankyu Kyoto Line
Kawaramachi
Gion-Shijō
Jōkō-ji
Kyoto Gion
Yuzuya
Lamp Museum
UFJ Bank
Circle-K
Takashimaya Dept. Store
Hanaya
Hatsune-kōji
Kikuume
U's Yasaka Inn
Sakaimachi-dōri
Fuji Daimaru
Seiju-in
Ayanokōji-dōri
Kawashima
Monument of the Birthplace of the KABUKI
Gion-kobu Kaburenjo (Miyako-odori)
Shijō
Higashi-no-tōin-dōri
Nakajimaya
Nansho-in
Nishi-Kiyamachi-dōri
Karaku
Karasuma
Fukachō-dōri
Family Mart
Donguri-dōri
Lady's Hotel Nishijin
Shimogawara-dōri
Bukkōji-dōri
Kawabata-dōri
Minami-za Theater
Kawataro
Nikkō Princess
Bukko-ji
Kiyamachi-dōri
Miyagawachō-dōri
Kyoto Inn
Kamo River
Shinmichi-dōri
Kennin-ji
Yasuikitamon-dōri
Kinoe
Lawson
Okuda
Seven Eleven
Seven Eleven
Takatsuji-dōri
Yasui Konpira-gu
Seven Eleven
Hinomoto
Naha
0
500m
N
Akenobo PO
AJA
TAKUSHI
AMEKU
UCHIMA
MEKARU
Pipe Line-dōri
Asato Bypass
Ryukyu Shinpo
Naha Int'l HS
Salon de Awamori
SHURI ONACHŌ
SHURI SUEYOSHI CHŌ
Shurisueyoshi PO
Ekka
Tenkudai Hospital
Sport Depo
Ameku Ryubo
City Office
Shintoshinmekaru Branch
Furujima
Naha Port
Best Denki
AMEKU PARK
UENOYA
SUEYOSHI PARK
Shiritsubyoinmae
Apple Town
Okinawa Pref. Art Museum
FURUJIMA
Naha City Hospital
Omoromachi Medical Center
San-A Naha Mainplace
Omoromachi
MAKABI
Tomarifutō PO
Port Terminal
TOMARI
MATSUSHIMA
Naminoue Beach
WAKASA
City Court
Gibo Odōri
Tomari PO
Naminoue-gu Shrine
ASAHIGAOKA PARK
MAEJIMA
SHURIYAMAGAWACHŌ
Naha Beach Side
MATSUYAMA
Okinawa Monorail
ASATO
Asato Bypass
MATSUGAWA
Shuri Sakashita-dōri
Gokoku-ji
Rico Inn
TSUJI
MATSUYAMA PARK
Miebashi
MAKISHI
Makishi
Okinawa Miyako
SHURINJŌ PARK
KUME
Kume Odōri
Asato
Daido Odōri
Kenchomae
Jal City
Urizun
Pacific
Karakara
Kozakura
NISHI
Kokusai-dōri
MATSUO
Okinawa Technical HS
Awamori Kan
Route Inn
Yamanekoya
HIGASHIMACHI
Palette-Kumoji
Okinawa Prefectural Offices
TSUBOYA
MIHARA
HANTAGAWA PARK
Loisir
Asahibashi
Nikko
TONDOCHŌ
Nahatsuboya PO
HANTAGAWA
ASAHIMACHI
Himeyuri-dōri
Naha Port
Rainbow
YORIMIYA
Harborview Crowne Plaza
High Court
US ARMY PORT
NICHUMAE
YOGI PARK
Nahamihara PO
Public Prosecutors
Civic Hall
OISHI PARK
KAKINOHANACHŌ
Naha Central PO
CENTRAL PARK
Naha Byoin-dōri
SHIKINA
Shikina Rei-en Cemetery
Tsubogawa
SOBE
Okinawa Prepectural College of Nursing
NAGATA
Yogi Odōri
Nahanagata PO
OHNOYAMA PARK
YAMASHITACHŌ
SHIKINA EN GARDEN
KOKUBA
KANAGUSUKU
Onoyamakoen
Naha Inner Loop Route
KOHAGURA
Ichinichibashi PO
Kawahira Hospital
Okinawa University
Nahauema PO
ASHIMINE

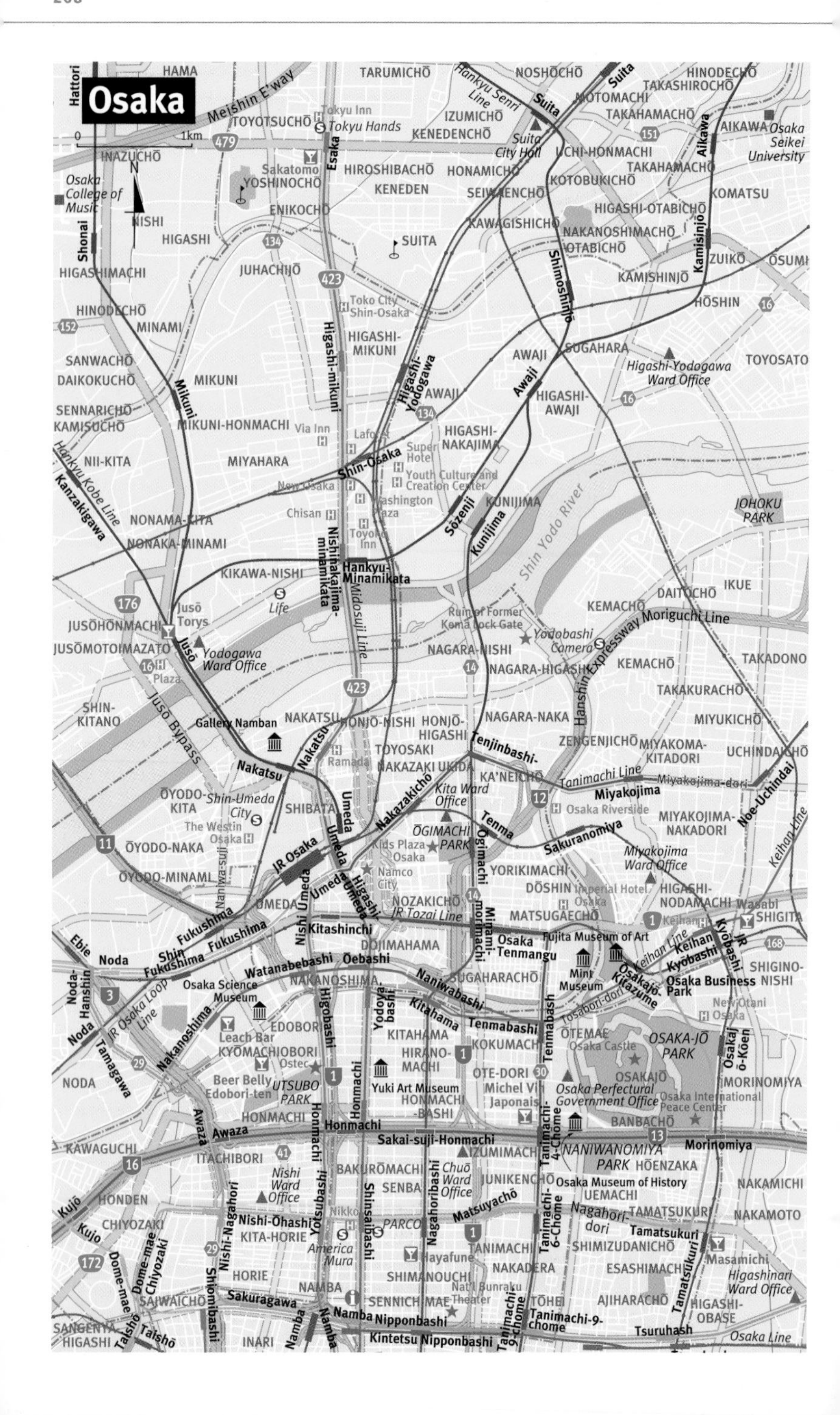
Osaka
0
1km
N
Hattori
HAMA
Meishin E'way
TARUMICHŌ
Hankyu Senri Line
NOSHŌCHŌ
Suita
HINODECHŌ
TAKASHIROCHŌ
MOTOMACHI
TAKAHAMACHŌ
AIKAWA
Osaka Seikei University
Aikawa
Tokyu Inn
Tokyu Hands
TOYOTSUCHŌ
IZUMICHŌ
KENEDENCHŌ
Suita City Hall
479
151
INAZUCHŌ
Sakatomo
Esaka
HIROSHIBACHŌ
HONAMICHŌ
UCHI-HONMACHI
TAKAHAMACHŌ
Osaka College of Music
YOSHINOCHŌ
KENEDEN
SEIWAENCHŌ
KOTOBUKICHŌ
KOMATSU
ENIKOCHŌ
KAWAGISHICHŌ
HIGASHI-OTABICHŌ
NISHI
HIGASHI
SUITA
NAKANOSHIMACHŌ
OTABICHŌ
Shonai
134
Shimoshinjō
Kamishinjō
ZUIKŌ
ŌSUMI
HIGASHIMACHI
JUHACHIJŌ
KAMISHINJŌ
423
Toko City Shin-Osaka
HŌSHIN
16
HINODECHŌ
MINAMI
152
HIGASHI-MIKUNI
SUGAHARA
Higashi-mikuni
AWAJI
Higashi-Yodogawa Ward Office
TOYOSATO
SANWACHŌ
DAIKOKUCHŌ
MIKUNI
Mikuni
Higashi-Yodogawa
AWAJI
Awaji
HIGASHI-AWAJI
SENNARICHŌ
KAMISUCHŌ
MIKUNI-HONMACHI
Via Inn
Laforet
HIGASHI-NAKAJIMA
Hankyu Kobe Line
NII-KITA
MIYAHARA
Super Hotel
Shin-Osaka
Youth Culture and Creation Center
New Osaka
Washington Plaza
Sōzenji
KUNIJIMA
Kanzakigawa
Chisan
Toyoko Inn
Kunijima
Shin Yodo River
JOHOKU PARK
NONAMA-KITA
NONAKA-MINAMI
Nishinakajima-minamikata
Hankyu-Minamikata
KIKAWA-NISHI
Midosuji Line
IKUE
DAITŌCHŌ
176
Life
KEMACHŌ
Jusō Torys
Ruin of Former Kema Lock Gate
JUSŌHONMACHI
Moriguchi Line
JUSŌMOTOIMAZATO
Jusō
Yodogawa Ward Office
Yodobashi Camera
Hanshin Expressway
Plaza
NAGARA-NISHI
NAGARA-HIGASHI
KEMACHŌ
TAKADONO
Jusō Bypass
TAKAKURACHŌ
SHIN-KITANO
Gallery Namban
NAKATSU
HONJŌ-NISHI
HONJŌ-HIGASHI
NAGARA-NAKA
MIYUKICHŌ
Nakatsu
TOYOSAKI
Tenjinbashi-
ZENGENJICHŌ
MIYAKOMA-KITADORI
UCHINDAICHŌ
Ramada
NAKAZAKI
UKIDA
Nakatsu
KA'NEICHŌ
Tanimachi Line
Miyakojima-dori
ŌYODO-KITA
Shin-Umeda City
SHIBATA
Umeda
Nakazakichō
Kita Ward Office
Miyakojima
Noe-Uchindai
12
Osaka Riverside
The Westin Osaka
Tenma
MIYAKOJIMA-NAKADORI
11
ŌYODO-NAKA
JR Osaka
Umeda
ŌGIMACHI PARK
Ōgimachi
Sakuranomiya
Keihan Line
Kids Plaza Osaka
Miyakojima Ward Office
ŌYODO-MINAMI
Namco City
YORIKIMACHI
DŌSHIN
Imperial Hotel Osaka
HIGASHI-NODAMACHI
Higashi-Umeda
Nishi Umeda
UMEDA
NOZAKICHŌ
JR Tozai Line
Minami-morimachi
MATSUGAECHŌ
Wasabi
SHIGITA
Fukushima
Kitashinchi
Keihan
Fujita Museum of Art
JR
Ebie
Shin Fukushima
Fukushima
DOJIMAHAMA
Osaka Tenmangu
Keihan Kyōbashi
Kyōbashi
168
Noda
Watanabebashi
Ōebashi
Mint Museum
Osakajō-Kitazume
SHIGINO-NISHI
Noda-Hanshin
JR Osaka Loop Line
Osaka Science Museum
NAKANOSHIMA
Naniwabashi
SUGAHARACHŌ
Osaka Business Park
3
Kitahama
Tosabori-dori
New Otani Osaka
Noda Hanshin
Nakanoshima
Leach Bar
EDOBORI
Higobashi
Yodoya-bashi
KITAHAMA
Tenmabashi
Tenmabashi
ŌTEMAE
Osaka Castle
OSAKA-JŌ PARK
Tamagawa
KYŌMACHIBORI
Ostec
HIRANO-MACHI
KOKUMACHI
Osakajō-kōen
29
OTE-DORI
30
OSAKAJŌ
NODA
Beer Belly Edobori-ten
UTSUBO PARK
Honmachi
Yuki Art Museum
Michel Vin Japonais
Osaka Perfectural Government Office
MORINOMIYA
HONMACHI-BASHI
Osaka International Peace Center
HONMACHI
Awaza
Honmachi
Awaza
BANBACHŌ
Sakai-suji-Honmachi
13
Morinomiya
KAWAGUCHI
ITACHIBORI
41
IZUMIMACHI
Tanimachi-4-Chome
NANIWANOMIYA PARK
HŌENZAKA
16
Nishi Ward Office
Honmachi
BAKURŌMACHI
Chuō Ward Office
JUNIKENCHŌ
Osaka Museum of History
NAKAMICHI
SENBA
UEMACHI
Kujō
HONDEN
Yotsubashi
Shinsaibashi
Nagahoribashi
Matsuyachō
Tanimachi-6-Chome
Nagahori-dori
TAMATSUKURI
NAKAMOTO
Nishi-Nagahori
Nishi-Ōhashi
Nikko
PARCO
1
CHIYOZAKI
KITA-HORIE
Tamatsukuri
Kujo
America Mura
TANIMACHI
SHIMIZUDANICHŌ
Masamichi
172
Dome-mae Chiyozaki
29
Hayafune
Higashinari Ward Office
HORIE
SHIMANOUCHI
NAKADERA
ESASHIMACHI
Shiomibashi
NAMBA
Nat'l Bunraku Theater
Tamatsukuri
Dome-mae
SAIWAICHŌ
Sakuragawa
SENNICHIMAE
TŌHEI
AJIHARACHŌ
HIGASHI-OBASE
SANGENYA-HIGASHI
Namba
Nipponbashi
Tanimachi-9-chome
Tanimachi-9-chome
Taishō
Taishō
INARI
Namba
Namba
Kintetsu Nipponbashi
Tsuruhashi
Osaka Line

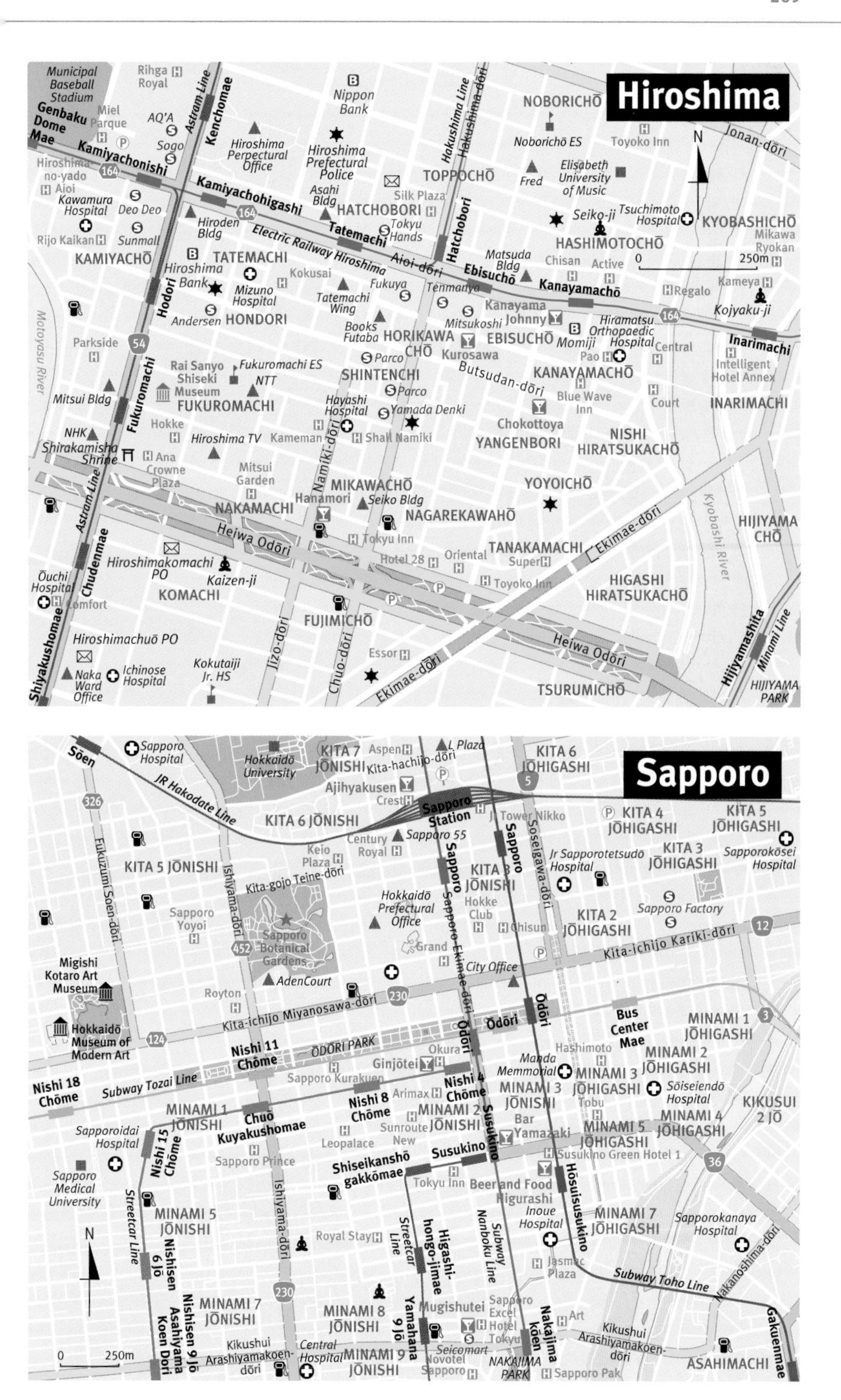
Hiroshima
Sapporo

Acknowledgments

I could not have written this book without the help of Itsuo Yoshino and Ayako Yoshino. Every word in these pages is the product of a group effort. I would like to thank them both for the weeks they spent helping me research in a language that is not my own. I would also like to thank Mitsue Yoshino for providing unstinting moral and practical support. The emotional space and encouragement given to me by my parents, Paul and Judith Bunting, allowed me to pursue this crooked, crazy "career" path of mine. Their eagle eyes spotted dozens of errors in my drafts.

Lee Yuen Kuan and Loh Sook Fan at Tuttle Publishing molded those drafts into what I think is both a visually stunning and functional book design. They showed extraordinary patience in dealing with my endless footering with the text. Tuttle's cartographers Fajar Wisnu Hardono and Amin Cahyadi created all the maps in the book. Noor Azlina Yunus edited the manuscript with an exceedingly sharp pen, succeeded in the daunting task of changing my British English into US English and somehow managed not to be sent round the bend by my last-minute changes. I would also like to thank June Chong in Tuttle's Singapore office, who dragged *Drinking Japan* over the finish line, and Eric Oey, my publisher, who honed my original concept for the book into this guidebook and gave me unwavering support.

The beer chapter of this guide was helped immeasurably by Chris "Chuwy" Philips, who was the source for almost everything I wrote about contemporary Japanese craft beer. Taylor Smisson opened my eyes to the richness of Japanese bar culture. Takeshi Mogi taught me about Japanese whisky (though he claims he did not!). Phred Kaufman showed me Sapporo and gave me a thundering hangover. John Davis and Akiyoshi Miyagi took me around Okinawa. The folks at Tsukayama, Helios and Zuisen distilleries gave me a privileged look at *awamori* making. Yusaku Takenouchi at Shirakane distillery and Toshihiro Manzen at Manzen distillery showed me craft *shōchū* distilling at its best. Serge Valentin, Davin de Kergommeaux, Dave Broom, Marcin Miller and Nicholas Sikorski-Mazur taught me about whisky and distilled spirits. Denis Gastin helped me get my head around Japanese wine.

At Suntory Holdings Ltd, Aoi Kojima was tireless and her ability to communicate in English was a great boon. Kazumasa Nishizaki, Hiroyoshi Miyamoto, Seiichi Koshimizu and Makoto Sumita all took time out of very busy schedules to show me around Suntory's facilities. At Asahi, Aiko Shima was extremely helpful, and the staff at the Yoichi and Miyagikyō distilleries could not have been more welcoming. I would particularly like to thank Minoru Miake at Miyagikyō and Koichi Nishikawa and Inoru Kohara at Yoichi. Mikio Hiraishi, president of Eigashima Shuzō, spent hours with me at the White Oak whisky distillery. Eri Todokoro at Kirin Brewery Ltd, Shigeharu Asagiri at Coedo Ltd and Kazue Matsushima at Fuji Kankō Kaihatsu also provided crucial assistance.

I visited hundreds of bars while researching this guide. Almost everyone was incredibly welcoming. There are too many people to thank individually but, of course, this book would not exist without them. Numerous bars did not, in the end, make it into the guide. I would like to apologize to their owners and staff, who spent time answering my questions and allowing me to take photographs of their establishments.

As my book began to take shape, Brian Harrell, John Gauntner and www.tokyofoodcast.com's Et-chan and Te-chan gave expert guidance, rooting out numerous errors in my early drafts. Nicholas Coldicott at the *Japan Times* provided much-needed perspective and nuance to my ideas about the Japanese drinks scene and shared his compendious knowledge of Tōkyō's bars.

Bibliography

The format of this guide has not allowed detailed academic-style referencing when I have used another's work as a source for my writing, but the following books were all invaluable.

Aoi Hiroyuki, *Biiru no Kyōkasho* (Kodansha, 2003)

Beer and Pub Magazine No. 3 (2005)

Buxrud, Ulf, *Japanese Whisky: Facts, Figures and Taste* (DataAnalys, 2008)

Checkland, Olive, *Japanese Whisky, Scotch Blend* (Scottish Cultural Press, 1998)

Cooper, Michael, ed., *They Came To Japan* (University of Michigan, 1995)

Dower, John, *Embracing Defeat* (Penguin, 2000)

Edagawa Kōichi, *Shin Tōkyō no Bar* (President sha, 2002)

Gauntner, John, *The Sake Handbook* (Tuttle, 2002)

Hagio Toshiaki, *Awamori no Bunkashi* (Border Ink, 2004)

Harada Nobuo, "A Peek at the Meals of the People of Edo," in *Kikkoman Food Culture No. 12* (Kikkoman Institute for International Food Culture, 2006)

Harper, Philip, *The Insider's Guide to Sake* (Kodansha, 1998)

Inomata Yoshitaka, *Imojōchū Kiwamekata Jiten* (Oizumi Shoten, 2005)

Kanzaki Noritake, ed., *Kampai no Bunkashi* (Domesu Shuppan, 2007)

Kusama Shunrō, *Yokohama Yōshoku Bunka Hajime* (Yūsankaku Shuppan, 1999)

Nagai Takashi, *Biiru Saishū Sensō* (Nikkei, 2006)

Nagayama Hisao, *Nihon no Sake Unchiku* (Kawade Shobō Shinsha, 2008)

Narita Ittetsu, *To the Bar* (Asahi Shimbunsha, 2006)

Nihon no Meishu Jiten (Kodansha, 2005)

Nihon Shohisha Renmei, *Honmono no Sake wo* (Sanichi Shobo, 1982)

Nihon Shurui Kenkyūkai, *Chishiki Zero Kara no Awamori Nyūmon* (Gentōsha, 2008)

Nōka ga Oshieru Doburoku no Tsukurikata (Nōbunkyo, 2007)

Ogawa Kihachirō and Nakashima Katsumi, *Honkaku Shōchū no Kitamichi* (Kinyōsha, 2007)

Okinawan Spirits: The Awamori (Okinawa Prefectural Government, 2003)

Ōta Kazuhiko, *Nippon no Jibiiru* (ASCII, 2007)

Ōta Kazuhiko, *Izakaya Mishuran* (Shinchōsha, 2008)

Oze Akira, *Chishiki Zero Kara no Nihonshu Nyūmon* (Gentōsha, 2001)

Oze Akira, *Sara ni Kiwameru Nihonshu Ajiwai Nyūmon* (Gentōsha, 2003)

Ronde, Ingvar, ed., *Malt Whisky Yearbook 2010* (MagDig Media, 2009)

Sakaguchi Kin'ichirō, *Nihon no Sake* (Iwanami, 2007)

Sarai ga Eranda Shinise Bar (Shōgakukan, 2004)

Seidensticker, Edward, *Low City High City* (Penguin, 1985)

Sekai ga Mitometa Nihon no Wain (Leed, 2006)

Shirakawa, Waku, *Honkaku Shōchū wo Marugoto Tanoshimu* (Shimpuushu, 2007)

Shochu 50 (Nihon Keizai Shimbun, 2005)

Smith, Robert J. and Wiswell, Ella Lury, *The Women of Suye Mura* (University of Chicago Press, 1982)

Tasaki Shinya, *Tasaki Shinya no Imakoso Shimajōchū* (Jitsugyō no Nihonsha, 2007)

Umesao Tadao, Yoshida Shuji and Schalow, Paul, eds., *Japanese Civilization in the Modern World: XVIII Alcoholic Beverages* (National Museum of Ethnology, 2003)

The Whisky World Vol. 16

Ueno Nobuhiro, *Nihon no Koshu* (Jitsugyō no Nihonsha, 2008)

Yamamoto Hiroshi, *Nihon no Wain* (Hayakawa Shobō, 2003)

Yamazaki Tatsurō, *Bar Yamazaki* (Hokkaido Shimbunsha, 2009)

Yanaka Jimusho, *Nonde Mitai! Honkaku Umeshu Katarogu* (Natsumesha, 2006)

Willett, Robert L., *Russian Sideshow: America's Undeclared War 1918–20* (Brassey's, 2004)

Yoshiba Katsuo, *Budōshu to Wain no Hakubutsukan* (Kankandō, 1983)

In this Bibliography, I have ignored the convention adopted in the rest of this book of putting Japanese names in the Western order. The Japanese habit of putting family names first works better in an alphabetical list. For more detailed referencing of the sources for particular parts of the text, please visit www.drinkingjapan.com.

Photo Credits

Many of the images in this book were provided by others. Without their generosity, it would have been a very dull guide indeed. Tony McNicol's photographs of Terada Honke brewery are beautiful. You can see more of his work at www.tonymcnicol.com. Stefano Bassetti's images of Tōkyō's drinking districts capture the atmosphere of these places in a way my modest photographic talents could not. Ysbrand Rogge's and Hans Brinckmann's photos give a unique view of the drinking culture of the past. Brinckmann's book *Showa Japan: The Post-War Golden Age and Its Troubled Legacy* (Tuttle, 2008) features more of the images and an excellent chapter on eating and drinking in Shōwa Japan.

I would also like to thank the following individuals for providing images for use in the book: Nathan A. Keirn, John Hawkins, Akyo Kondo, Sake Kobayashi (sake-kobayasi.cocolog-nifty.com), Jordon Cheung, Et-chan and Te-chan at www.tokyofoodcast.com, "kozyndan" on Flickr, "459i" on Flickr, Yoshi Dazai, Toshihiro Manzen, Yusaku Takenouchi and the staff at Nikka Whisky's Miyagikyō distillery. Not all of the images made the final volume, but their help was greatly appreciated.

Front cover main photo: © 2009 Stefano Bassetti
Pages 4–5: © 2009 Stefano Bassetti
Page 7: © 2009 Stefano Bassetti
Page 15: Provided by and © Hagi Uragami Museum, Yamaguchi Prefecture
Page 19: © Nick Peters
Page 25: © 2009 Stefano Bassetti
Page 26: © Jordon Cheung
Page 30: © Q. Sawami/JNTO
Page 31: © Tony McNicol
Pages 32–3 (above): © Tony McNicol
Page 33 (bottom): © Ysbrand Rogge
Page 34: © Hans Brinckmann
Page 36 (left): © Tony McNicol
Pages 36–7 (top right): © Saga Prefecture/JNTO
Page 37 (center): © Tony McNicol
Page 37 (below right): © Tokyofoodcast.com
Page 39: © Tony McNicol
Page 40: © Gifu Prefecture Tourist Federation
Page 41: © Gifu Prefecture Tourist Federation
Page 44: Courtesy of the American Friends of the British Museum. Photo © The Trustees of the British Museum
Page 45: © Gifu Prefecture Tourist Federation
Page 59: © Izakaya Kaasan
Page 75 (top left): © Okinawa Convention & Visitors Bureau/JNTO
Page 76: Provided by Toshihiro Manzen
Page 78 (top left) © Sake Kobayashi (sake-kobayasi.cocolog-nifty.com)
Page 78 (top center): Provided by Shirakane Shuzō
Page 79 (top right and center): Provided by Shirakane Shuzō
Pages 82–3: © Kagoshima Prefectural Tourist Federation/JNTO
Page 85 (top left): Provided by Shirakane Shuzō
Page 106: © Yoshi Dazai Photography (www.yoshidazaiphotos.com)
Page 108: © Sentir Co. Ltd
Page 111 (top): © Nathan A. Keirn
Page 114: Provided by and © Waseda University Library
Page 116: © 459i, Flickr
Page 118: Reproduced with permission of Tsukayama distillery
Page 119: © (2007) Helios Distillery Company Ltd
Page 120: © (2007) Helios Distillery Company Ltd
Page 121: © (2007) Helios Distillery Company Ltd
Page 135: © Michael Rougier, Time and Life Pictures; Provided by Getty Images
Page 137: © Asahi Beer
Page 138 (top left and bottom): © Coedo Brewery
Page 138 (top right): © Fuji Kankō Kaihatsu
Page 139: © Fuji Kankō Kaihatsu
Page 140: Provided by Sapporo Lion
Page 144 (bottom left): Provided by Baird Beer
Page 163 (top left, top center and center right): © Suntory Holdings Ltd
Page 165: © Suntory Holdings Ltd
Page 166: © Suntory Holdings Ltd
Page 168 (top left and right): © Suntory Holdings Ltd
Page 169: © Suntory Holdings Ltd
Pages 172–3: © Suntory Holdings Ltd
Page 174 (top): © Suntory Holdings Ltd
Page 176: © Akyo Kondo
Page 195: © Sentir Co. Ltd
Page 196: © Suntory Holdings Ltd
Page 199: © Suntory Holdings Ltd
Page 200: © Suntory Holdings Ltd
Page 210: Provided by Park Hyatt Tokyo
Page 215: Provided by Wine Bar Mayu
Page 234: Provided by Hisayo Miyakoshi
Page 242: Provided by NAA Retailing

Japan's Best Bars
LISTED ALPHABETICALLY